CASE CLOSED

VOLUME 27

Gosho Aoyama

Case Briefing:

Subject:
Occupation:
Special Skills:
Equipment:

Jimmy Kudo, a.k.a. Conan Edogawa
High School Student/Detective
Analytical thinking and deductive reasoning, Soccer
Bow Tie Voice Transmitter, Super Sneakers,
Homing Glasses, Stretchy Suspenders

The subject is hot on the trail of a pair of suspicious men in black when he is attacked from behind and administered a strange substance which physically transforms him into a first grader. When the subject confides in the eccentric inventor Dr. Agasa, they decide to keep the subject's true identity a secret for the safety of everyone around him. Assuming the new identity of first-grader Conan Edogawa, the subject continues to assist the police force on their most baffling cases. The only problem is that most crime-solving professionals won't take a little kid's advice!

Table of Contents

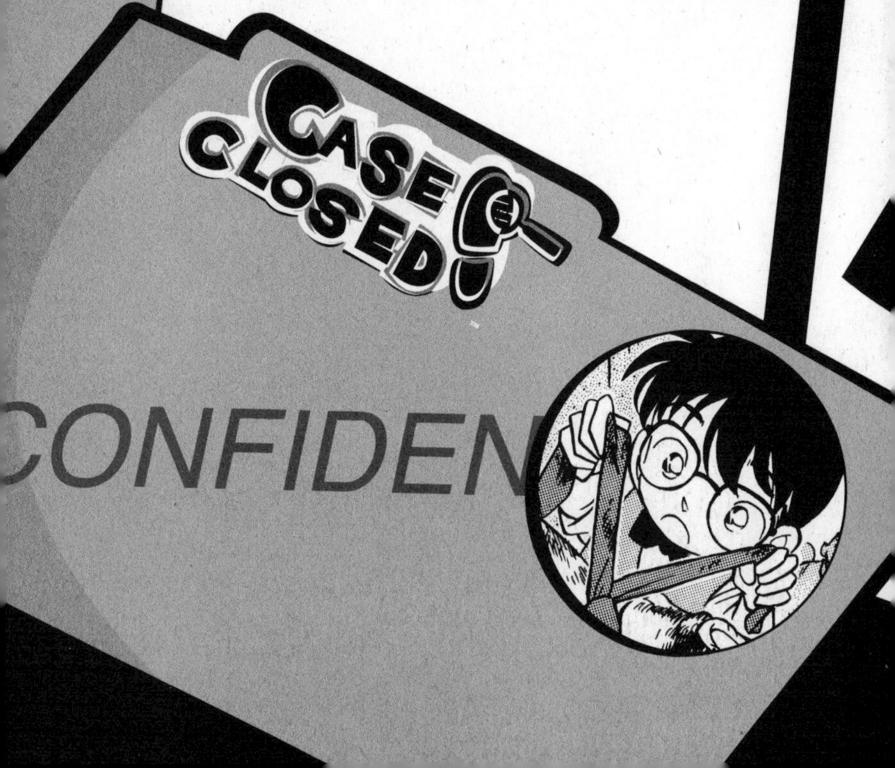

CASE CLOSED
CONFIDEN

CASE CLOSED

Volume 27 • VIZ Media Edition

GOSHO AOYAMA

Translation
Tetsuichiro Miyaki

Touch-up & Lettering
Freeman Wong

Cover & Graphic Design
Andrea Rice

Editor
Shaenon K. Garrity

Editor in Chief, Books **Alvin Lu**
Editor in Chief, Magazines **Marc Weidenbaum**
VP, Publishing Licensing **Rika Inouye**
VP, Sales & Product Marketing **Gonzalo Ferreyra**
VP, Creative **Linda Espinosa**
Publisher **Hyoe Narita**

MEITANTEI CONAN 27 by Gosho AOYAMA © 2000 Gosho AOYAMA
All rights reserved. Original Japanese edition published in 2000 by Shogakukan Inc., Tokyo.
The stories, characters and incidents mentioned in this publication are entirely fictional.

store.viz.com

Printed in the U.S.A.
Published by VIZ Media, LLC
P.O. Box 77010
San Francisco, CA 94107

10 9 8 7 6 5 4 3 2 1
First printing, January 2009

www.viz.com

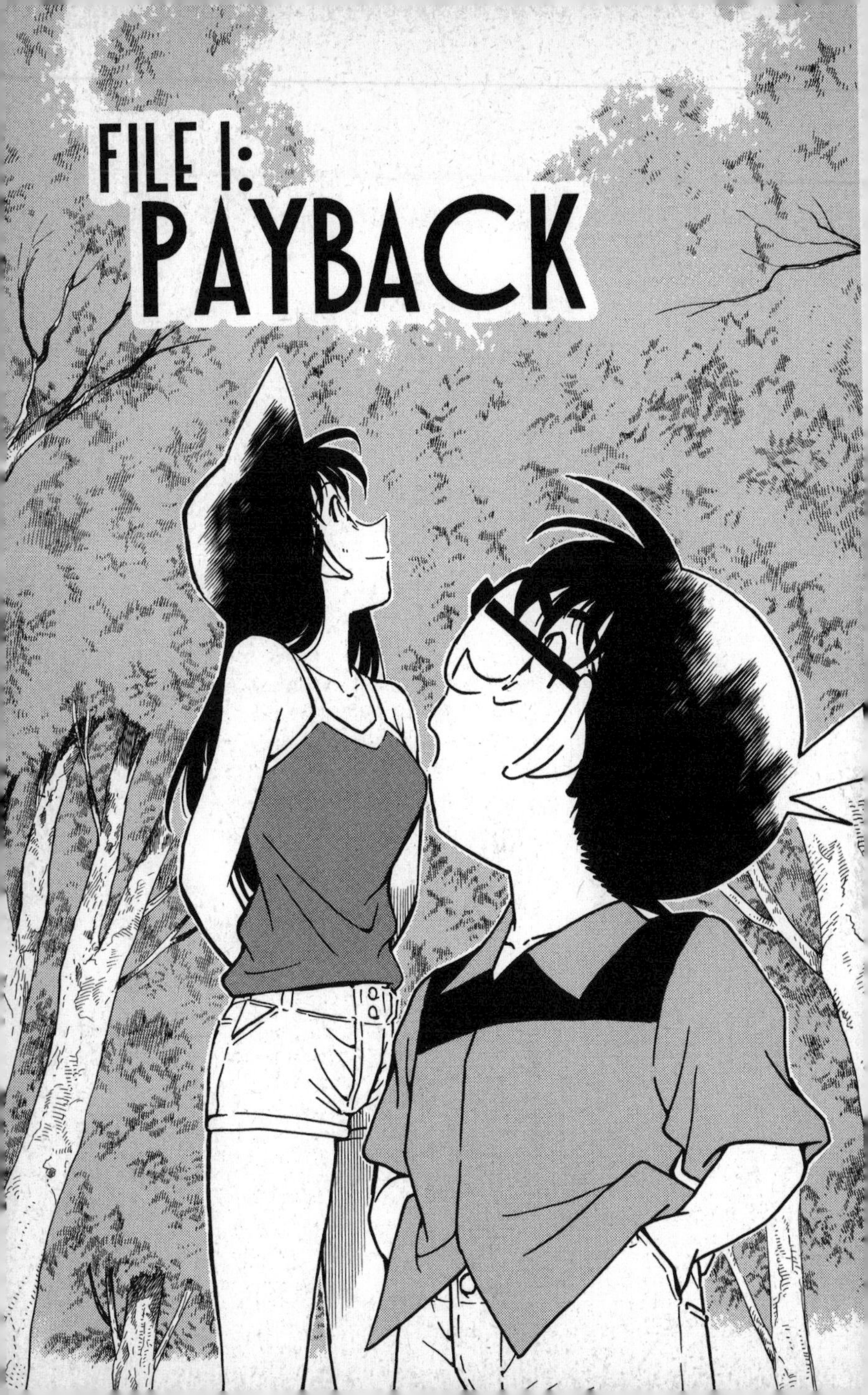
FILE 1:
PAYBACK

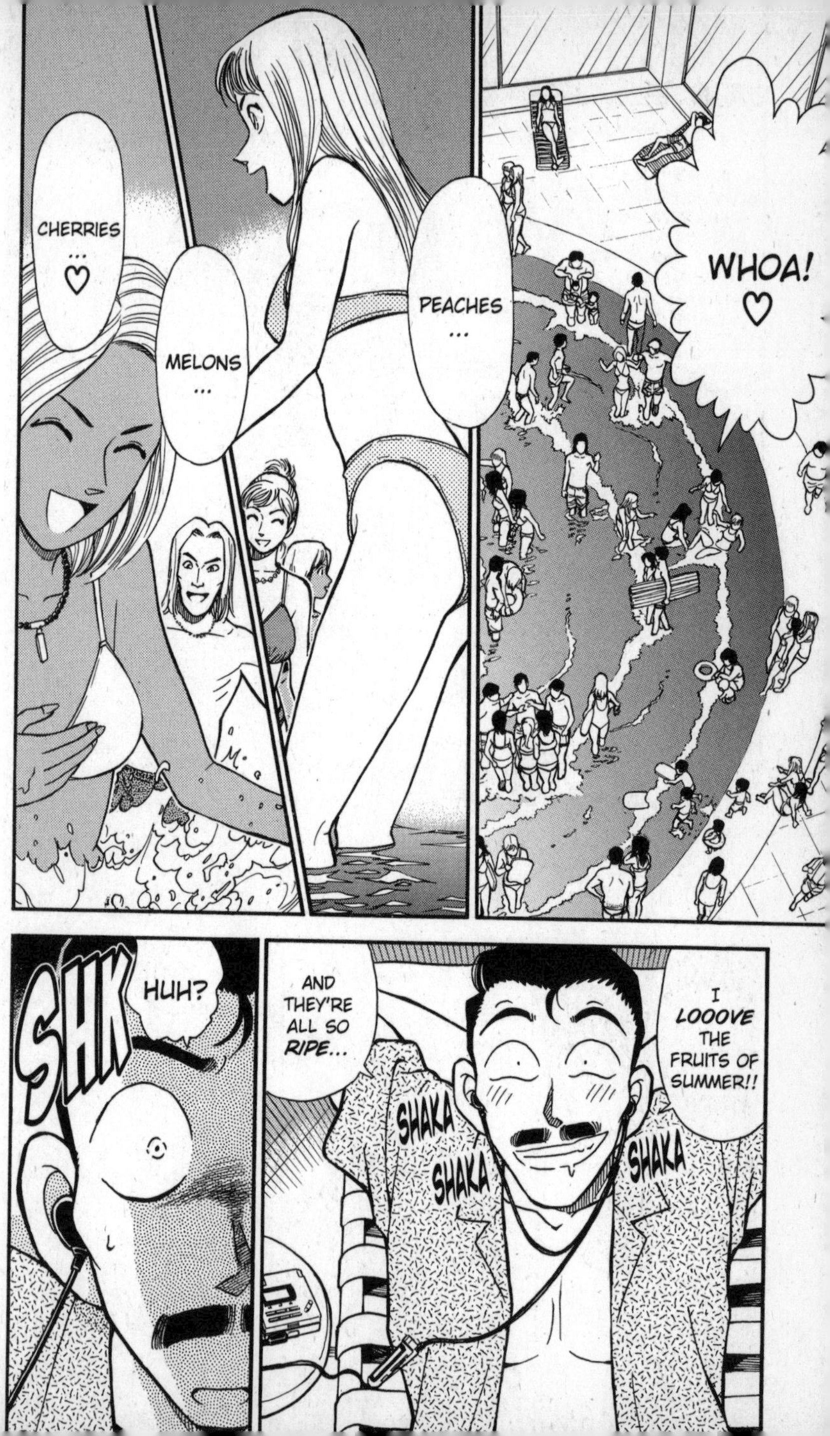
WHOA! ♡
PEACHES ...
MELONS ...
CHERRIES ... ♡
I LOOOVE THE FRUITS OF SUMMER!!
AND THEY'RE ALL SO RIPE...
SHAKA SHAKA SHAKA
HUH?
SHK

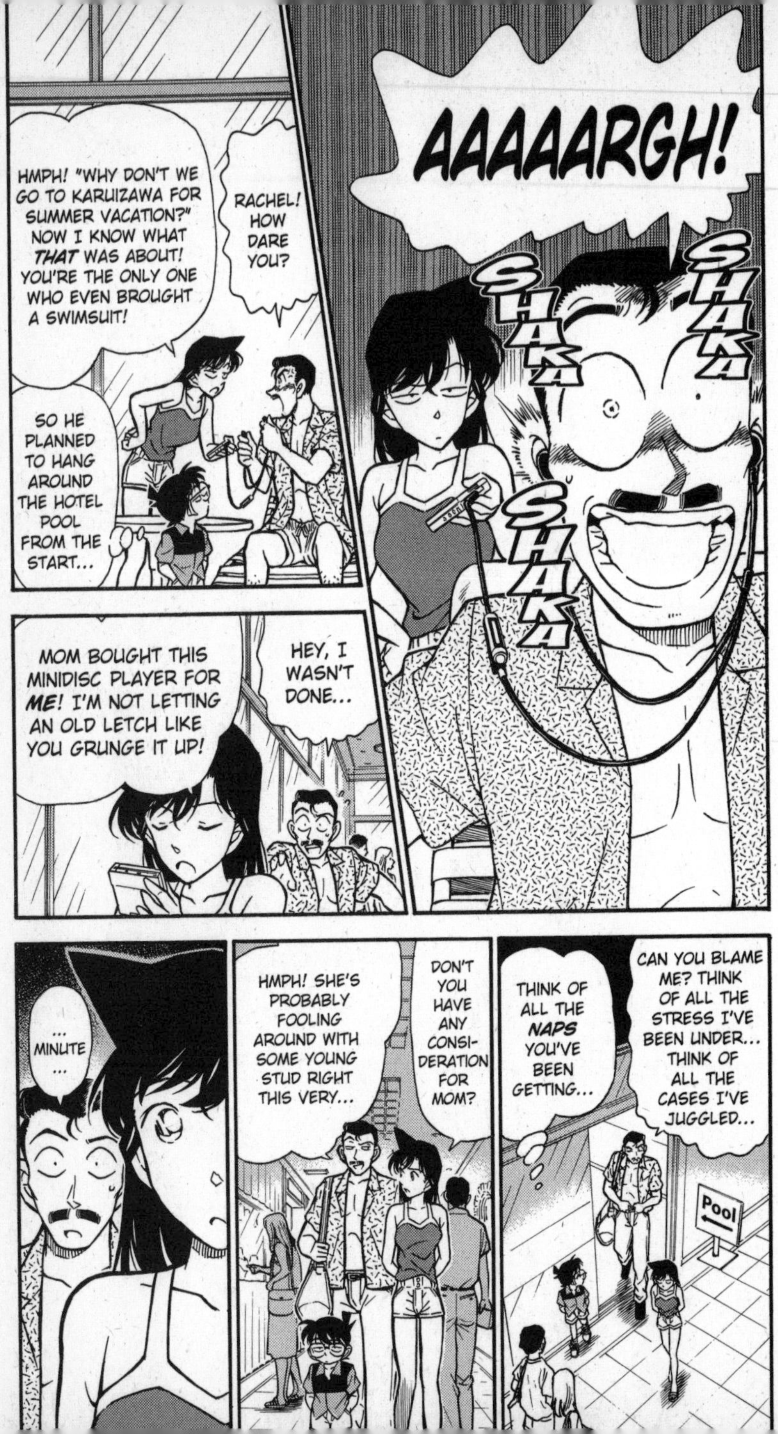
AAAAARGH!
SHAKA
SHAKA
SHAKA
SHAKA
RACHEL! HOW DARE YOU?
HMPH! "WHY DON'T WE GO TO KARUIZAWA FOR SUMMER VACATION?" NOW I KNOW WHAT THAT WAS ABOUT! YOU'RE THE ONLY ONE WHO EVEN BROUGHT A SWIMSUIT!
SO HE PLANNED TO HANG AROUND THE HOTEL POOL FROM THE START...
HEY, I WASN'T DONE...
MOM BOUGHT THIS MINIDISC PLAYER FOR ME! I'M NOT LETTING AN OLD LETCH LIKE YOU GRUNGE IT UP!
CAN YOU BLAME ME? THINK OF ALL THE STRESS I'VE BEEN UNDER... THINK OF ALL THE CASES I'VE JUGGLED...
THINK OF ALL THE NAPS YOU'VE BEEN GETTING...
Pool
DON'T YOU HAVE ANY CONSIDERATION FOR MOM?
HMPH! SHE'S PROBABLY FOOLING AROUND WITH SOME YOUNG STUD RIGHT THIS VERY...
... MINUTE ...

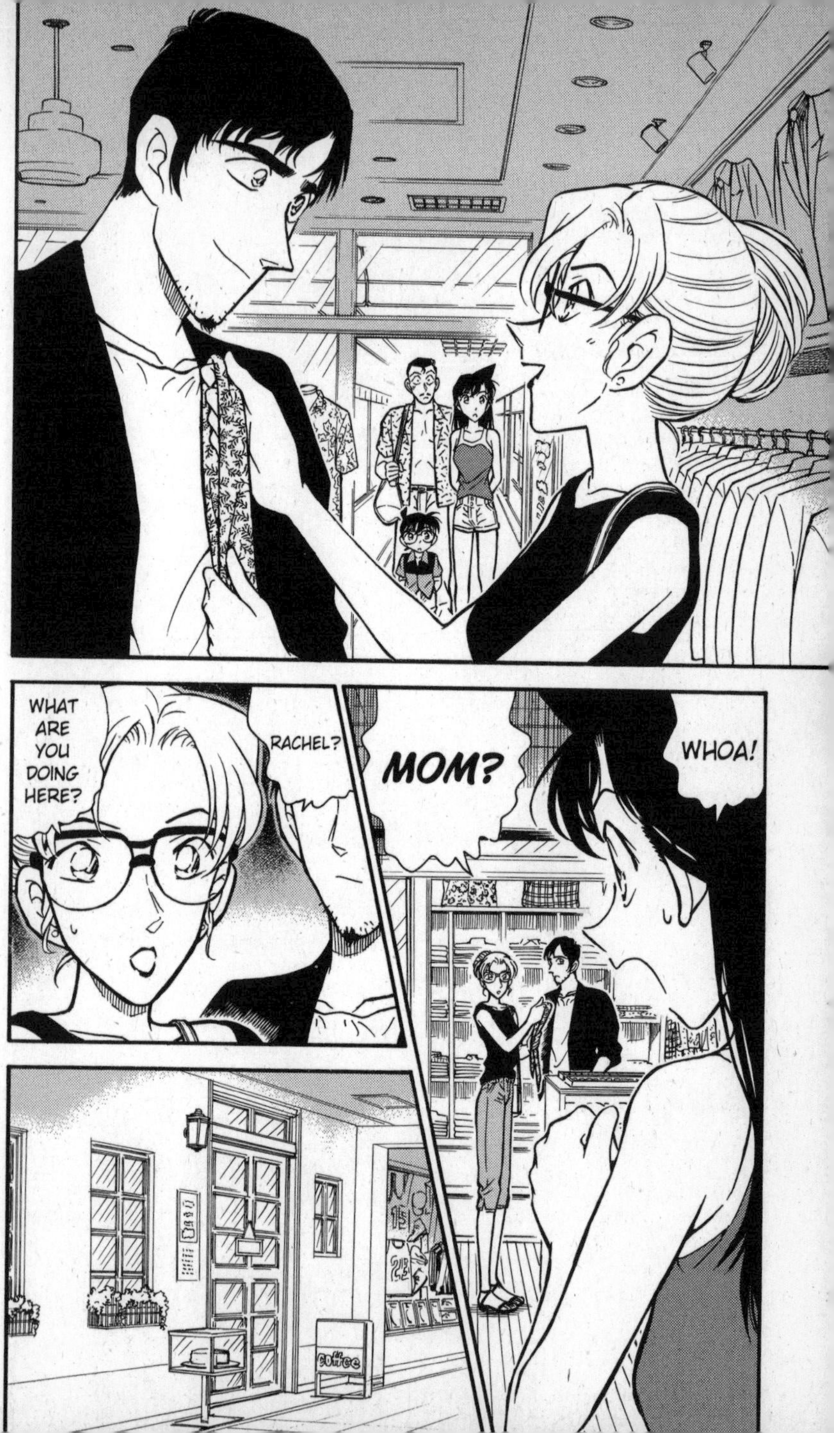
WHOA!
MOM?
RACHEL?
WHAT ARE YOU DOING HERE?
coffee

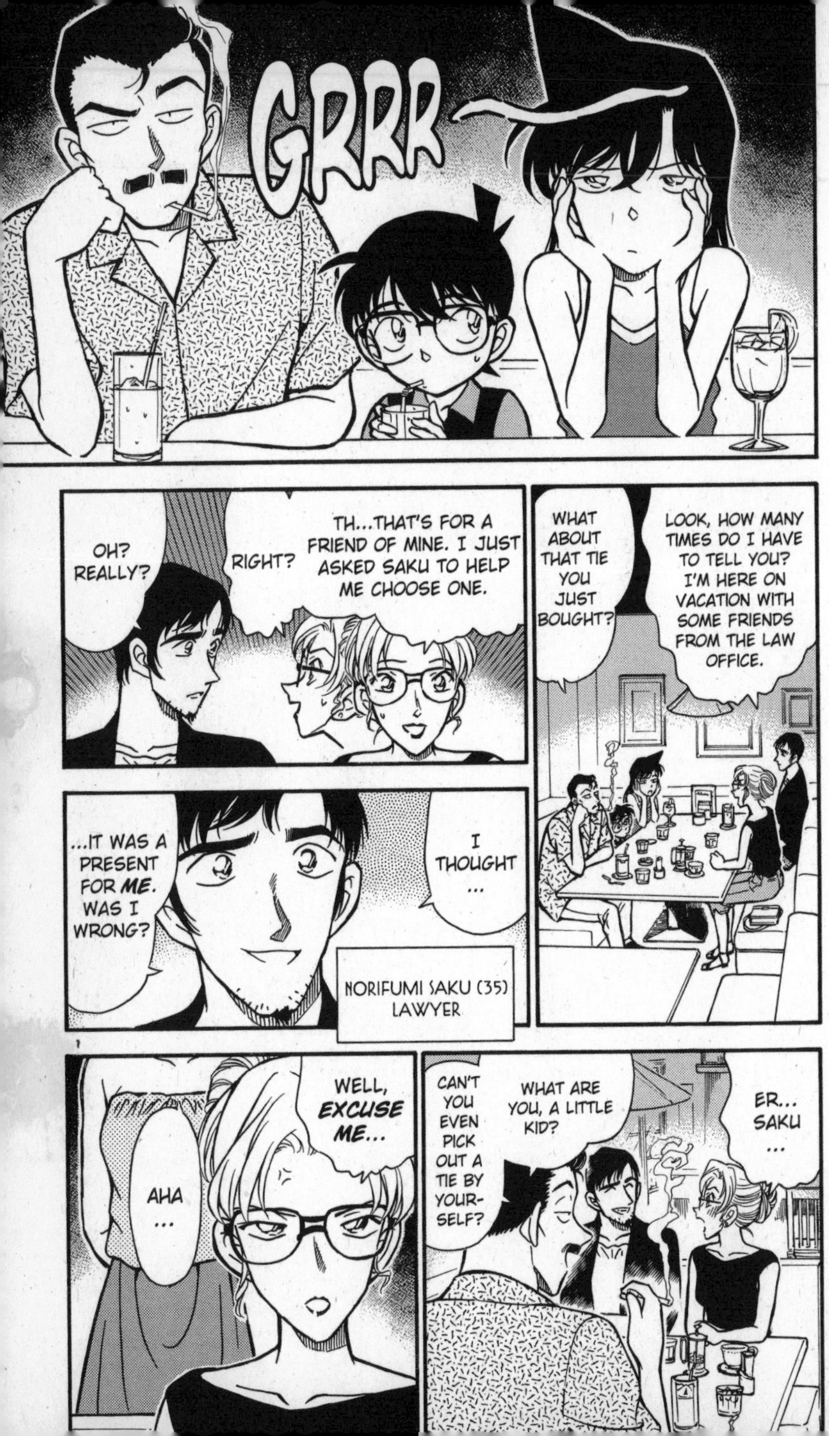
GRRR
LOOK, HOW MANY TIMES DO I HAVE TO TELL YOU? I'M HERE ON VACATION WITH SOME FRIENDS FROM THE LAW OFFICE.
WHAT ABOUT THAT TIE YOU JUST BOUGHT?
TH...THAT'S FOR A FRIEND OF MINE. I JUST ASKED SAKU TO HELP ME CHOOSE ONE.
RIGHT?
OH? REALLY?
I THOUGHT ...
...IT WAS A PRESENT FOR **ME**. WAS I WRONG?
NORIFUMI SAKU (35) LAWYER
ER... SAKU ...
WHAT ARE YOU, A LITTLE KID?
CAN'T YOU EVEN PICK OUT A TIE BY YOURSELF?
WELL, **EXCUSE ME**...
AHA ...

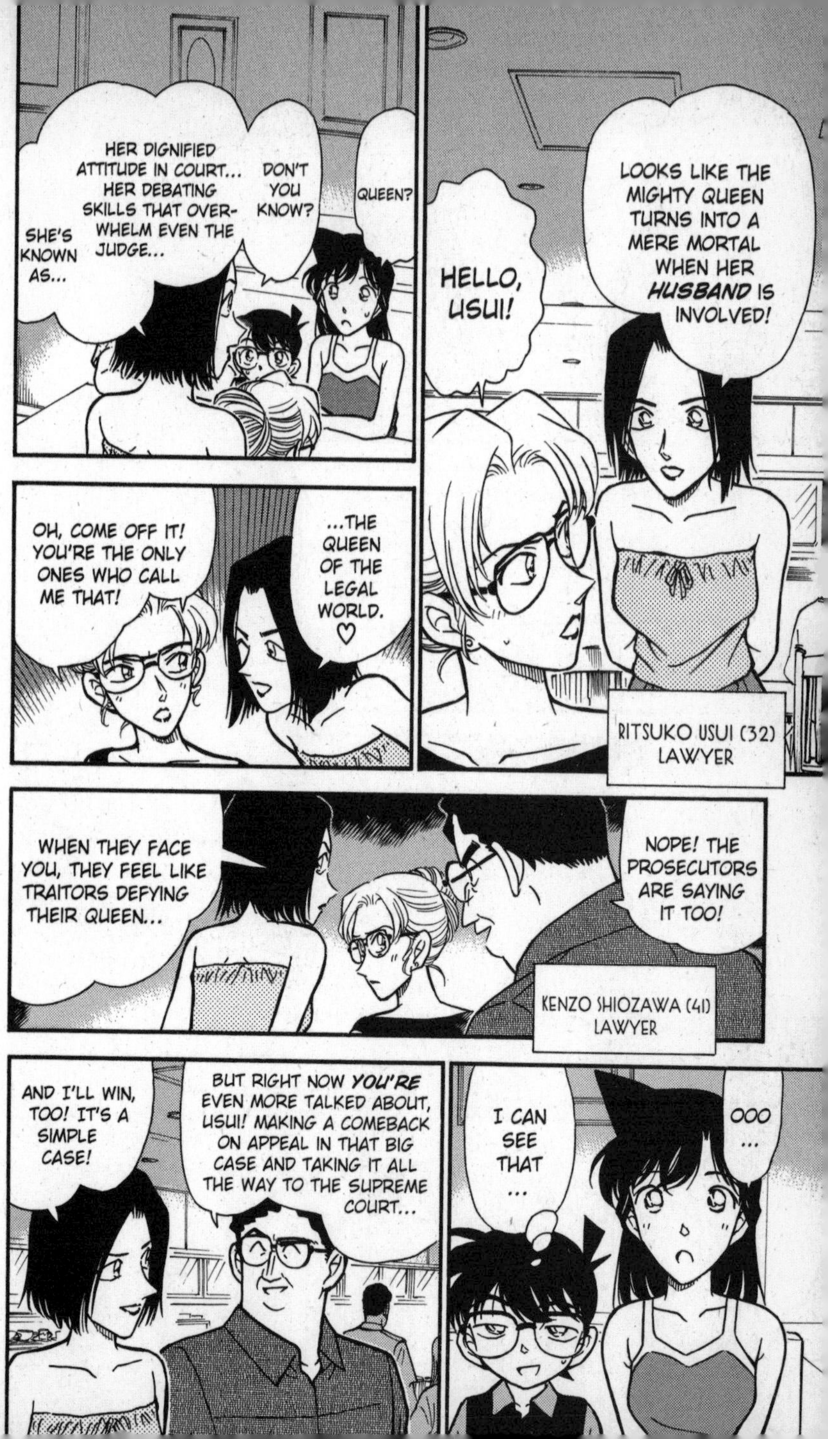
LOOKS LIKE THE MIGHTY QUEEN TURNS INTO A MERE MORTAL WHEN HER HUSBAND IS INVOLVED!
HELLO, USUI!
RITSUKO USUI (32) LAWYER
QUEEN?
DON'T YOU KNOW?
HER DIGNIFIED ATTITUDE IN COURT... HER DEBATING SKILLS THAT OVER-WHELM EVEN THE JUDGE...
SHE'S KNOWN AS...
...THE QUEEN OF THE LEGAL WORLD. ♡
OH, COME OFF IT! YOU'RE THE ONLY ONES WHO CALL ME THAT!
NOPE! THE PROSECUTORS ARE SAYING IT TOO!
WHEN THEY FACE YOU, THEY FEEL LIKE TRAITORS DEFYING THEIR QUEEN...
KENZO SHIOZAWA (41) LAWYER
OOO ...
I CAN SEE THAT ...
BUT RIGHT NOW YOU'RE EVEN MORE TALKED ABOUT, USUI! MAKING A COMEBACK ON APPEAL IN THAT BIG CASE AND TAKING IT ALL THE WAY TO THE SUPREME COURT...
AND I'LL WIN, TOO! IT'S A SIMPLE CASE!

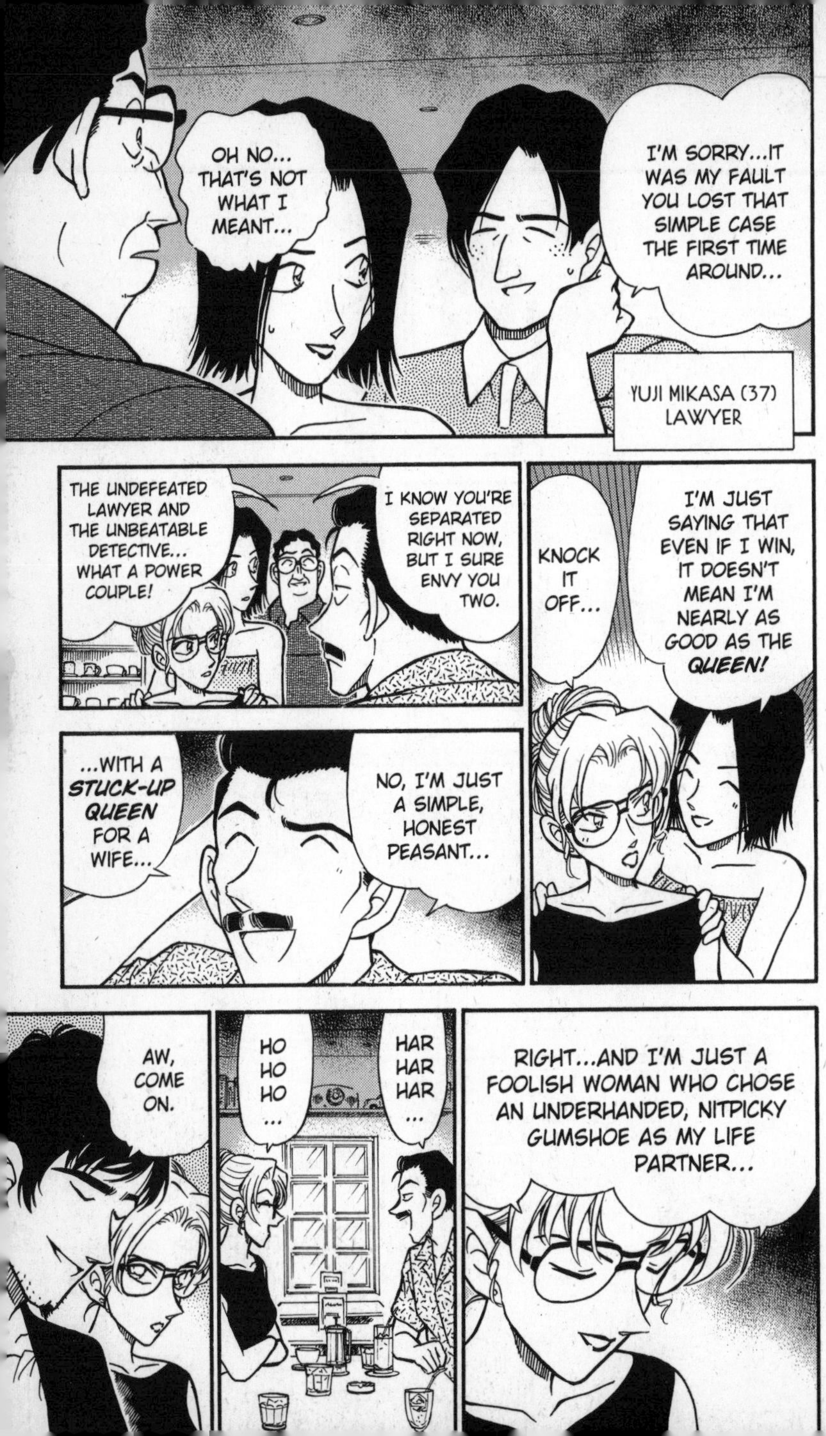
I'M SORRY...IT WAS MY FAULT YOU LOST THAT SIMPLE CASE THE FIRST TIME AROUND...
YUJI MIKASA (37) LAWYER
OH NO... THAT'S NOT WHAT I MEANT...
I'M JUST SAYING THAT EVEN IF I WIN, IT DOESN'T MEAN I'M NEARLY AS GOOD AS THE **QUEEN!**
KNOCK IT OFF...
I KNOW YOU'RE SEPARATED RIGHT NOW, BUT I SURE ENVY YOU TWO.
THE UNDEFEATED LAWYER AND THE UNBEATABLE DETECTIVE... WHAT A POWER COUPLE!
NO, I'M JUST A SIMPLE, HONEST PEASANT...
...WITH A **STUCK-UP QUEEN** FOR A WIFE...
RIGHT...AND I'M JUST A FOOLISH WOMAN WHO CHOSE AN UNDERHANDED, NITPICKY GUMSHOE AS MY LIFE PARTNER...
HAR HAR HAR ...
HO HO HO ...
AW, COME ON.

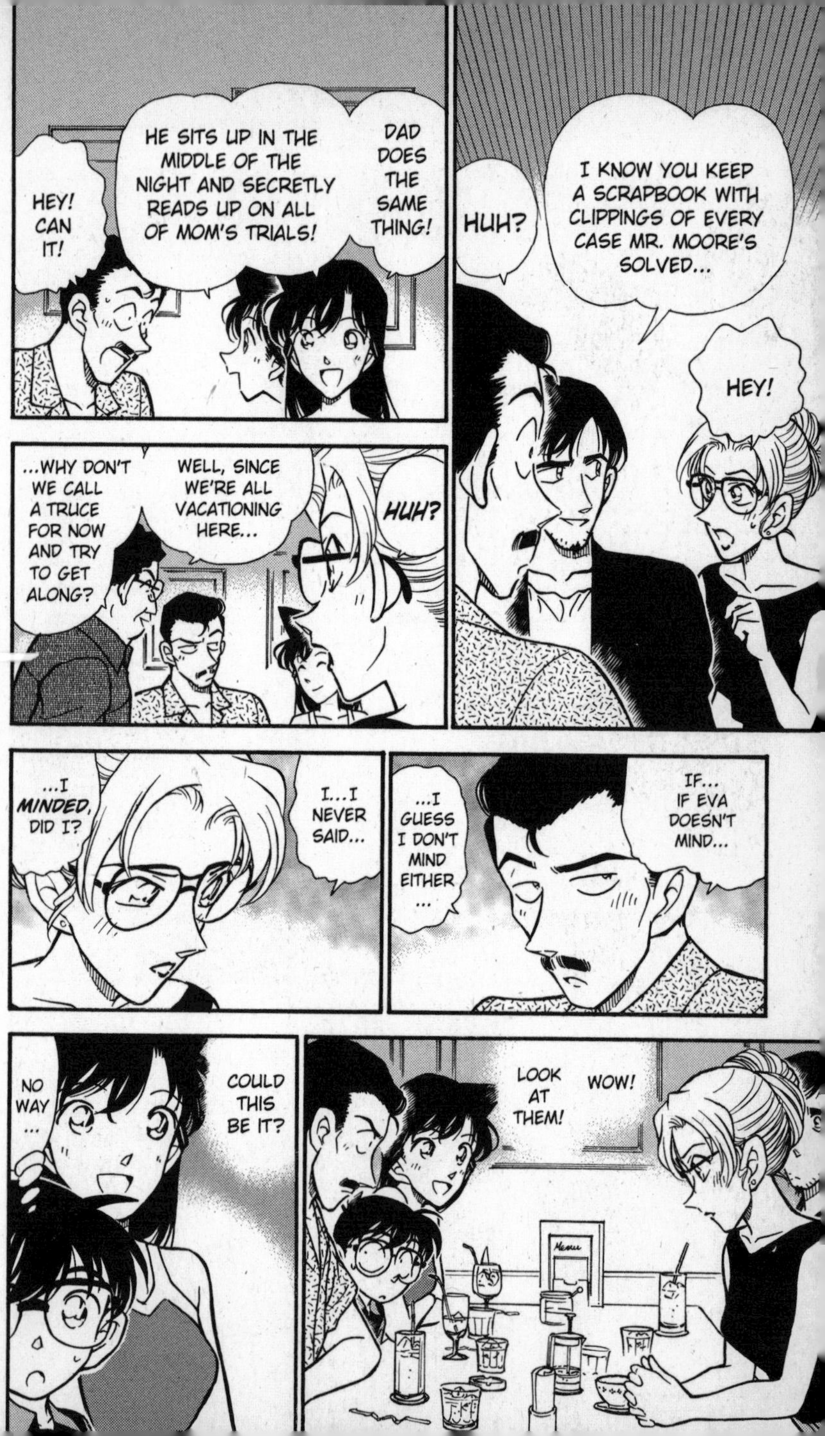
I KNOW YOU KEEP A SCRAPBOOK WITH CLIPPINGS OF EVERY CASE MR. MOORE'S SOLVED...
HUH?
HEY!
DAD DOES THE SAME THING!
HE SITS UP IN THE MIDDLE OF THE NIGHT AND SECRETLY READS UP ON ALL OF MOM'S TRIALS!
HEY! CAN IT!
HUH?
WELL, SINCE WE'RE ALL VACATIONING HERE...
...WHY DON'T WE CALL A TRUCE FOR NOW AND TRY TO GET ALONG?
IF... IF EVA DOESN'T MIND...
...I GUESS I DON'T MIND EITHER ...
I...I NEVER SAID...
...I *MINDED*, DID I?
WOW!
LOOK AT THEM!
COULD THIS BE IT?
NO WAY ...

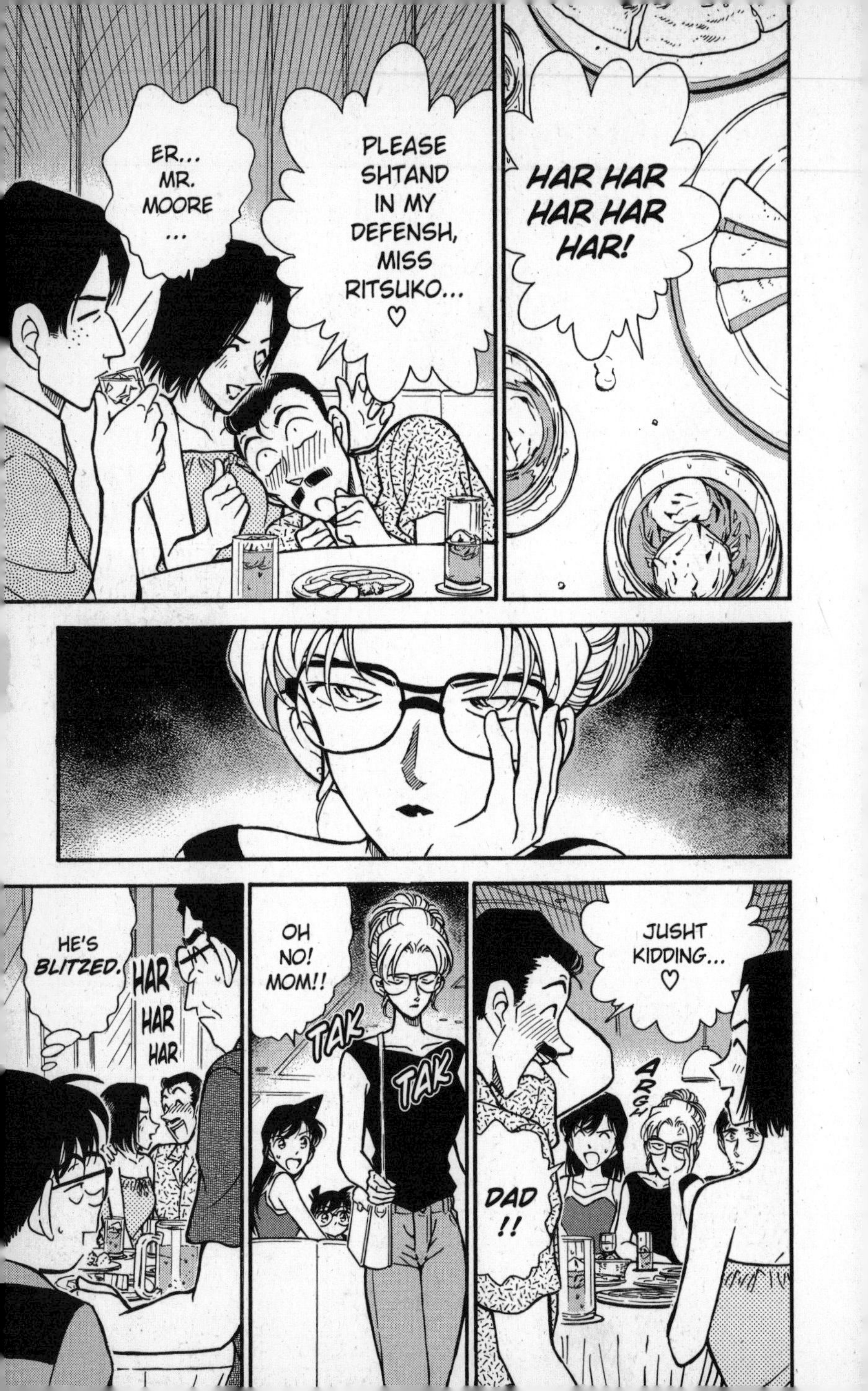
HAR HAR HAR HAR HAR!
PLEASE SHTAND IN MY DEFENSH, MISS RITSUKO... ♡
ER... MR. MOORE...
JUSHT KIDDING... ♡
ARGH
DAD!!
OH NO! MOM!!
TAK
TAK
HE'S BLITZED.
HAR HAR HAR

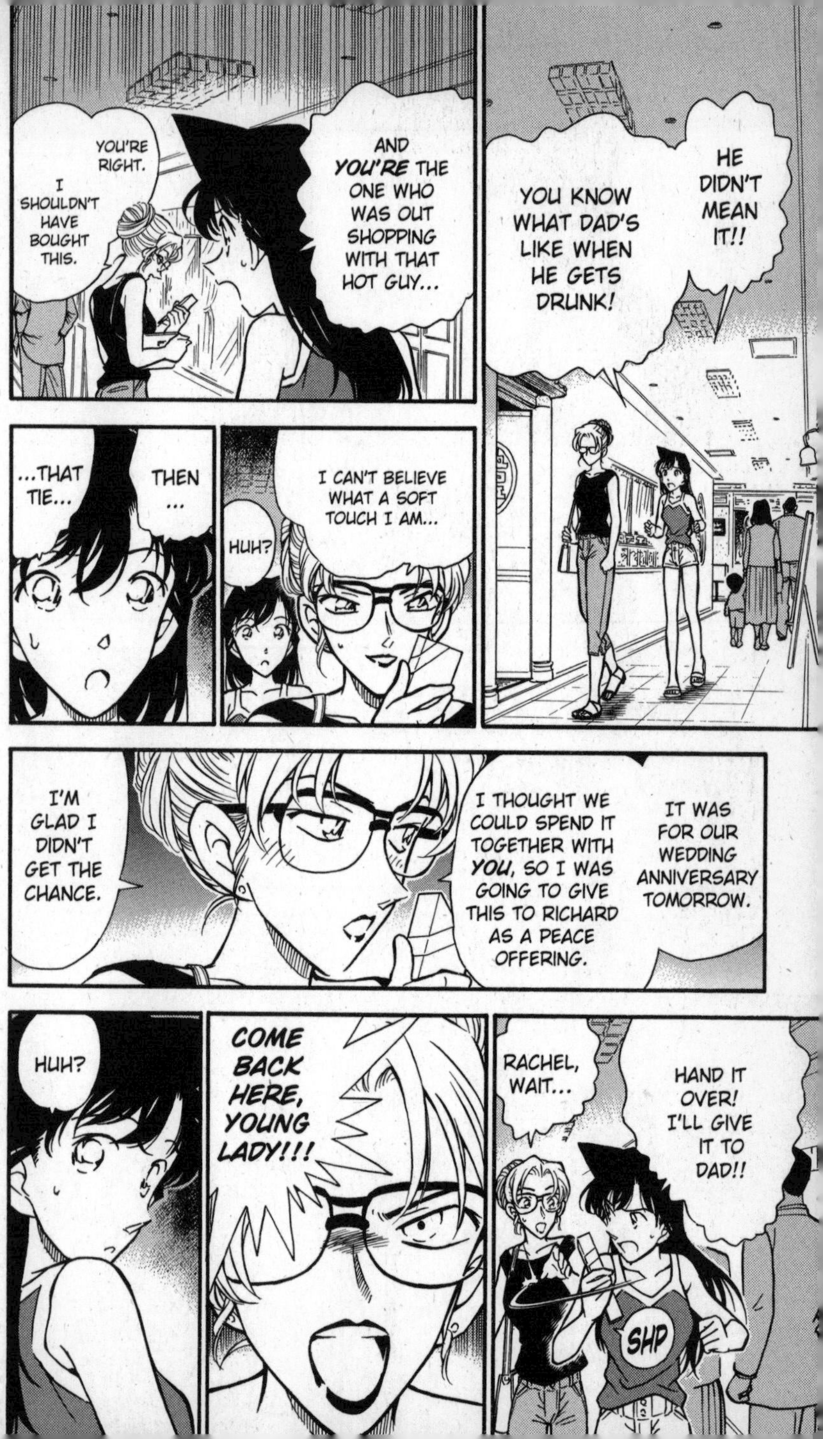
HE DIDN'T MEAN IT!!
YOU KNOW WHAT DAD'S LIKE WHEN HE GETS DRUNK!
AND *YOU'RE* THE ONE WHO WAS OUT SHOPPING WITH THAT HOT GUY...
YOU'RE RIGHT.
I SHOULDN'T HAVE BOUGHT THIS.
I CAN'T BELIEVE WHAT A SOFT TOUCH I AM...
HUH?
THEN ...
...THAT TIE...
IT WAS FOR OUR WEDDING ANNIVERSARY TOMORROW.
I THOUGHT WE COULD SPEND IT TOGETHER WITH *YOU*, SO I WAS GOING TO GIVE THIS TO RICHARD AS A PEACE OFFERING.
I'M GLAD I DIDN'T GET THE CHANCE.
HAND IT OVER! I'LL GIVE IT TO DAD!!
RACHEL, WAIT...
SHP
COME BACK HERE, YOUNG LADY!!!
HUH?

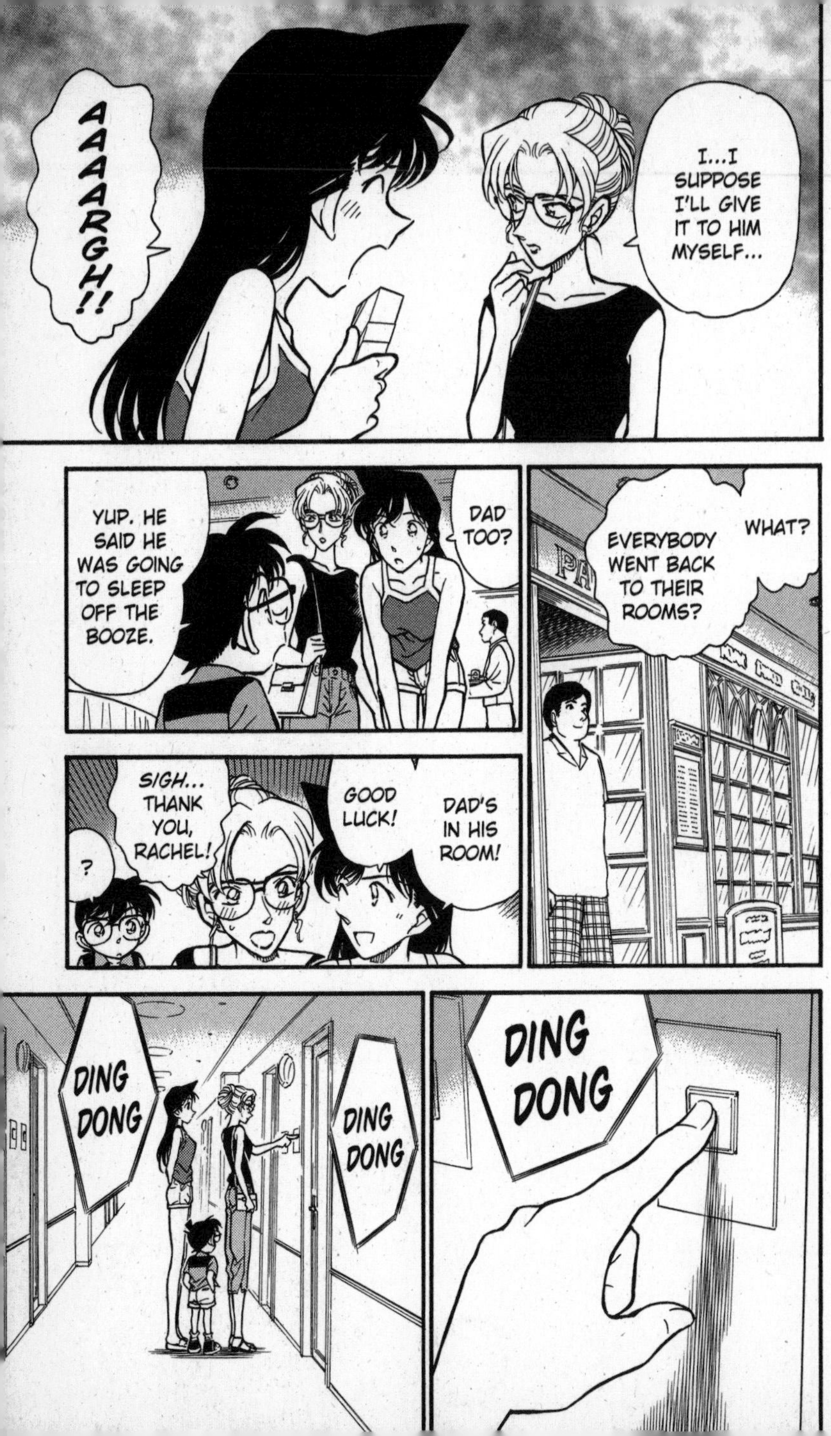

I...I SUPPOSE I'LL GIVE IT TO HIM MYSELF...
AAAARGH!!
WHAT?
EVERYBODY WENT BACK TO THEIR ROOMS?
DAD TOO?
YUP. HE SAID HE WAS GOING TO SLEEP OFF THE BOOZE.
DAD'S IN HIS ROOM!
GOOD LUCK!
SIGH... THANK YOU, RACHEL!
?
DING DONG
DING DONG
DING DONG

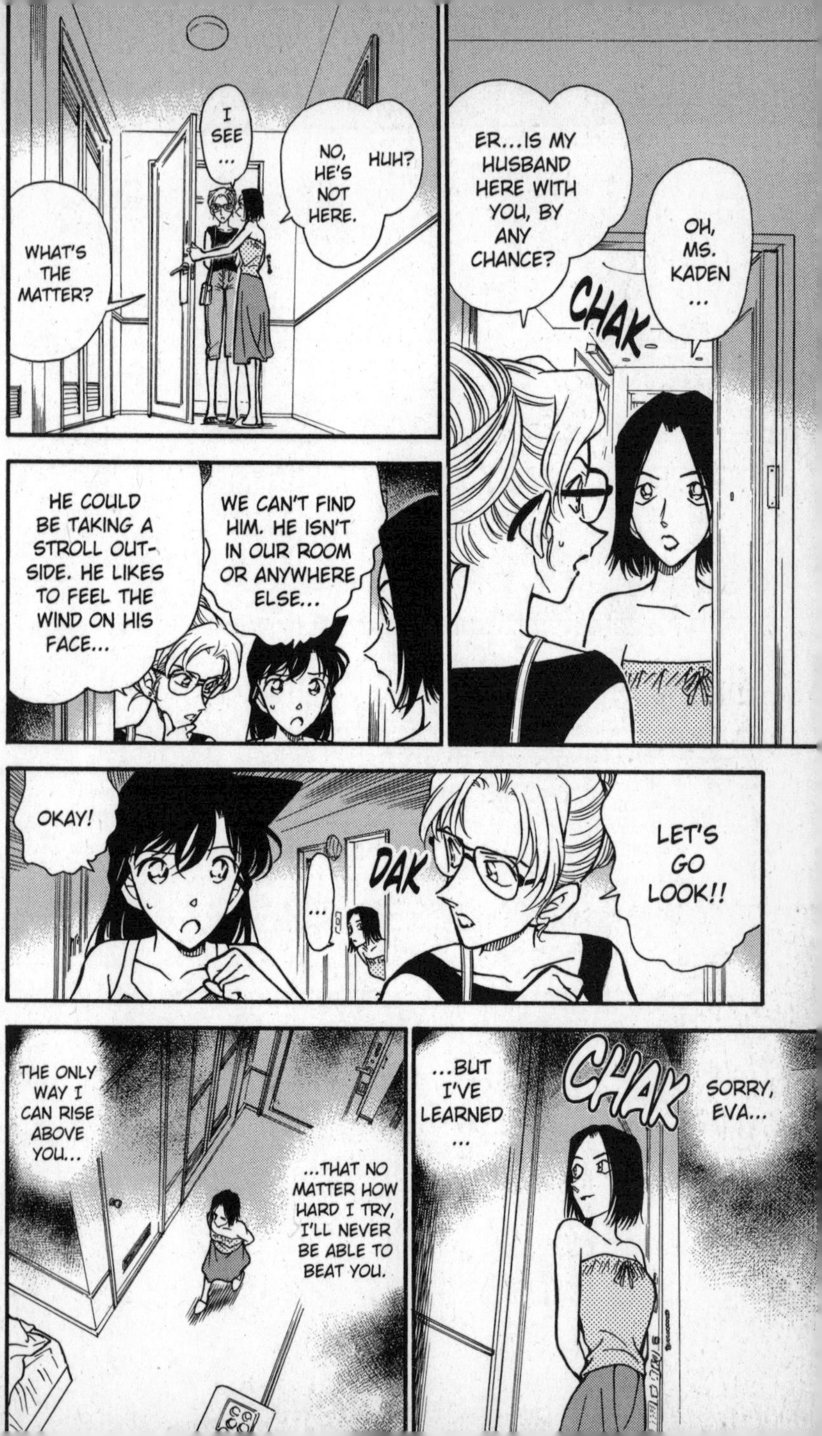
OH, MS. KADEN...
CHAK
ER...IS MY HUSBAND HERE WITH YOU, BY ANY CHANCE?
HUH?
NO, HE'S NOT HERE.
I SEE...
WHAT'S THE MATTER?
WE CAN'T FIND HIM. HE ISN'T IN OUR ROOM OR ANYWHERE ELSE...
HE COULD BE TAKING A STROLL OUT-SIDE. HE LIKES TO FEEL THE WIND ON HIS FACE...
LET'S GO LOOK!!
DAK
...
OKAY!
SORRY, EVA...
CHAK
...BUT I'VE LEARNED...
...THAT NO MATTER HOW HARD I TRY, I'LL NEVER BE ABLE TO BEAT YOU.
THE ONLY WAY I CAN RISE ABOVE YOU...

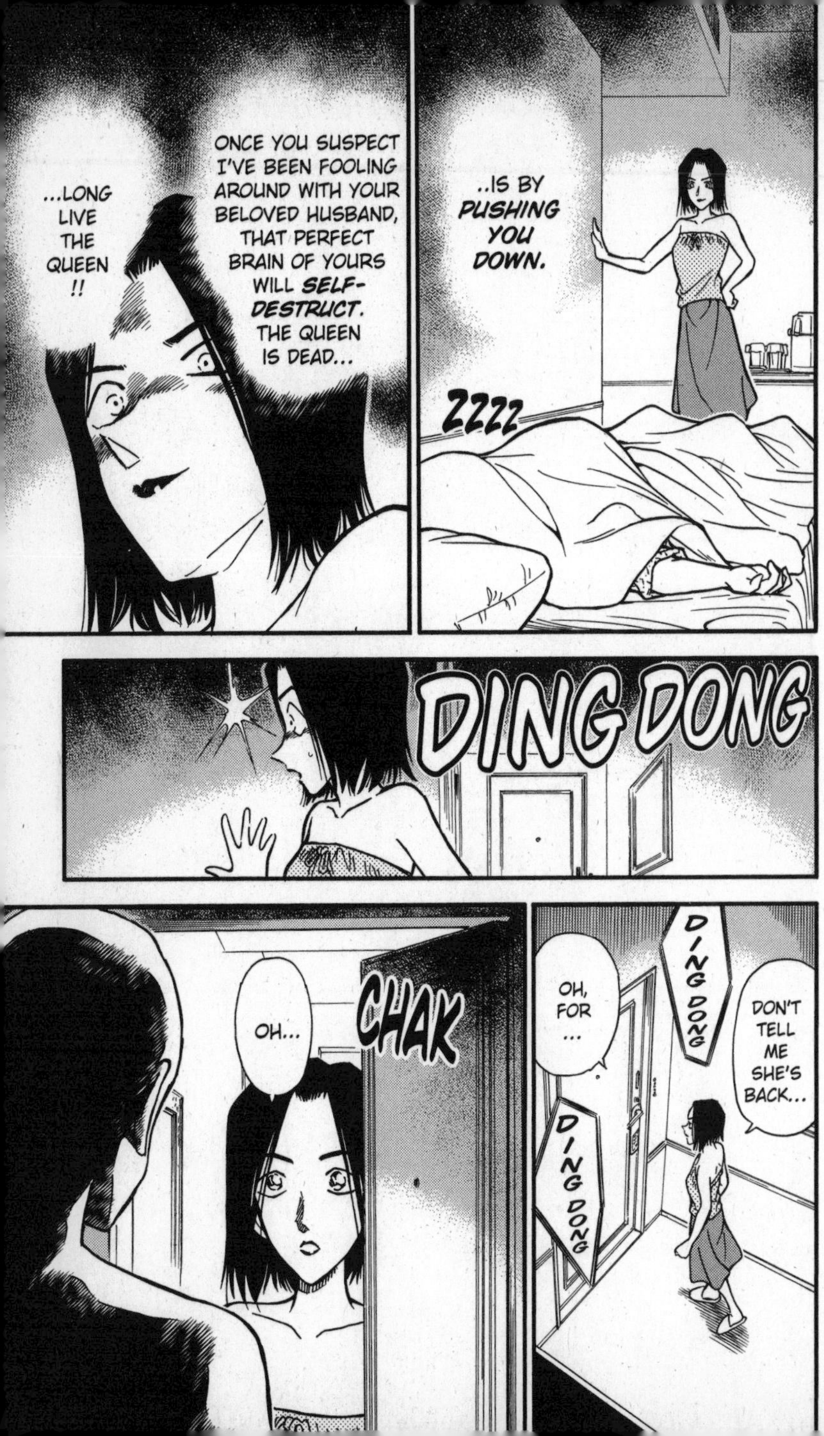
..IS BY PUSHING YOU DOWN.
ZZZZ
ONCE YOU SUSPECT I'VE BEEN FOOLING AROUND WITH YOUR BELOVED HUSBAND, THAT PERFECT BRAIN OF YOURS WILL SELF-DESTRUCT. THE QUEEN IS DEAD...
...LONG LIVE THE QUEEN !!
DING DONG
DING DONG
DON'T TELL ME SHE'S BACK...
OH, FOR ...
DING DONG
CHAK
OH...

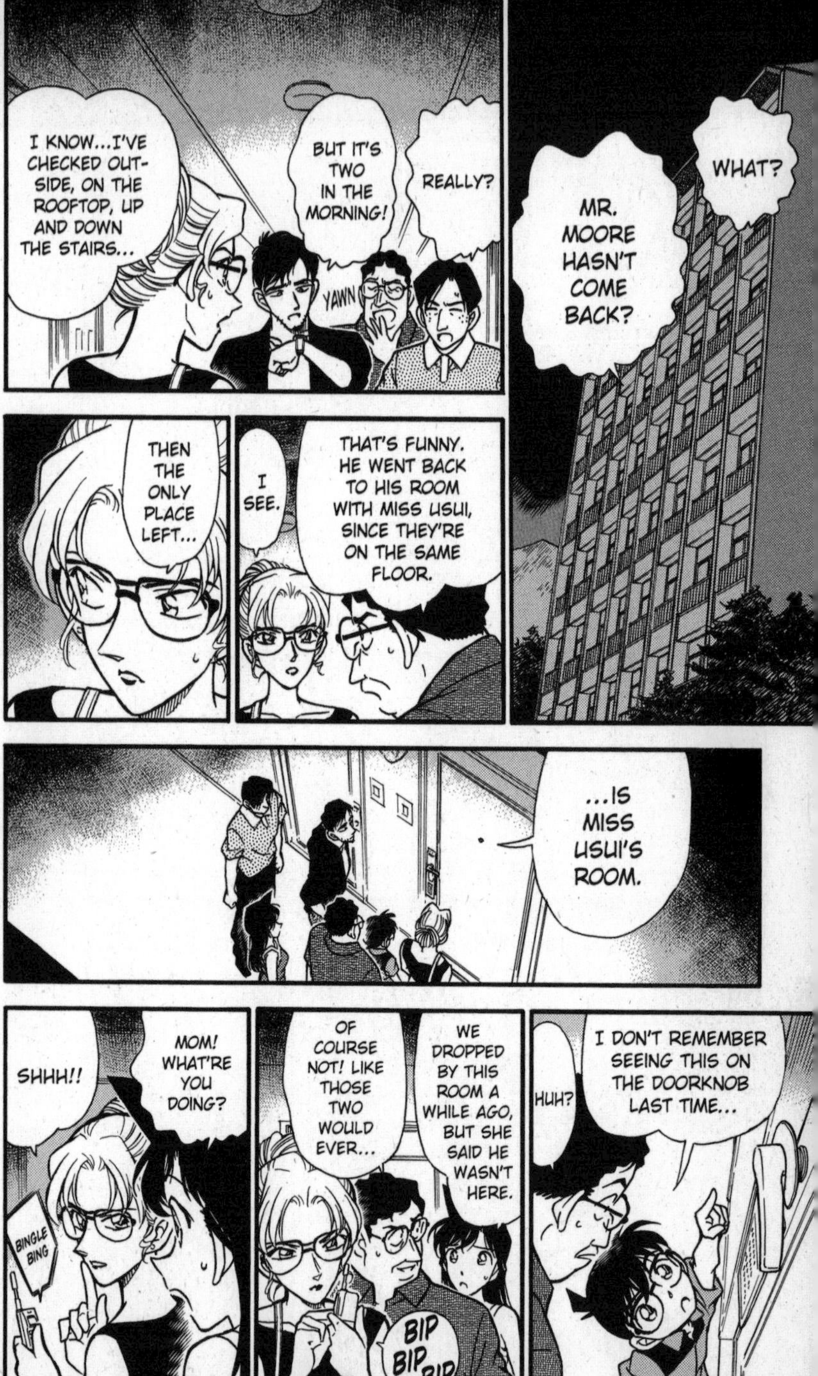
WHAT?
MR. MOORE HASN'T COME BACK?
REALLY?
BUT IT'S TWO IN THE MORNING!
YAWN
I KNOW...I'VE CHECKED OUT-SIDE, ON THE ROOFTOP, UP AND DOWN THE STAIRS...
THAT'S FUNNY. HE WENT BACK TO HIS ROOM WITH MISS USUI, SINCE THEY'RE ON THE SAME FLOOR.
I SEE.
THEN THE ONLY PLACE LEFT...
...IS MISS USUI'S ROOM.
I DON'T REMEMBER SEEING THIS ON THE DOORKNOB LAST TIME...
HUH?
WE DROPPED BY THIS ROOM A WHILE AGO, BUT SHE SAID HE WASN'T HERE.
OF COURSE NOT! LIKE THOSE TWO WOULD EVER...
BIP BIP BIP
MOM! WHAT'RE YOU DOING?
SHHH!!
BINGLE BING

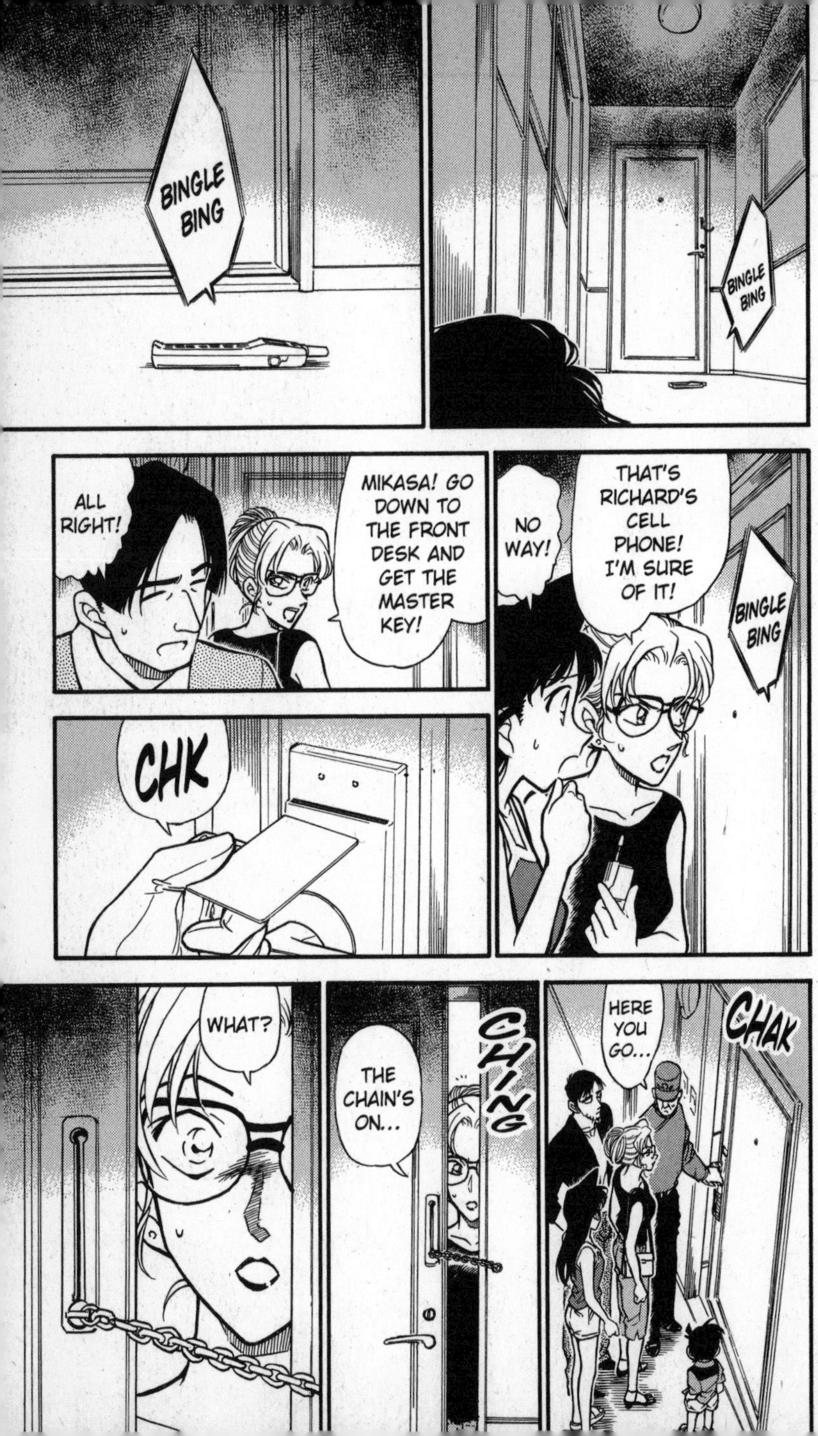
BINGLE BING
BINGLE BING
THAT'S RICHARD'S CELL PHONE! I'M SURE OF IT!
NO WAY!
BINGLE BING
MIKASA! GO DOWN TO THE FRONT DESK AND GET THE MASTER KEY!
ALL RIGHT!
CHK
CHAK
HERE YOU GO...
CHING
THE CHAIN'S ON...
WHAT?

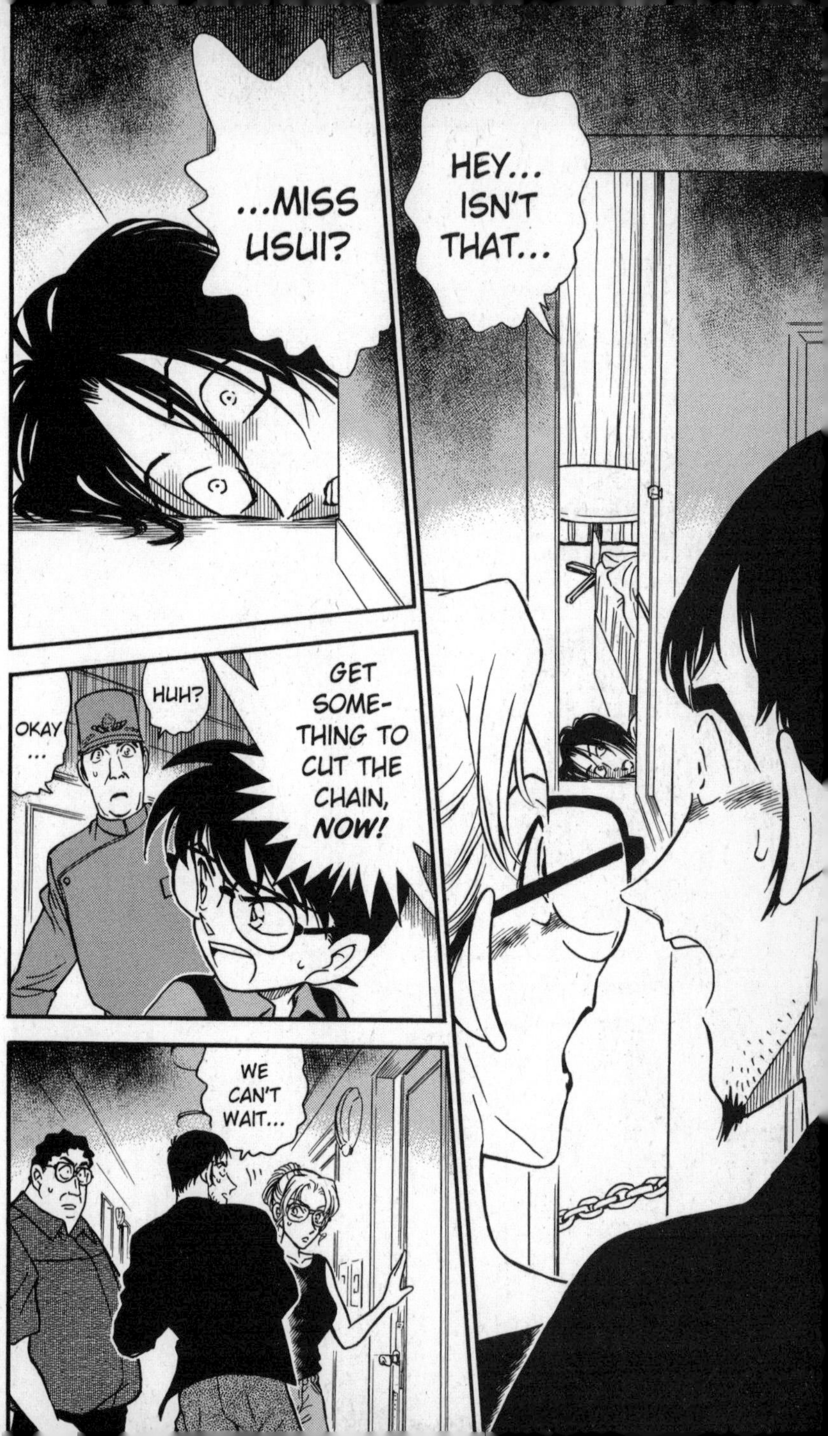
HEY... ISN'T THAT...
...MISS USUI?
GET SOME-THING TO CUT THE CHAIN, *NOW!*
HUH?
OKAY...
WE CAN'T WAIT...

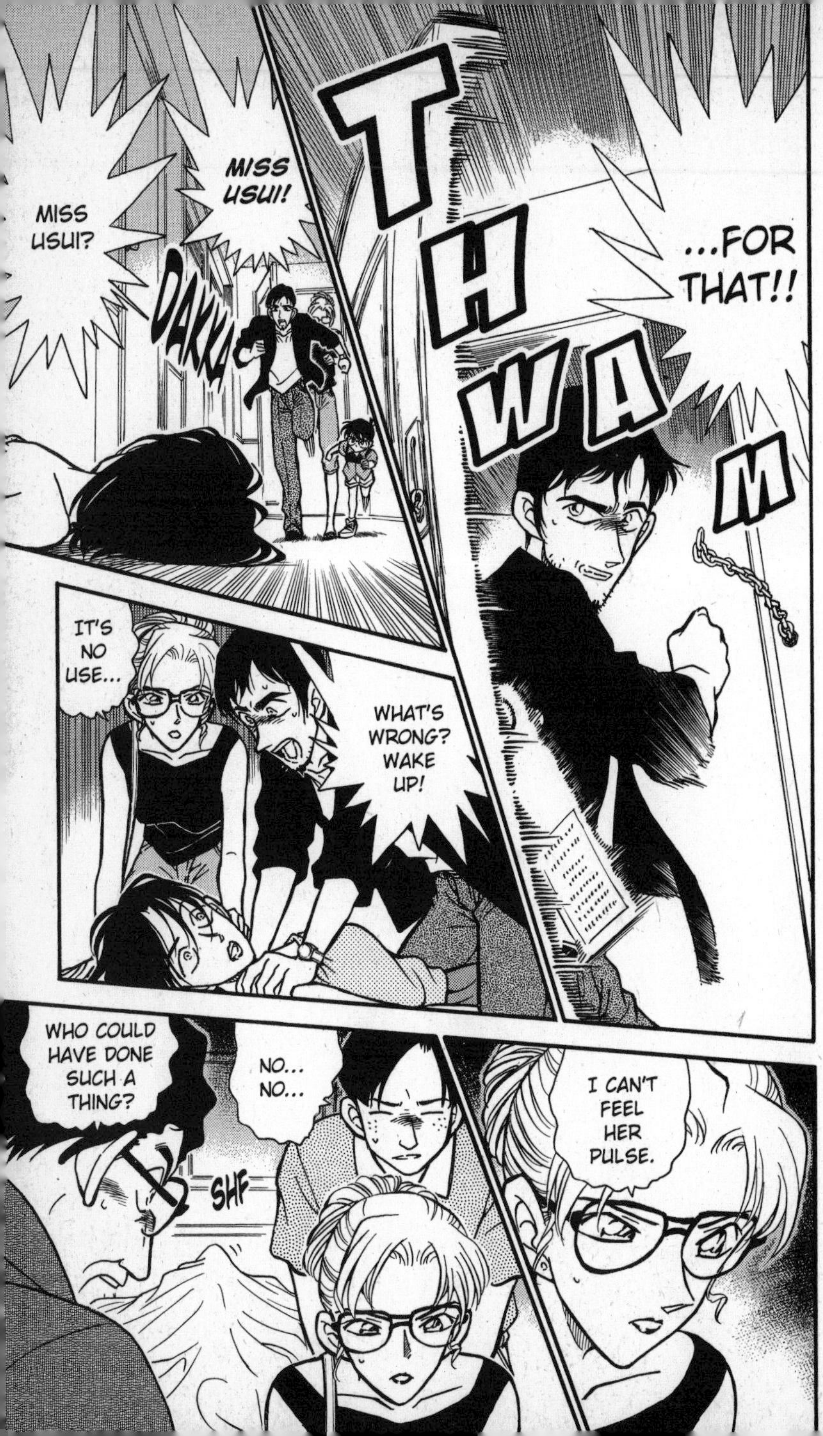
...FOR THAT!!
THWAM
MISS USUI!
DAKKA
MISS USUI?
WHAT'S WRONG? WAKE UP!
IT'S NO USE...
I CAN'T FEEL HER PULSE.
NO... NO...
WHO COULD HAVE DONE SUCH A THING?
SHF

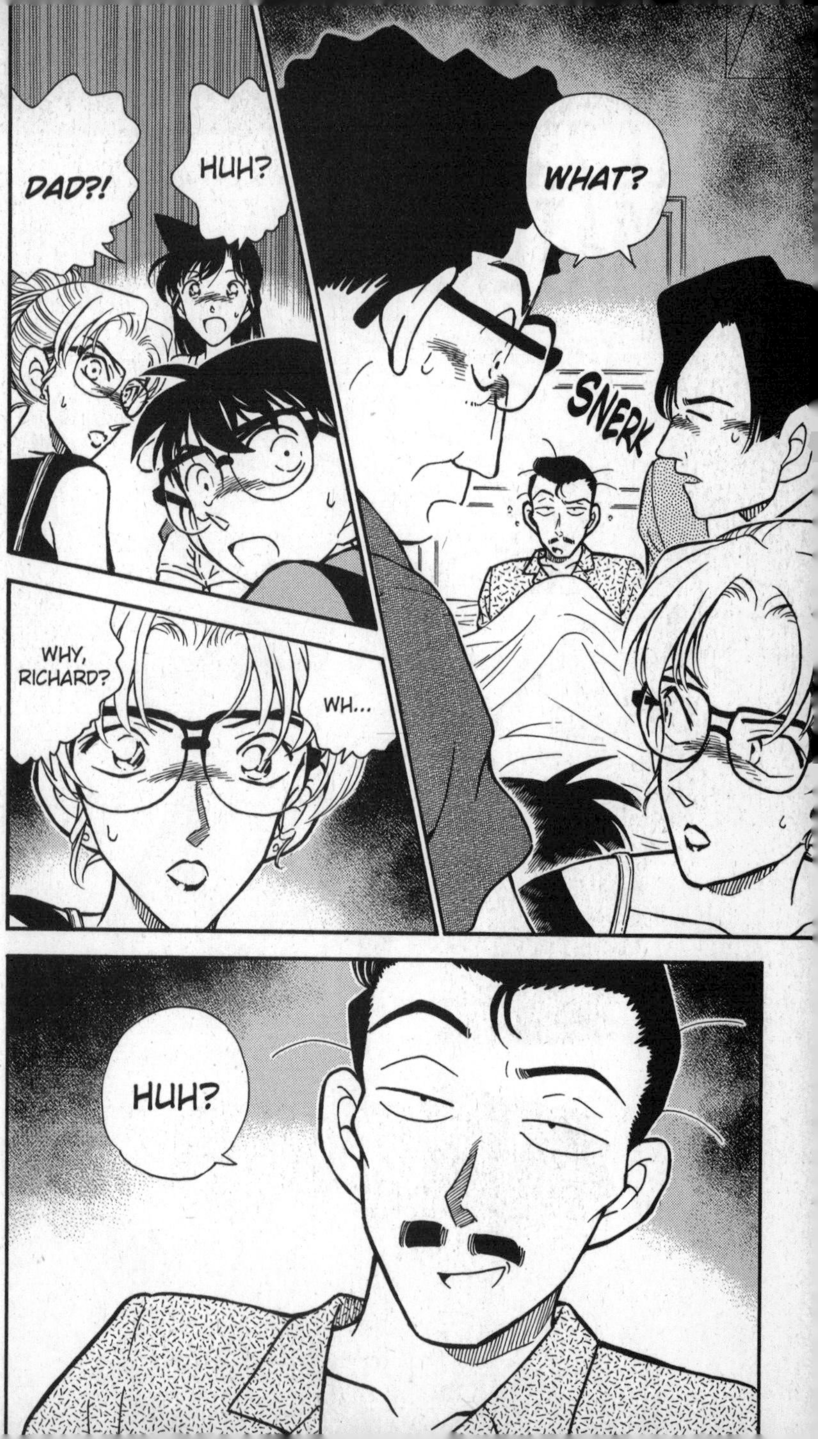
WHAT?
SNERK
HUH?
DAD?!
WHY, RICHARD?
WH...
HUH?

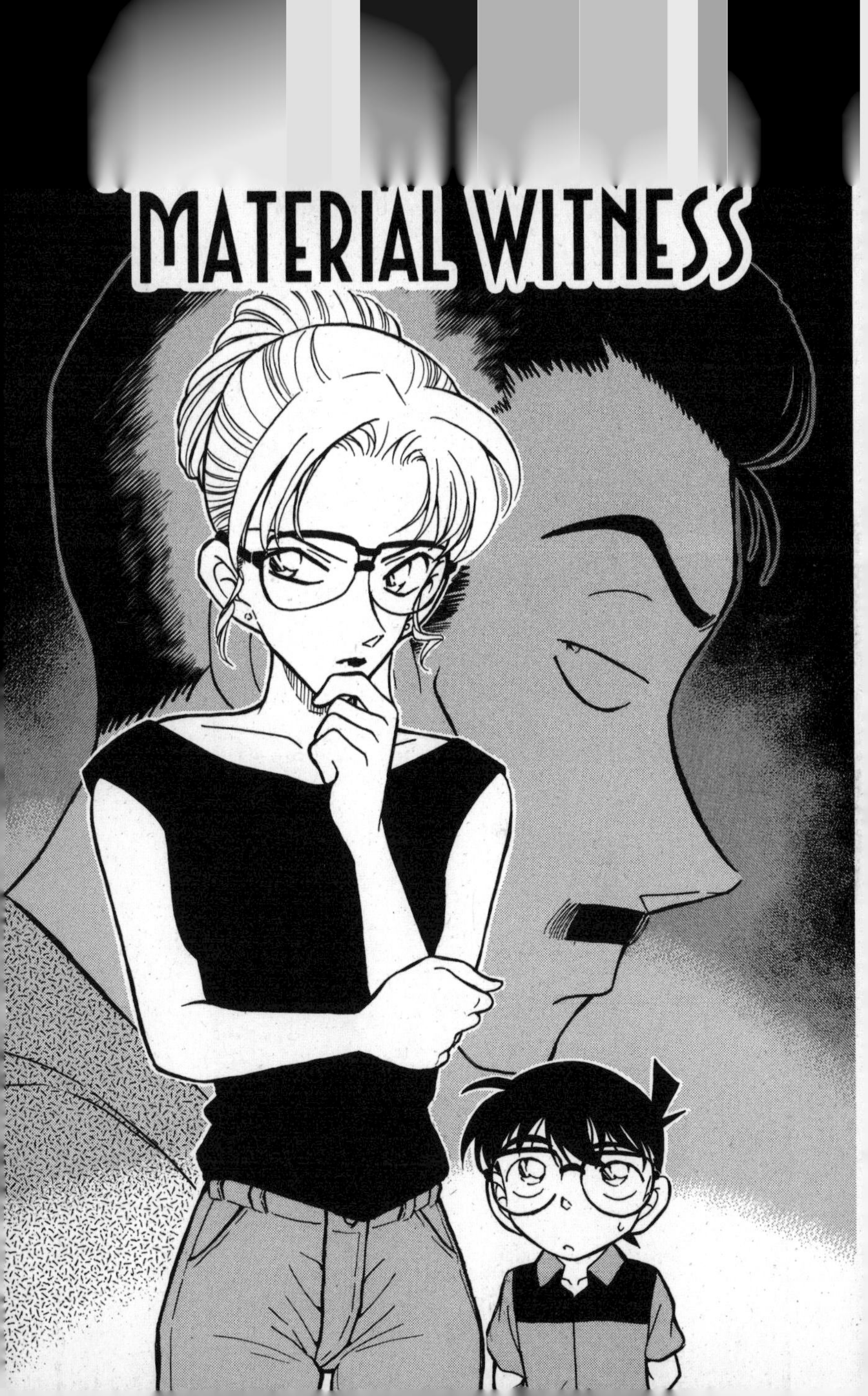
MATERIAL WITNESS

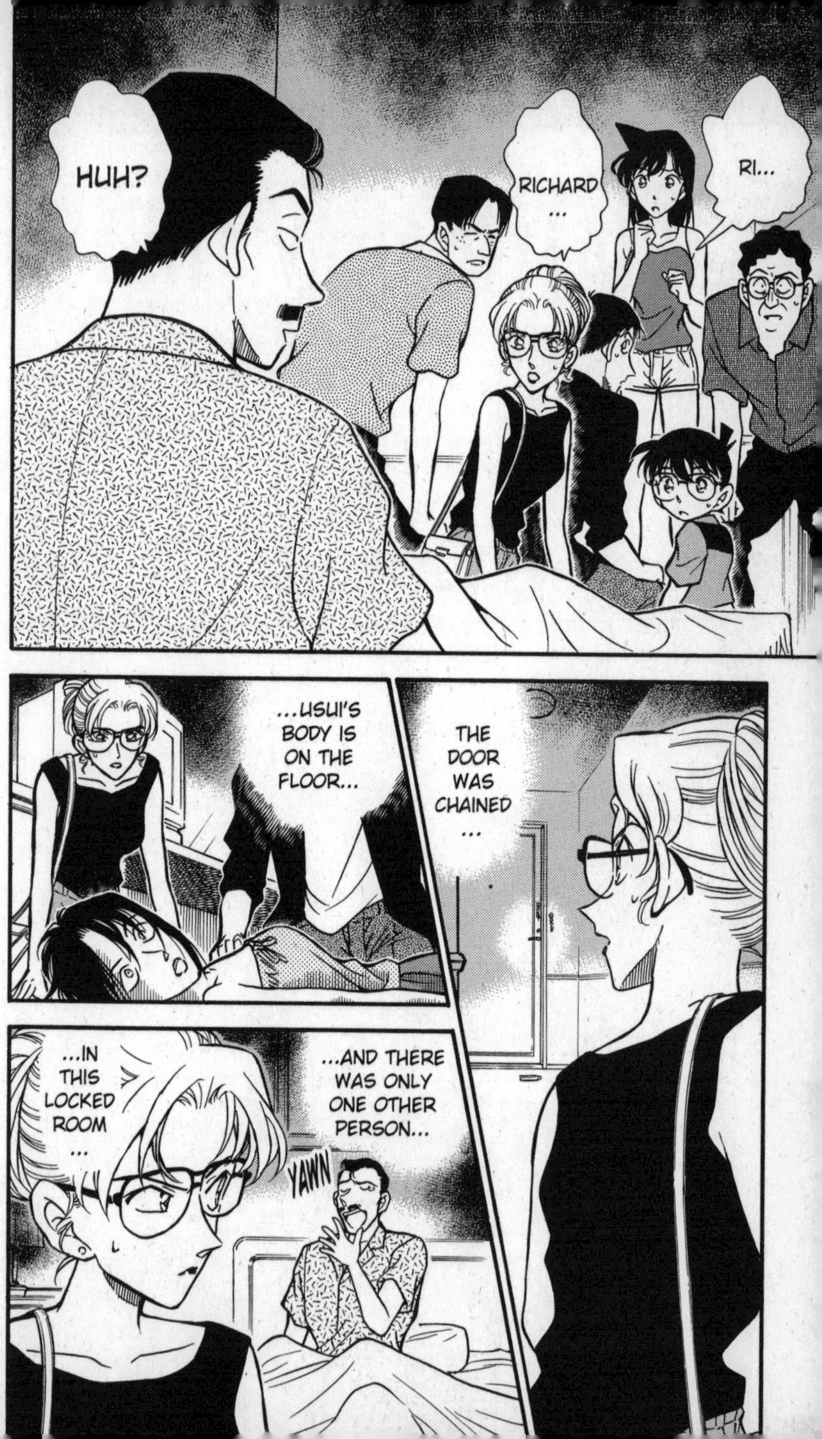
RI...
RICHARD ...
HUH?
THE DOOR WAS CHAINED ...
...USUI'S BODY IS ON THE FLOOR...
...AND THERE WAS ONLY ONE OTHER PERSON...
YAWN
...IN THIS LOCKED ROOM ...

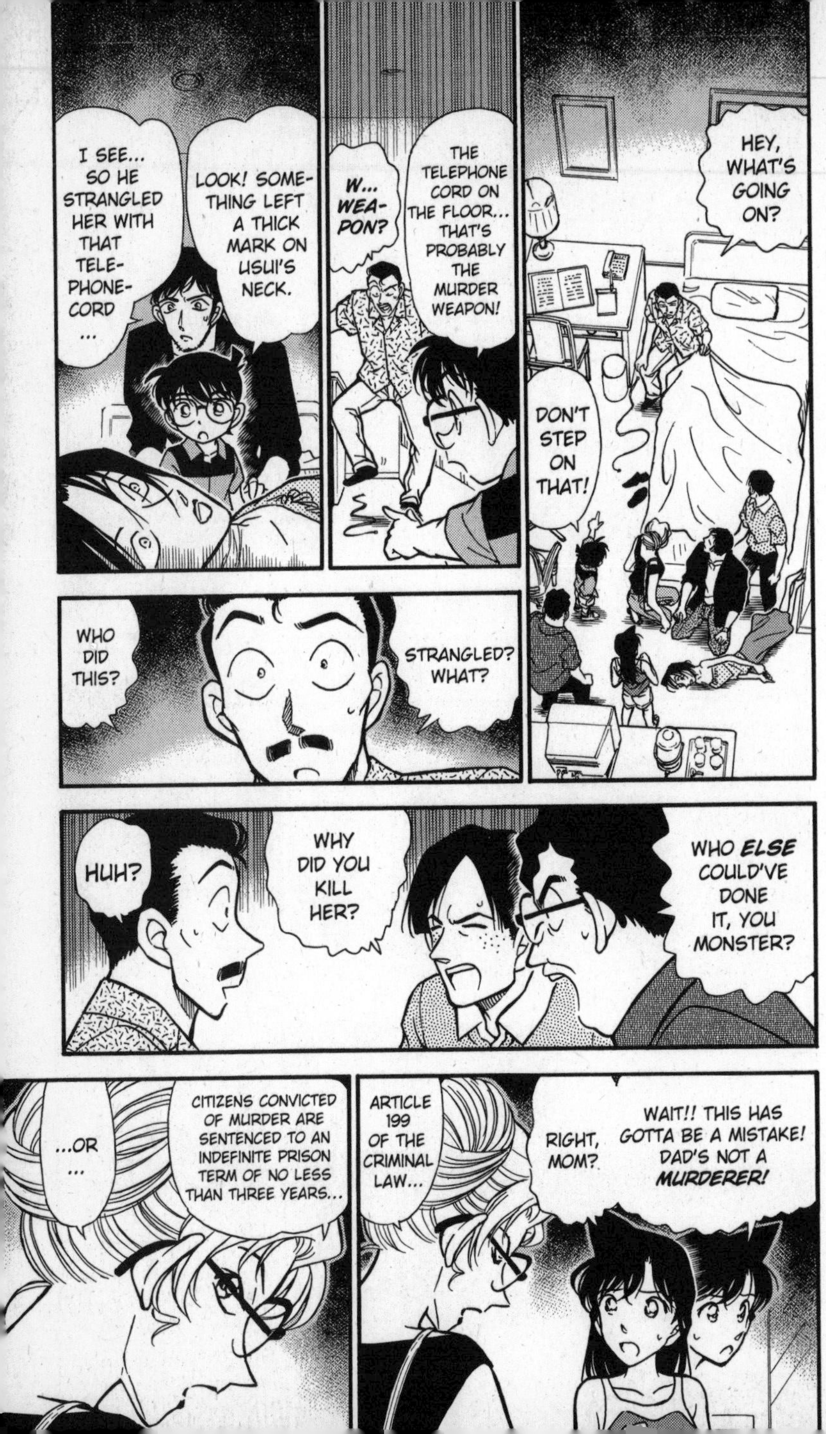
HEY, WHAT'S GOING ON?
DON'T STEP ON THAT!
THE TELEPHONE CORD ON THE FLOOR... THAT'S PROBABLY THE MURDER WEAPON!
W... WEAPON?
LOOK! SOMETHING LEFT A THICK MARK ON USUI'S NECK.
I SEE... SO HE STRANGLED HER WITH THAT TELEPHONE-CORD ...
STRANGLED? WHAT?
WHO DID THIS?
WHO *ELSE* COULD'VE DONE IT, YOU MONSTER?
WHY DID YOU KILL HER?
HUH?
WAIT!! THIS HAS GOTTA BE A MISTAKE! DAD'S NOT A ***MURDERER!***
RIGHT, MOM?
ARTICLE 199 OF THE CRIMINAL LAW...
CITIZENS CONVICTED OF MURDER ARE SENTENCED TO AN INDEFINITE PRISON TERM OF NO LESS THAN THREE YEARS...
...OR ...

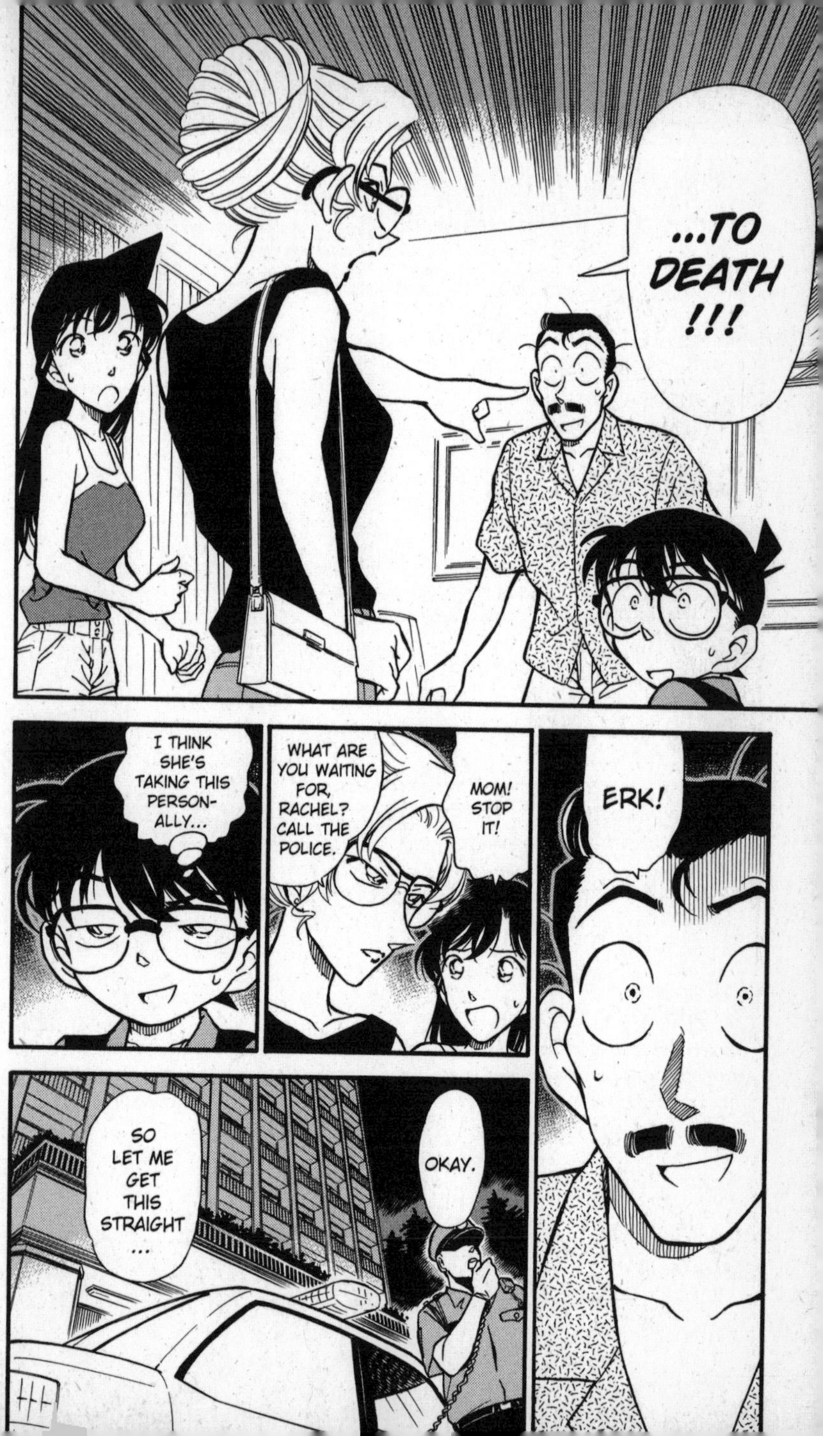
...TO DEATH !!!
ERK!
WHAT ARE YOU WAITING FOR, RACHEL? CALL THE POLICE.
MOM! STOP IT!
I THINK SHE'S TAKING THIS PERSON-ALLY...
OKAY.
SO LET ME GET THIS STRAIGHT ...

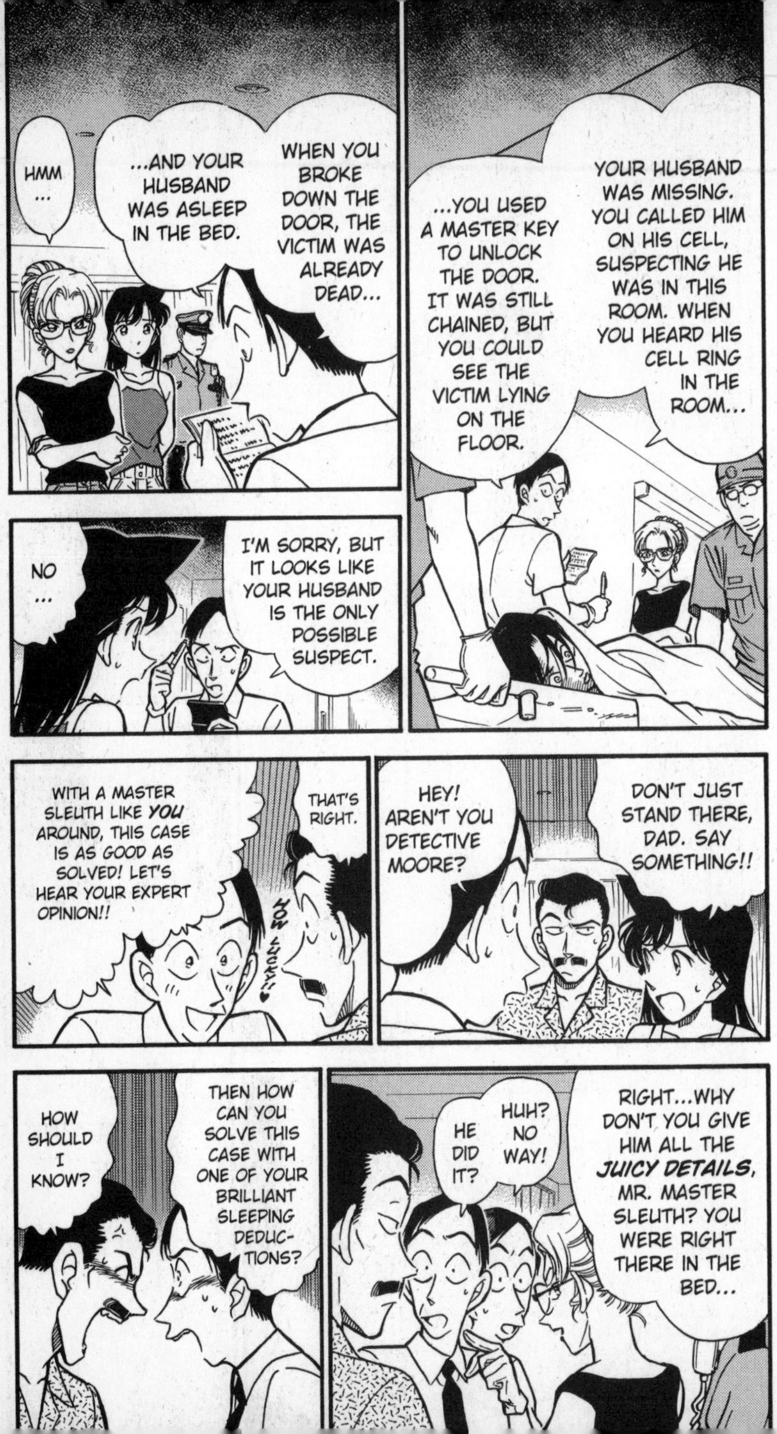
YOUR HUSBAND WAS MISSING. YOU CALLED HIM ON HIS CELL, SUSPECTING HE WAS IN THIS ROOM. WHEN YOU HEARD HIS CELL RING IN THE ROOM...
...YOU USED A MASTER KEY TO UNLOCK THE DOOR. IT WAS STILL CHAINED, BUT YOU COULD SEE THE VICTIM LYING ON THE FLOOR.
WHEN YOU BROKE DOWN THE DOOR, THE VICTIM WAS ALREADY DEAD...
...AND YOUR HUSBAND WAS ASLEEP IN THE BED.
HMM...
I'M SORRY, BUT IT LOOKS LIKE YOUR HUSBAND IS THE ONLY POSSIBLE SUSPECT.
NO...
DON'T JUST STAND THERE, DAD. SAY SOMETHING!!
HEY! AREN'T YOU DETECTIVE MOORE?
THAT'S RIGHT.
HOW LUCKY!!
WITH A MASTER SLEUTH LIKE *YOU* AROUND, THIS CASE IS AS GOOD AS SOLVED! LET'S HEAR YOUR EXPERT OPINION!!
RIGHT...WHY DON'T YOU GIVE HIM ALL THE ***JUICY DETAILS***, MR. MASTER SLEUTH? YOU WERE RIGHT THERE IN THE BED...
HUH? NO WAY!
HE DID IT?
THEN HOW CAN YOU SOLVE THIS CASE WITH ONE OF YOUR BRILLIANT SLEEPING DEDUCTIONS?
HOW SHOULD I KNOW?

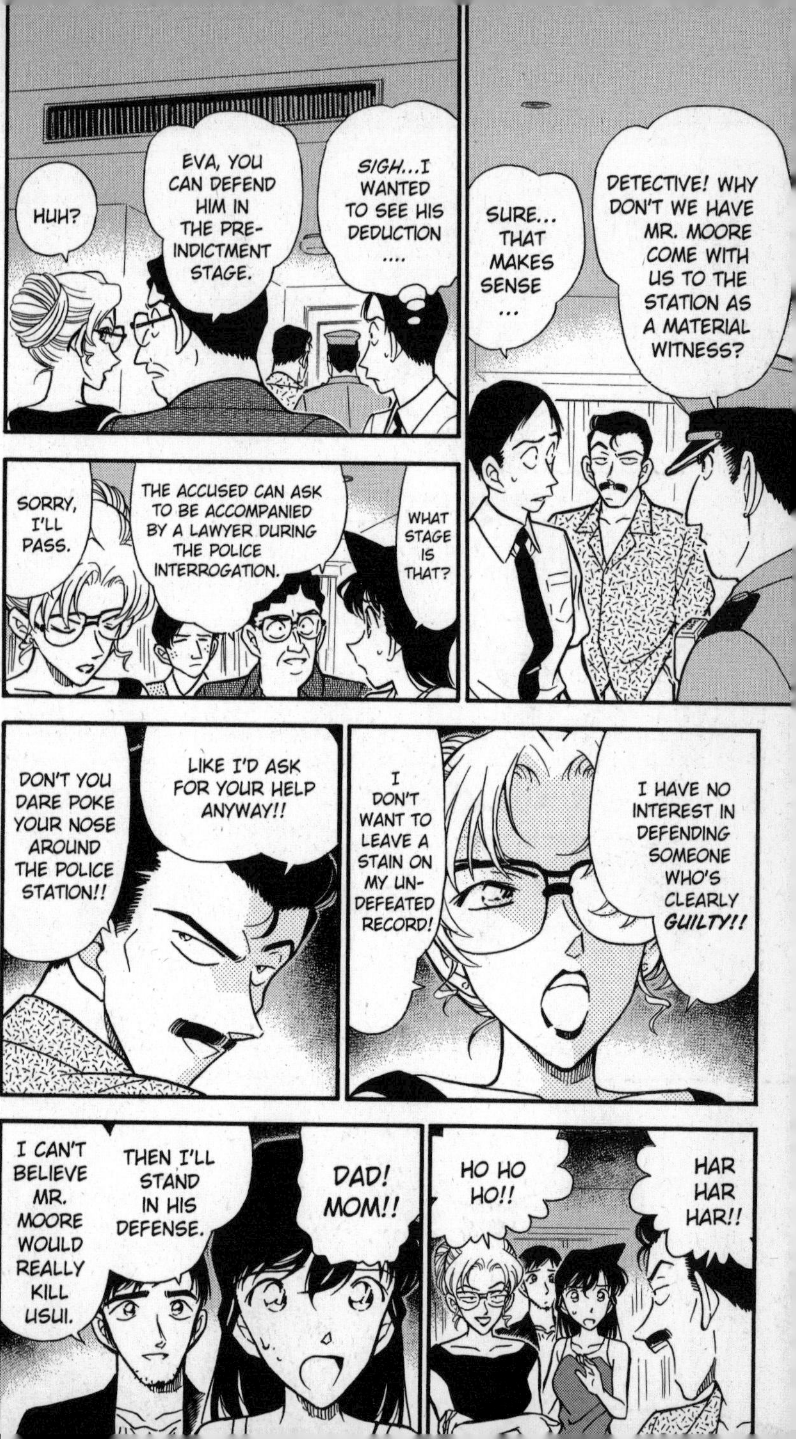
DETECTIVE! WHY DON'T WE HAVE MR. MOORE COME WITH US TO THE STATION AS A MATERIAL WITNESS?
SURE... THAT MAKES SENSE ...
SIGH...I WANTED TO SEE HIS DEDUCTION ....
EVA, YOU CAN DEFEND HIM IN THE PRE-INDICTMENT STAGE.
HUH?
WHAT STAGE IS THAT?
THE ACCUSED CAN ASK TO BE ACCOMPANIED BY A LAWYER DURING THE POLICE INTERROGATION.
SORRY, I'LL PASS.
I HAVE NO INTEREST IN DEFENDING SOMEONE WHO'S CLEARLY ***GUILTY!!***
I DON'T WANT TO LEAVE A STAIN ON MY UNDEFEATED RECORD!
LIKE I'D ASK FOR YOUR HELP ANYWAY!!
DON'T YOU DARE POKE YOUR NOSE AROUND THE POLICE STATION!!
HAR HAR HAR!!
HO HO HO!!
DAD! MOM!!
THEN I'LL STAND IN HIS DEFENSE.
I CAN'T BELIEVE MR. MOORE WOULD REALLY KILL USUI.

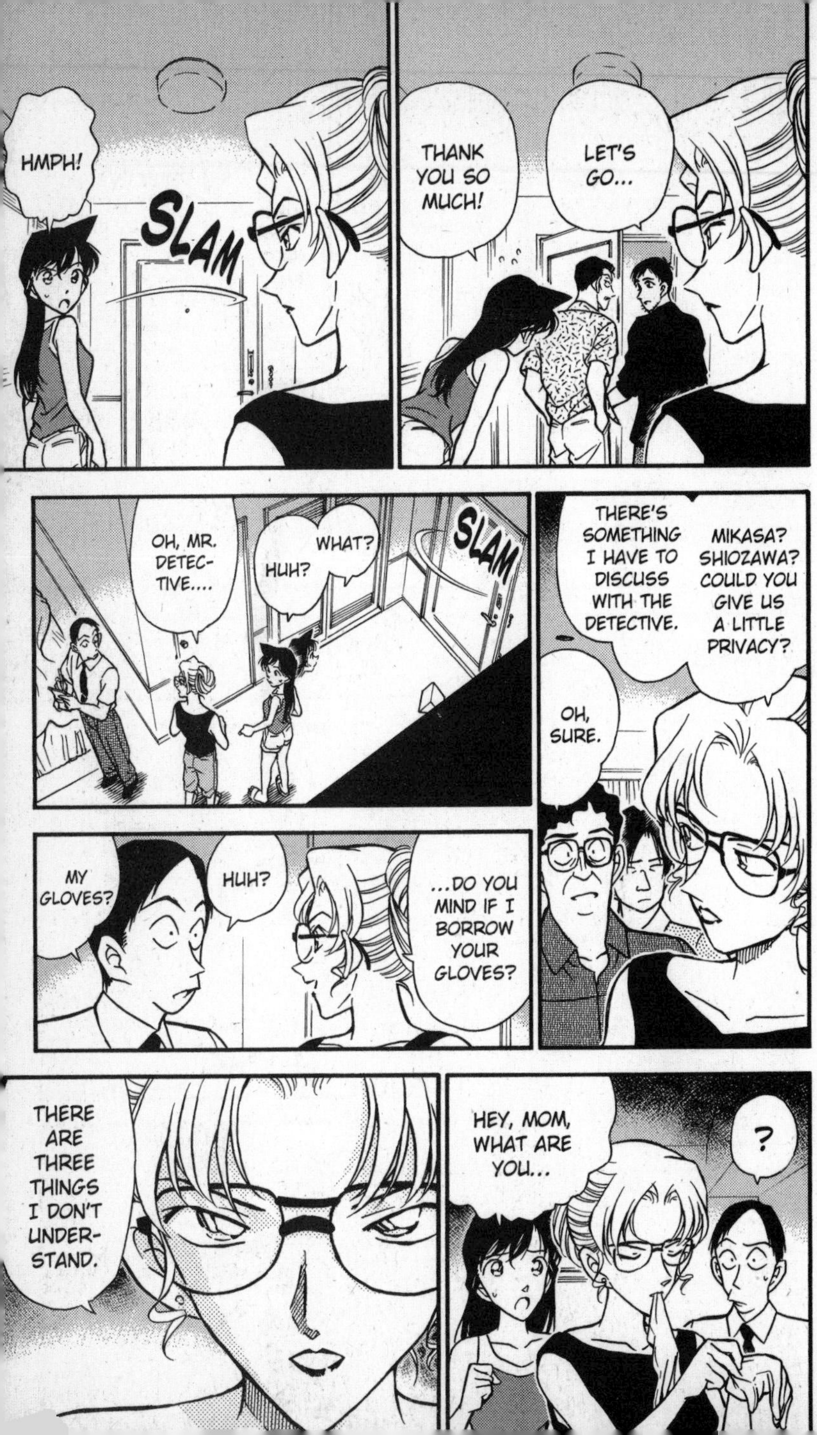
LET'S GO...
THANK YOU SO MUCH!
SLAM
HMPH!
MIKASA? SHIOZAWA? COULD YOU GIVE US A LITTLE PRIVACY?
THERE'S SOMETHING I HAVE TO DISCUSS WITH THE DETECTIVE.
OH, SURE.
SLAM
WHAT?
HUH?
OH, MR. DETEC-TIVE....
...DO YOU MIND IF I BORROW YOUR GLOVES?
HUH?
MY GLOVES?
?
HEY, MOM, WHAT ARE YOU...
THERE ARE THREE THINGS I DON'T UNDER-STAND.

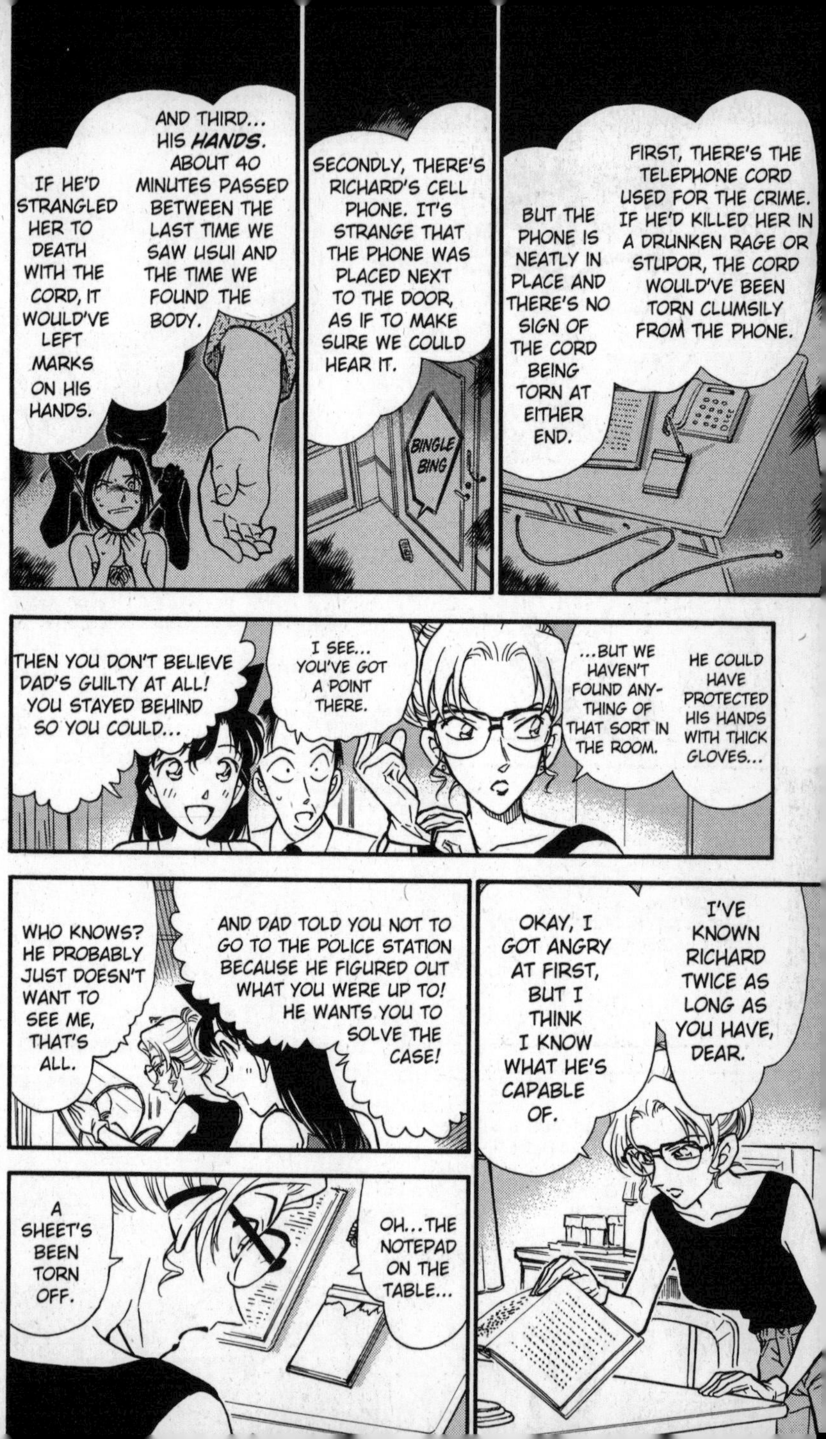
FIRST, THERE'S THE TELEPHONE CORD USED FOR THE CRIME. IF HE'D KILLED HER IN A DRUNKEN RAGE OR STUPOR, THE CORD WOULD'VE BEEN TORN CLUMSILY FROM THE PHONE.
BUT THE PHONE IS NEATLY IN PLACE AND THERE'S NO SIGN OF THE CORD BEING TORN AT EITHER END.
SECONDLY, THERE'S RICHARD'S CELL PHONE. IT'S STRANGE THAT THE PHONE WAS PLACED NEXT TO THE DOOR, AS IF TO MAKE SURE WE COULD HEAR IT.
BINGLE BING
AND THIRD... HIS ***HANDS***. ABOUT 40 MINUTES PASSED BETWEEN THE LAST TIME WE SAW USUI AND THE TIME WE FOUND THE BODY.
IF HE'D STRANGLED HER TO DEATH WITH THE CORD, IT WOULD'VE LEFT MARKS ON HIS HANDS.
HE COULD HAVE PROTECTED HIS HANDS WITH THICK GLOVES...
...BUT WE HAVEN'T FOUND ANYTHING OF THAT SORT IN THE ROOM.
I SEE... YOU'VE GOT A POINT THERE.
THEN YOU DON'T BELIEVE DAD'S GUILTY AT ALL! YOU STAYED BEHIND SO YOU COULD...
I'VE KNOWN RICHARD TWICE AS LONG AS YOU HAVE, DEAR.
OKAY, I GOT ANGRY AT FIRST, BUT I THINK I KNOW WHAT HE'S CAPABLE OF.
AND DAD TOLD YOU NOT TO GO TO THE POLICE STATION BECAUSE HE FIGURED OUT WHAT YOU WERE UP TO! HE WANTS YOU TO SOLVE THE CASE!
WHO KNOWS? HE PROBABLY JUST DOESN'T WANT TO SEE ME, THAT'S ALL.
OH...THE NOTEPAD ON THE TABLE...
A SHEET'S BEEN TORN OFF.

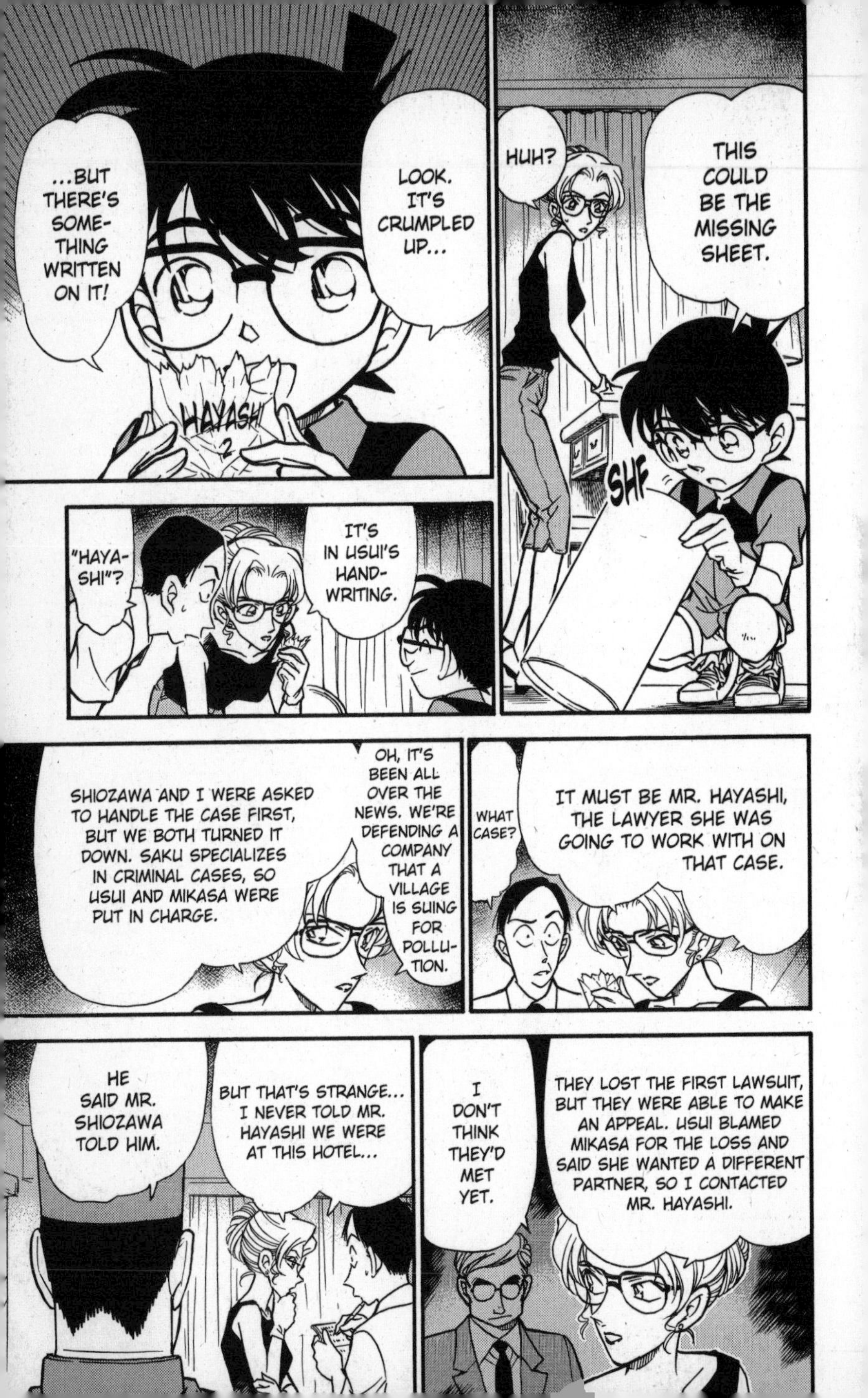
THIS COULD BE THE MISSING SHEET.
HUH?
SHF
LOOK. IT'S CRUMPLED UP...
...BUT THERE'S SOME-THING WRITTEN ON IT!
HAYASHI
2
IT'S IN USUI'S HAND-WRITING.
"HAYA-SHI"?
IT MUST BE MR. HAYASHI, THE LAWYER SHE WAS GOING TO WORK WITH ON THAT CASE.
WHAT CASE?
OH, IT'S BEEN ALL OVER THE NEWS. WE'RE DEFENDING A COMPANY THAT A VILLAGE IS SUING FOR POLLU-TION.
SHIOZAWA AND I WERE ASKED TO HANDLE THE CASE FIRST, BUT WE BOTH TURNED IT DOWN. SAKU SPECIALIZES IN CRIMINAL CASES, SO USUI AND MIKASA WERE PUT IN CHARGE.
THEY LOST THE FIRST LAWSUIT, BUT THEY WERE ABLE TO MAKE AN APPEAL. USUI BLAMED MIKASA FOR THE LOSS AND SAID SHE WANTED A DIFFERENT PARTNER, SO I CONTACTED MR. HAYASHI.
I DON'T THINK THEY'D MET YET.
BUT THAT'S STRANGE... I NEVER TOLD MR. HAYASHI WE WERE AT THIS HOTEL...
HE SAID MR. SHIOZAWA TOLD HIM.

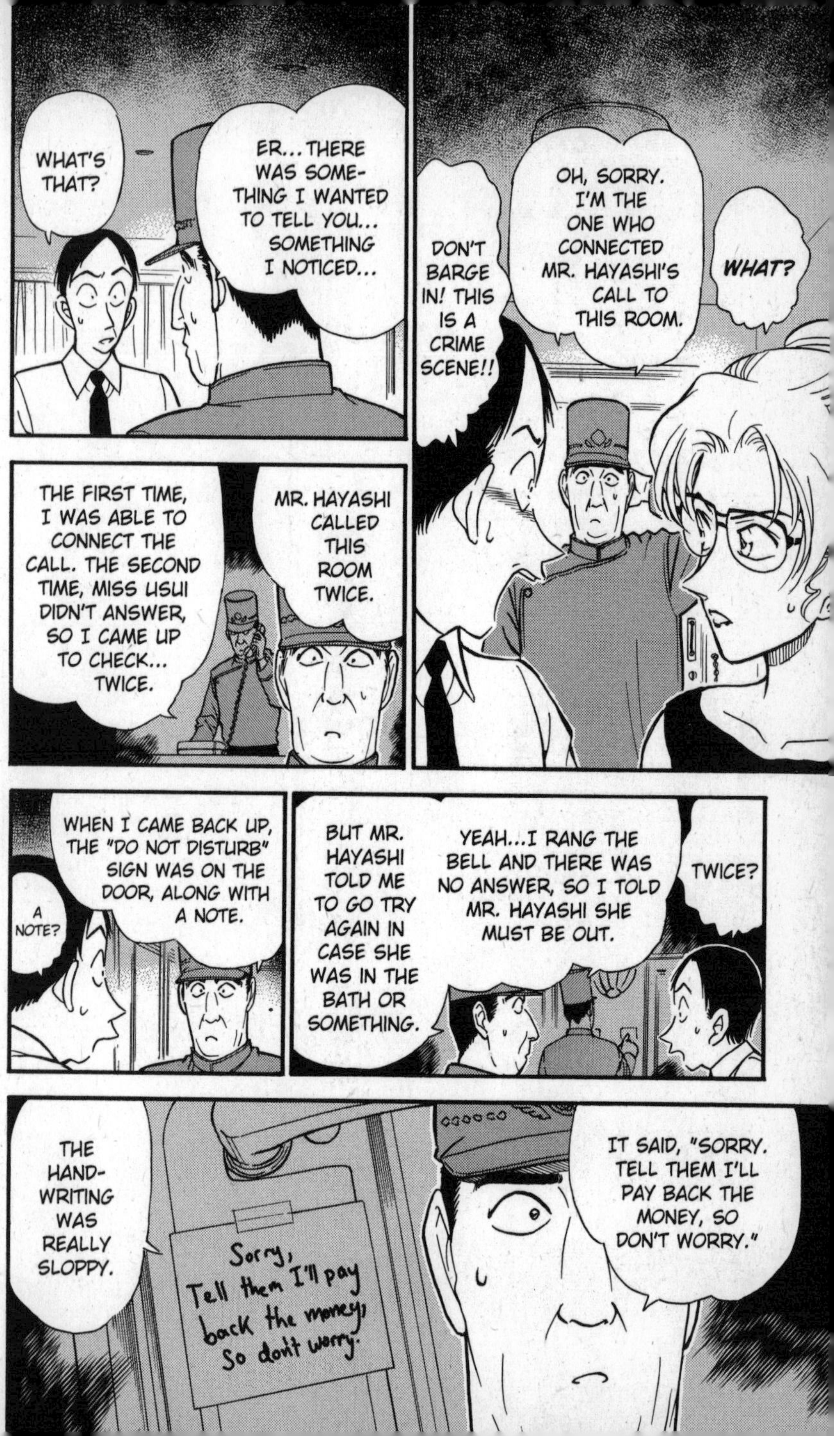
OH, SORRY. I'M THE ONE WHO CONNECTED MR. HAYASHI'S CALL TO THIS ROOM.
WHAT?
DON'T BARGE IN! THIS IS A CRIME SCENE!!
ER... THERE WAS SOMETHING I WANTED TO TELL YOU... SOMETHING I NOTICED...
WHAT'S THAT?
MR. HAYASHI CALLED THIS ROOM TWICE.
THE FIRST TIME, I WAS ABLE TO CONNECT THE CALL. THE SECOND TIME, MISS USUI DIDN'T ANSWER, SO I CAME UP TO CHECK... TWICE.
TWICE?
YEAH...I RANG THE BELL AND THERE WAS NO ANSWER, SO I TOLD MR. HAYASHI SHE MUST BE OUT.
BUT MR. HAYASHI TOLD ME TO GO TRY AGAIN IN CASE SHE WAS IN THE BATH OR SOMETHING.
WHEN I CAME BACK UP, THE "DO NOT DISTURB" SIGN WAS ON THE DOOR, ALONG WITH A NOTE.
A NOTE?
IT SAID, "SORRY. TELL THEM I'LL PAY BACK THE MONEY, SO DON'T WORRY."
Sorry, Tell them I'll pay back the money, So don't worry.
THE HAND-WRITING WAS REALLY SLOPPY.

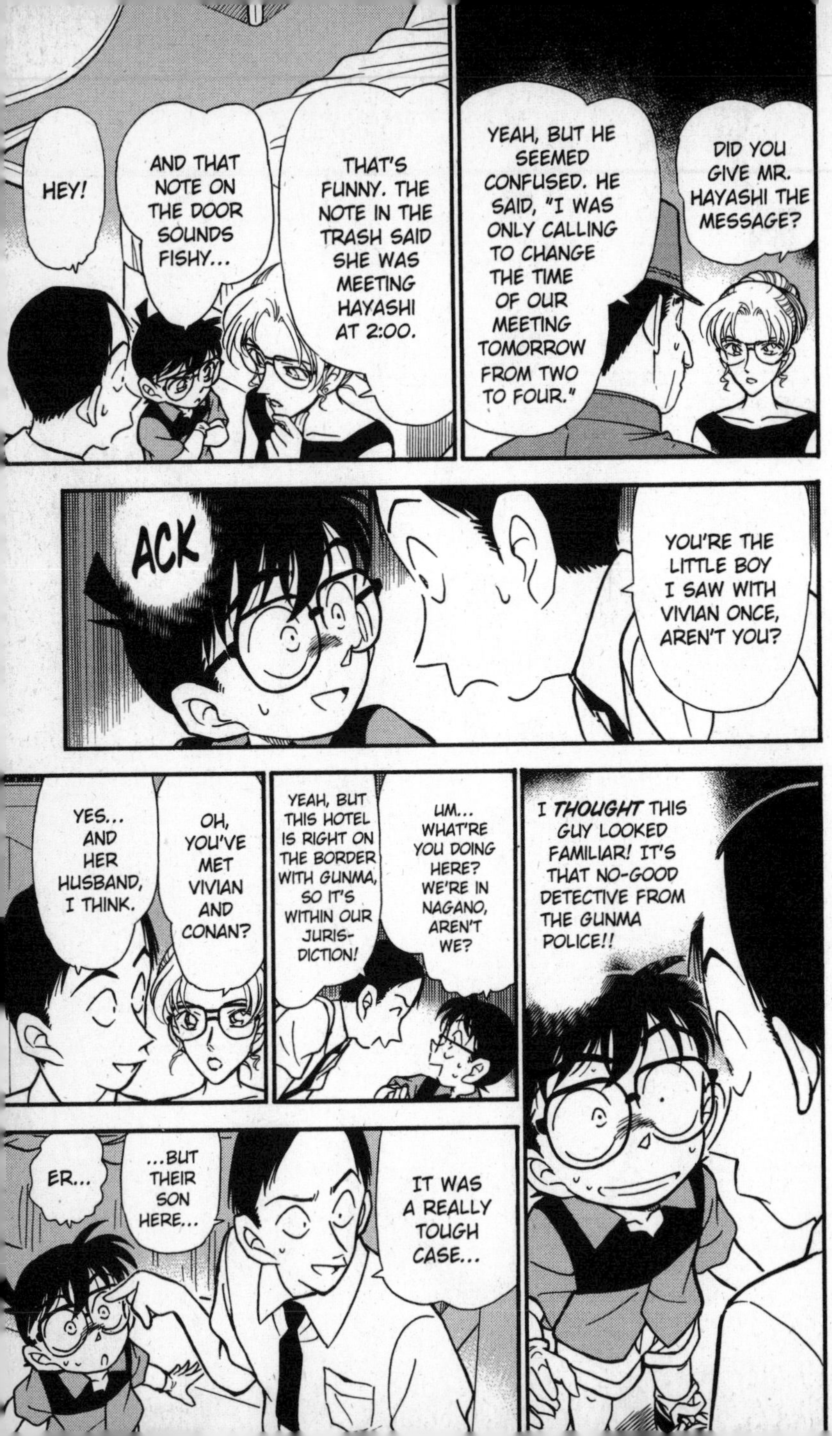
DID YOU GIVE MR. HAYASHI THE MESSAGE?
YEAH, BUT HE SEEMED CONFUSED. HE SAID, "I WAS ONLY CALLING TO CHANGE THE TIME OF OUR MEETING TOMORROW FROM TWO TO FOUR."
THAT'S FUNNY. THE NOTE IN THE TRASH SAID SHE WAS MEETING HAYASHI AT 2:00.
AND THAT NOTE ON THE DOOR SOUNDS FISHY...
HEY!
YOU'RE THE LITTLE BOY I SAW WITH VIVIAN ONCE, AREN'T YOU?
ACK
I THOUGHT THIS GUY LOOKED FAMILIAR! IT'S THAT NO-GOOD DETECTIVE FROM THE GUNMA POLICE!!
UM... WHAT'RE YOU DOING HERE? WE'RE IN NAGANO, AREN'T WE?
YEAH, BUT THIS HOTEL IS RIGHT ON THE BORDER WITH GUNMA, SO IT'S WITHIN OUR JURIS-DICTION!
OH, YOU'VE MET VIVIAN AND CONAN?
YES... AND HER HUSBAND, I THINK.
IT WAS A REALLY TOUGH CASE...
...BUT THEIR SON HERE...
ER...

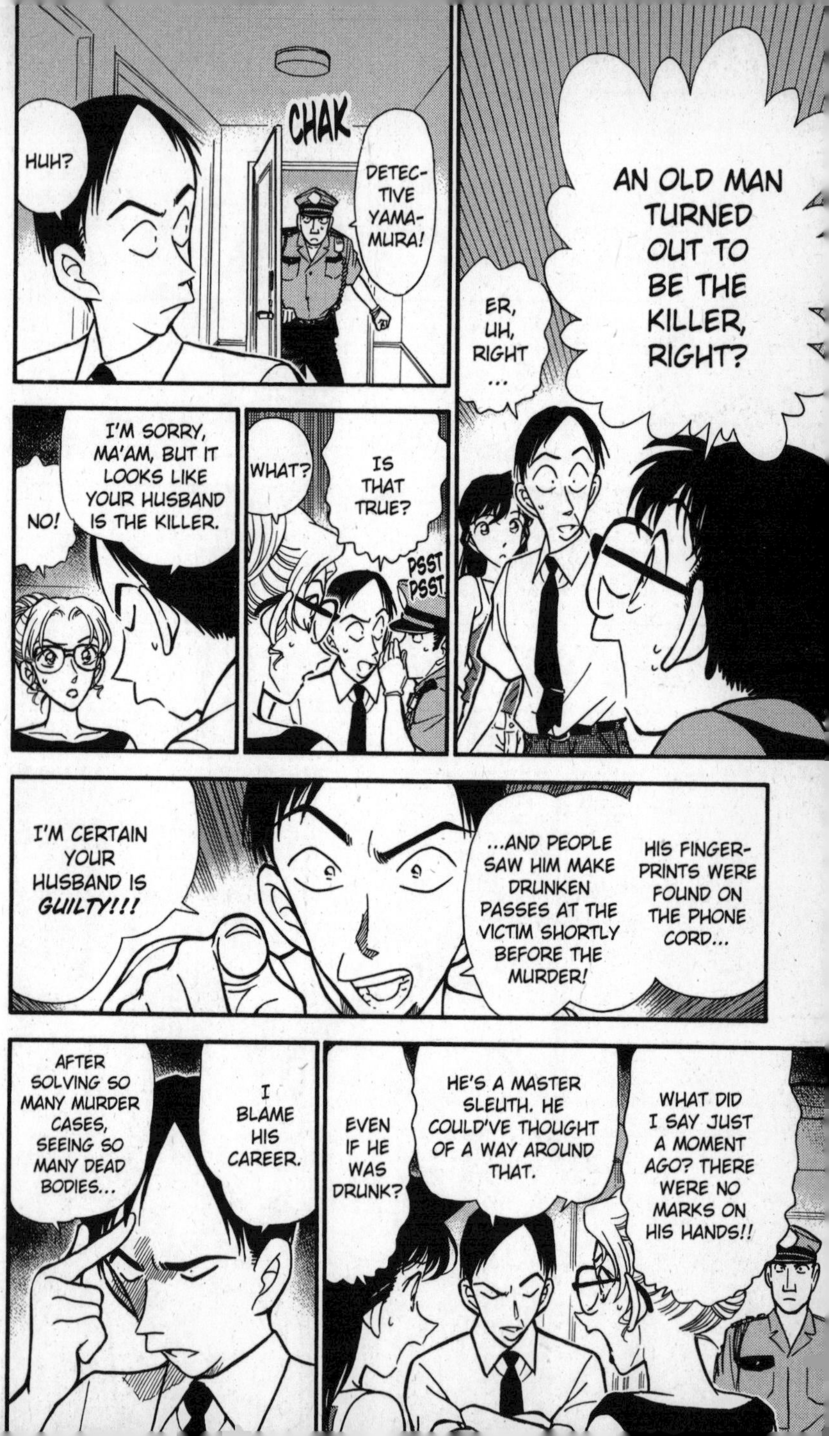
AN OLD MAN TURNED OUT TO BE THE KILLER, RIGHT?
ER, UH, RIGHT...
DETECTIVE YAMAMURA!
CHAK
HUH?
IS THAT TRUE?
PSST PSST
WHAT?
I'M SORRY, MA'AM, BUT IT LOOKS LIKE YOUR HUSBAND IS THE KILLER.
NO!
HIS FINGERPRINTS WERE FOUND ON THE PHONE CORD...
...AND PEOPLE SAW HIM MAKE DRUNKEN PASSES AT THE VICTIM SHORTLY BEFORE THE MURDER!
I'M CERTAIN YOUR HUSBAND IS *GUILTY!!!*
WHAT DID I SAY JUST A MOMENT AGO? THERE WERE NO MARKS ON HIS HANDS!!
HE'S A MASTER SLEUTH. HE COULD'VE THOUGHT OF A WAY AROUND THAT.
EVEN IF HE WAS DRUNK?
I BLAME HIS CAREER.
AFTER SOLVING SO MANY MURDER CASES, SEEING SO MANY DEAD BODIES...

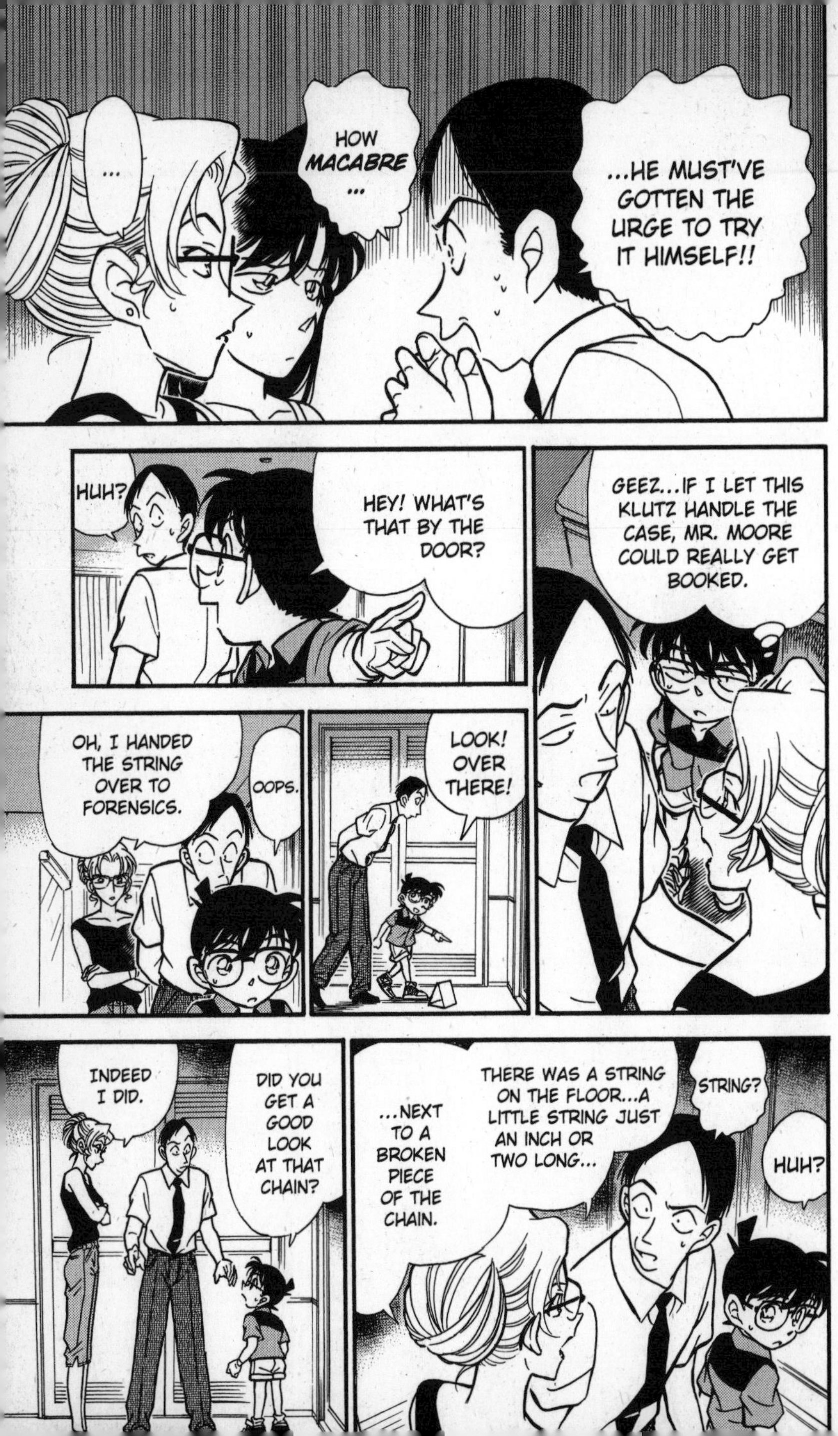
...HE MUST'VE GOTTEN THE URGE TO TRY IT HIMSELF!!
HOW *MACABRE* ...
...
GEEZ...IF I LET THIS KLUTZ HANDLE THE CASE, MR. MOORE COULD REALLY GET BOOKED.
HEY! WHAT'S THAT BY THE DOOR?
HUH?
LOOK! OVER THERE!
OH, I HANDED THE STRING OVER TO FORENSICS.
OOPS.
STRING?
HUH?
THERE WAS A STRING ON THE FLOOR...A LITTLE STRING JUST AN INCH OR TWO LONG...
...NEXT TO A BROKEN PIECE OF THE CHAIN.
DID YOU GET A GOOD LOOK AT THAT CHAIN?
INDEED I DID.

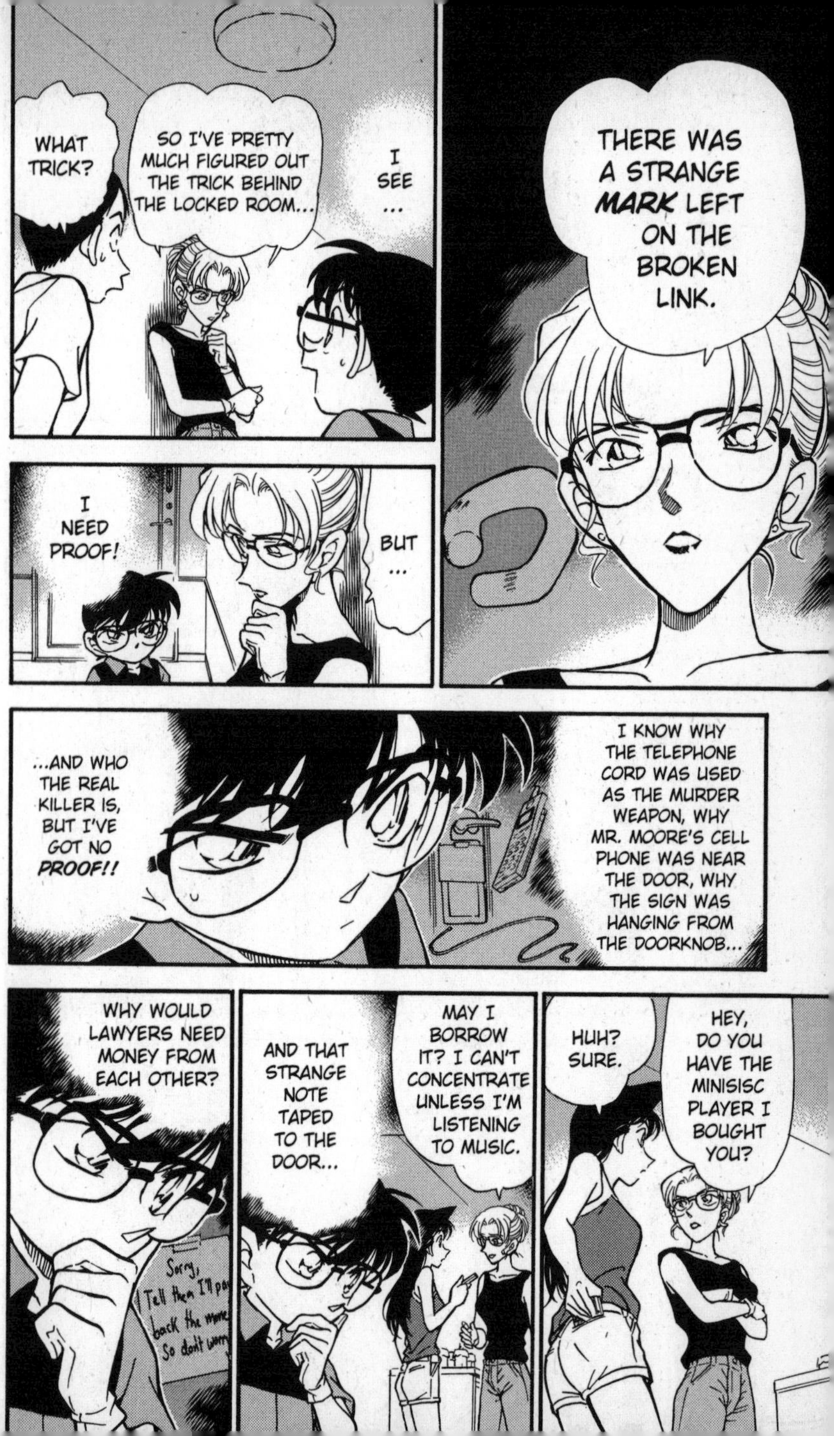
THERE WAS A STRANGE **MARK** LEFT ON THE BROKEN LINK.
I SEE ...
SO I'VE PRETTY MUCH FIGURED OUT THE TRICK BEHIND THE LOCKED ROOM...
WHAT TRICK?
BUT ...
I NEED PROOF!
I KNOW WHY THE TELEPHONE CORD WAS USED AS THE MURDER WEAPON, WHY MR. MOORE'S CELL PHONE WAS NEAR THE DOOR, WHY THE SIGN WAS HANGING FROM THE DOORKNOB...
...AND WHO THE REAL KILLER IS, BUT I'VE GOT NO ***PROOF!!***
HEY, DO YOU HAVE THE MINISISC PLAYER I BOUGHT YOU?
HUH? SURE.
MAY I BORROW IT? I CAN'T CONCENTRATE UNLESS I'M LISTENING TO MUSIC.
AND THAT STRANGE NOTE TAPED TO THE DOOR...
WHY WOULD LAWYERS NEED MONEY FROM EACH OTHER?
Sorry,
Tell them I'll pa
back the mone
So don't worr

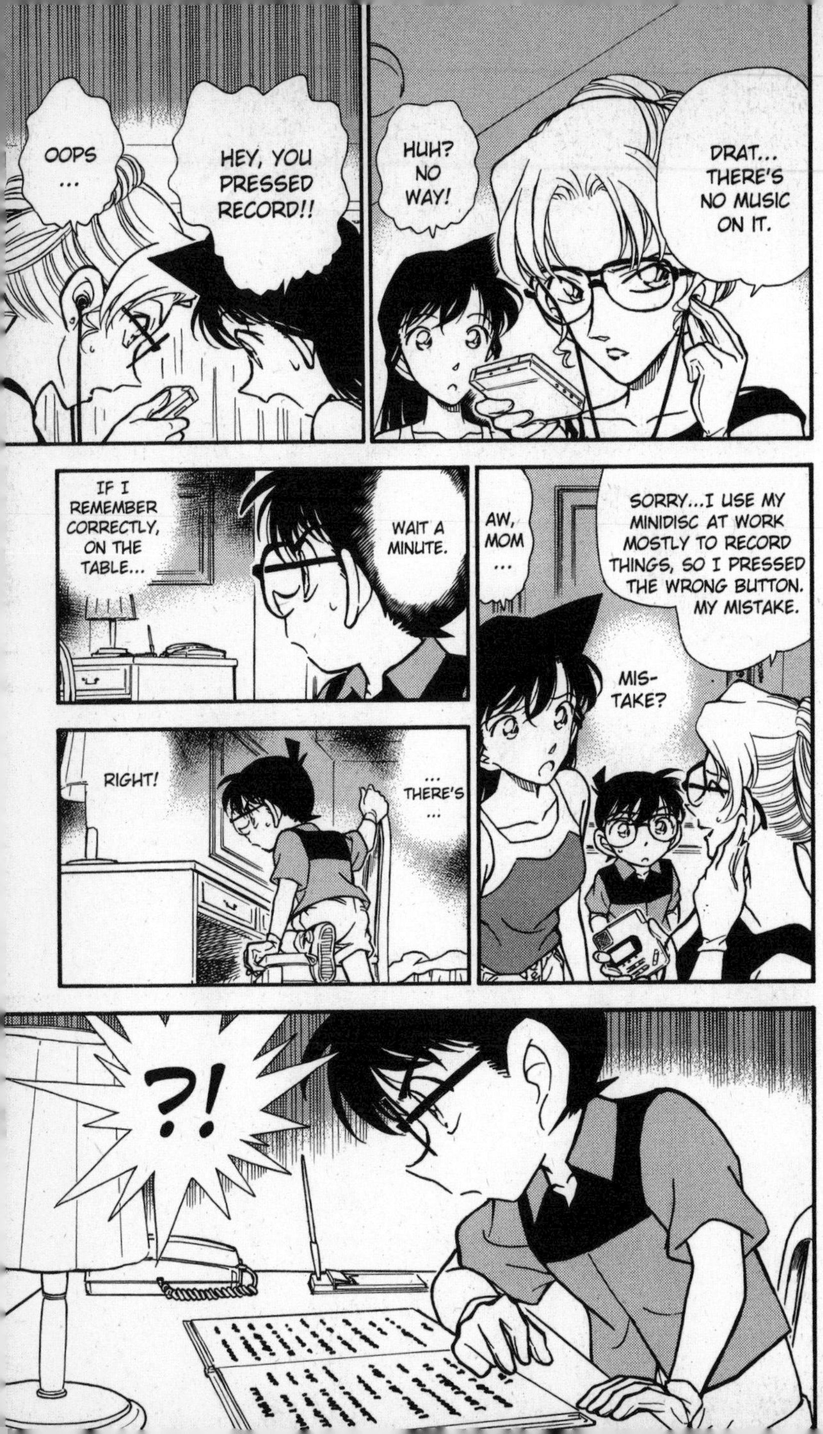
DRAT... THERE'S NO MUSIC ON IT.
HUH? NO WAY!
HEY, YOU PRESSED RECORD!!
OOPS ...
SORRY...I USE MY MINIDISC AT WORK MOSTLY TO RECORD THINGS, SO I PRESSED THE WRONG BUTTON. MY MISTAKE.
AW, MOM ...
MIS-TAKE?
WAIT A MINUTE.
IF I REMEMBER CORRECTLY, ON THE TABLE...
... THERE'S ...
RIGHT!
?!

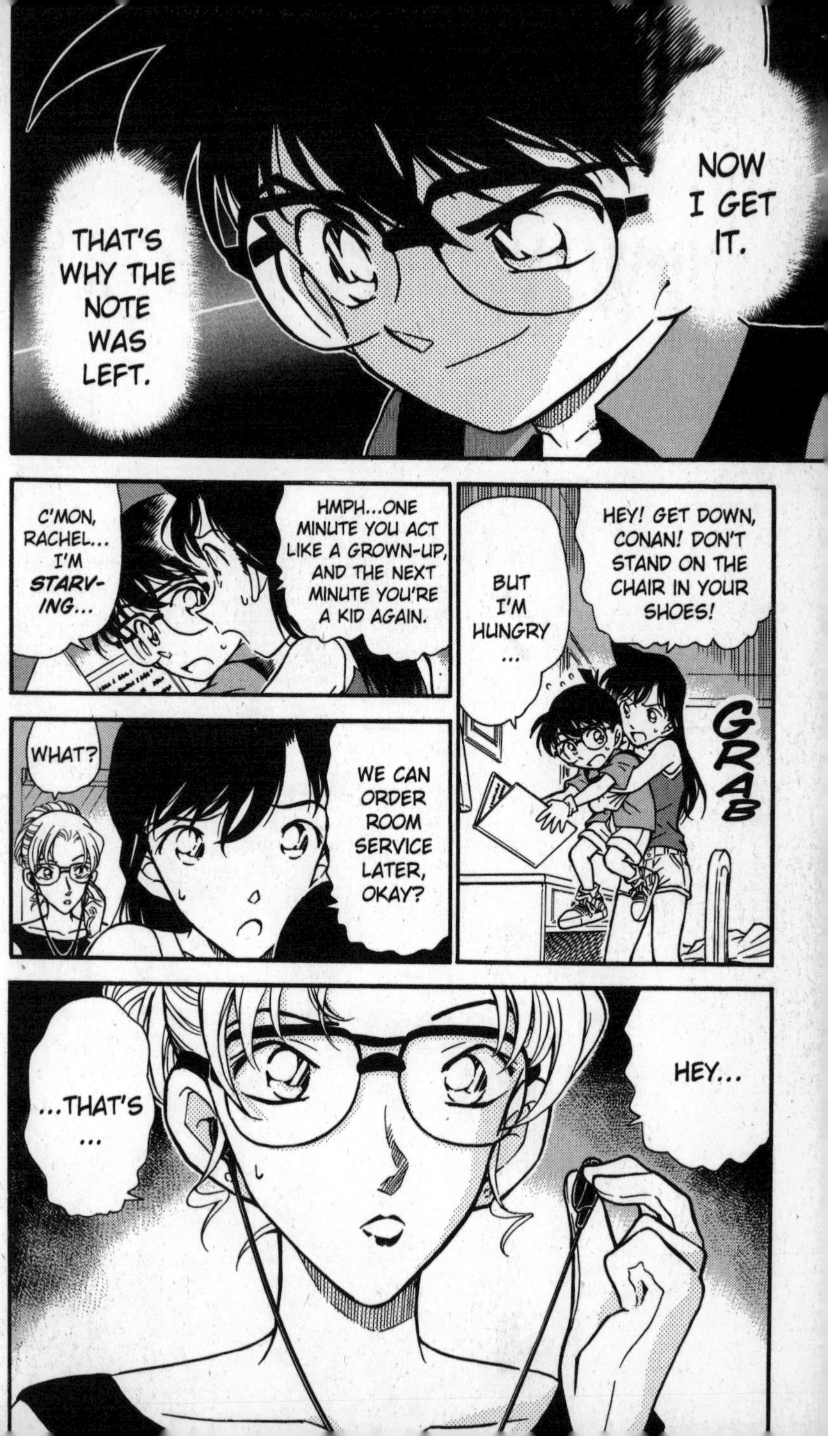
NOW I GET IT.
THAT'S WHY THE NOTE WAS LEFT.
HEY! GET DOWN, CONAN! DON'T STAND ON THE CHAIR IN YOUR SHOES!
BUT I'M HUNGRY...
GRAB
HMPH...ONE MINUTE YOU ACT LIKE A GROWN-UP, AND THE NEXT MINUTE YOU'RE A KID AGAIN.
C'MON, RACHEL... I'M *STARVING*...
WE CAN ORDER ROOM SERVICE LATER, OKAY?
WHAT?
HEY...
...THAT'S ...

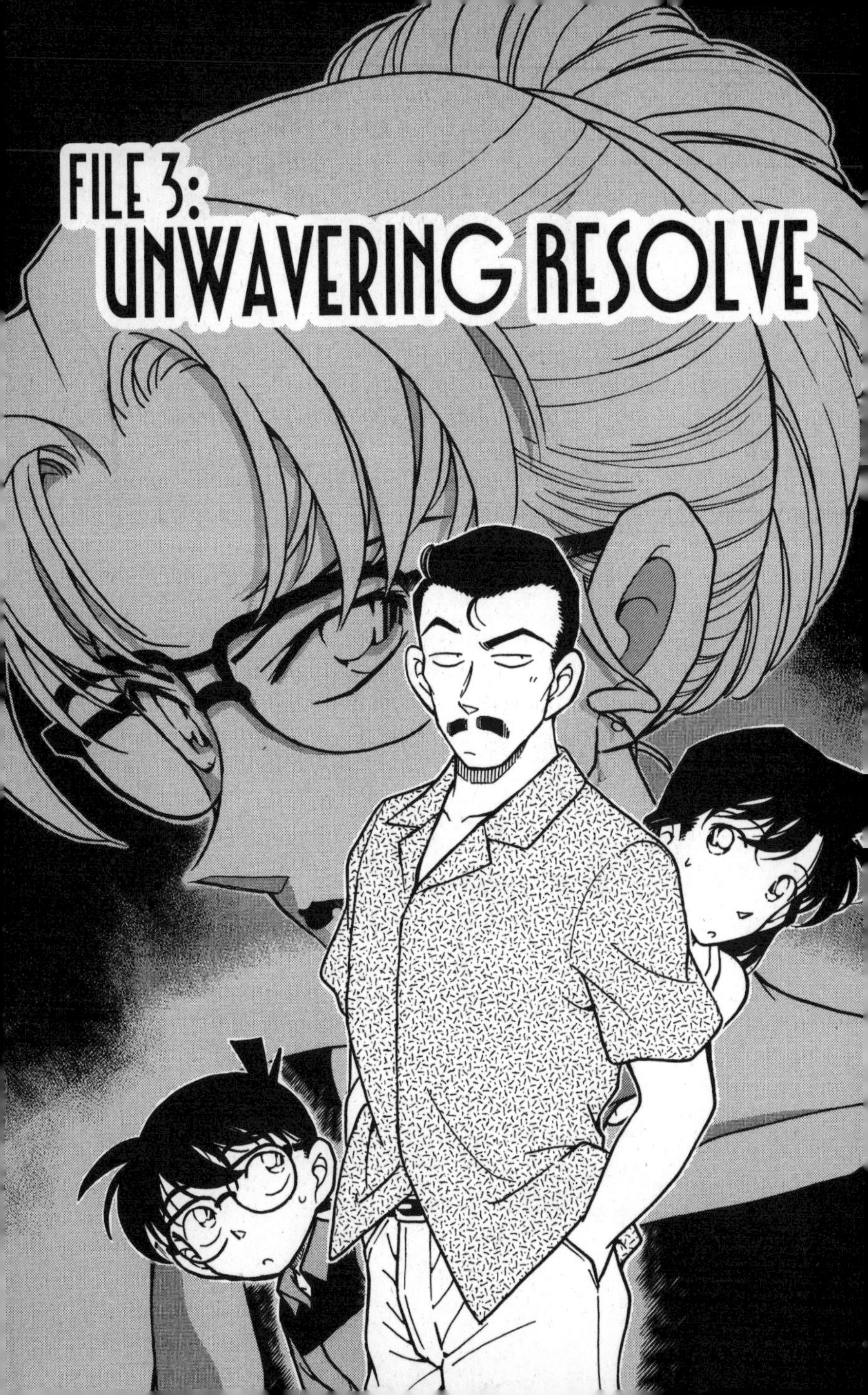
FILE 3:
UNWAVERING RESOLVE

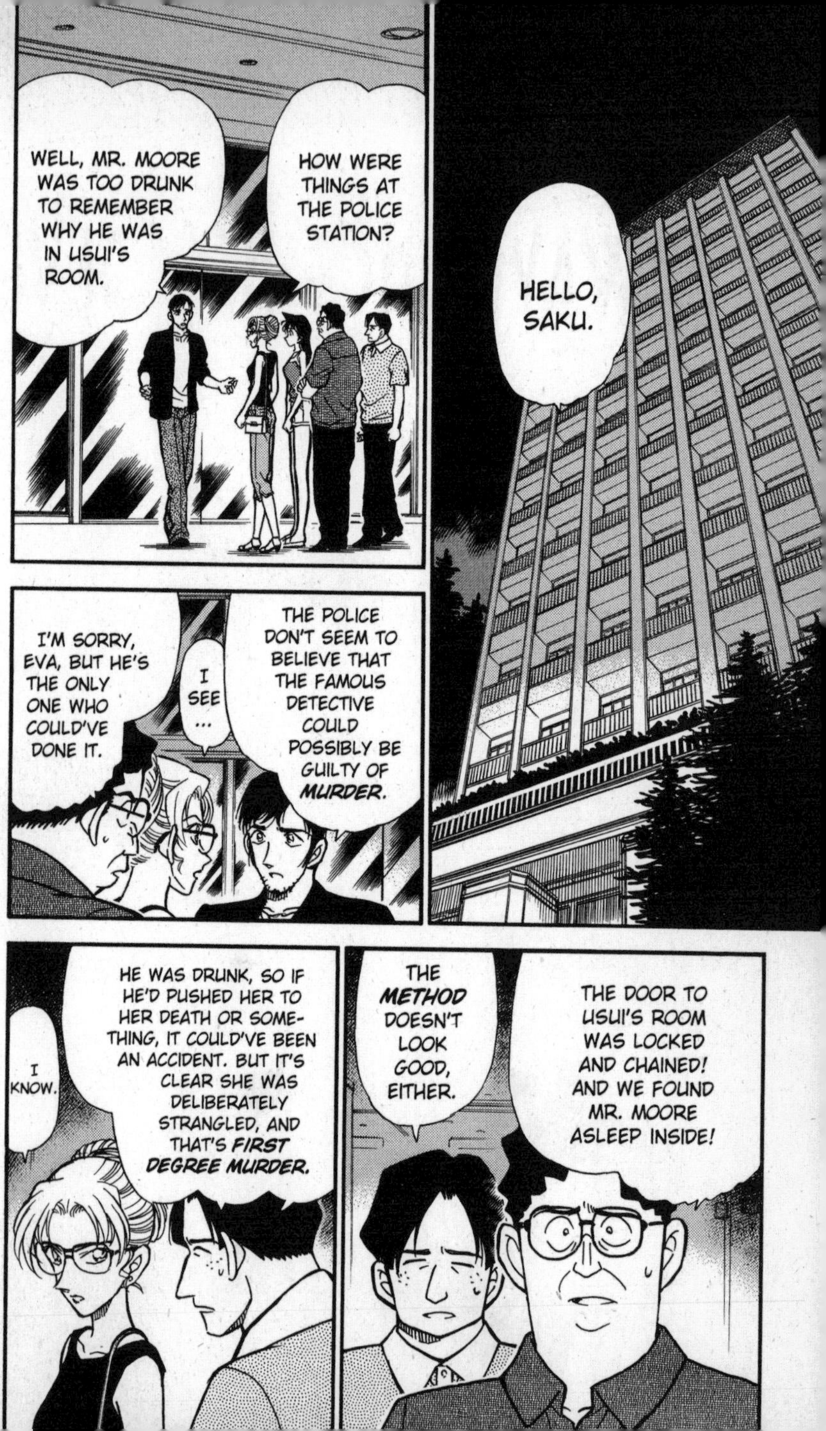
HELLO, SAKU.
HOW WERE THINGS AT THE POLICE STATION?
WELL, MR. MOORE WAS TOO DRUNK TO REMEMBER WHY HE WAS IN USUI'S ROOM.
THE POLICE DON'T SEEM TO BELIEVE THAT THE FAMOUS DETECTIVE COULD POSSIBLY BE GUILTY OF MURDER.
I SEE...
I'M SORRY, EVA, BUT HE'S THE ONLY ONE WHO COULD'VE DONE IT.
THE DOOR TO USUI'S ROOM WAS LOCKED AND CHAINED! AND WE FOUND MR. MOORE ASLEEP INSIDE!
THE METHOD DOESN'T LOOK GOOD, EITHER.
HE WAS DRUNK, SO IF HE'D PUSHED HER TO HER DEATH OR SOME-THING, IT COULD'VE BEEN AN ACCIDENT. BUT IT'S CLEAR SHE WAS DELIBERATELY STRANGLED, AND THAT'S FIRST DEGREE MURDER.
I KNOW.

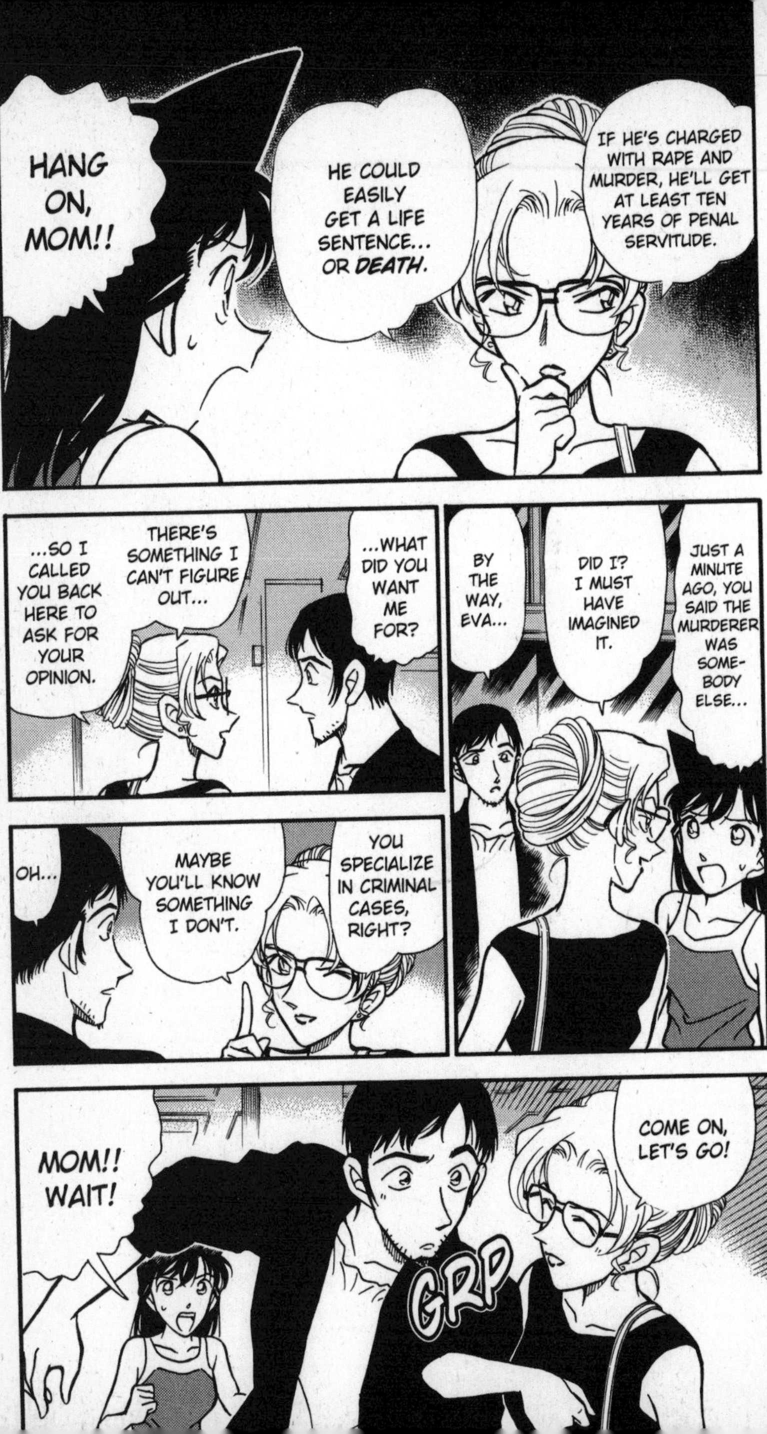
IF HE'S CHARGED WITH RAPE AND MURDER, HE'LL GET AT LEAST TEN YEARS OF PENAL SERVITUDE.
HE COULD EASILY GET A LIFE SENTENCE... OR *DEATH*.
HANG ON, MOM!!
JUST A MINUTE AGO, YOU SAID THE MURDERER WAS SOME-BODY ELSE...
DID I? I MUST HAVE IMAGINED IT.
BY THE WAY, EVA...
...WHAT DID YOU WANT ME FOR?
THERE'S SOMETHING I CAN'T FIGURE OUT...
...SO I CALLED YOU BACK HERE TO ASK FOR YOUR OPINION.
YOU SPECIALIZE IN CRIMINAL CASES, RIGHT?
MAYBE YOU'LL KNOW SOMETHING I DON'T.
OH...
COME ON, LET'S GO!
GRP
MOM!! WAIT!

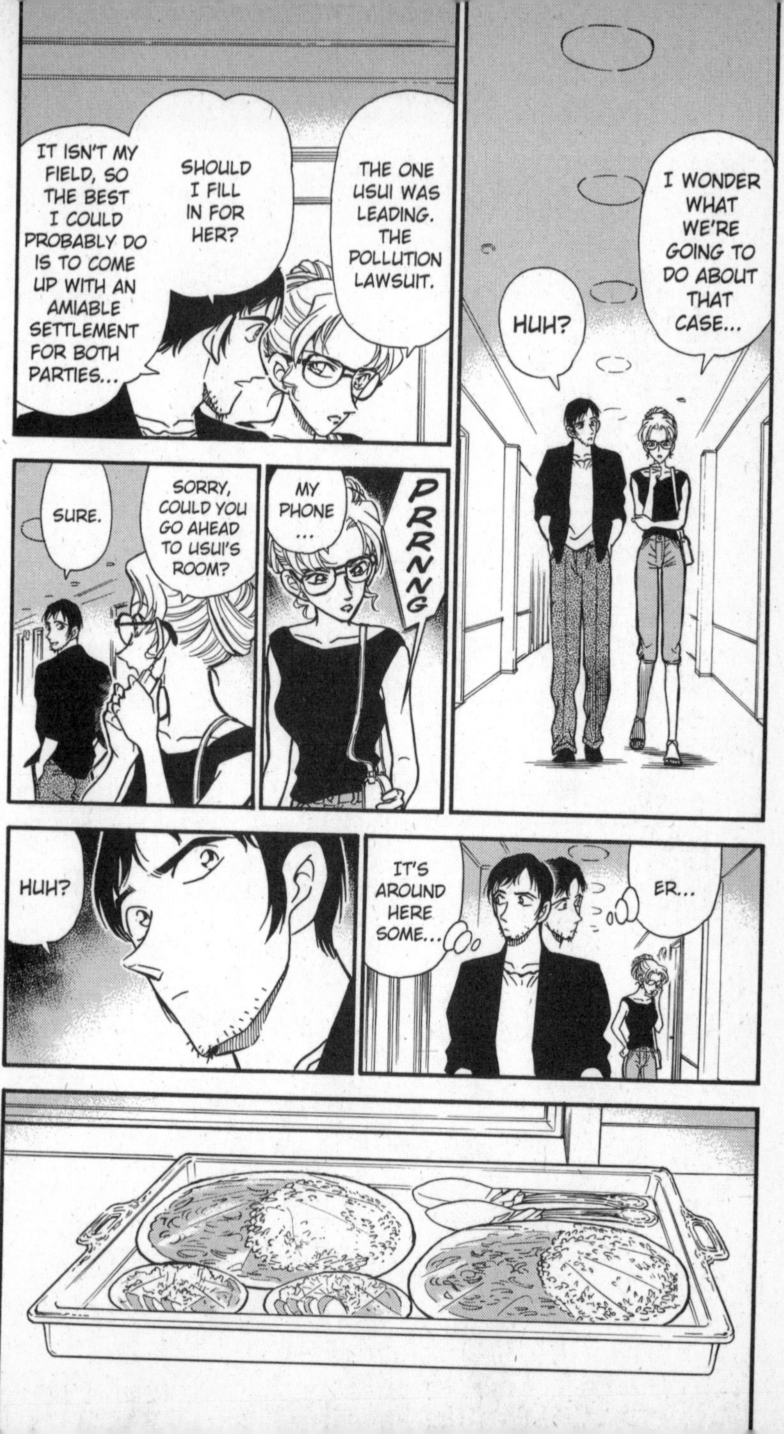
I WONDER WHAT WE'RE GOING TO DO ABOUT THAT CASE...
HUH?
THE ONE USUI WAS LEADING. THE POLLUTION LAWSUIT.
SHOULD I FILL IN FOR HER?
IT ISN'T MY FIELD, SO THE BEST I COULD PROBABLY DO IS TO COME UP WITH AN AMIABLE SETTLEMENT FOR BOTH PARTIES...
PRRNNG
MY PHONE ...
SORRY, COULD YOU GO AHEAD TO USUI'S ROOM?
SURE.
ER...
IT'S AROUND HERE SOME...
HUH?

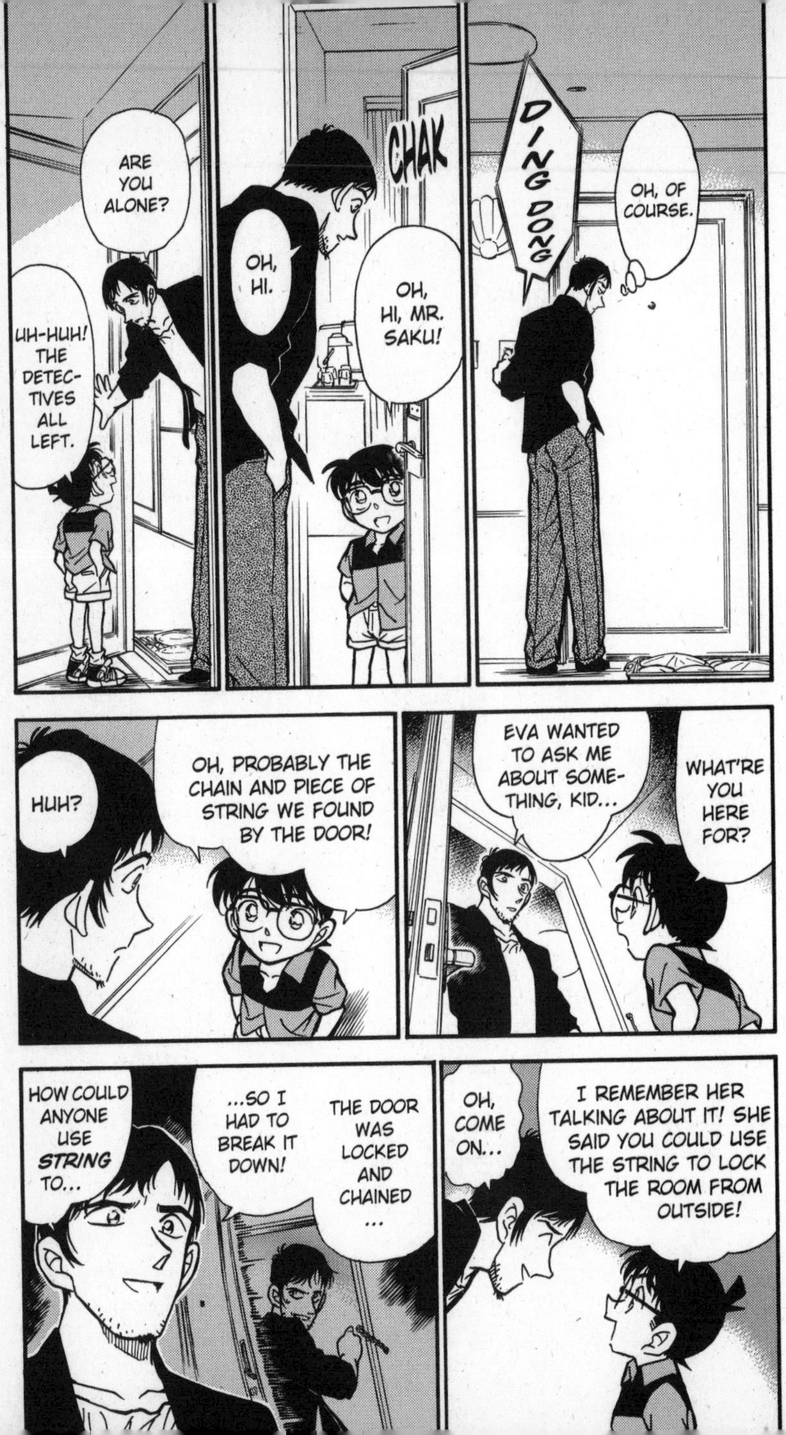
DING DONG
OH, OF COURSE.
CHAK
OH, HI, MR. SAKU!
OH, HI.
ARE YOU ALONE?
UH-HUH! THE DETECTIVES ALL LEFT.
WHAT'RE YOU HERE FOR?
EVA WANTED TO ASK ME ABOUT SOMETHING, KID...
OH, PROBABLY THE CHAIN AND PIECE OF STRING WE FOUND BY THE DOOR!
HUH?
I REMEMBER HER TALKING ABOUT IT! SHE SAID YOU COULD USE THE STRING TO LOCK THE ROOM FROM OUTSIDE!
OH, COME ON...
THE DOOR WAS LOCKED AND CHAINED ...
...SO I HAD TO BREAK IT DOWN!
HOW COULD ANYONE USE STRING TO...

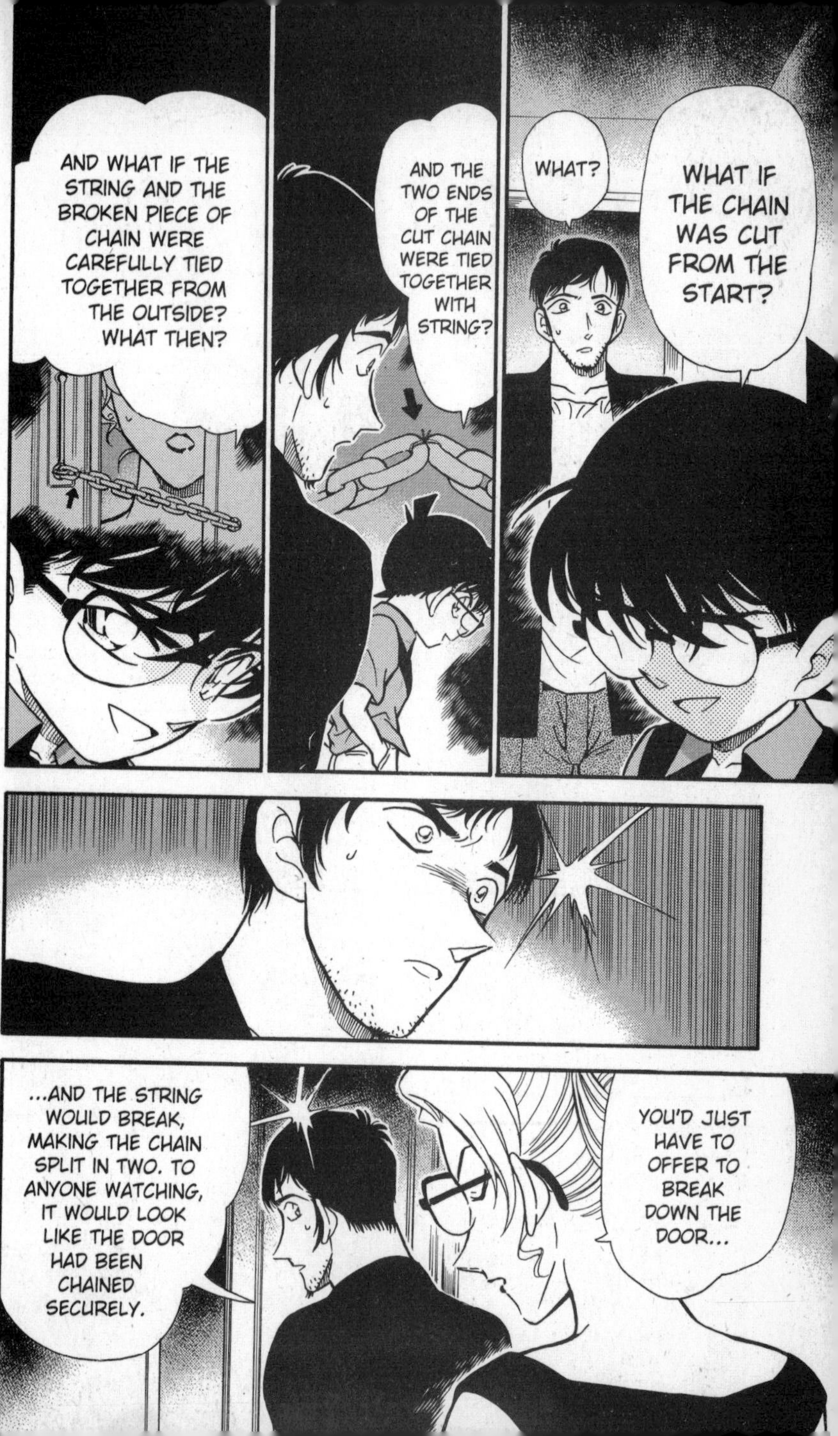
WHAT IF THE CHAIN WAS CUT FROM THE START?
WHAT?
AND THE TWO ENDS OF THE CUT CHAIN WERE TIED TOGETHER WITH STRING?
AND WHAT IF THE STRING AND THE BROKEN PIECE OF CHAIN WERE CAREFULLY TIED TOGETHER FROM THE OUTSIDE? WHAT THEN?
YOU'D JUST HAVE TO OFFER TO BREAK DOWN THE DOOR...
...AND THE STRING WOULD BREAK, MAKING THE CHAIN SPLIT IN TWO. TO ANYONE WATCHING, IT WOULD LOOK LIKE THE DOOR HAD BEEN CHAINED SECURELY.

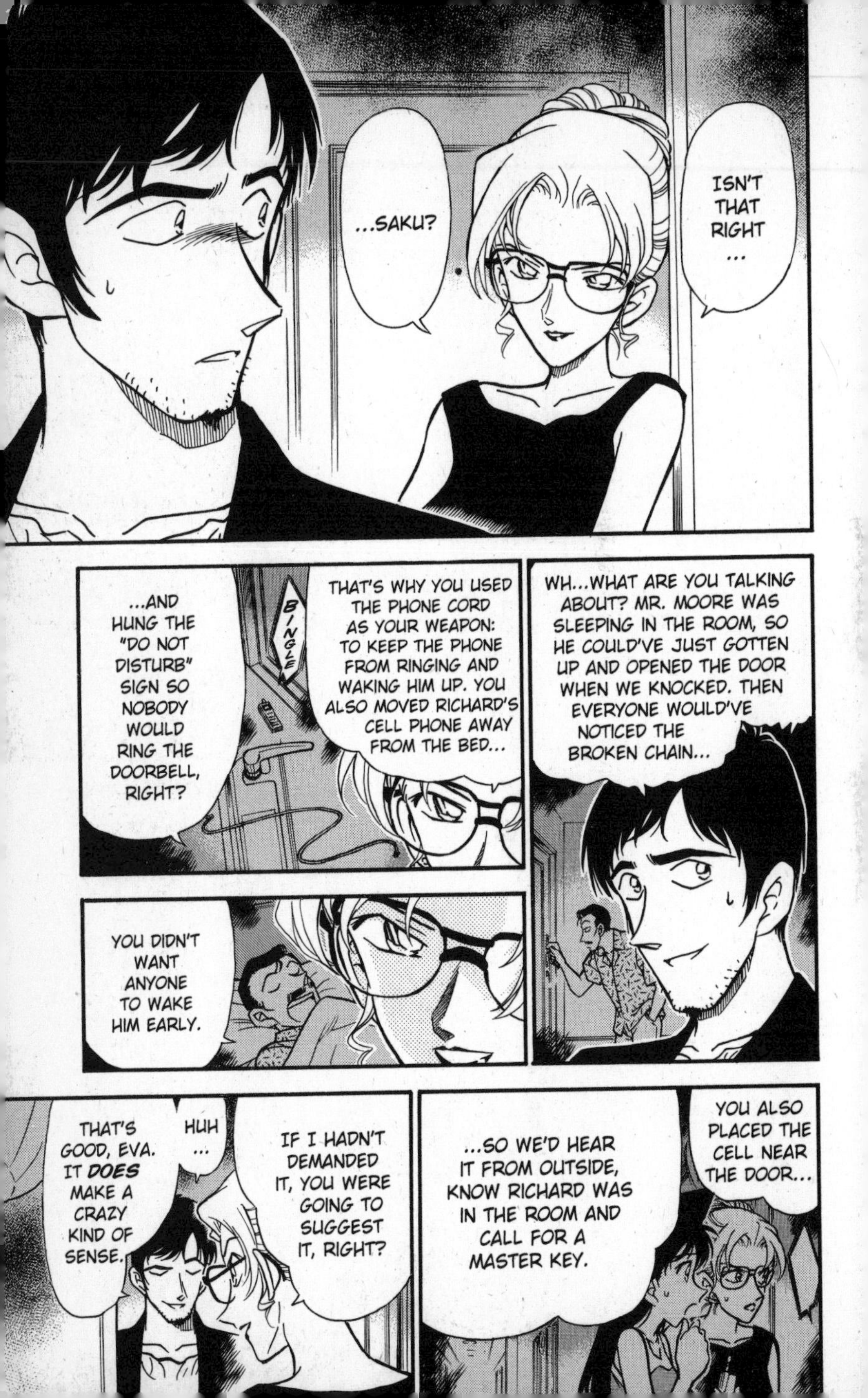
ISN'T THAT RIGHT...
...SAKU?
WH...WHAT ARE YOU TALKING ABOUT? MR. MOORE WAS SLEEPING IN THE ROOM, SO HE COULD'VE JUST GOTTEN UP AND OPENED THE DOOR WHEN WE KNOCKED. THEN EVERYONE WOULD'VE NOTICED THE BROKEN CHAIN...
THAT'S WHY YOU USED THE PHONE CORD AS YOUR WEAPON: TO KEEP THE PHONE FROM RINGING AND WAKING HIM UP. YOU ALSO MOVED RICHARD'S CELL PHONE AWAY FROM THE BED...
BINGLE
...AND HUNG THE "DO NOT DISTURB" SIGN SO NOBODY WOULD RING THE DOORBELL, RIGHT?
YOU DIDN'T WANT ANYONE TO WAKE HIM EARLY.
YOU ALSO PLACED THE CELL NEAR THE DOOR...
...SO WE'D HEAR IT FROM OUTSIDE, KNOW RICHARD WAS IN THE ROOM AND CALL FOR A MASTER KEY.
IF I HADN'T DEMANDED IT, YOU WERE GOING TO SUGGEST IT, RIGHT?
HUH...
THAT'S GOOD, EVA. IT DOES MAKE A CRAZY KIND OF SENSE.

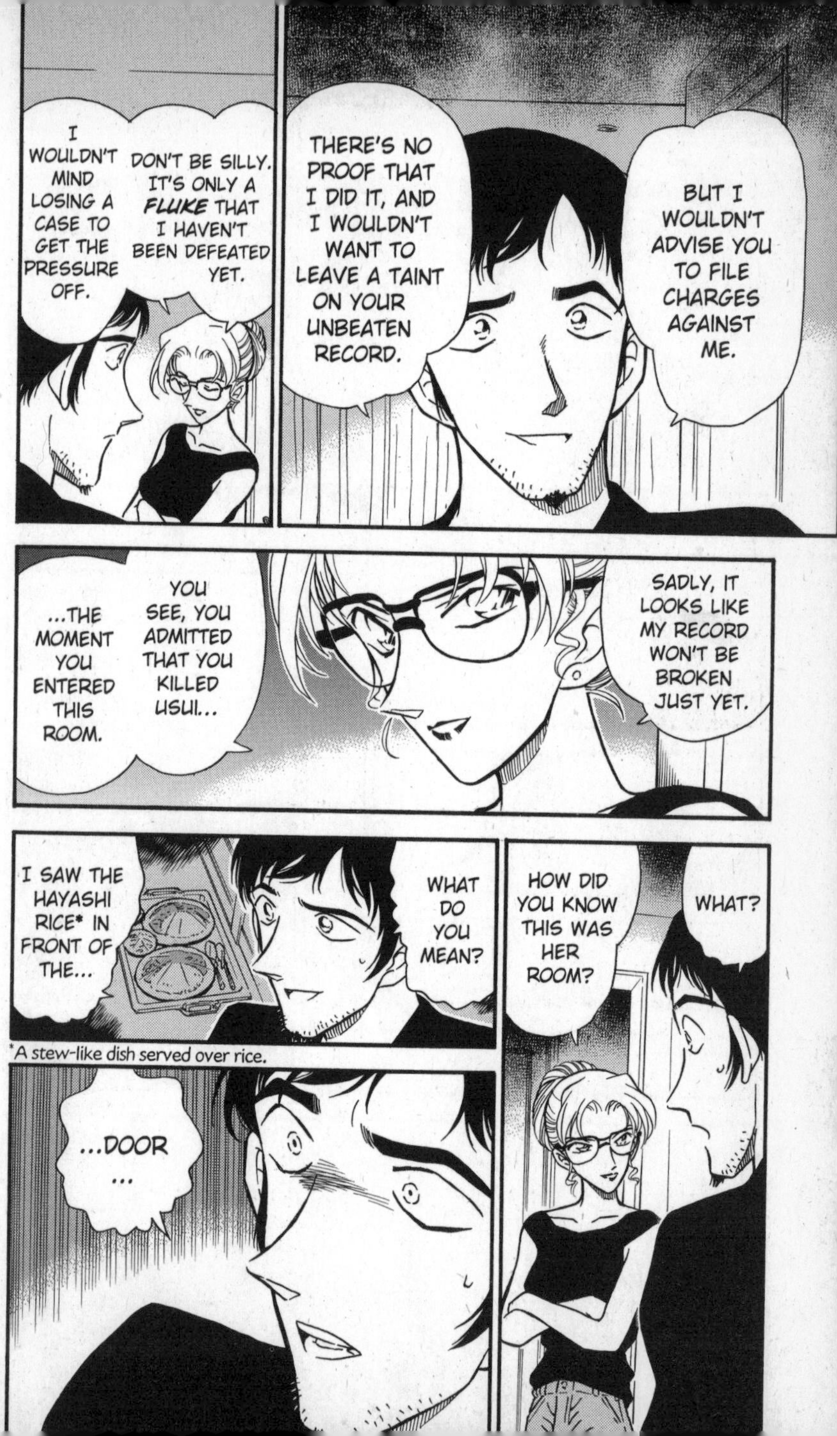
BUT I WOULDN'T ADVISE YOU TO FILE CHARGES AGAINST ME.
THERE'S NO PROOF THAT I DID IT, AND I WOULDN'T WANT TO LEAVE A TAINT ON YOUR UNBEATEN RECORD.
DON'T BE SILLY. IT'S ONLY A FLUKE THAT I HAVEN'T BEEN DEFEATED YET.
I WOULDN'T MIND LOSING A CASE TO GET THE PRESSURE OFF.
SADLY, IT LOOKS LIKE MY RECORD WON'T BE BROKEN JUST YET.
YOU SEE, YOU ADMITTED THAT YOU KILLED USUI...
...THE MOMENT YOU ENTERED THIS ROOM.
WHAT?
HOW DID YOU KNOW THIS WAS HER ROOM?
WHAT DO YOU MEAN?
I SAW THE HAYASHI RICE* IN FRONT OF THE...
...DOOR ...
*A stew-like dish served over rice.

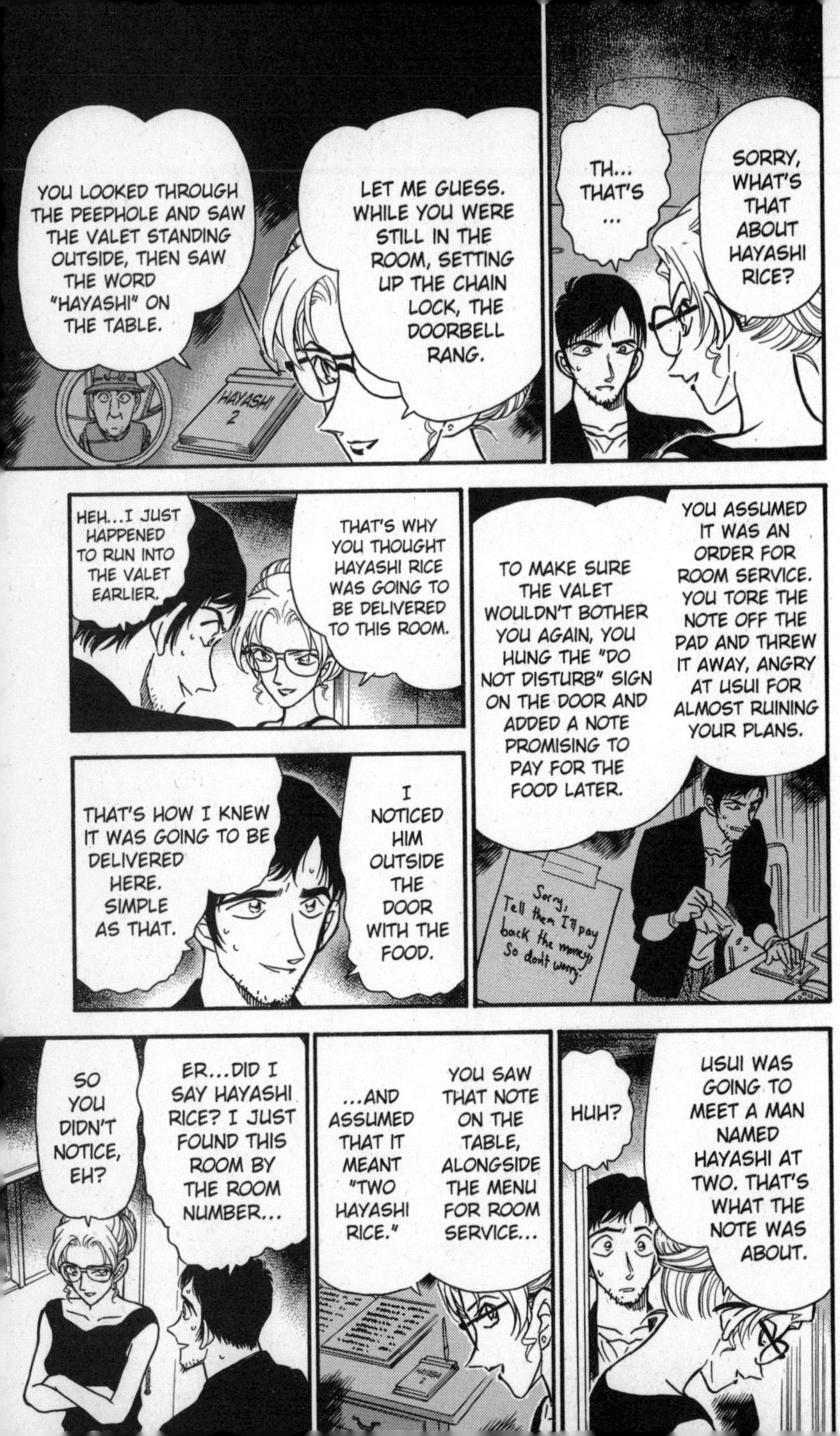
SORRY, WHAT'S THAT ABOUT HAYASHI RICE?
TH... THAT'S ...
LET ME GUESS. WHILE YOU WERE STILL IN THE ROOM, SETTING UP THE CHAIN LOCK, THE DOORBELL RANG.
YOU LOOKED THROUGH THE PEEPHOLE AND SAW THE VALET STANDING OUTSIDE, THEN SAW THE WORD "HAYASHI" ON THE TABLE.
HAYASHI 2
YOU ASSUMED IT WAS AN ORDER FOR ROOM SERVICE. YOU TORE THE NOTE OFF THE PAD AND THREW IT AWAY, ANGRY AT USUI FOR ALMOST RUINING YOUR PLANS.
TO MAKE SURE THE VALET WOULDN'T BOTHER YOU AGAIN, YOU HUNG THE "DO NOT DISTURB" SIGN ON THE DOOR AND ADDED A NOTE PROMISING TO PAY FOR THE FOOD LATER.
Sorry, Tell them I'll pay back the money, So don't worry.
THAT'S WHY YOU THOUGHT HAYASHI RICE WAS GOING TO BE DELIVERED TO THIS ROOM.
HEH...I JUST HAPPENED TO RUN INTO THE VALET EARLIER.
I NOTICED HIM OUTSIDE THE DOOR WITH THE FOOD.
THAT'S HOW I KNEW IT WAS GOING TO BE DELIVERED HERE. SIMPLE AS THAT.
USUI WAS GOING TO MEET A MAN NAMED HAYASHI AT TWO. THAT'S WHAT THE NOTE WAS ABOUT.
HUH?
YOU SAW THAT NOTE ON THE TABLE, ALONGSIDE THE MENU FOR ROOM SERVICE...
...AND ASSUMED THAT IT MEANT "TWO HAYASHI RICE."
ER...DID I SAY HAYASHI RICE? I JUST FOUND THIS ROOM BY THE ROOM NUMBER...
SO YOU DIDN'T NOTICE, EH?

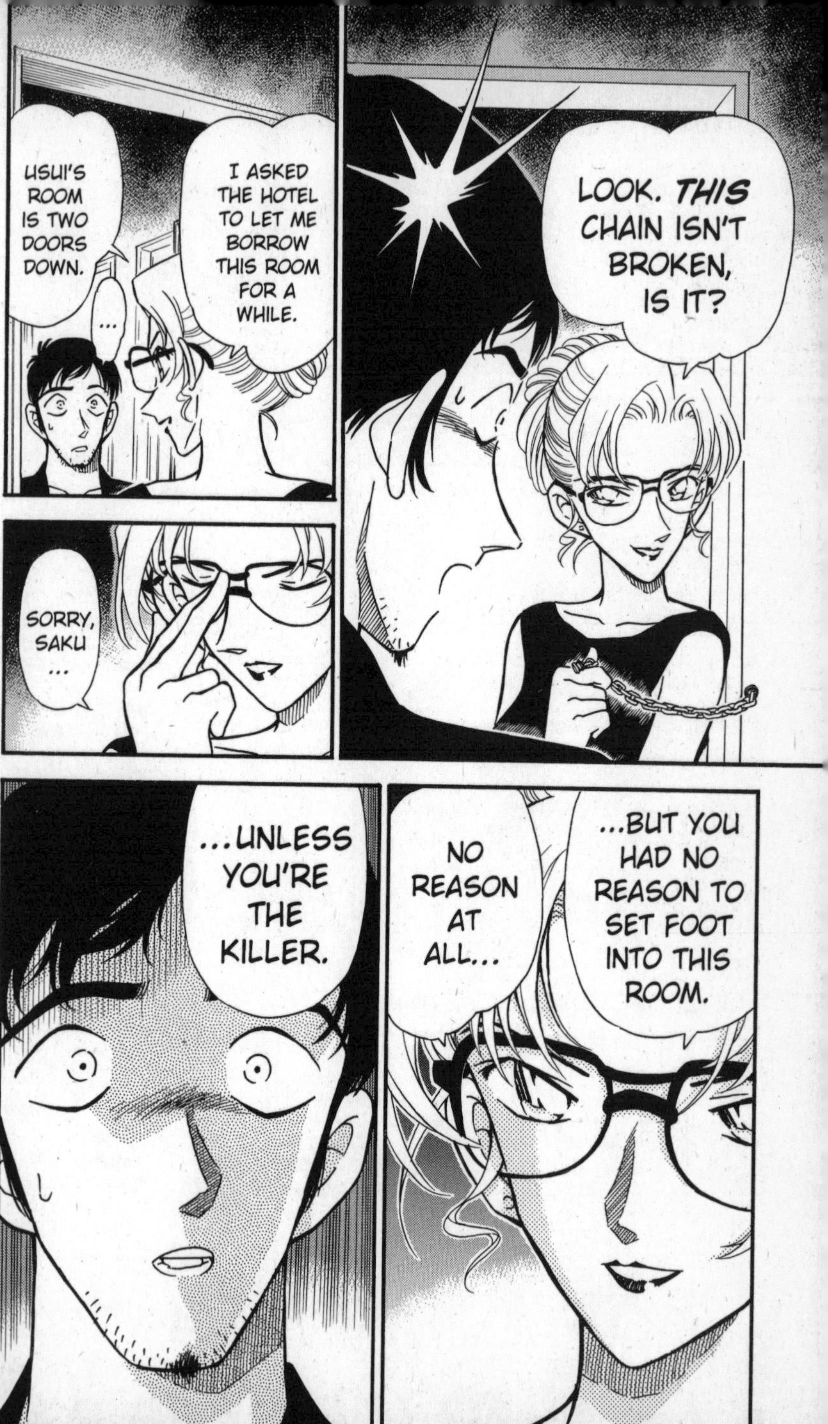
LOOK. *THIS* CHAIN ISN'T BROKEN, IS IT?
I ASKED THE HOTEL TO LET ME BORROW THIS ROOM FOR A WHILE.
USUI'S ROOM IS TWO DOORS DOWN.
...
SORRY, SAKU ...
...BUT YOU HAD NO REASON TO SET FOOT INTO THIS ROOM.
NO REASON AT ALL...
...UNLESS YOU'RE THE KILLER.

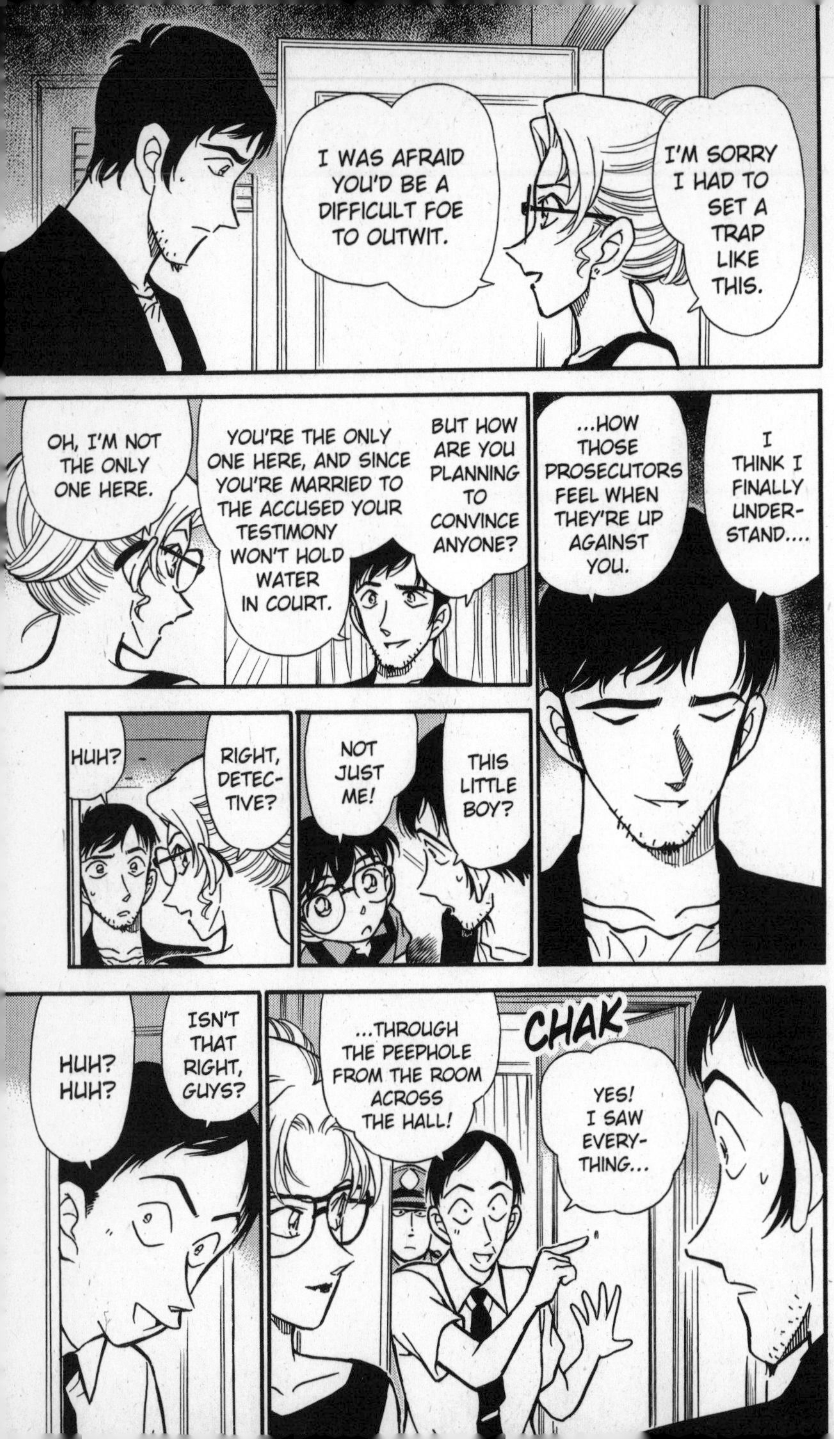
I'M SORRY I HAD TO SET A TRAP LIKE THIS.
I WAS AFRAID YOU'D BE A DIFFICULT FOE TO OUTWIT.
I THINK I FINALLY UNDER-STAND....
...HOW THOSE PROSECUTORS FEEL WHEN THEY'RE UP AGAINST YOU.
BUT HOW ARE YOU PLANNING TO CONVINCE ANYONE?
YOU'RE THE ONLY ONE HERE, AND SINCE YOU'RE MARRIED TO THE ACCUSED YOUR TESTIMONY WON'T HOLD WATER IN COURT.
OH, I'M NOT THE ONLY ONE HERE.
THIS LITTLE BOY?
NOT JUST ME!
RIGHT, DETEC-TIVE?
HUH?
CHAK
YES! I SAW EVERY-THING...
...THROUGH THE PEEPHOLE FROM THE ROOM ACROSS THE HALL!
ISN'T THAT RIGHT, GUYS?
HUH? HUH?

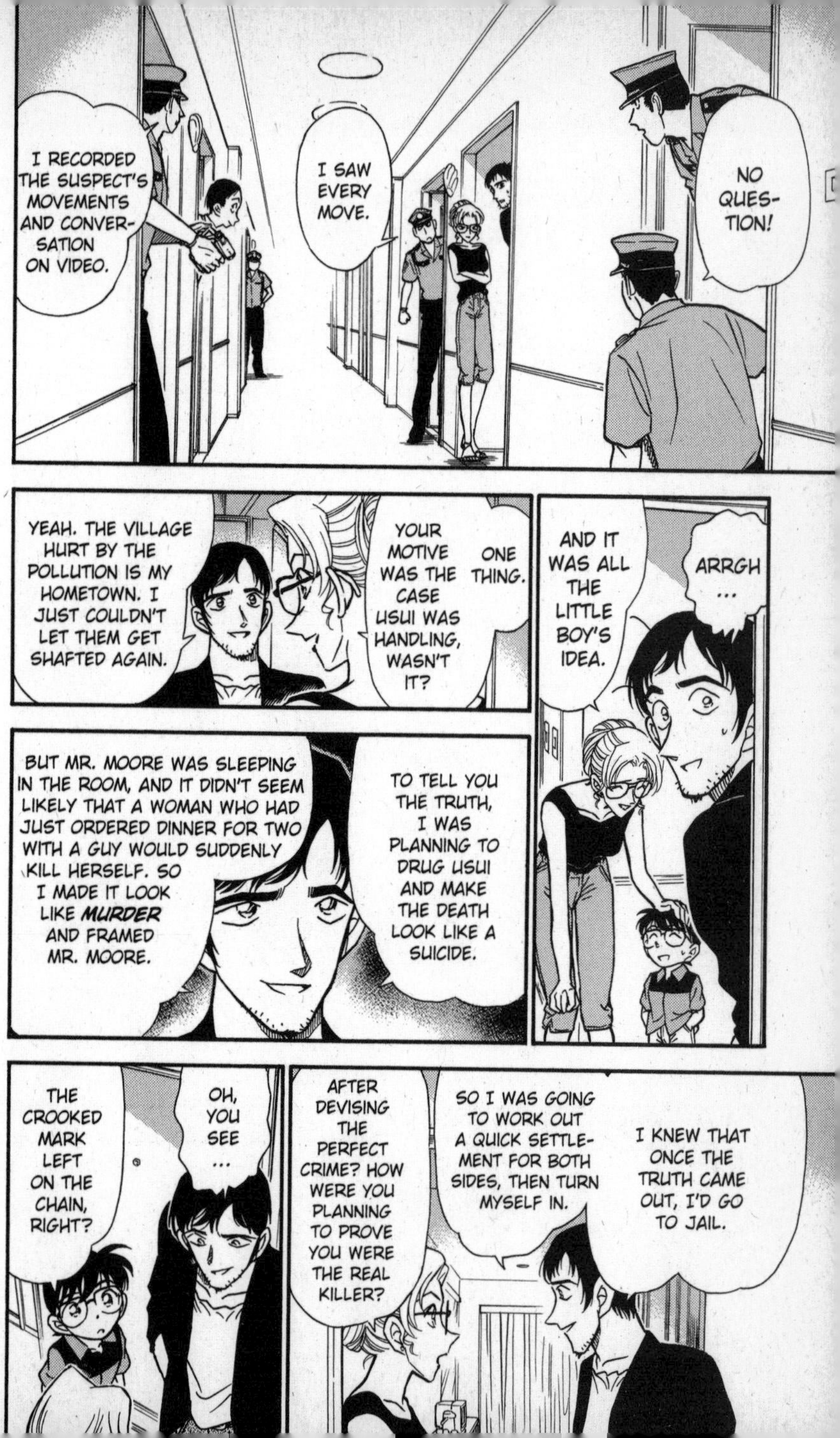

NO QUESTION!
I SAW EVERY MOVE.
I RECORDED THE SUSPECT'S MOVEMENTS AND CONVERSATION ON VIDEO.
ARRGH ...
AND IT WAS ALL THE LITTLE BOY'S IDEA.
ONE THING.
YOUR MOTIVE WAS THE CASE USUI WAS HANDLING, WASN'T IT?
YEAH. THE VILLAGE HURT BY THE POLLUTION IS MY HOMETOWN. I JUST COULDN'T LET THEM GET SHAFTED AGAIN.
TO TELL YOU THE TRUTH, I WAS PLANNING TO DRUG USUI AND MAKE THE DEATH LOOK LIKE A SUICIDE.
BUT MR. MOORE WAS SLEEPING IN THE ROOM, AND IT DIDN'T SEEM LIKELY THAT A WOMAN WHO HAD JUST ORDERED DINNER FOR TWO WITH A GUY WOULD SUDDENLY KILL HERSELF. SO I MADE IT LOOK LIKE MURDER AND FRAMED MR. MOORE.
I KNEW THAT ONCE THE TRUTH CAME OUT, I'D GO TO JAIL.
SO I WAS GOING TO WORK OUT A QUICK SETTLEMENT FOR BOTH SIDES, THEN TURN MYSELF IN.
AFTER DEVISING THE PERFECT CRIME? HOW WERE YOU PLANNING TO PROVE YOU WERE THE REAL KILLER?
OH, YOU SEE ...
THE CROOKED MARK LEFT ON THE CHAIN, RIGHT?

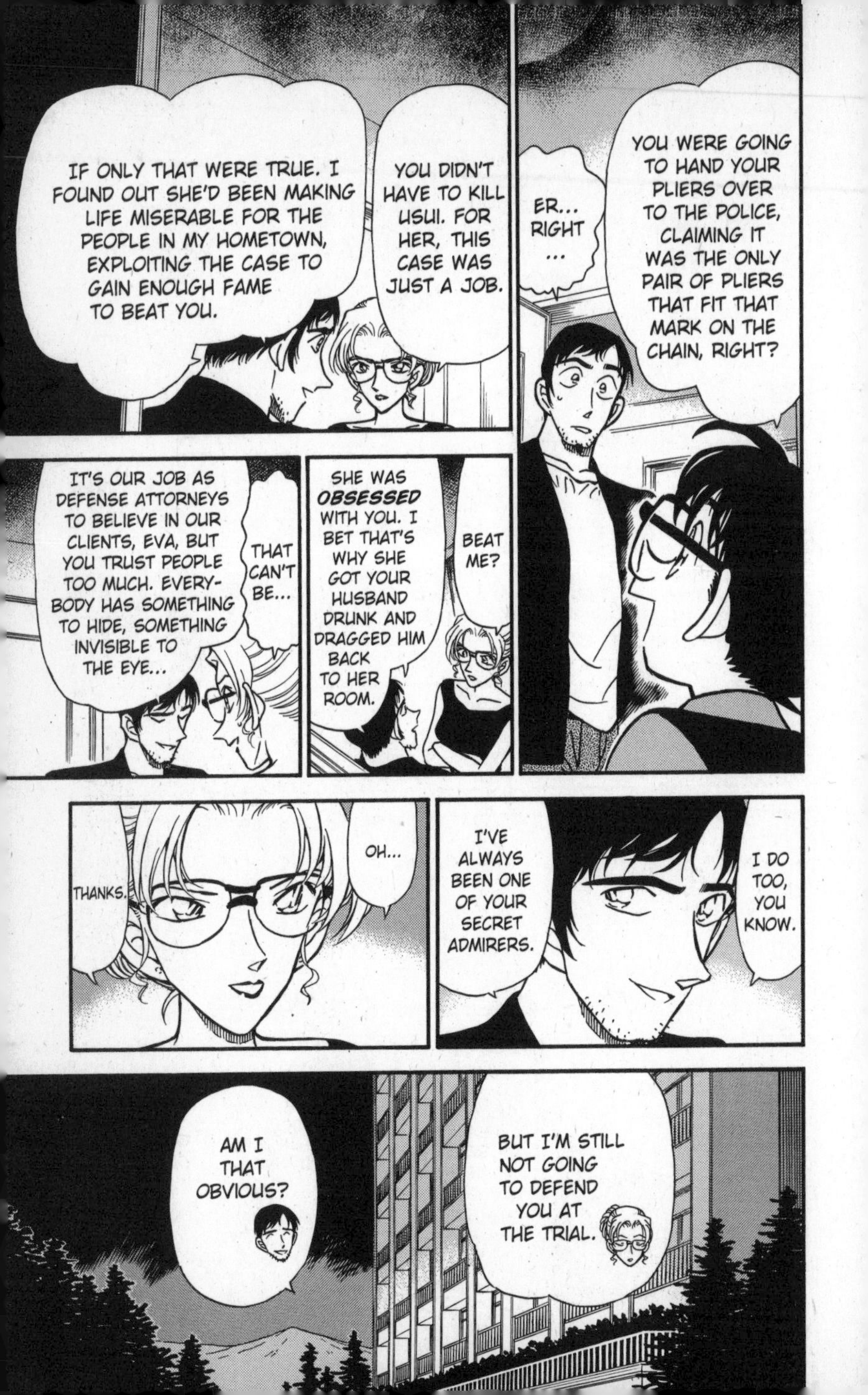
YOU WERE GOING TO HAND YOUR PLIERS OVER TO THE POLICE, CLAIMING IT WAS THE ONLY PAIR OF PLIERS THAT FIT THAT MARK ON THE CHAIN, RIGHT?
ER... RIGHT ...
YOU DIDN'T HAVE TO KILL USUI. FOR HER, THIS CASE WAS JUST A JOB.
IF ONLY THAT WERE TRUE. I FOUND OUT SHE'D BEEN MAKING LIFE MISERABLE FOR THE PEOPLE IN MY HOMETOWN, EXPLOITING THE CASE TO GAIN ENOUGH FAME TO BEAT YOU.
BEAT ME?
SHE WAS *OBSESSED* WITH YOU. I BET THAT'S WHY SHE GOT YOUR HUSBAND DRUNK AND DRAGGED HIM BACK TO HER ROOM.
THAT CAN'T BE...
IT'S OUR JOB AS DEFENSE ATTORNEYS TO BELIEVE IN OUR CLIENTS, EVA, BUT YOU TRUST PEOPLE TOO MUCH. EVERY-BODY HAS SOMETHING TO HIDE, SOMETHING INVISIBLE TO THE EYE...
I DO TOO, YOU KNOW.
I'VE ALWAYS BEEN ONE OF YOUR SECRET ADMIRERS.
OH...
THANKS.
BUT I'M STILL NOT GOING TO DEFEND YOU AT THE TRIAL.
AM I THAT OBVIOUS?

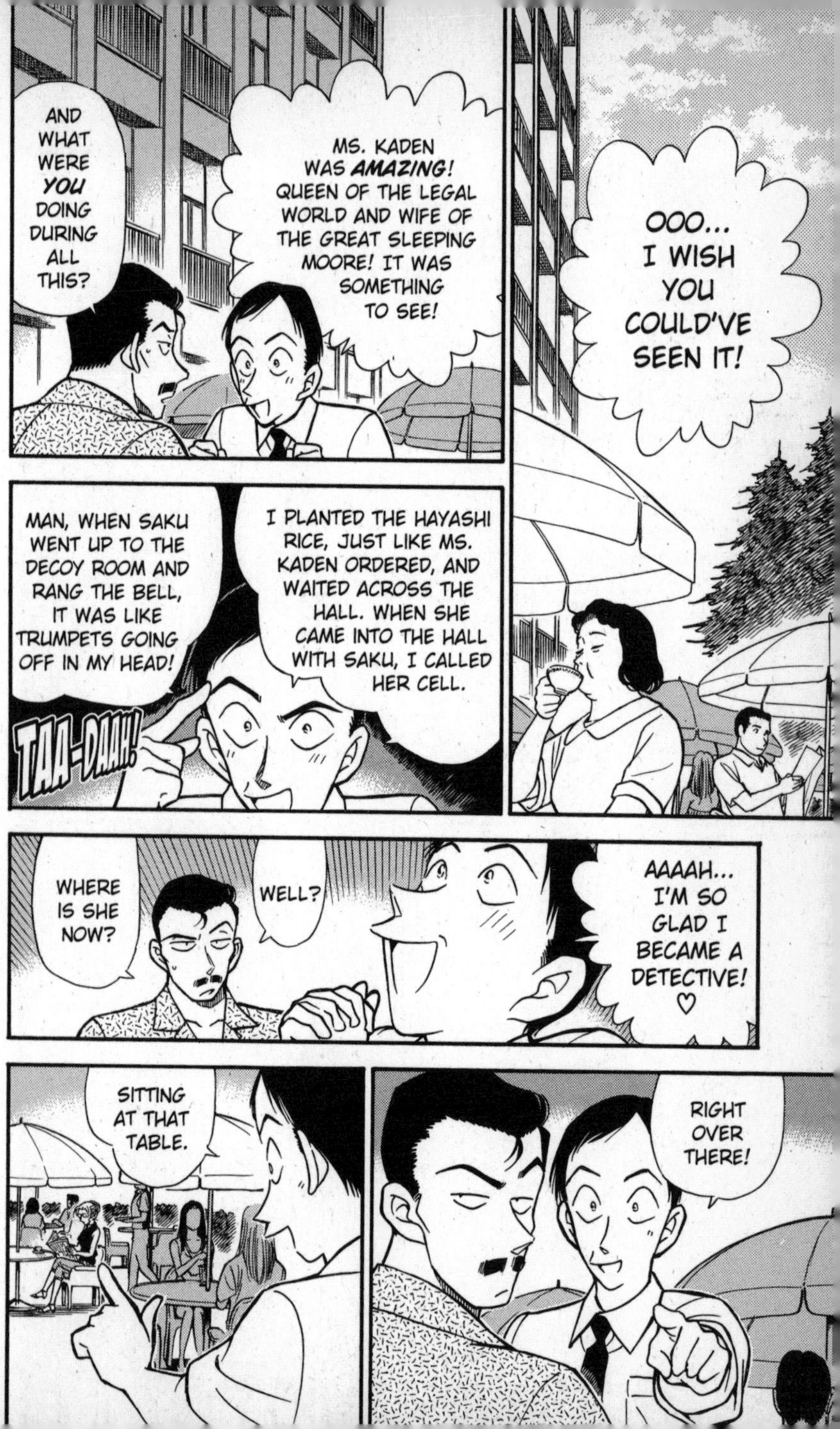
OOO... I WISH YOU COULD'VE SEEN IT!
MS. KADEN WAS *AMAZING*! QUEEN OF THE LEGAL WORLD AND WIFE OF THE GREAT SLEEPING MOORE! IT WAS SOMETHING TO SEE!
AND WHAT WERE *YOU* DOING DURING ALL THIS?
I PLANTED THE HAYASHI RICE, JUST LIKE MS. KADEN ORDERED, AND WAITED ACROSS THE HALL. WHEN SHE CAME INTO THE HALL WITH SAKU, I CALLED HER CELL.
MAN, WHEN SAKU WENT UP TO THE DECOY ROOM AND RANG THE BELL, IT WAS LIKE TRUMPETS GOING OFF IN MY HEAD!
TAA-DAAH!
AAAAH... I'M SO GLAD I BECAME A DETECTIVE! ♡
WELL?
WHERE IS SHE NOW?
RIGHT OVER THERE!
SITTING AT THAT TABLE.

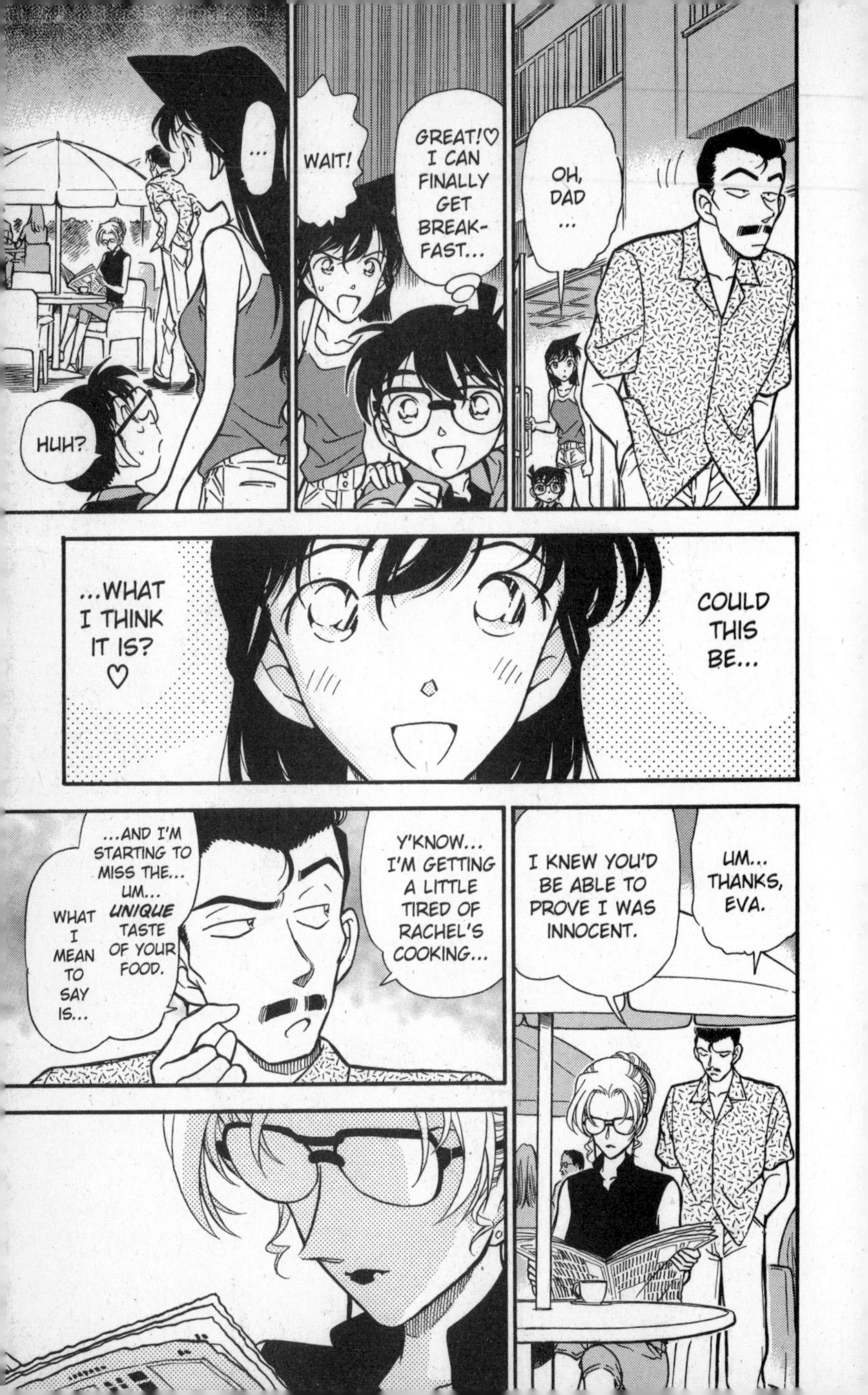
OH, DAD ...
GREAT!♡ I CAN FINALLY GET BREAKFAST...
WAIT!
...
HUH?
COULD THIS BE...
...WHAT I THINK IT IS? ♡
UM... THANKS, EVA.
I KNEW YOU'D BE ABLE TO PROVE I WAS INNOCENT.
Y'KNOW... I'M GETTING A LITTLE TIRED OF RACHEL'S COOKING...
...AND I'M STARTING TO MISS THE... UM... **UNIQUE** TASTE OF YOUR FOOD.
WHAT I MEAN TO SAY IS...

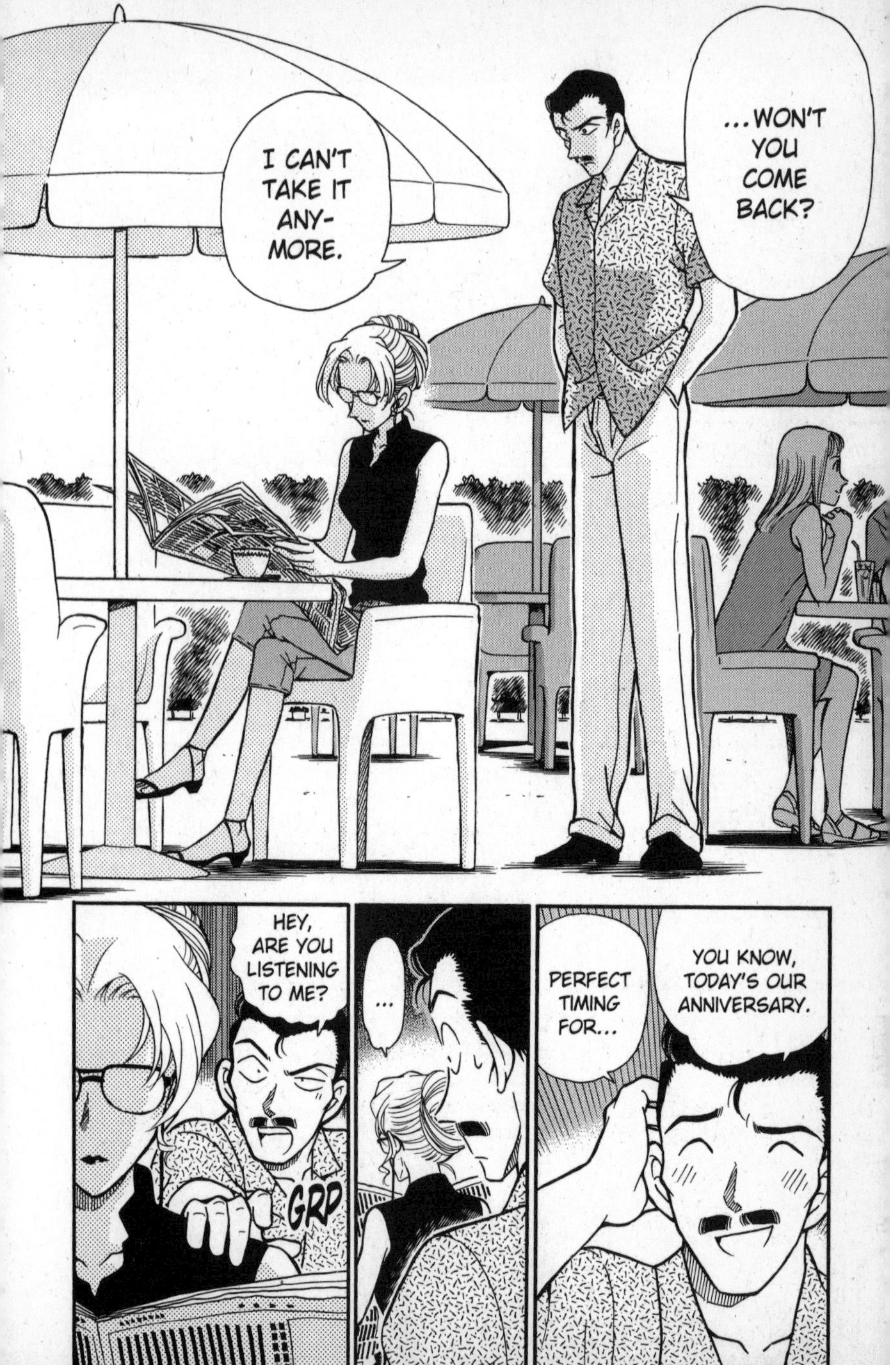
...WON'T YOU COME BACK?
I CAN'T TAKE IT ANYMORE.
YOU KNOW, TODAY'S OUR ANNIVERSARY.
PERFECT TIMING FOR...
...
HEY, ARE YOU LISTENING TO ME?
GRP

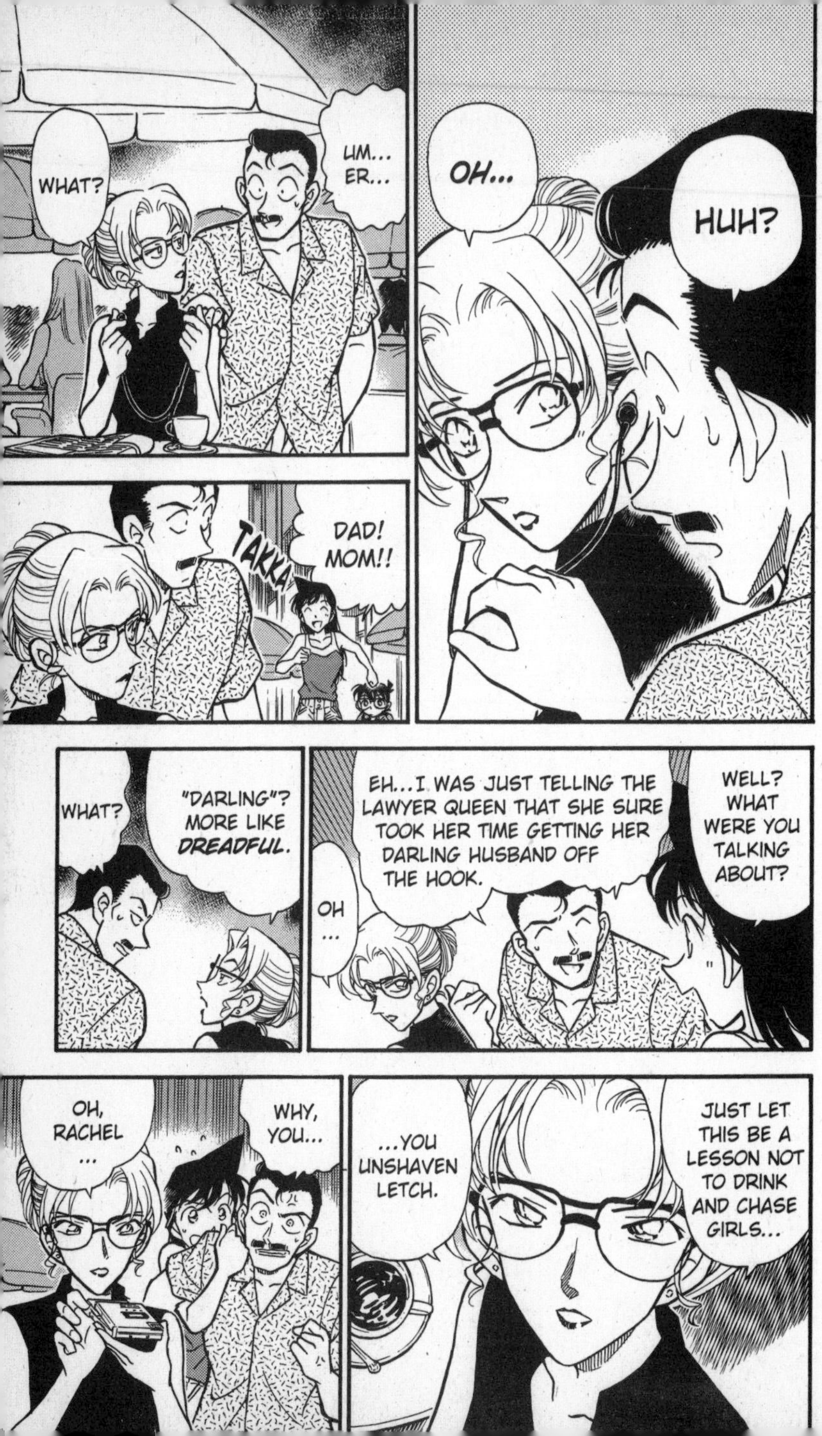
HUH?
OH...
UM... ER...
WHAT?
DAD! MOM!!
TAKKA
WELL? WHAT WERE YOU TALKING ABOUT?
EH...I WAS JUST TELLING THE LAWYER QUEEN THAT SHE SURE TOOK HER TIME GETTING HER DARLING HUSBAND OFF THE HOOK.
OH ...
"DARLING"? MORE LIKE DREADFUL.
WHAT?
JUST LET THIS BE A LESSON NOT TO DRINK AND CHASE GIRLS...
...YOU UNSHAVEN LETCH.
WHY, YOU...
OH, RACHEL ...

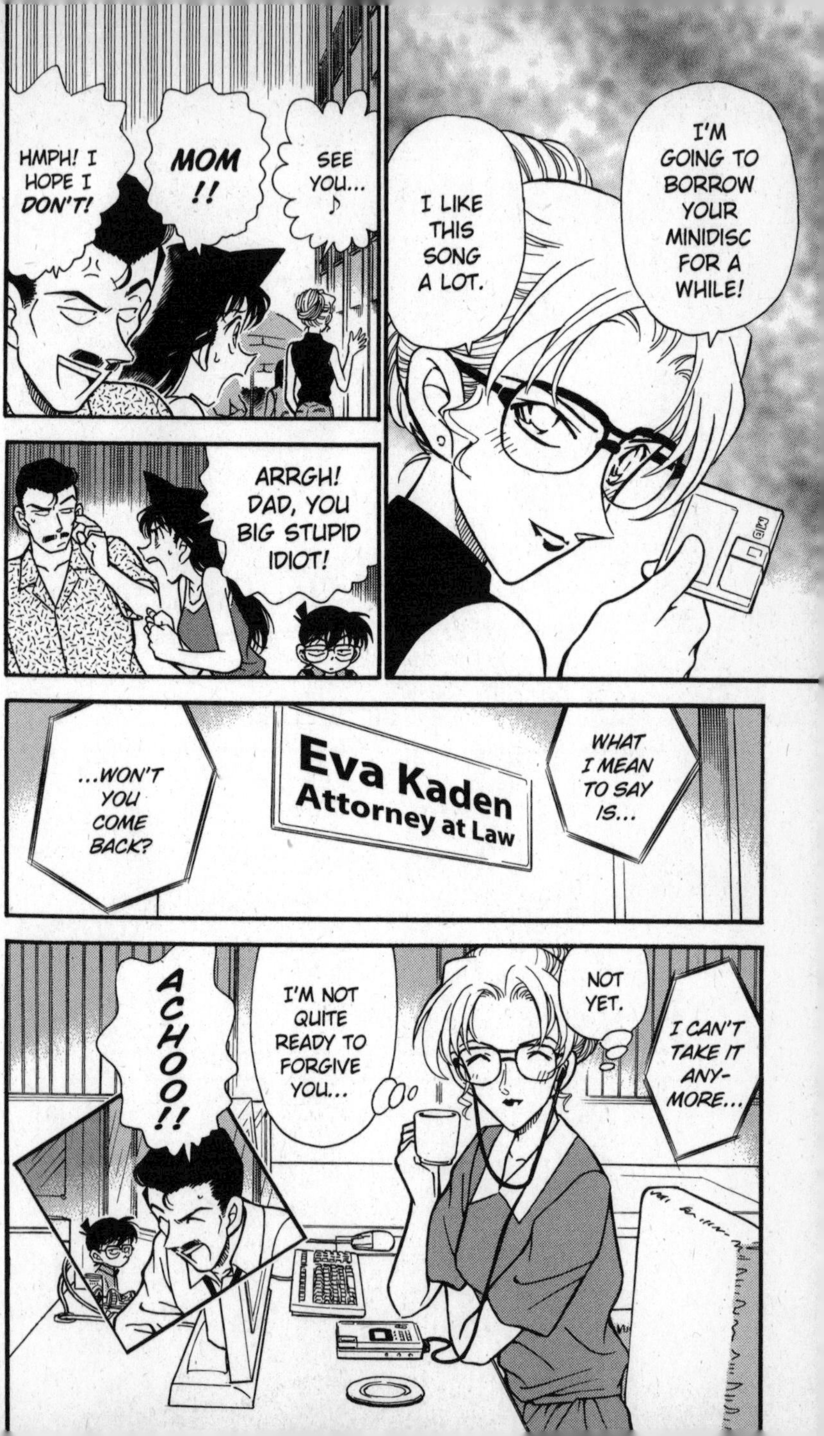
I'M GOING TO BORROW YOUR MINIDISC FOR A WHILE!
I LIKE THIS SONG A LOT.
SEE YOU... ♪
MOM!!
HMPH! I HOPE I DON'T!
ARRGH! DAD, YOU BIG STUPID IDIOT!
WHAT I MEAN TO SAY IS...
Eva Kaden
Attorney at Law
...WON'T YOU COME BACK?
NOT YET.
I'M NOT QUITE READY TO FORGIVE YOU...
I CAN'T TAKE IT ANY-MORE...
ACHOO!!

FILE 4: THE MAN FROM 18 YEARS AGO

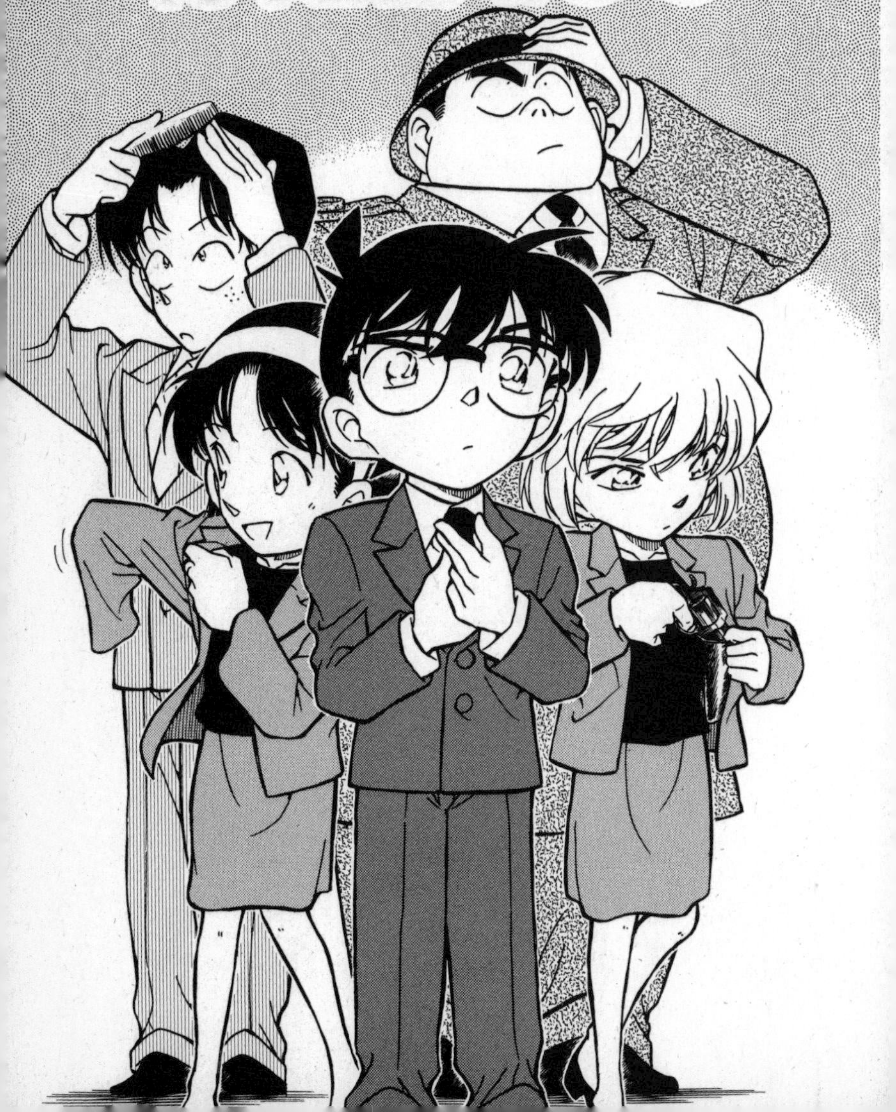

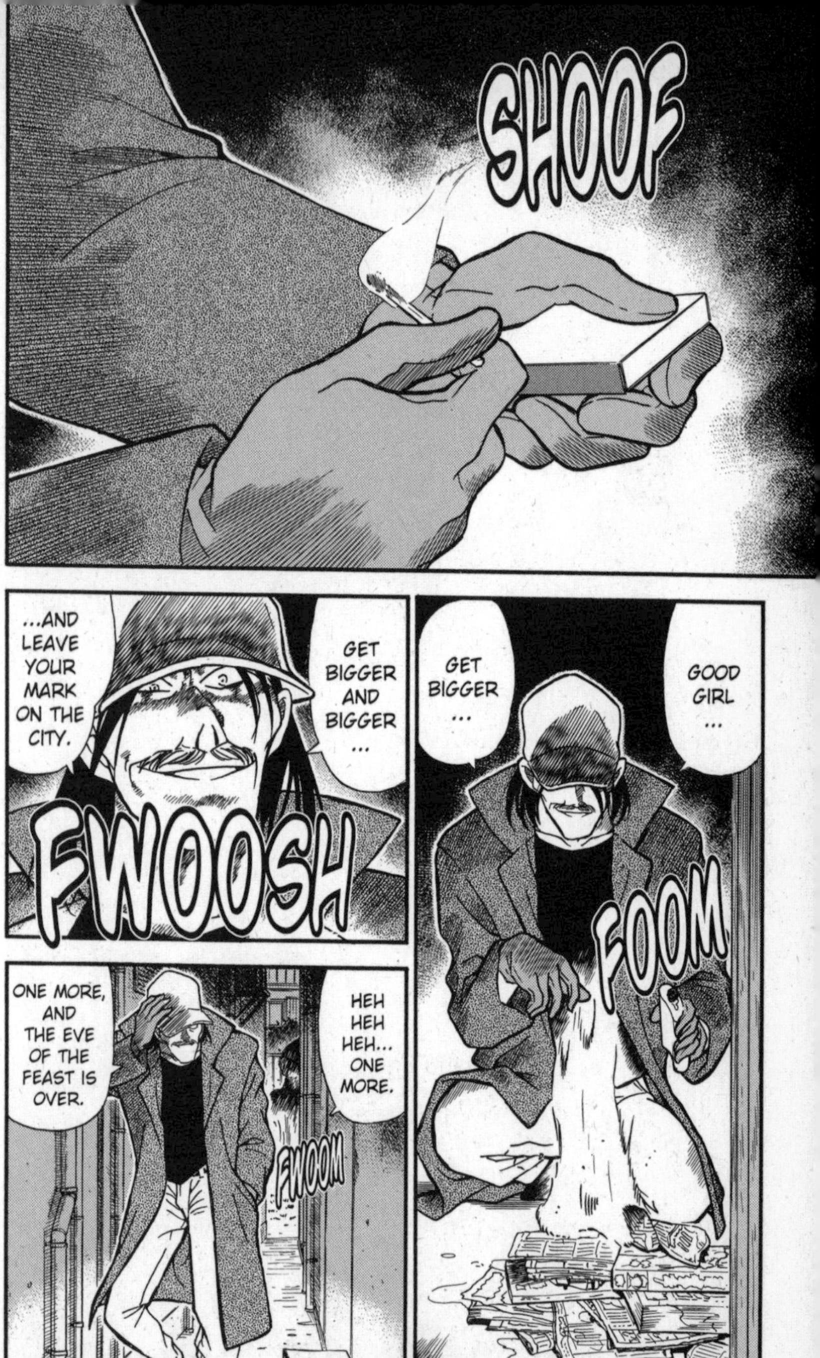
SHOOF
GOOD GIRL...
GET BIGGER...
FOOM
GET BIGGER AND BIGGER...
...AND LEAVE YOUR MARK ON THE CITY.
FWOOSH
HEH HEH HEH... ONE MORE.
ONE MORE, AND THE EVE OF THE FEAST IS OVER.
FWOOM

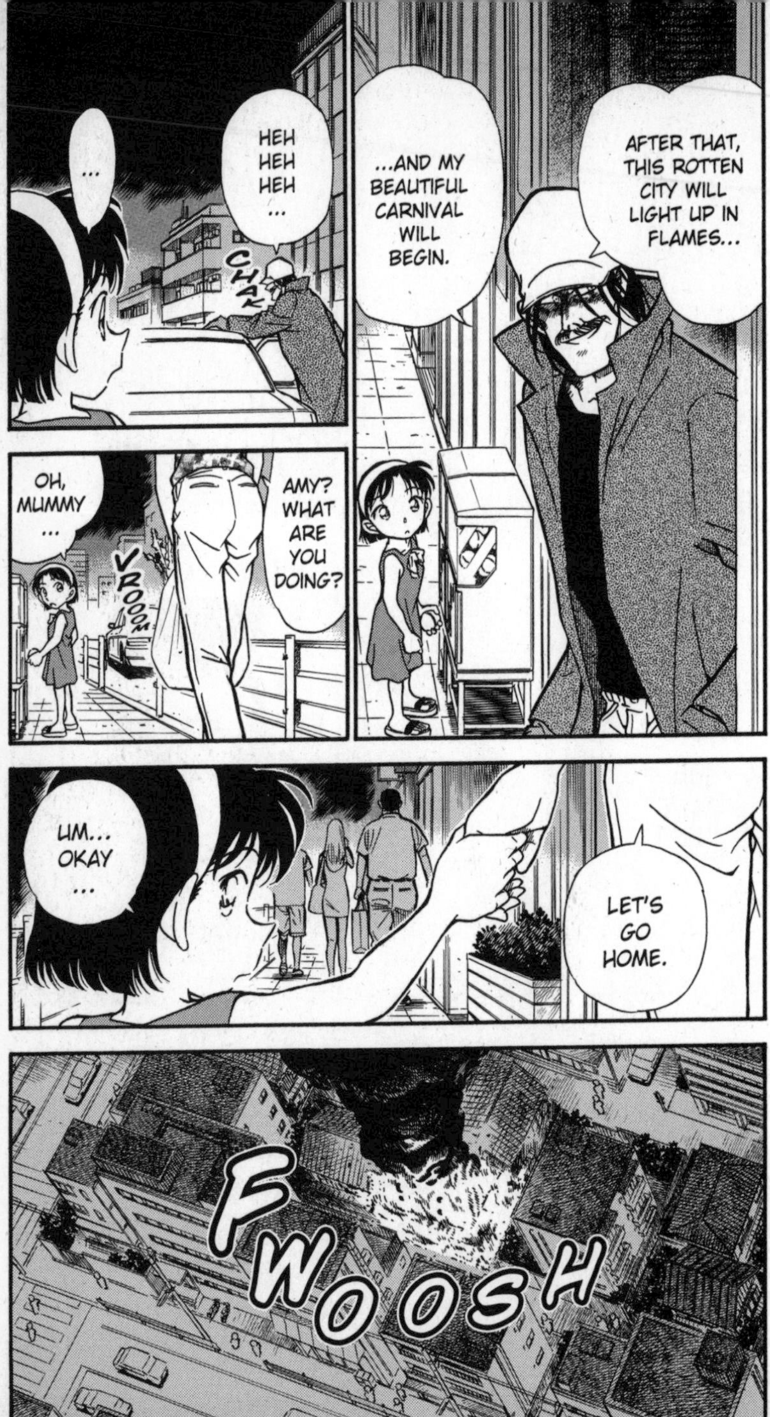
AFTER THAT, THIS ROTTEN CITY WILL LIGHT UP IN FLAMES...
...AND MY BEAUTIFUL CARNIVAL WILL BEGIN.
HEH HEH HEH ...
CHAK
...
AMY? WHAT ARE YOU DOING?
VROOOM
OH, MUMMY ...
LET'S GO HOME.
UM... OKAY ...
FWOOSH

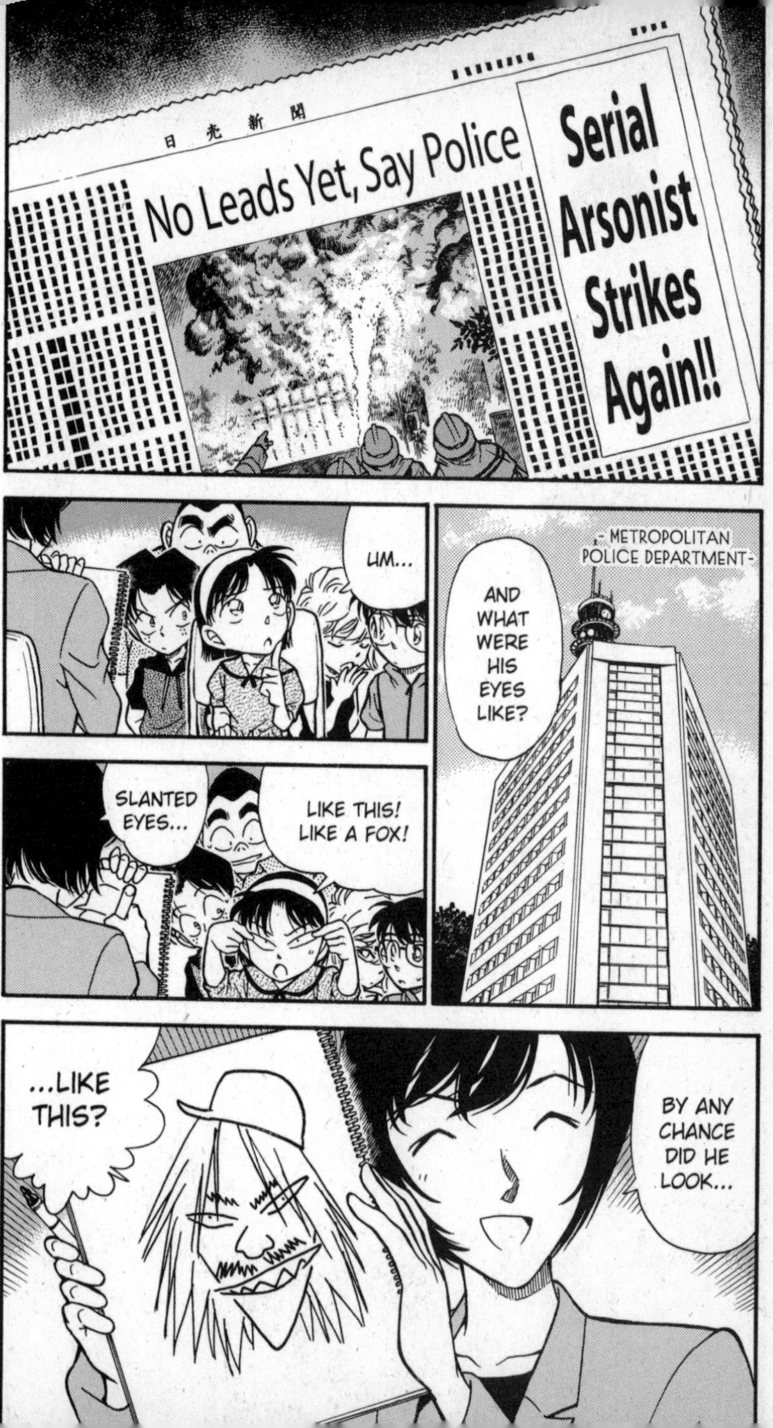

日売新聞
Serial Arsonist Strikes Again!!
No Leads Yet, Say Police
- METROPOLITAN POLICE DEPARTMENT -
AND WHAT WERE HIS EYES LIKE?
UM...
LIKE THIS! LIKE A FOX!
SLANTED EYES...
BY ANY CHANCE DID HE LOOK...
...LIKE THIS?

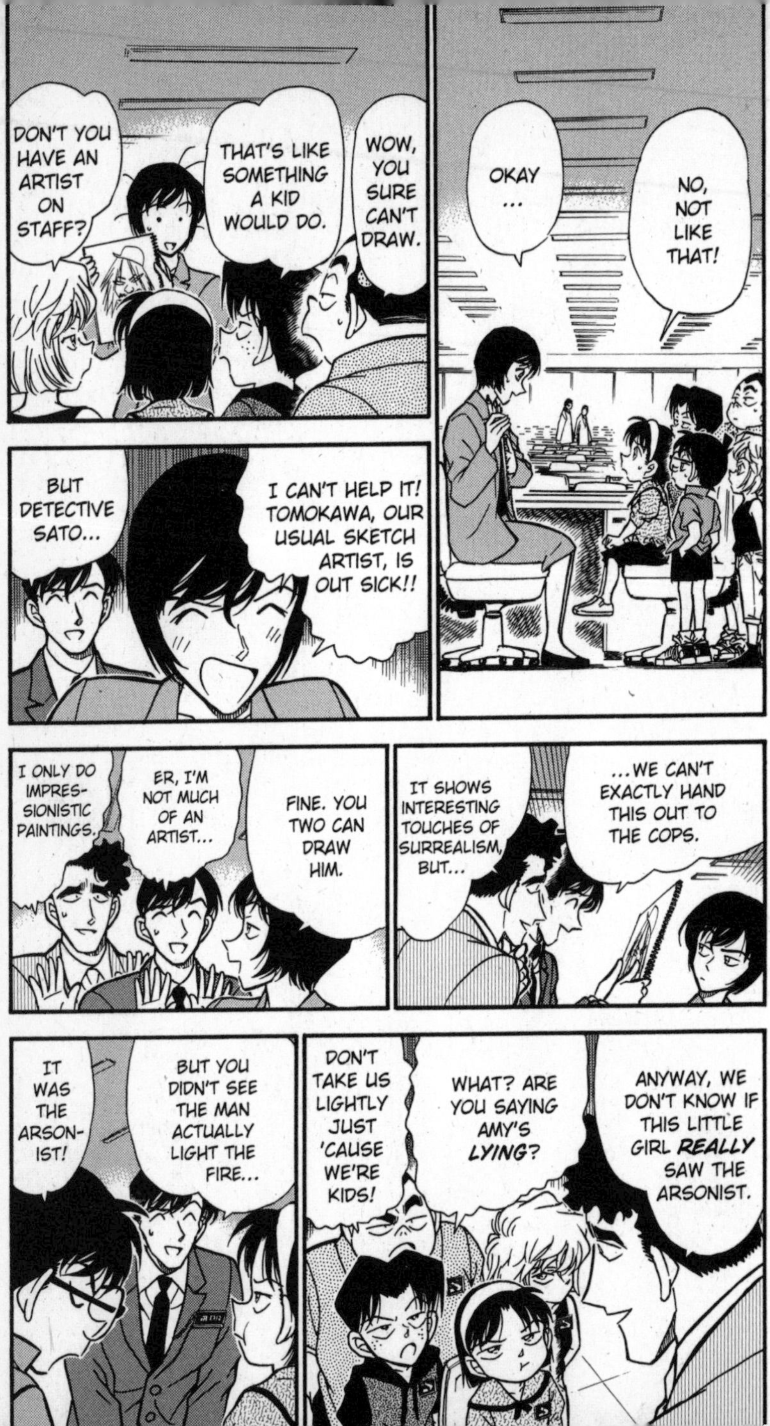
NO, NOT LIKE THAT!
OKAY ...
WOW, YOU SURE CAN'T DRAW.
THAT'S LIKE SOMETHING A KID WOULD DO.
DON'T YOU HAVE AN ARTIST ON STAFF?
I CAN'T HELP IT! TOMOKAWA, OUR USUAL SKETCH ARTIST, IS OUT SICK!!
BUT DETECTIVE SATO...
...WE CAN'T EXACTLY HAND THIS OUT TO THE COPS.
IT SHOWS INTERESTING TOUCHES OF SURREALISM, BUT...
FINE. YOU TWO CAN DRAW HIM.
ER, I'M NOT MUCH OF AN ARTIST...
I ONLY DO IMPRESSIONISTIC PAINTINGS.
ANYWAY, WE DON'T KNOW IF THIS LITTLE GIRL ***REALLY*** SAW THE ARSONIST.
WHAT? ARE YOU SAYING AMY'S ***LYING***?
DON'T TAKE US LIGHTLY JUST 'CAUSE WE'RE KIDS!
BUT YOU DIDN'T SEE THE MAN ACTUALLY LIGHT THE FIRE...
IT WAS THE ARSONIST!

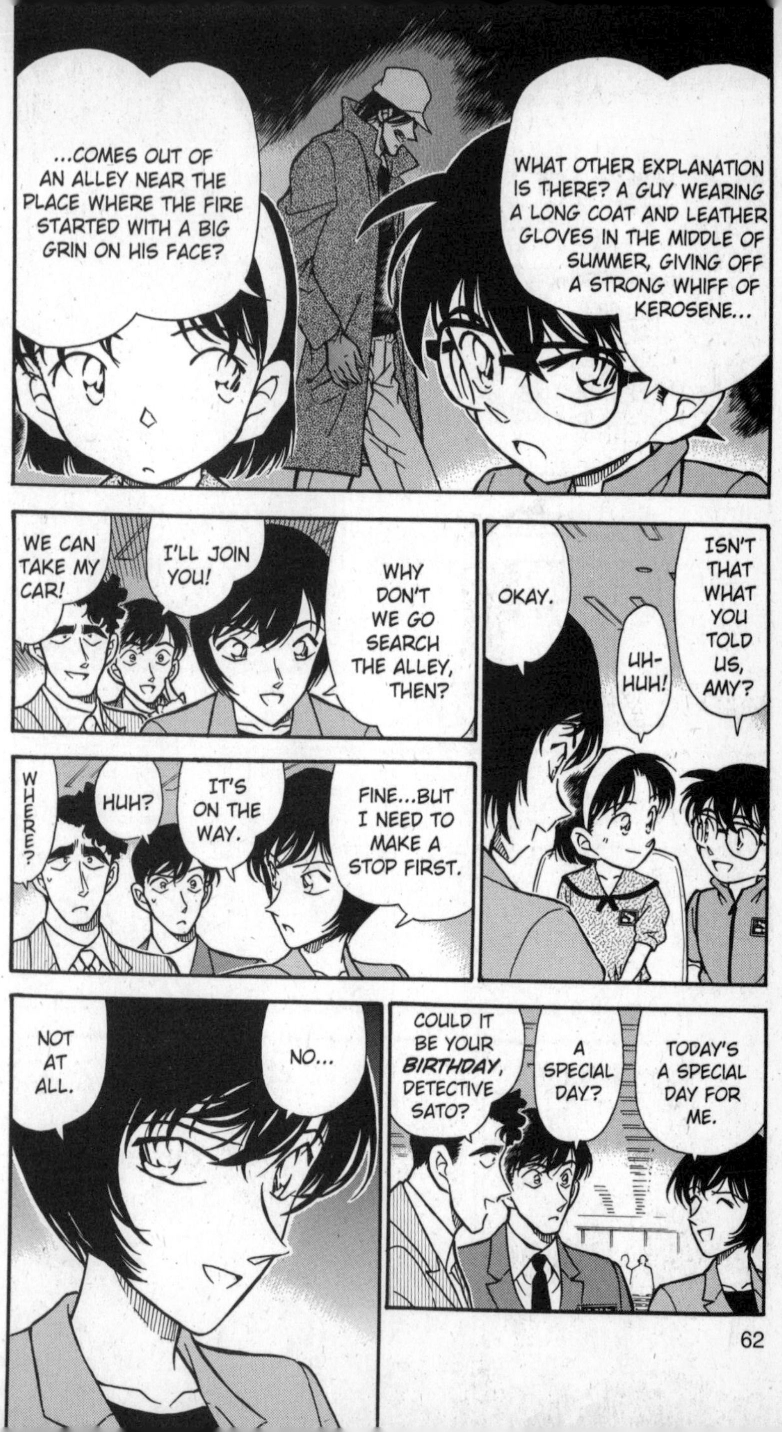
WHAT OTHER EXPLANATION IS THERE? A GUY WEARING A LONG COAT AND LEATHER GLOVES IN THE MIDDLE OF SUMMER, GIVING OFF A STRONG WHIFF OF KEROSENE...
...COMES OUT OF AN ALLEY NEAR THE PLACE WHERE THE FIRE STARTED WITH A BIG GRIN ON HIS FACE?
ISN'T THAT WHAT YOU TOLD US, AMY?
UH-HUH!
OKAY.
WHY DON'T WE GO SEARCH THE ALLEY, THEN?
I'LL JOIN YOU!
WE CAN TAKE MY CAR!
FINE...BUT I NEED TO MAKE A STOP FIRST.
IT'S ON THE WAY.
HUH?
WHERE?
TODAY'S A SPECIAL DAY FOR ME.
A SPECIAL DAY?
COULD IT BE YOUR ***BIRTHDAY***, DETECTIVE SATO?
NO...
NOT AT ALL.

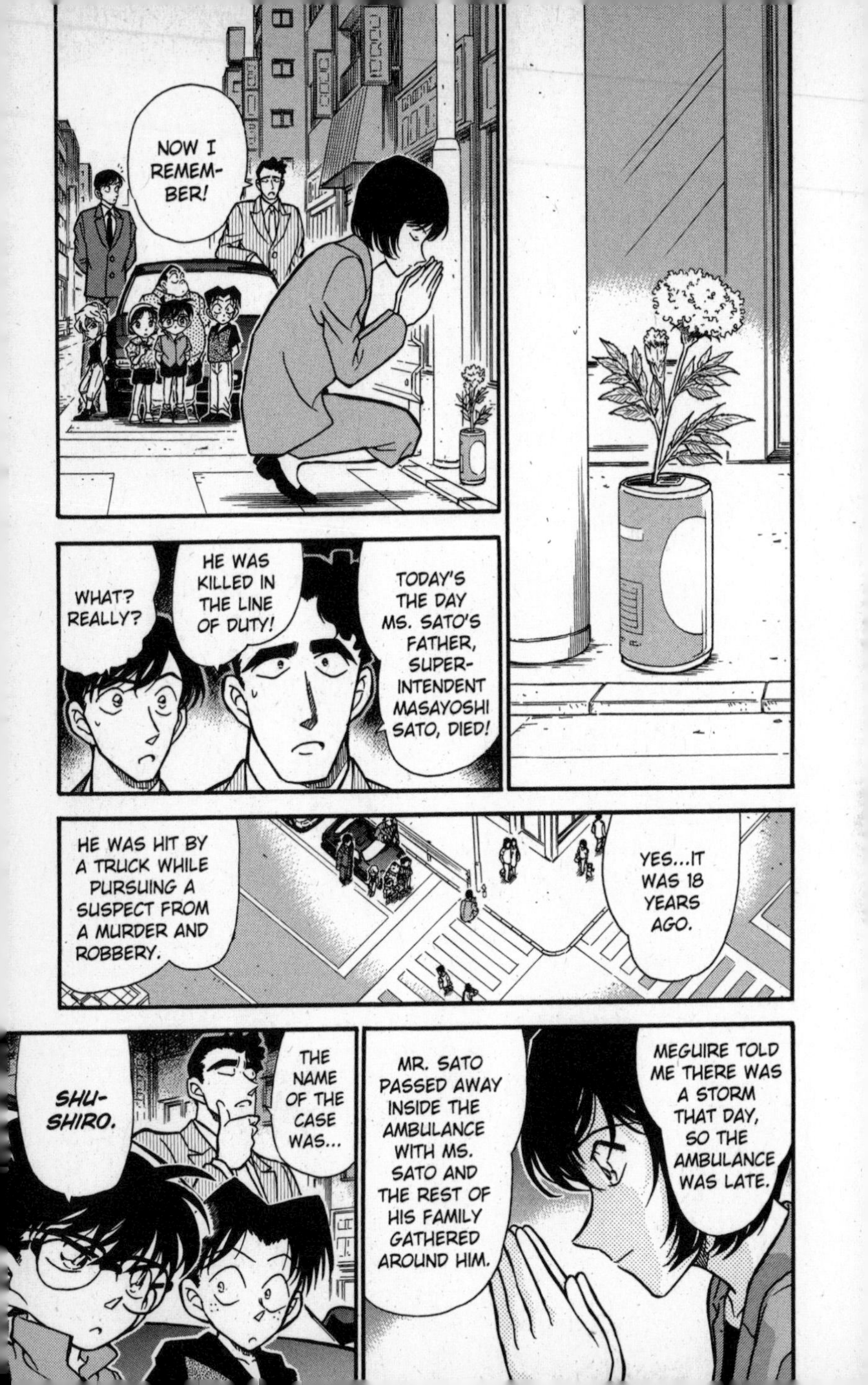
NOW I REMEMBER!
TODAY'S THE DAY MS. SATO'S FATHER, SUPERINTENDENT MASAYOSHI SATO, DIED!
HE WAS KILLED IN THE LINE OF DUTY!
WHAT? REALLY?
YES...IT WAS 18 YEARS AGO.
HE WAS HIT BY A TRUCK WHILE PURSUING A SUSPECT FROM A MURDER AND ROBBERY.
MEGUIRE TOLD ME THERE WAS A STORM THAT DAY, SO THE AMBULANCE WAS LATE.
MR. SATO PASSED AWAY INSIDE THE AMBULANCE WITH MS. SATO AND THE REST OF HIS FAMILY GATHERED AROUND HIM.
THE NAME OF THE CASE WAS...
SHUSHIRO.

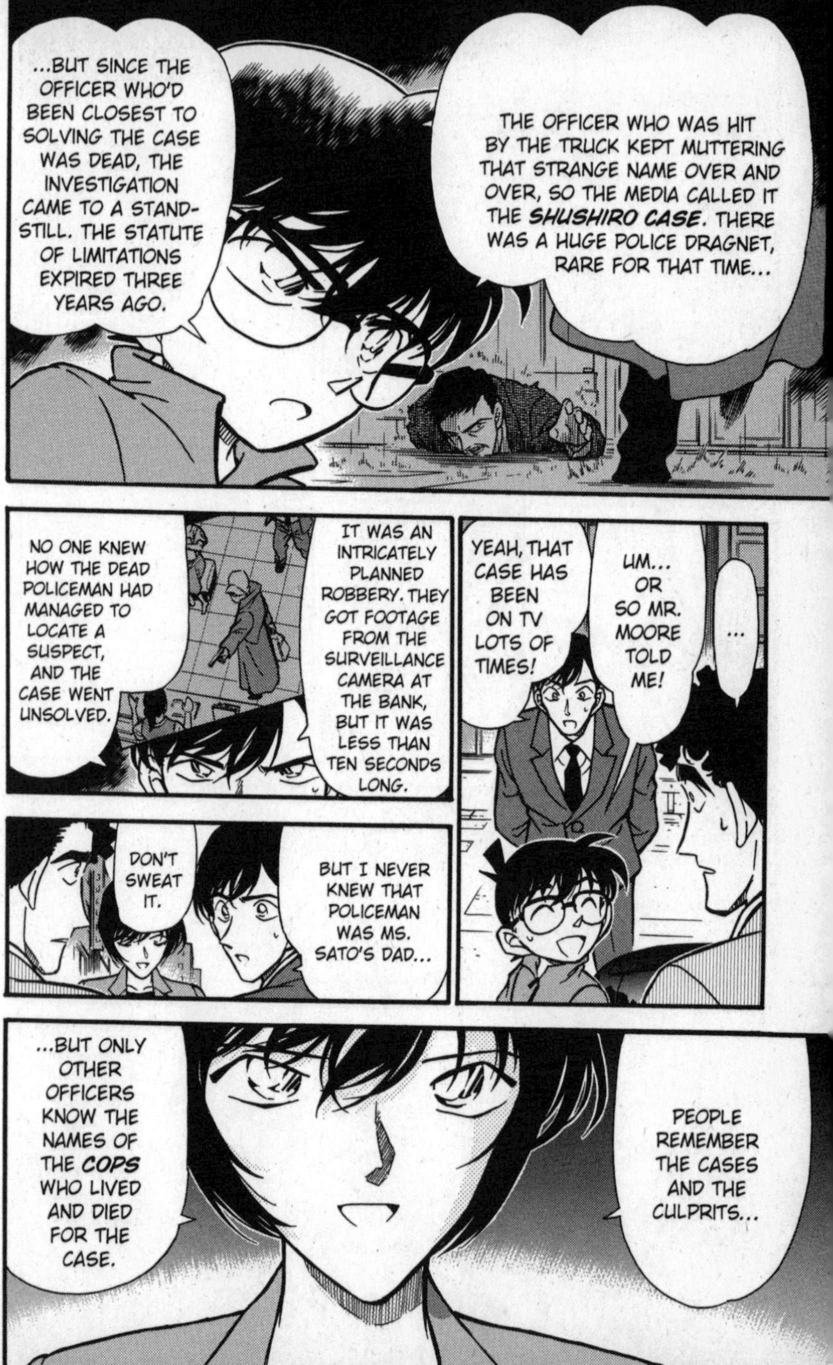
THE OFFICER WHO WAS HIT BY THE TRUCK KEPT MUTTERING THAT STRANGE NAME OVER AND OVER, SO THE MEDIA CALLED IT THE ***SHUSHIRO CASE***. THERE WAS A HUGE POLICE DRAGNET, RARE FOR THAT TIME...
...BUT SINCE THE OFFICER WHO'D BEEN CLOSEST TO SOLVING THE CASE WAS DEAD, THE INVESTIGATION CAME TO A STAND-STILL. THE STATUTE OF LIMITATIONS EXPIRED THREE YEARS AGO.
...
UM... OR SO MR. MOORE TOLD ME!
YEAH, THAT CASE HAS BEEN ON TV LOTS OF TIMES!
IT WAS AN INTRICATELY PLANNED ROBBERY. THEY GOT FOOTAGE FROM THE SURVEILLANCE CAMERA AT THE BANK, BUT IT WAS LESS THAN TEN SECONDS LONG.
NO ONE KNEW HOW THE DEAD POLICEMAN HAD MANAGED TO LOCATE A SUSPECT, AND THE CASE WENT UNSOLVED.
BUT I NEVER KNEW THAT POLICEMAN WAS MS. SATO'S DAD...
DON'T SWEAT IT.
PEOPLE REMEMBER THE CASES AND THE CULPRITS...
...BUT ONLY OTHER OFFICERS KNOW THE NAMES OF THE ***COPS*** WHO LIVED AND DIED FOR THE CASE.

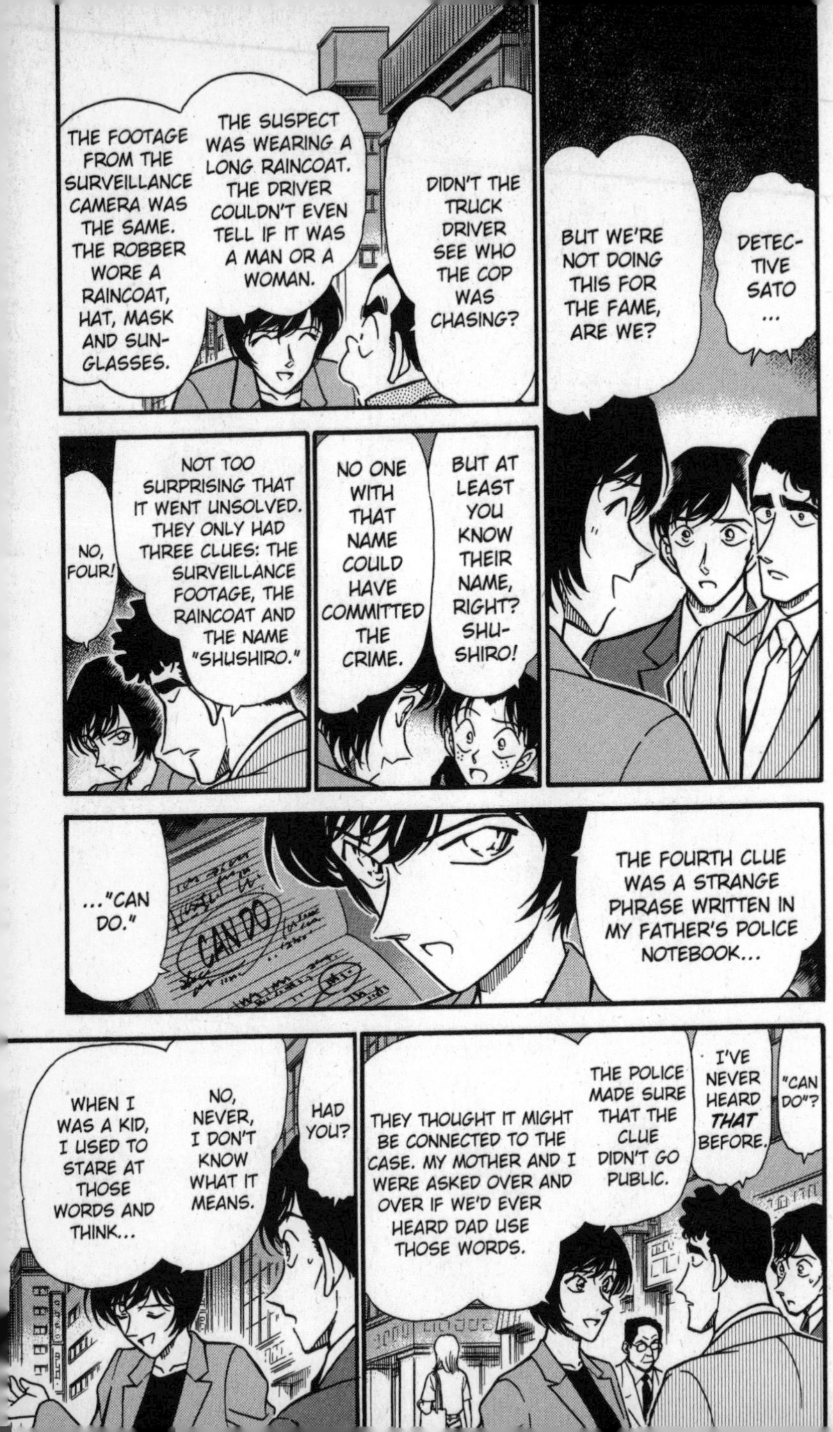
DETECTIVE SATO...
BUT WE'RE NOT DOING THIS FOR THE FAME, ARE WE?
DIDN'T THE TRUCK DRIVER SEE WHO THE COP WAS CHASING?
THE SUSPECT WAS WEARING A LONG RAINCOAT. THE DRIVER COULDN'T EVEN TELL IF IT WAS A MAN OR A WOMAN.
THE FOOTAGE FROM THE SURVEILLANCE CAMERA WAS THE SAME. THE ROBBER WORE A RAINCOAT, HAT, MASK AND SUNGLASSES.
BUT AT LEAST YOU KNOW THEIR NAME, RIGHT? SHUSHIRO!
NO ONE WITH THAT NAME COULD HAVE COMMITTED THE CRIME.
NOT TOO SURPRISING THAT IT WENT UNSOLVED. THEY ONLY HAD THREE CLUES: THE SURVEILLANCE FOOTAGE, THE RAINCOAT AND THE NAME "SHUSHIRO."
NO, FOUR!
THE FOURTH CLUE WAS A STRANGE PHRASE WRITTEN IN MY FATHER'S POLICE NOTEBOOK...
CAN DO
..."CAN DO."
"CAN DO"?
I'VE NEVER HEARD *THAT* BEFORE.
THE POLICE MADE SURE THAT THE CLUE DIDN'T GO PUBLIC.
THEY THOUGHT IT MIGHT BE CONNECTED TO THE CASE. MY MOTHER AND I WERE ASKED OVER AND OVER IF WE'D EVER HEARD DAD USE THOSE WORDS.
HAD YOU?
NO, NEVER, I DON'T KNOW WHAT IT MEANS.
WHEN I WAS A KID, I USED TO STARE AT THOSE WORDS AND THINK...

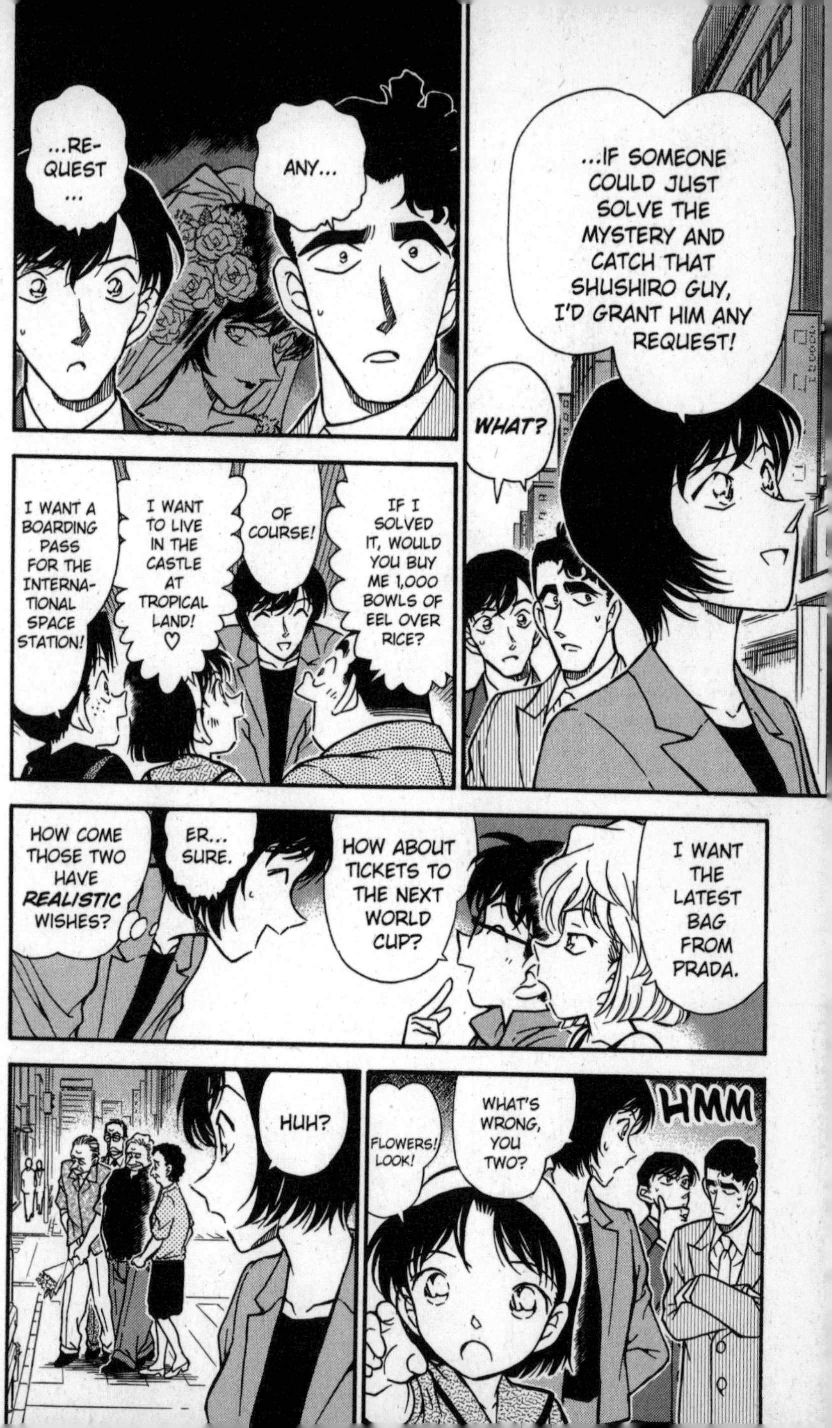
...IF SOMEONE COULD JUST SOLVE THE MYSTERY AND CATCH THAT SHUSHIRO GUY, I'D GRANT HIM ANY REQUEST!
WHAT?
ANY...
...RE-QUEST ...
IF I SOLVED IT, WOULD YOU BUY ME 1,000 BOWLS OF EEL OVER RICE?
OF COURSE!
I WANT TO LIVE IN THE CASTLE AT TROPICAL LAND! ♡
I WANT A BOARDING PASS FOR THE INTERNA-TIONAL SPACE STATION!
I WANT THE LATEST BAG FROM PRADA.
HOW ABOUT TICKETS TO THE NEXT WORLD CUP?
ER... SURE.
HOW COME THOSE TWO HAVE REALISTIC WISHES?
HMM
WHAT'S WRONG, YOU TWO?
FLOWERS! LOOK!
HUH?

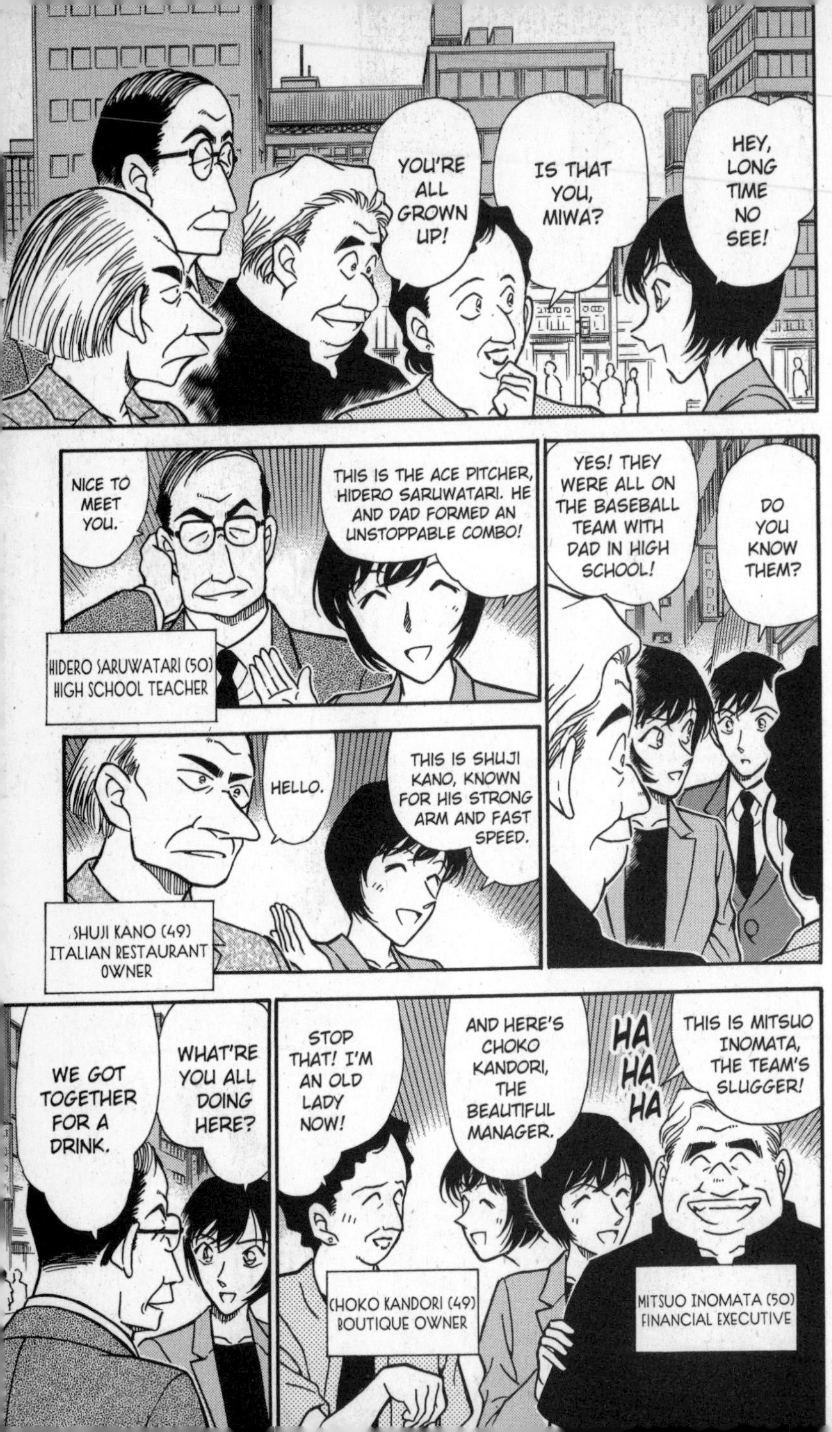
HEY, LONG TIME NO SEE!
IS THAT YOU, MIWA?
YOU'RE ALL GROWN UP!
DO YOU KNOW THEM?
YES! THEY WERE ALL ON THE BASEBALL TEAM WITH DAD IN HIGH SCHOOL!
THIS IS THE ACE PITCHER, HIDERO SARUWATARI. HE AND DAD FORMED AN UNSTOPPABLE COMBO!
NICE TO MEET YOU.
HIDERO SARUWATARI (50) HIGH SCHOOL TEACHER
THIS IS SHUJI KANO, KNOWN FOR HIS STRONG ARM AND FAST SPEED.
HELLO.
SHUJI KANO (49) ITALIAN RESTAURANT OWNER
THIS IS MITSUO INOMATA, THE TEAM'S SLUGGER!
HA HA HA
AND HERE'S CHOKO KANDORI, THE BEAUTIFUL MANAGER.
STOP THAT! I'M AN OLD LADY NOW!
MITSUO INOMATA (50) FINANCIAL EXECUTIVE
CHOKO KANDORI (49) BOUTIQUE OWNER
WHAT'RE YOU ALL DOING HERE?
WE GOT TOGETHER FOR A DRINK.

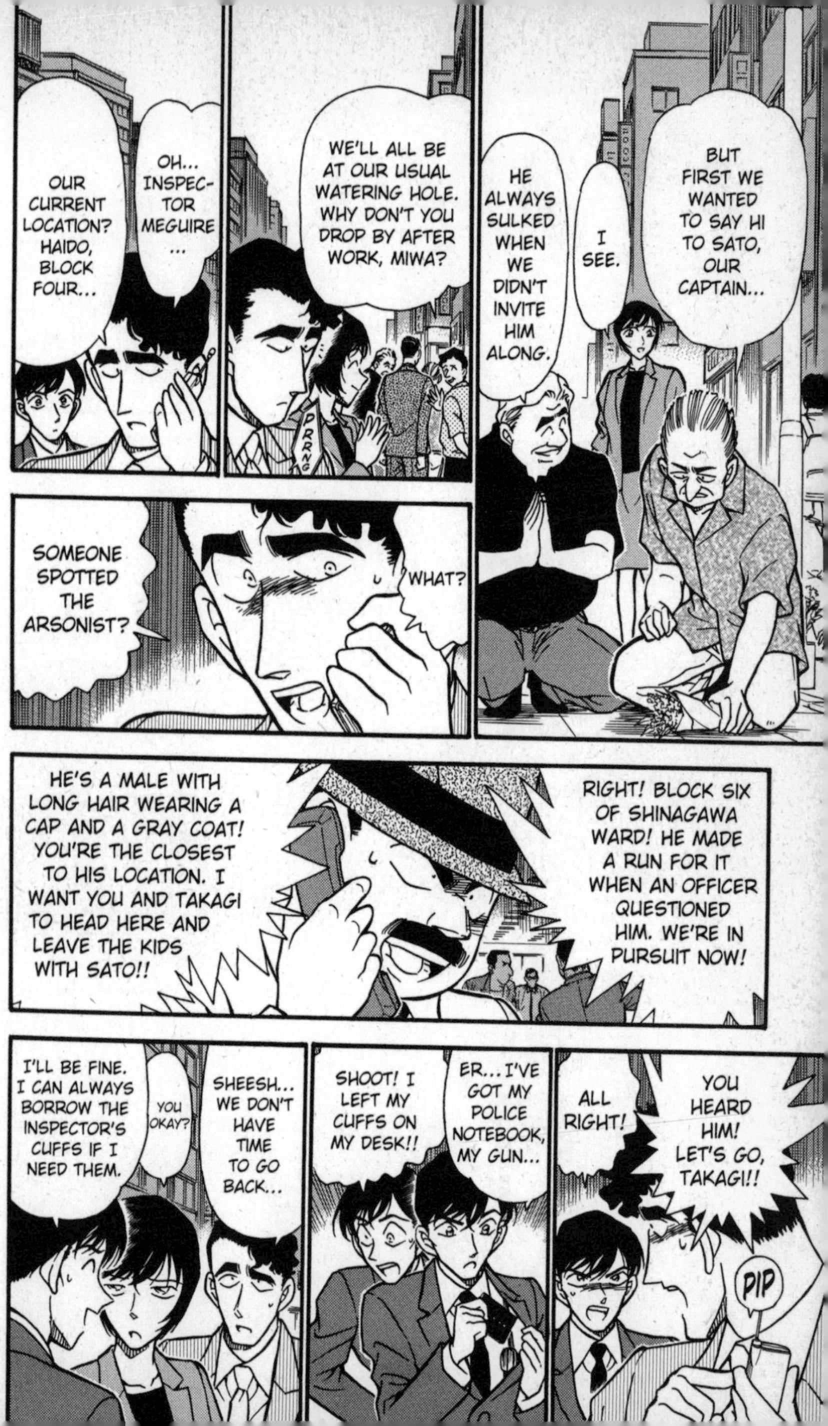
BUT FIRST WE WANTED TO SAY HI TO SATO, OUR CAPTAIN...
I SEE.
HE ALWAYS SULKED WHEN WE DIDN'T INVITE HIM ALONG.
PRRNG
WE'LL ALL BE AT OUR USUAL WATERING HOLE. WHY DON'T YOU DROP BY AFTER WORK, MIWA?
OH... INSPECTOR MEGUIRE ...
OUR CURRENT LOCATION? HAIDO, BLOCK FOUR...
WHAT?
SOMEONE SPOTTED THE ARSONIST?
RIGHT! BLOCK SIX OF SHINAGAWA WARD! HE MADE A RUN FOR IT WHEN AN OFFICER QUESTIONED HIM. WE'RE IN PURSUIT NOW!
HE'S A MALE WITH LONG HAIR WEARING A CAP AND A GRAY COAT! YOU'RE THE CLOSEST TO HIS LOCATION. I WANT YOU AND TAKAGI TO HEAD HERE AND LEAVE THE KIDS WITH SATO!!
YOU HEARD HIM! LET'S GO, TAKAGI!!
ALL RIGHT!
PIP
ER... I'VE GOT MY POLICE NOTEBOOK, MY GUN...
SHOOT! I LEFT MY CUFFS ON MY DESK!!
SHEESH... WE DON'T HAVE TIME TO GO BACK...
YOU OKAY?
I'LL BE FINE. I CAN ALWAYS BORROW THE INSPECTOR'S CUFFS IF I NEED THEM.

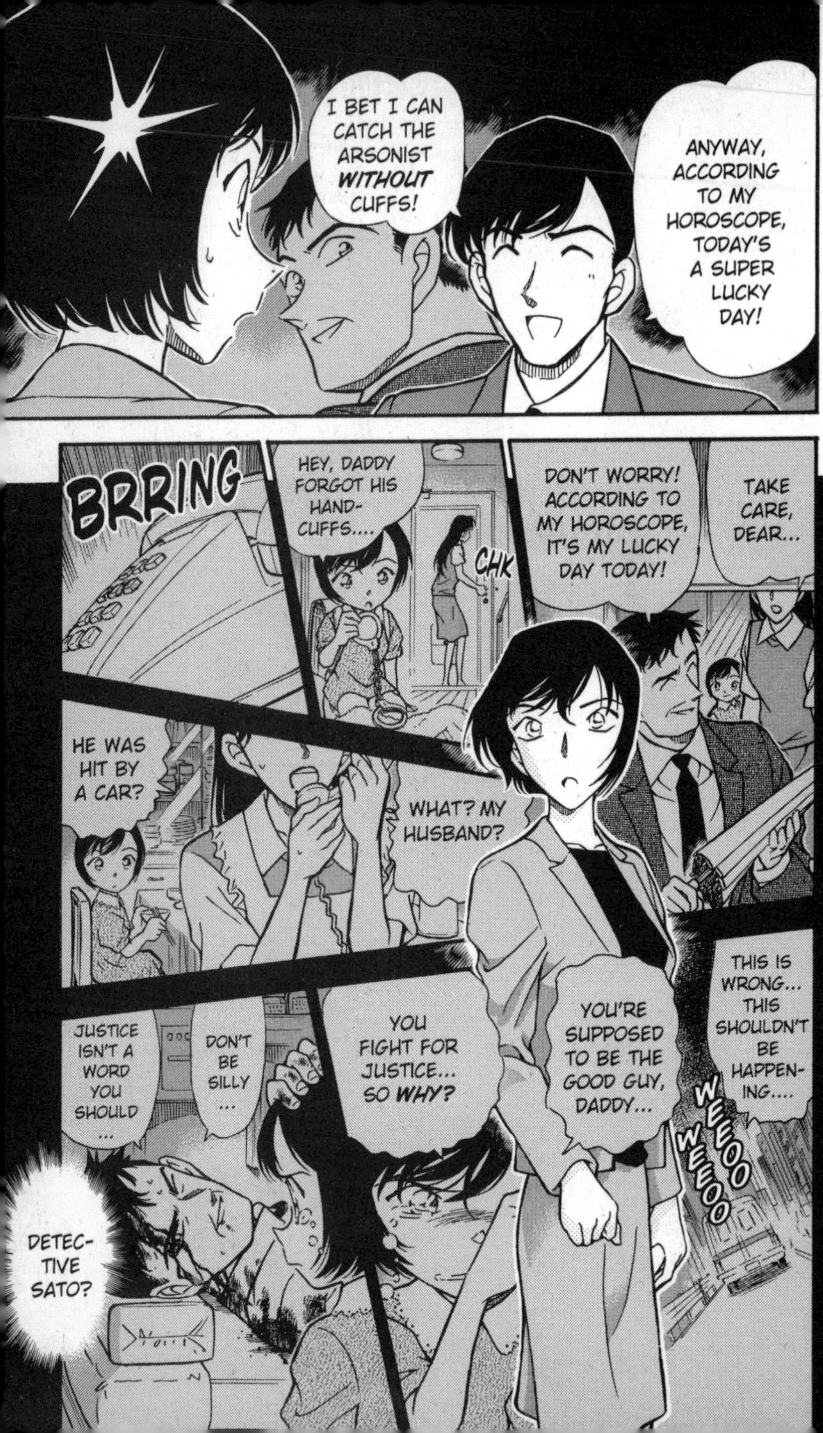
ANYWAY, ACCORDING TO MY HOROSCOPE, TODAY'S A SUPER LUCKY DAY!
I BET I CAN CATCH THE ARSONIST ***WITHOUT*** CUFFS!
TAKE CARE, DEAR...
DON'T WORRY! ACCORDING TO MY HOROSCOPE, IT'S MY LUCKY DAY TODAY!
CHK
HEY, DADDY FORGOT HIS HAND-CUFFS....
BRRING
WHAT? MY HUSBAND?
HE WAS HIT BY A CAR?
THIS IS WRONG... THIS SHOULDN'T BE HAPPEN-ING....
YOU'RE SUPPOSED TO BE THE GOOD GUY, DADDY...
WEEOO WEEOO
YOU FIGHT FOR JUSTICE... SO ***WHY?***
DON'T BE SILLY ...
JUSTICE ISN'T A WORD YOU SHOULD ...
DETEC-TIVE SATO?

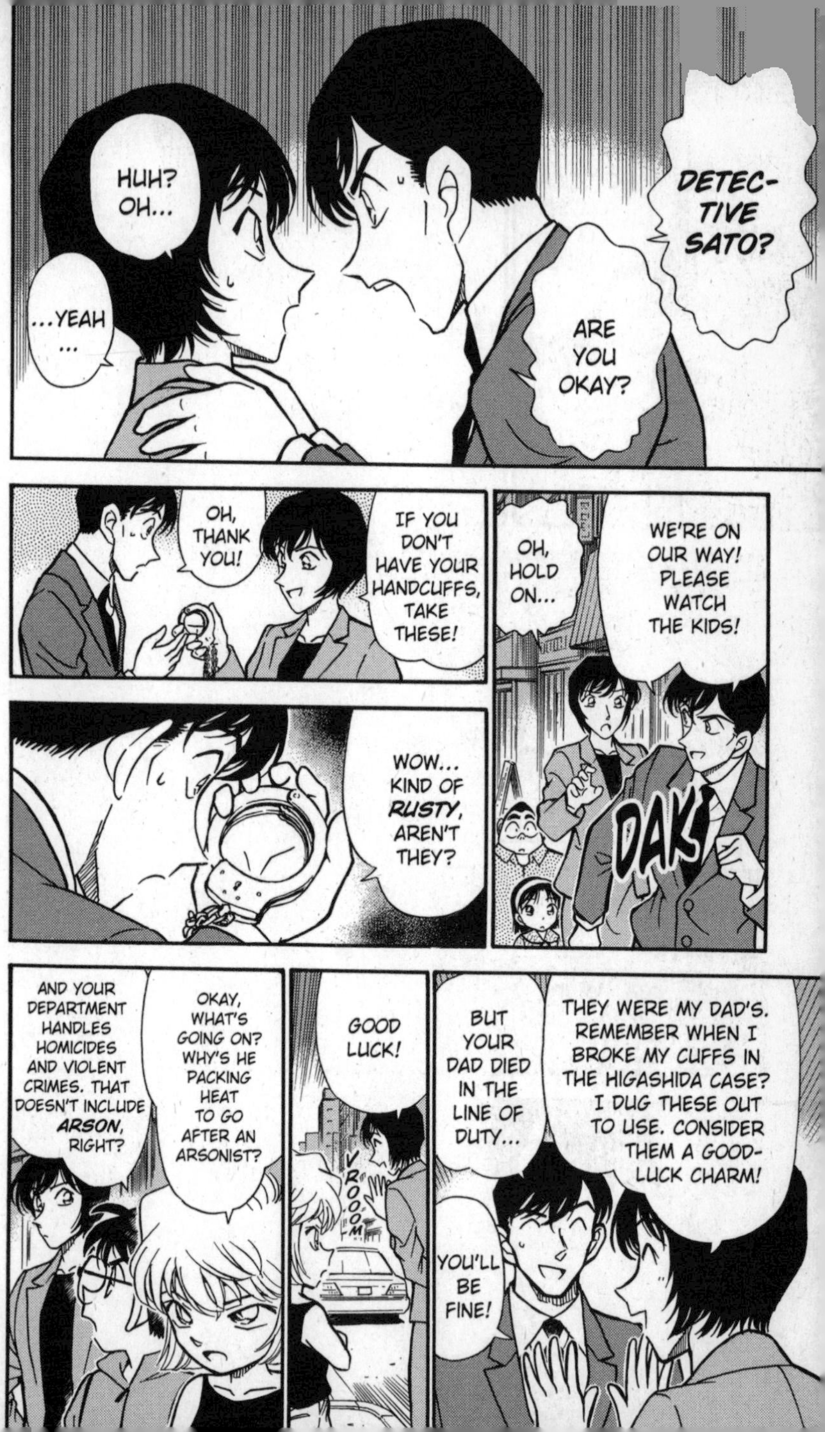
DETEC-TIVE SATO?
ARE YOU OKAY?
HUH? OH...
...YEAH ...
WE'RE ON OUR WAY! PLEASE WATCH THE KIDS!
OH, HOLD ON...
DAK
IF YOU DON'T HAVE YOUR HANDCUFFS, TAKE THESE!
OH, THANK YOU!
WOW... KIND OF *RUSTY*, AREN'T THEY?
THEY WERE MY DAD'S. REMEMBER WHEN I BROKE MY CUFFS IN THE HIGASHIDA CASE? I DUG THESE OUT TO USE. CONSIDER THEM A GOOD-LUCK CHARM!
BUT YOUR DAD DIED IN THE LINE OF DUTY...
YOU'LL BE FINE!
GOOD LUCK!
VROOOOM
OKAY, WHAT'S GOING ON? WHY'S HE PACKING HEAT TO GO AFTER AN ARSONIST?
AND YOUR DEPARTMENT HANDLES HOMICIDES AND VIOLENT CRIMES. THAT DOESN'T INCLUDE *ARSON*, RIGHT?

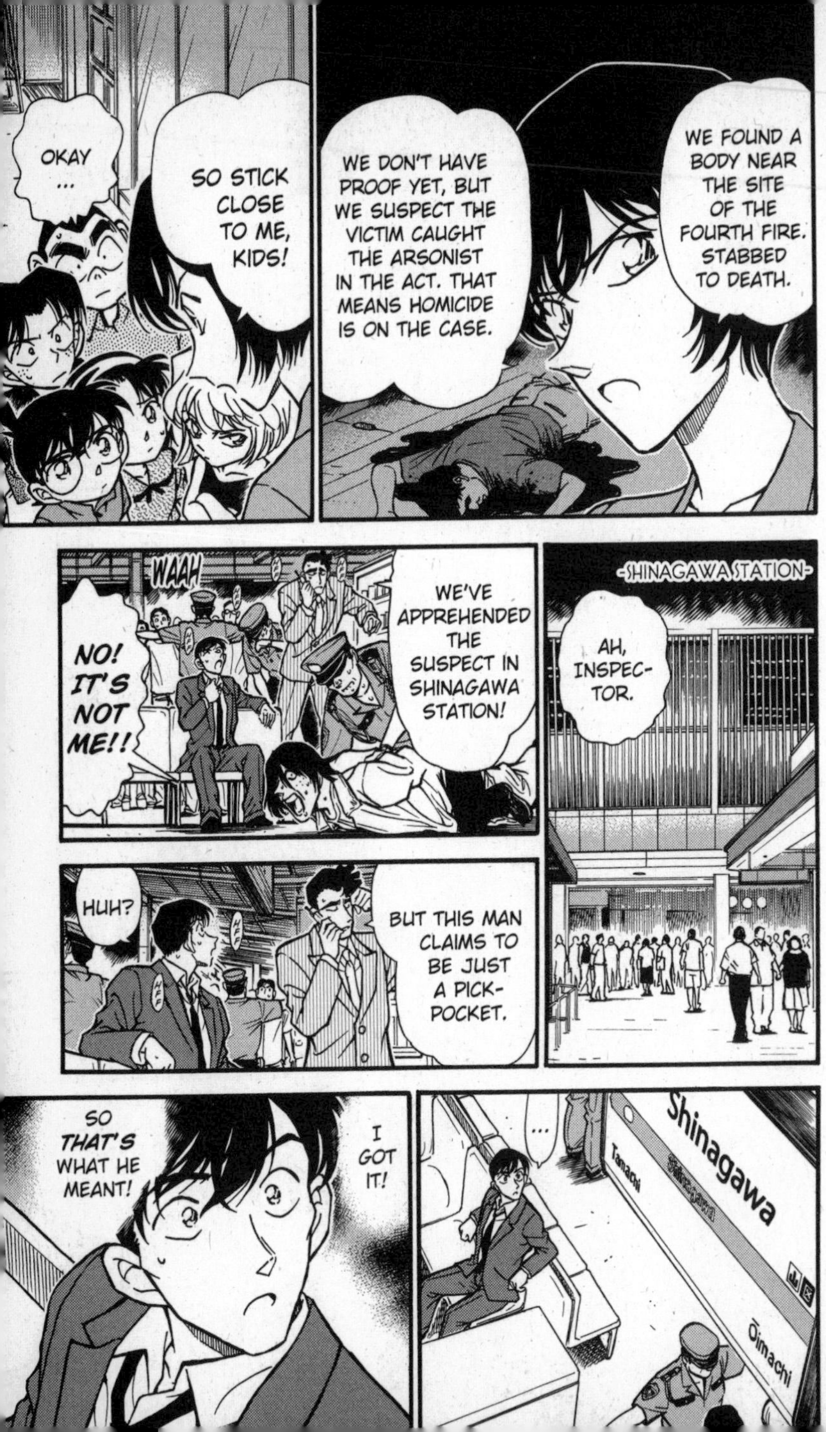
WE FOUND A BODY NEAR THE SITE OF THE FOURTH FIRE. STABBED TO DEATH.
WE DON'T HAVE PROOF YET, BUT WE SUSPECT THE VICTIM CAUGHT THE ARSONIST IN THE ACT. THAT MEANS HOMICIDE IS ON THE CASE.
SO STICK CLOSE TO ME, KIDS!
OKAY ...
-SHINAGAWA STATION-
AH, INSPECTOR.
WE'VE APPREHENDED THE SUSPECT IN SHINAGAWA STATION!
WAAH
NO! IT'S NOT ME!!
BUT THIS MAN CLAIMS TO BE JUST A PICK-POCKET.
HUH?
...
Shinagawa
Tamachi
Oimachi
I GOT IT!
SO THAT'S WHAT HE MEANT!

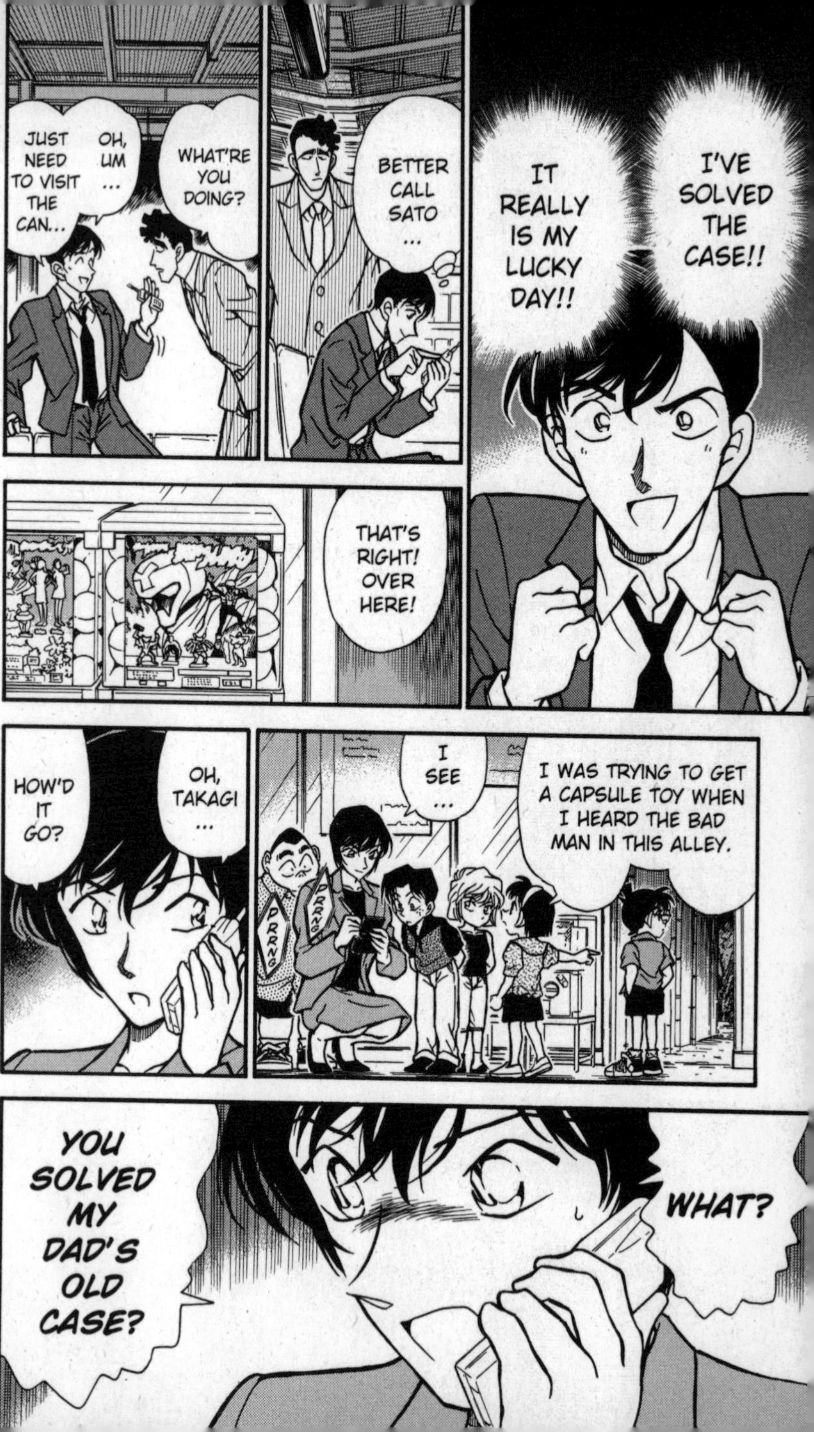
I'VE SOLVED THE CASE!!
IT REALLY IS MY LUCKY DAY!!
BETTER CALL SATO ...
WHAT'RE YOU DOING?
OH, UM ...
JUST NEED TO VISIT THE CAN...
THAT'S RIGHT! OVER HERE!
I WAS TRYING TO GET A CAPSULE TOY WHEN I HEARD THE BAD MAN IN THIS ALLEY.
I SEE ...
PRRNG
PRRNG
OH, TAKAGI ...
HOW'D IT GO?
WHAT?
YOU SOLVED MY DAD'S OLD CASE?

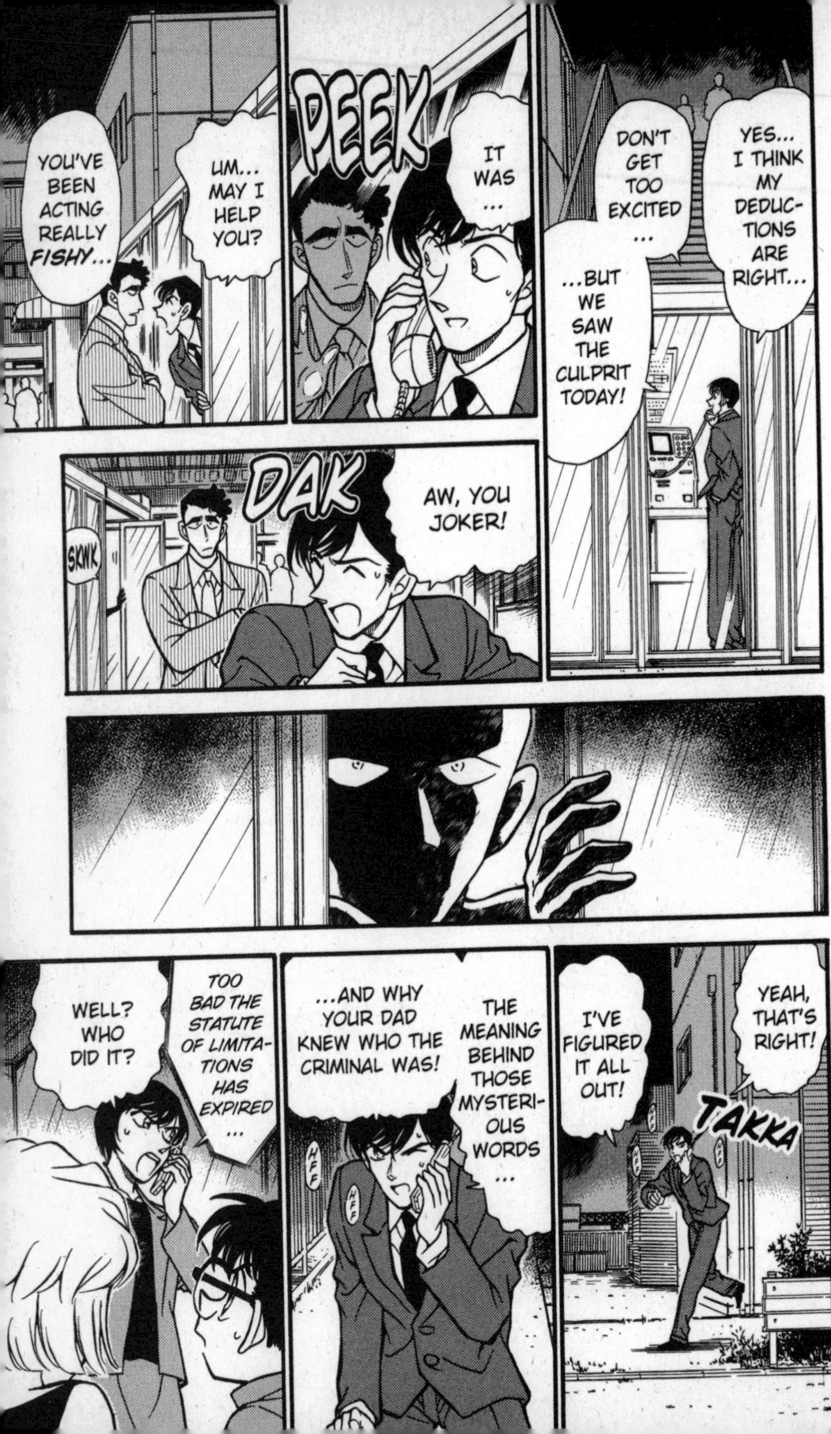
YES... I THINK MY DEDUCTIONS ARE RIGHT...
DON'T GET TOO EXCITED...
...BUT WE SAW THE CULPRIT TODAY!
PEEK
IT WAS...
UM... MAY I HELP YOU?
YOU'VE BEEN ACTING REALLY FISHY...
AW, YOU JOKER!
DAK
SKWK
YEAH, THAT'S RIGHT!
I'VE FIGURED IT ALL OUT!
TAKKA
HFF
THE MEANING BEHIND THOSE MYSTERIOUS WORDS...
...AND WHY YOUR DAD KNEW WHO THE CRIMINAL WAS!
HFF
TOO BAD THE STATUTE OF LIMITATIONS HAS EXPIRED...
WELL? WHO DID IT?

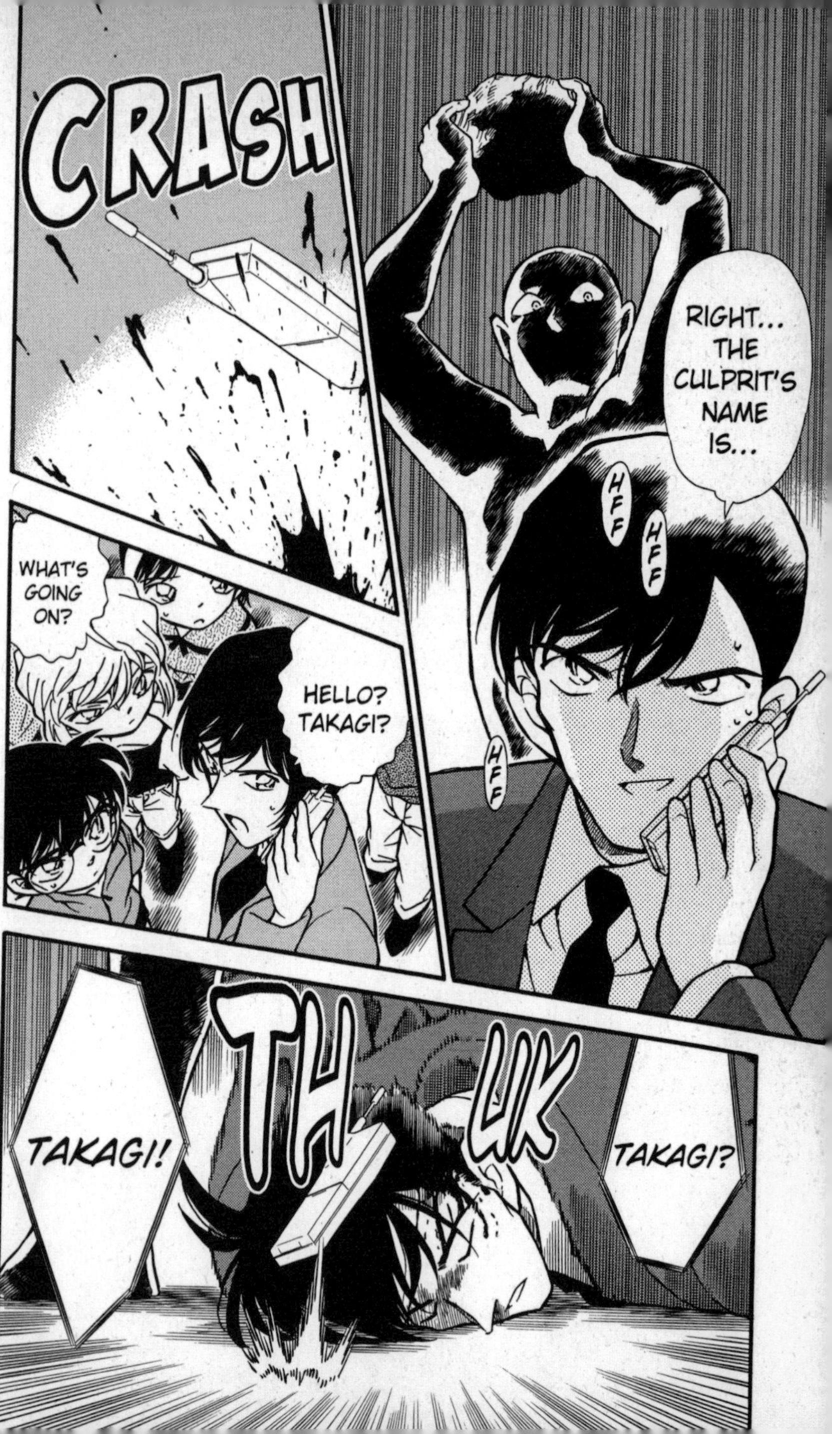
RIGHT... THE CULPRIT'S NAME IS...
HFF
HFF
HFF
CRASH
HELLO? TAKAGI?
WHAT'S GOING ON?
TAKAGI?
THUK
TAKAGI!

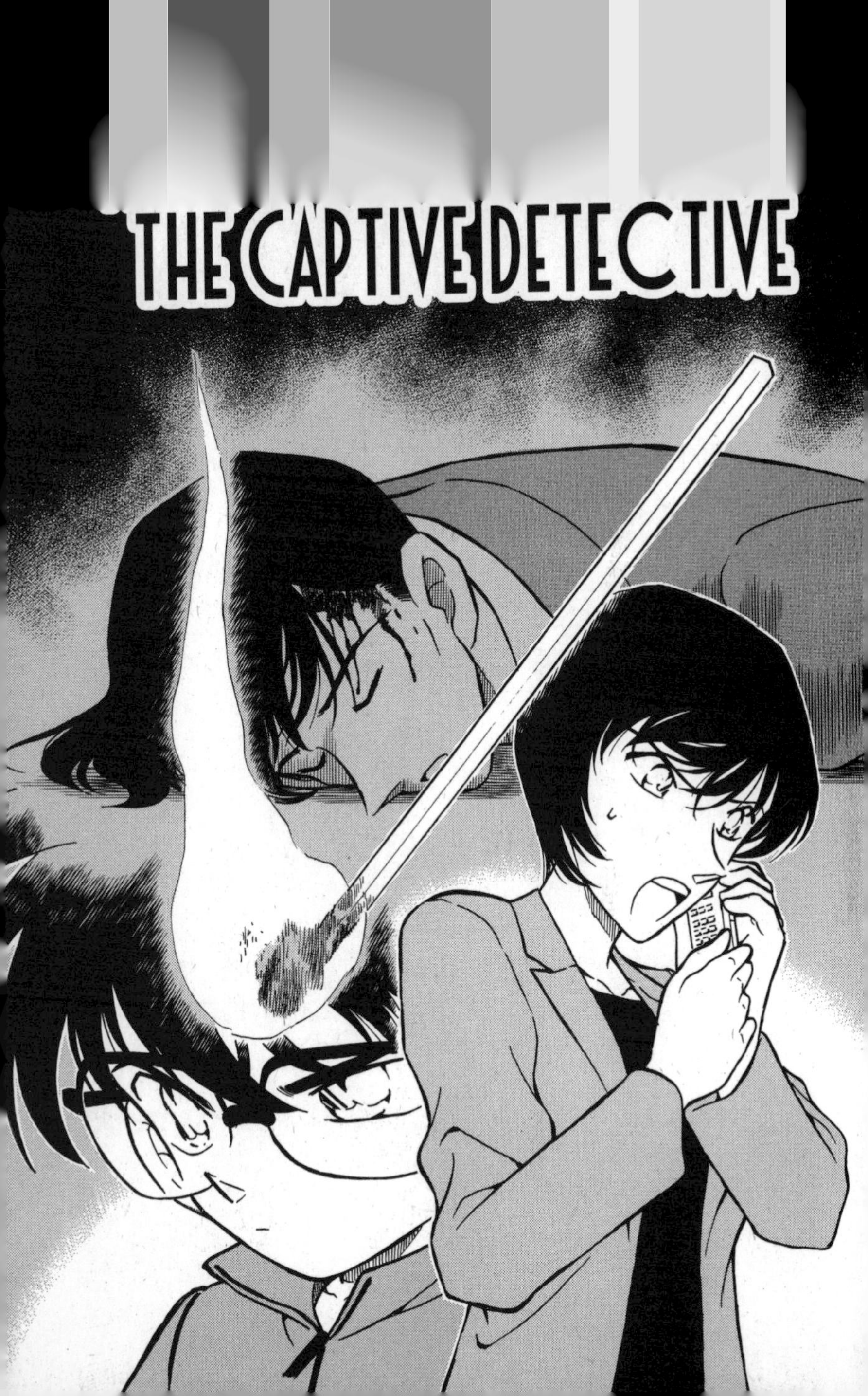
THE CAPTIVE DETECTIVE

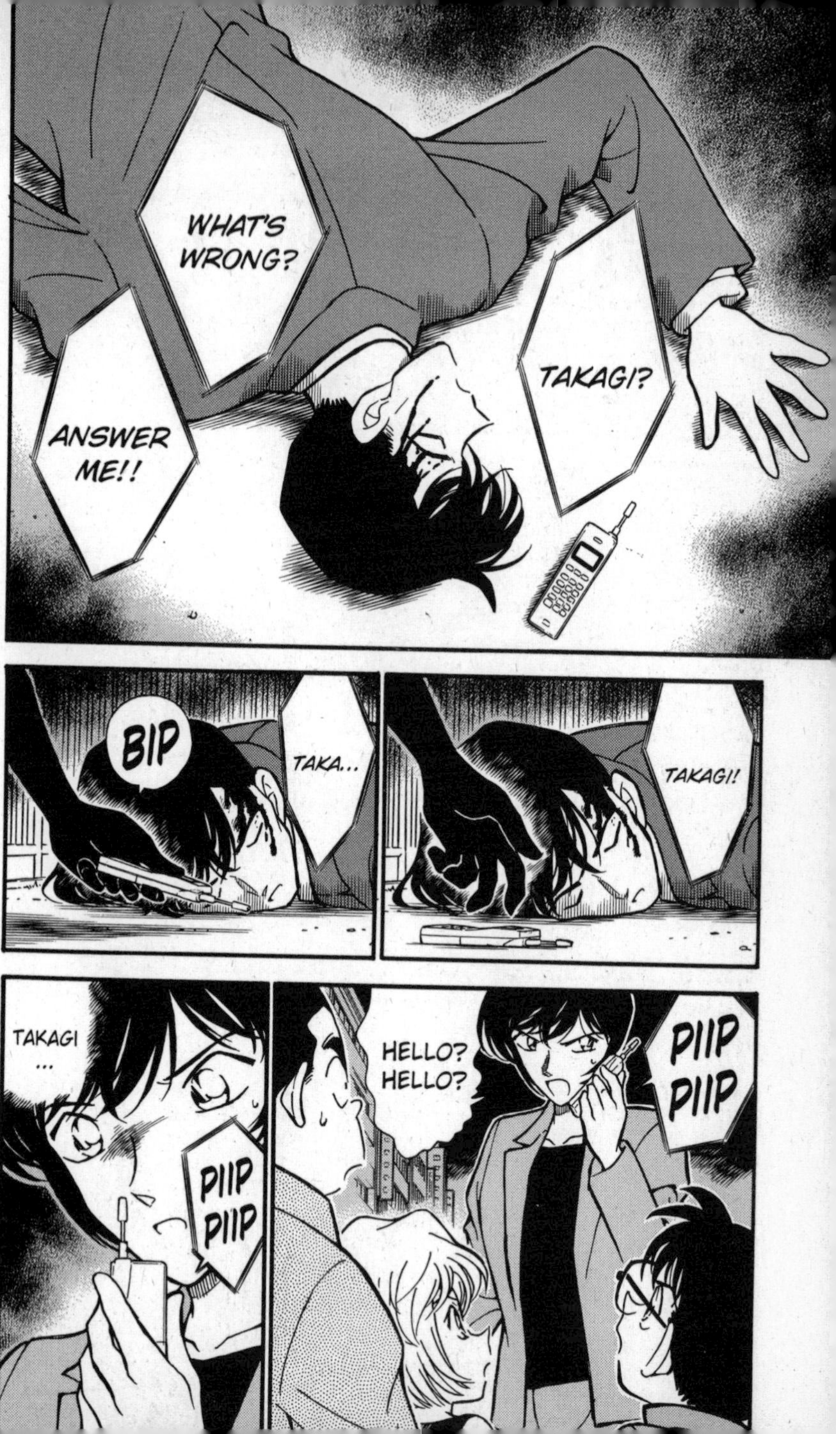
TAKAGI?
WHAT'S WRONG?
ANSWER ME!!
TAKAGI!
BIP
TAKA...
PIIP PIIP
HELLO? HELLO?
TAKAGI ...
PIIP PIIP

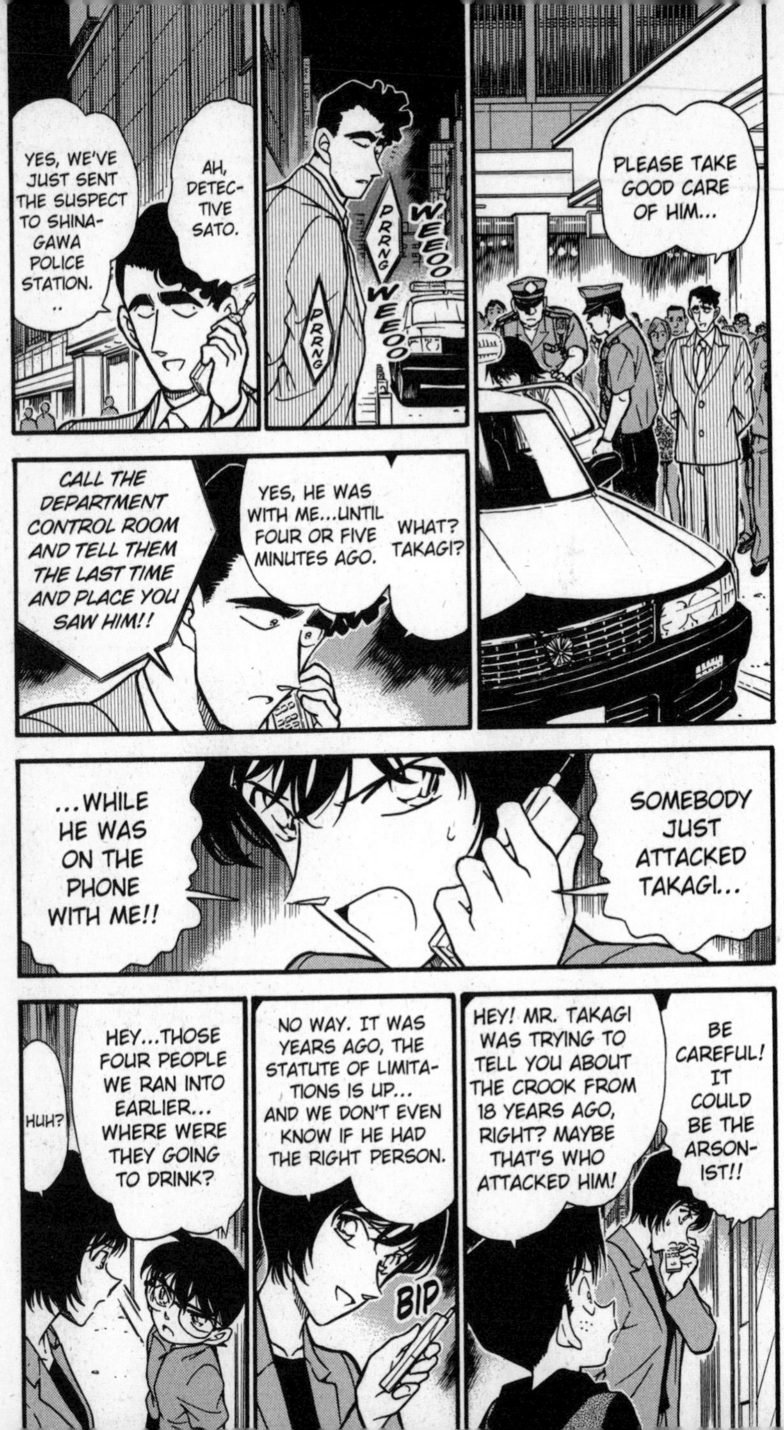
PLEASE TAKE GOOD CARE OF HIM...
WEEOO
WEEOO
PRRNG
PRRNG
AH, DETECTIVE SATO.
YES, WE'VE JUST SENT THE SUSPECT TO SHINAGAWA POLICE STATION...
WHAT? TAKAGI?
YES, HE WAS WITH ME...UNTIL FOUR OR FIVE MINUTES AGO.
CALL THE DEPARTMENT CONTROL ROOM AND TELL THEM THE LAST TIME AND PLACE YOU SAW HIM!!
SOMEBODY JUST ATTACKED TAKAGI...
...WHILE HE WAS ON THE PHONE WITH ME!!
BE CAREFUL! IT COULD BE THE ARSONIST!!
HEY! MR. TAKAGI WAS TRYING TO TELL YOU ABOUT THE CROOK FROM 18 YEARS AGO, RIGHT? MAYBE THAT'S WHO ATTACKED HIM!
BIP
NO WAY. IT WAS YEARS AGO, THE STATUTE OF LIMITATIONS IS UP... AND WE DON'T EVEN KNOW IF HE HAD THE RIGHT PERSON.
HEY...THOSE FOUR PEOPLE WE RAN INTO EARLIER... WHERE WERE THEY GOING TO DRINK?
HUH?

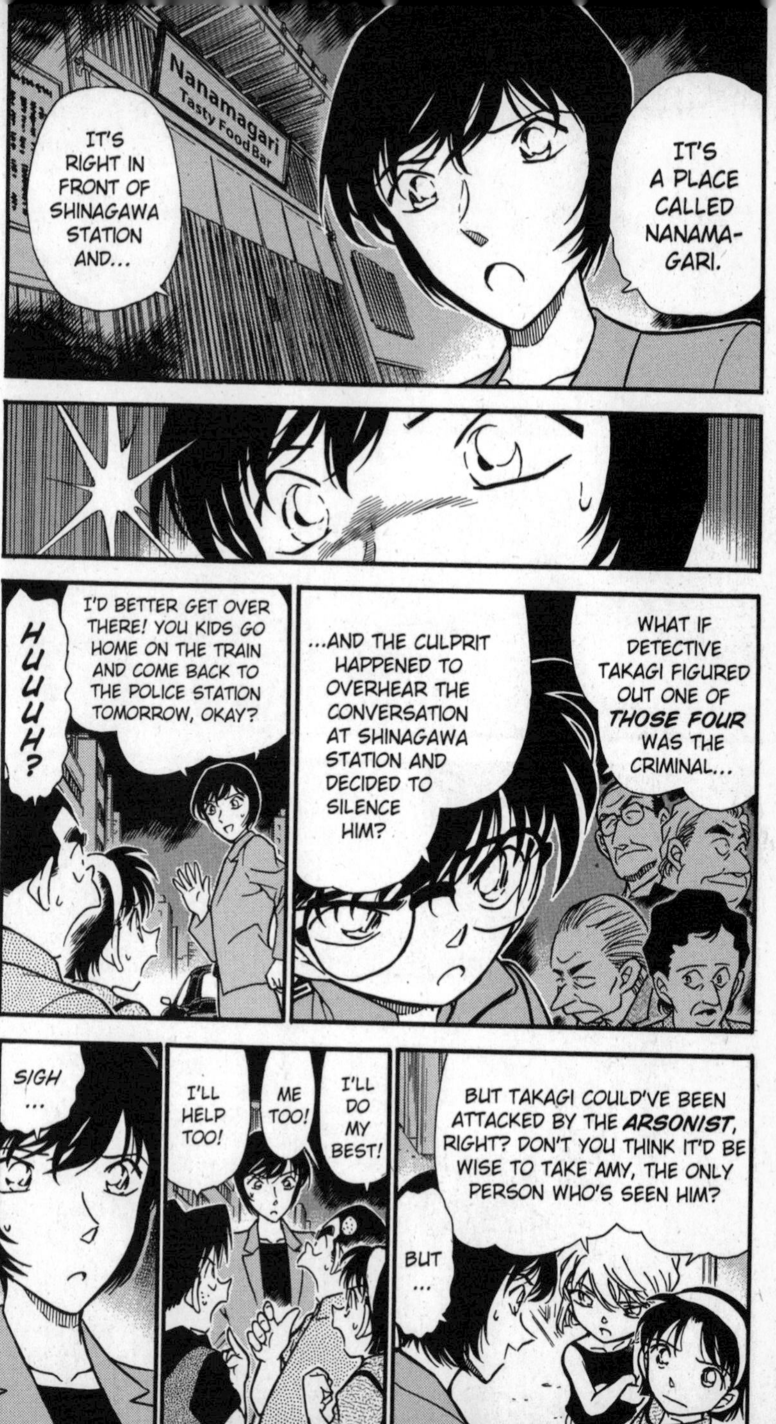
IT'S A PLACE CALLED NANAMA-GARI.
Nanamagari Tasty Food Bar
IT'S RIGHT IN FRONT OF SHINAGAWA STATION AND...
WHAT IF DETECTIVE TAKAGI FIGURED OUT ONE OF *THOSE FOUR* WAS THE CRIMINAL...
...AND THE CULPRIT HAPPENED TO OVERHEAR THE CONVERSATION AT SHINAGAWA STATION AND DECIDED TO SILENCE HIM?
I'D BETTER GET OVER THERE! YOU KIDS GO HOME ON THE TRAIN AND COME BACK TO THE POLICE STATION TOMORROW, OKAY?
HUUUH?
BUT TAKAGI COULD'VE BEEN ATTACKED BY THE *ARSONIST*, RIGHT? DON'T YOU THINK IT'D BE WISE TO TAKE AMY, THE ONLY PERSON WHO'S SEEN HIM?
BUT ...
I'LL DO MY BEST!
ME TOO!
I'LL HELP TOO!
SIGH ...

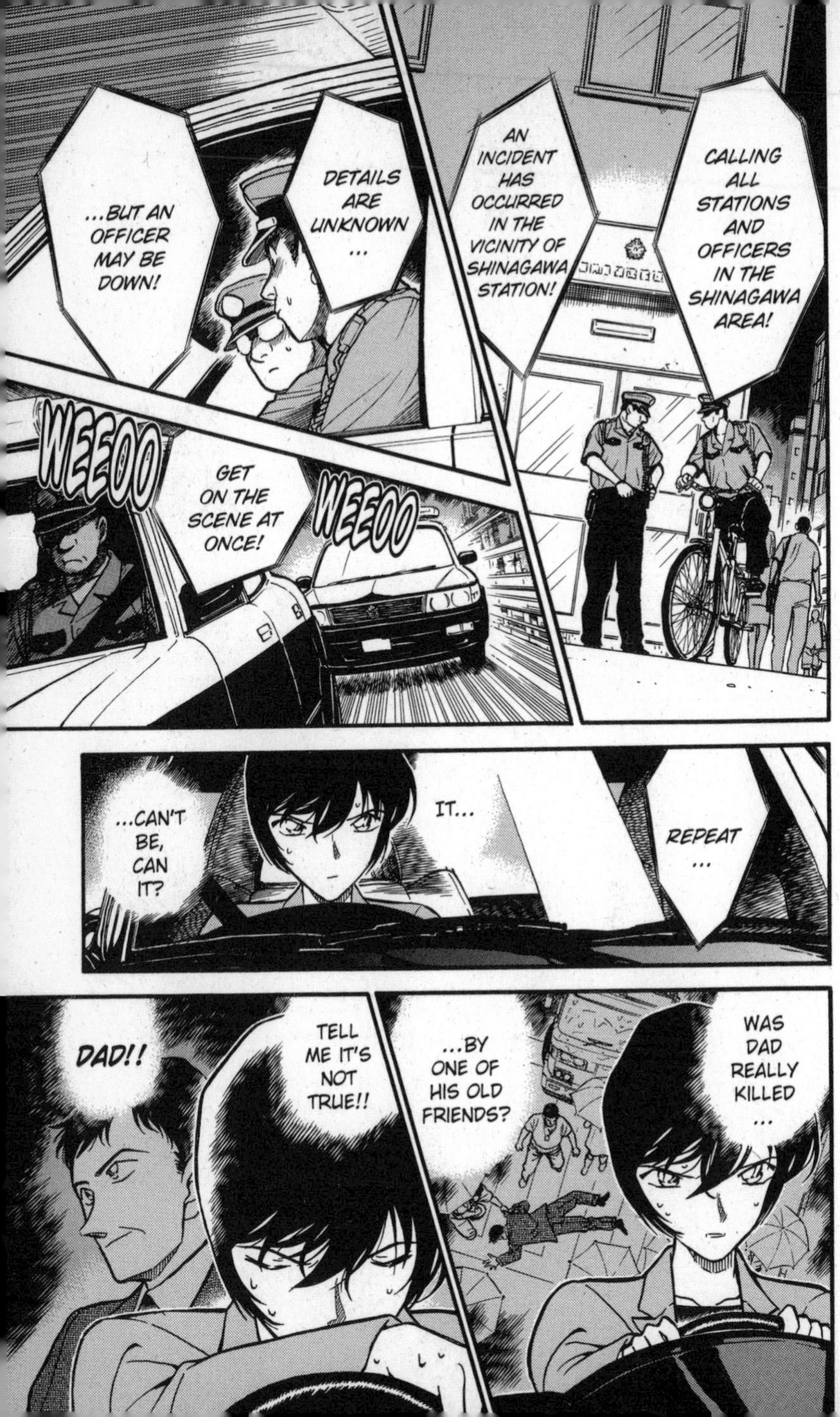
CALLING ALL STATIONS AND OFFICERS IN THE SHINAGAWA AREA!
AN INCIDENT HAS OCCURRED IN THE VICINITY OF SHINAGAWA STATION!
DETAILS ARE UNKNOWN...
...BUT AN OFFICER MAY BE DOWN!
WEEOO
GET ON THE SCENE AT ONCE!
WEEOO
REPEAT...
IT...
...CAN'T BE, CAN IT?
WAS DAD REALLY KILLED...
...BY ONE OF HIS OLD FRIENDS?
TELL ME IT'S NOT TRUE!!
DAD!!

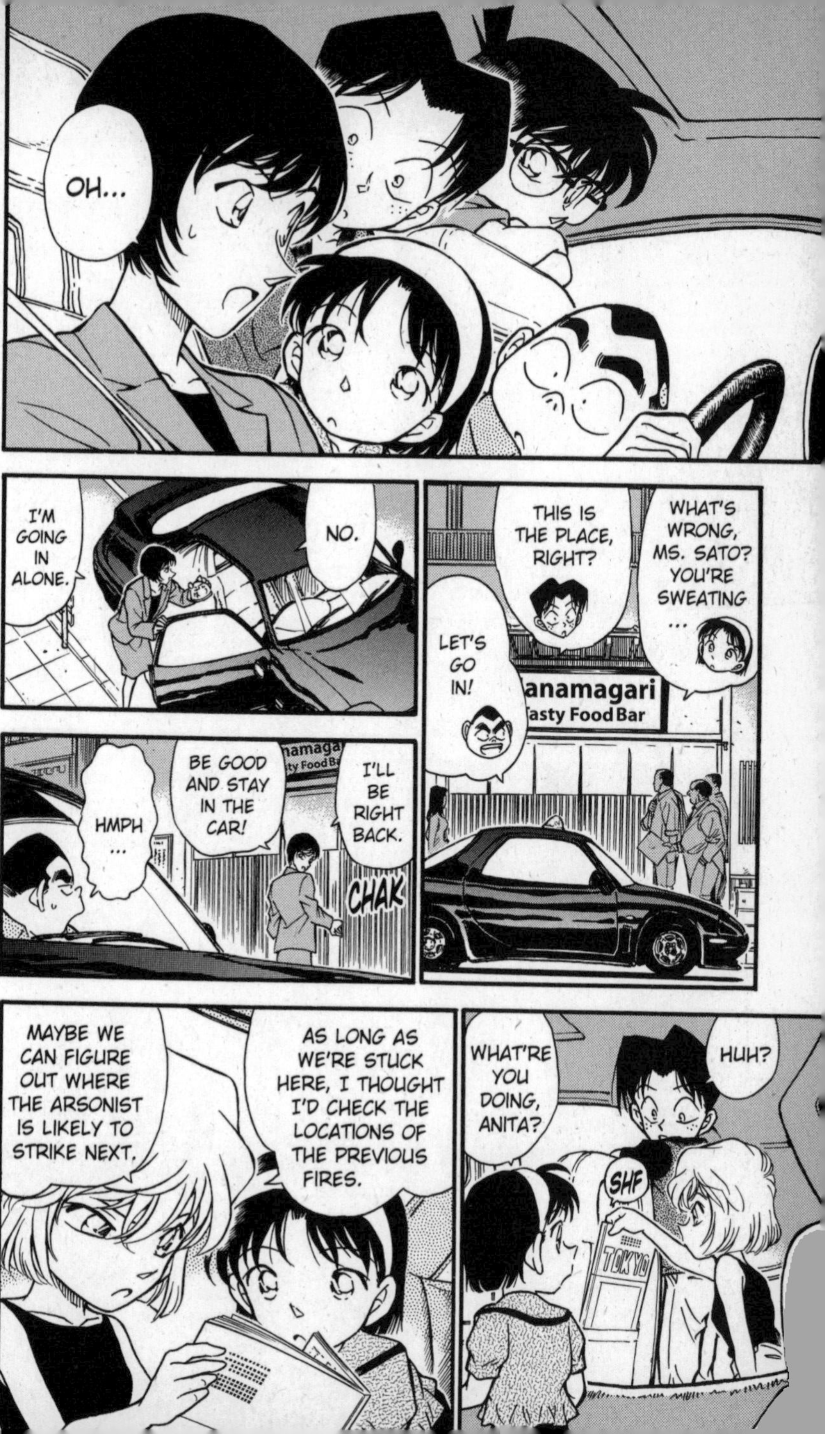
OH...
WHAT'S WRONG, MS. SATO? YOU'RE SWEATING ...
THIS IS THE PLACE, RIGHT?
LET'S GO IN!
anamagari
Tasty Food Bar
NO.
I'M GOING IN ALONE.
I'LL BE RIGHT BACK.
CHAK
BE GOOD AND STAY IN THE CAR!
HMPH ...
HUH?
WHAT'RE YOU DOING, ANITA?
SHF
TOKYO
AS LONG AS WE'RE STUCK HERE, I THOUGHT I'D CHECK THE LOCATIONS OF THE PREVIOUS FIRES.
MAYBE WE CAN FIGURE OUT WHERE THE ARSONIST IS LIKELY TO STRIKE NEXT.

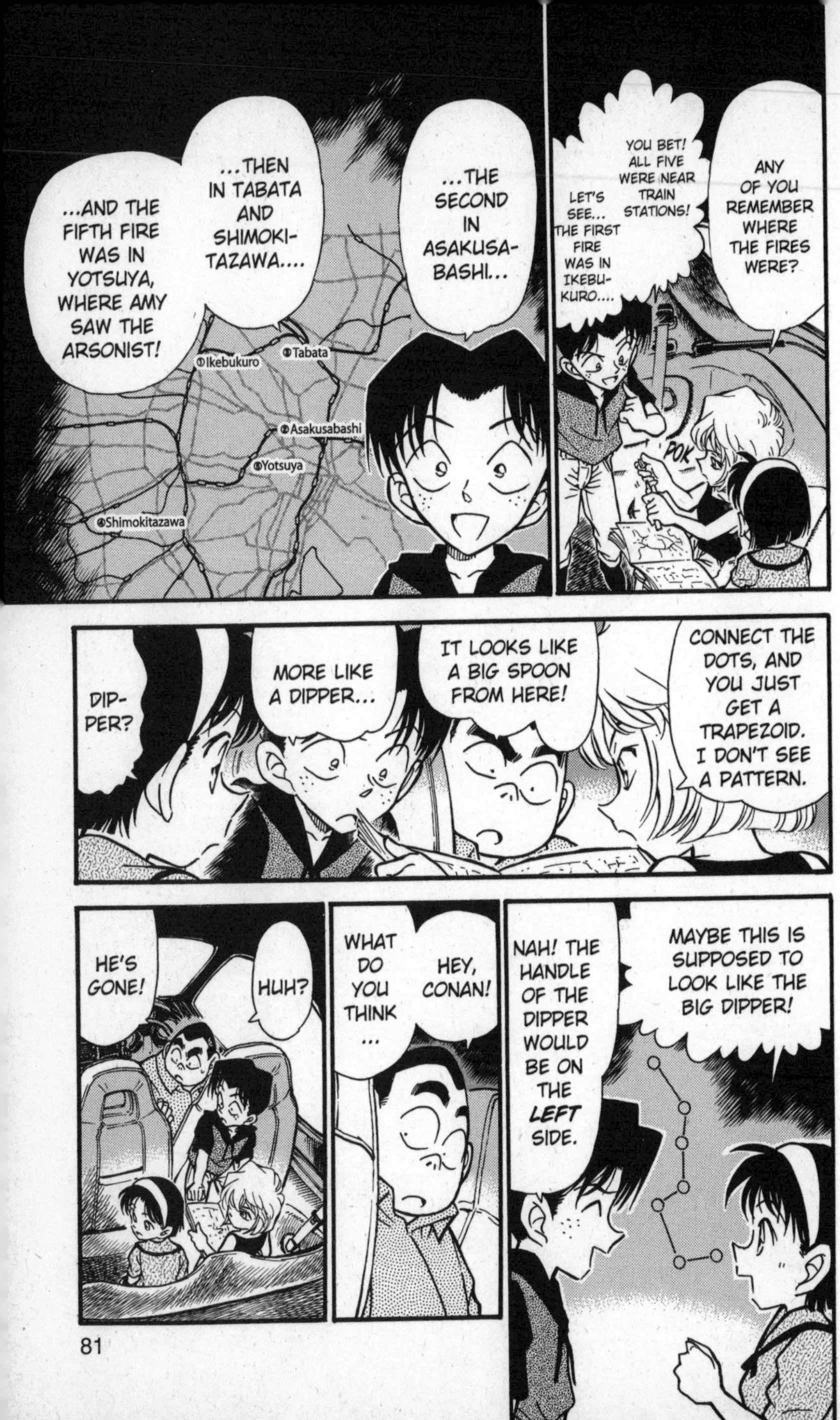
ANY OF YOU REMEMBER WHERE THE FIRES WERE?
YOU BET! ALL FIVE WERE NEAR TRAIN STATIONS!
LET'S SEE... THE FIRST FIRE WAS IN IKEBUKURO....
POK
...THE SECOND IN ASAKUSA-BASHI...
...THEN IN TABATA AND SHIMOKI-TAZAWA....
...AND THE FIFTH FIRE WAS IN YOTSUYA, WHERE AMY SAW THE ARSONIST!
①Ikebukuro
③Tabata
②Asakusabashi
⑤Yotsuya
④Shimokitazawa
CONNECT THE DOTS, AND YOU JUST GET A TRAPEZOID. I DON'T SEE A PATTERN.
IT LOOKS LIKE A BIG SPOON FROM HERE!
MORE LIKE A DIPPER...
DIP-PER?
MAYBE THIS IS SUPPOSED TO LOOK LIKE THE BIG DIPPER!
NAH! THE HANDLE OF THE DIPPER WOULD BE ON THE *LEFT* SIDE.
HEY, CONAN!
WHAT DO YOU THINK...
HUH?
HE'S GONE!

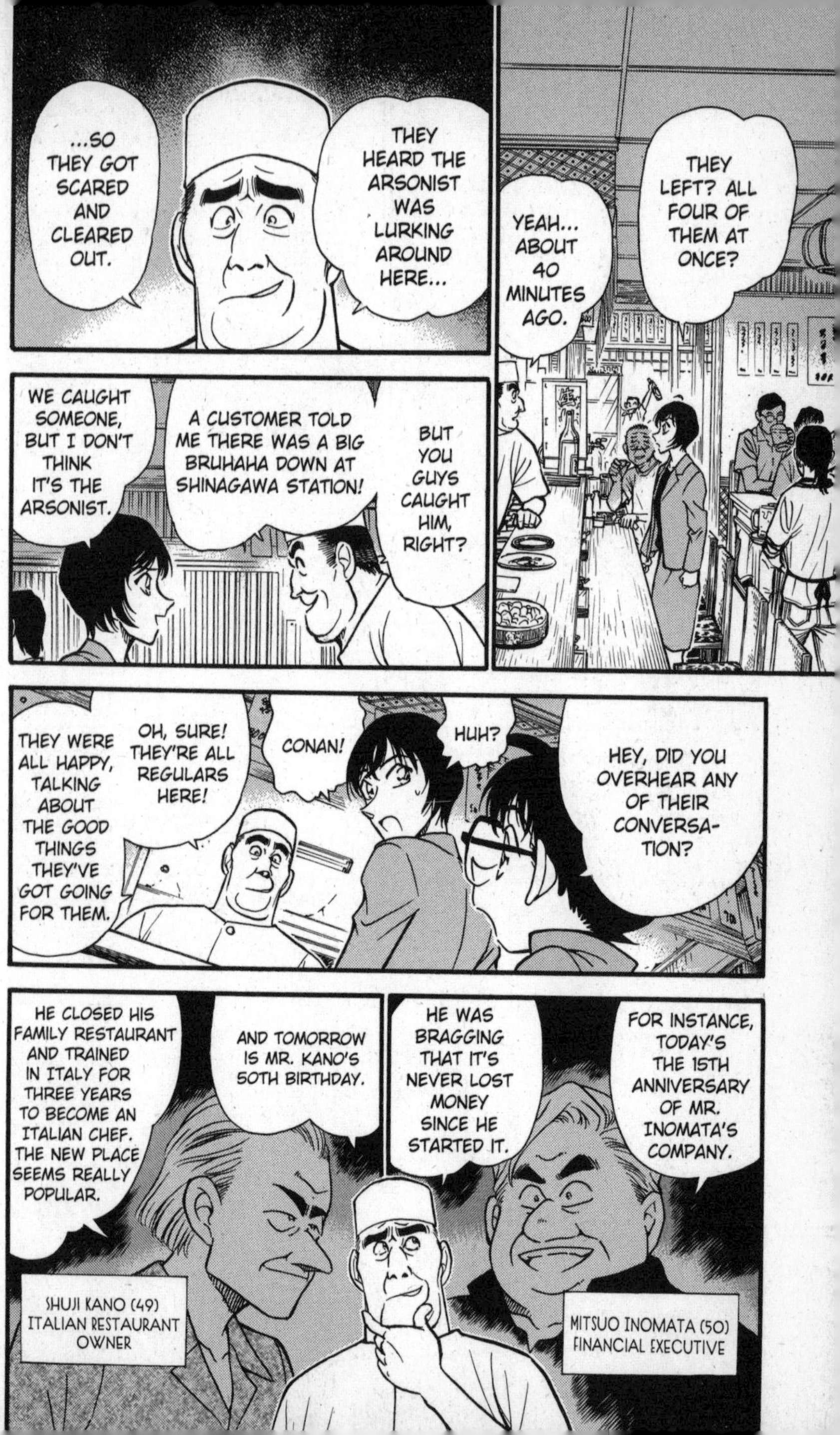
THEY LEFT? ALL FOUR OF THEM AT ONCE?
YEAH... ABOUT 40 MINUTES AGO.
THEY HEARD THE ARSONIST WAS LURKING AROUND HERE...
...SO THEY GOT SCARED AND CLEARED OUT.
BUT YOU GUYS CAUGHT HIM, RIGHT?
A CUSTOMER TOLD ME THERE WAS A BIG BRUHAHA DOWN AT SHINAGAWA STATION!
WE CAUGHT SOMEONE, BUT I DON'T THINK IT'S THE ARSONIST.
HEY, DID YOU OVERHEAR ANY OF THEIR CONVERSA-TION?
HUH?
CONAN!
OH, SURE! THEY'RE ALL REGULARS HERE!
THEY WERE ALL HAPPY, TALKING ABOUT THE GOOD THINGS THEY'VE GOT GOING FOR THEM.
FOR INSTANCE, TODAY'S THE 15TH ANNIVERSARY OF MR. INOMATA'S COMPANY.
HE WAS BRAGGING THAT IT'S NEVER LOST MONEY SINCE HE STARTED IT.
MITSUO INOMATA (50) FINANCIAL EXECUTIVE
AND TOMORROW IS MR. KANO'S 50TH BIRTHDAY.
HE CLOSED HIS FAMILY RESTAURANT AND TRAINED IN ITALY FOR THREE YEARS TO BECOME AN ITALIAN CHEF. THE NEW PLACE SEEMS REALLY POPULAR.
SHUJI KANO (49) ITALIAN RESTAURANT OWNER

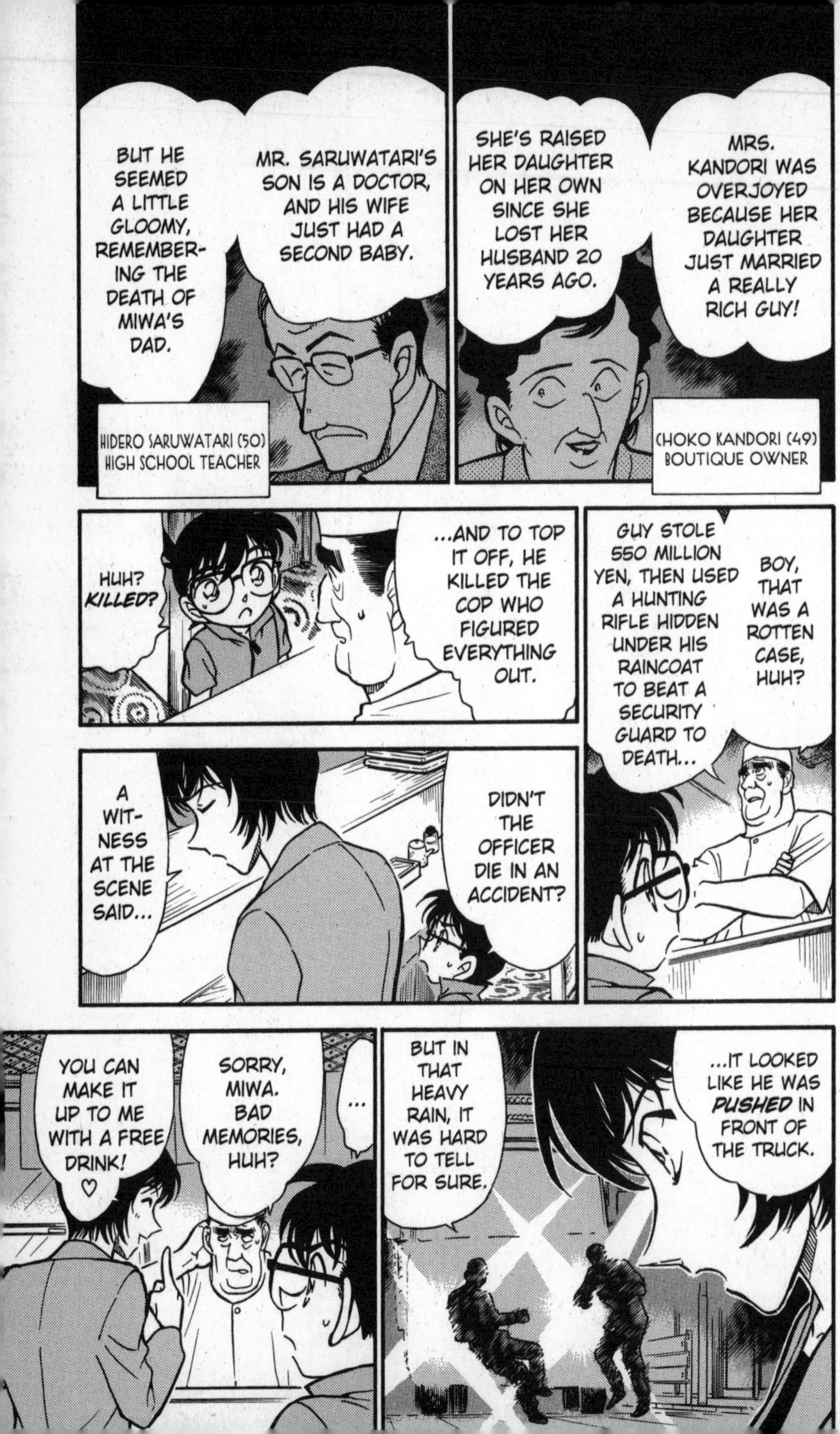
MRS. KANDORI WAS OVERJOYED BECAUSE HER DAUGHTER JUST MARRIED A REALLY RICH GUY!
SHE'S RAISED HER DAUGHTER ON HER OWN SINCE SHE LOST HER HUSBAND 20 YEARS AGO.
CHOKO KANDORI (49) BOUTIQUE OWNER
MR. SARUWATARI'S SON IS A DOCTOR, AND HIS WIFE JUST HAD A SECOND BABY.
BUT HE SEEMED A LITTLE GLOOMY, REMEMBERING THE DEATH OF MIWA'S DAD.
HIDERO SARUWATARI (50) HIGH SCHOOL TEACHER
BOY, THAT WAS A ROTTEN CASE, HUH?
GUY STOLE 550 MILLION YEN, THEN USED A HUNTING RIFLE HIDDEN UNDER HIS RAINCOAT TO BEAT A SECURITY GUARD TO DEATH...
...AND TO TOP IT OFF, HE KILLED THE COP WHO FIGURED EVERYTHING OUT.
HUH? *KILLED?*
DIDN'T THE OFFICER DIE IN AN ACCIDENT?
A WITNESS AT THE SCENE SAID...
...IT LOOKED LIKE HE WAS *PUSHED* IN FRONT OF THE TRUCK.
BUT IN THAT HEAVY RAIN, IT WAS HARD TO TELL FOR SURE.
...
SORRY, MIWA. BAD MEMORIES, HUH?
YOU CAN MAKE IT UP TO ME WITH A FREE DRINK! ♡

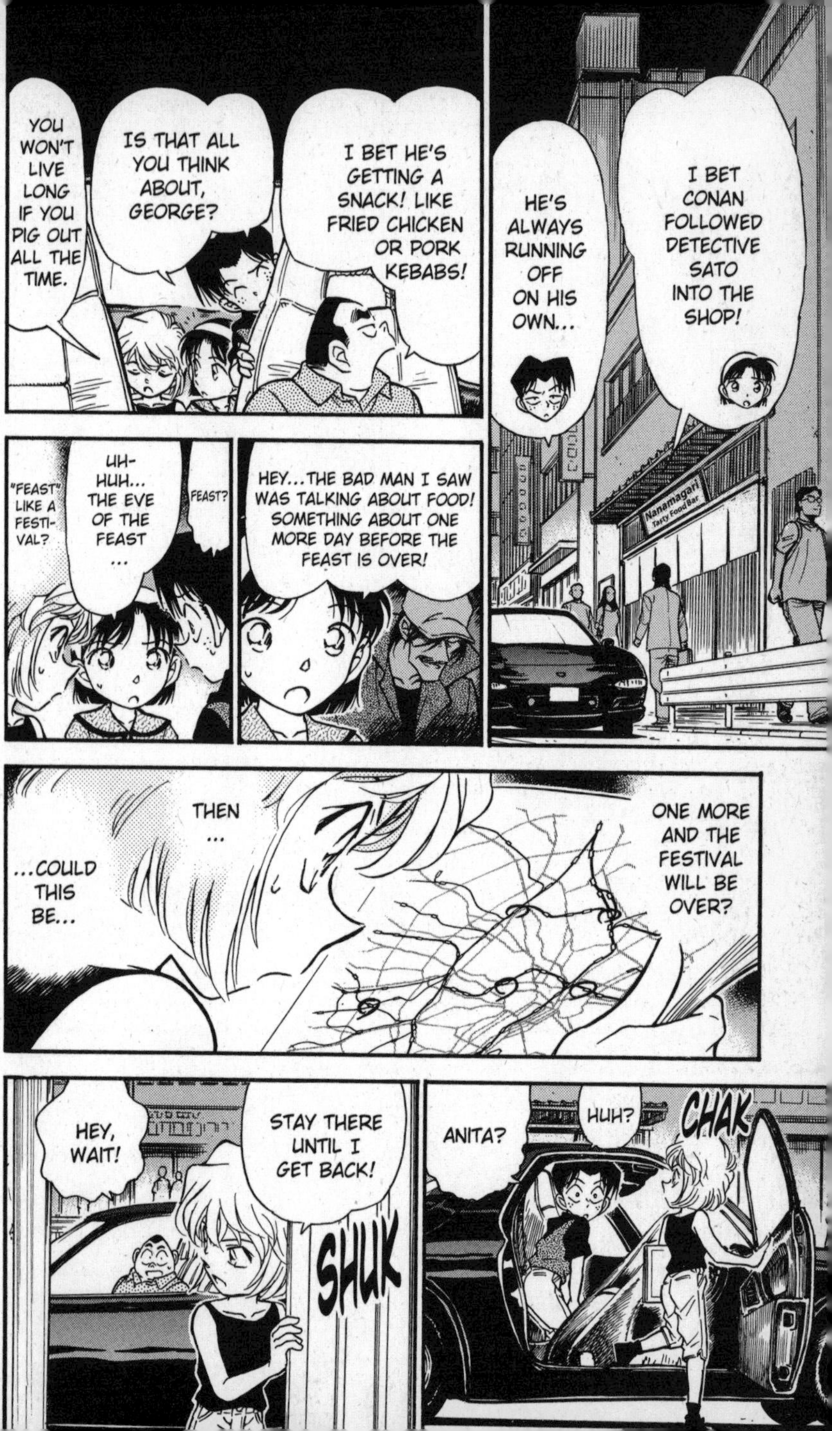
I BET CONAN FOLLOWED DETECTIVE SATO INTO THE SHOP!
HE'S ALWAYS RUNNING OFF ON HIS OWN...
Nanamagari Tasty Food Bar
I BET HE'S GETTING A SNACK! LIKE FRIED CHICKEN OR PORK KEBABS!
IS THAT ALL YOU THINK ABOUT, GEORGE?
YOU WON'T LIVE LONG IF YOU PIG OUT ALL THE TIME.
HEY...THE BAD MAN I SAW WAS TALKING ABOUT FOOD! SOMETHING ABOUT ONE MORE DAY BEFORE THE FEAST IS OVER!
FEAST?
UH-HUH... THE EVE OF THE FEAST...
"FEAST" LIKE A FESTIVAL?
ONE MORE AND THE FESTIVAL WILL BE OVER?
THEN...
...COULD THIS BE...
CHAK
HUH?
ANITA?
STAY THERE UNTIL I GET BACK!
HEY, WAIT!
SHUK

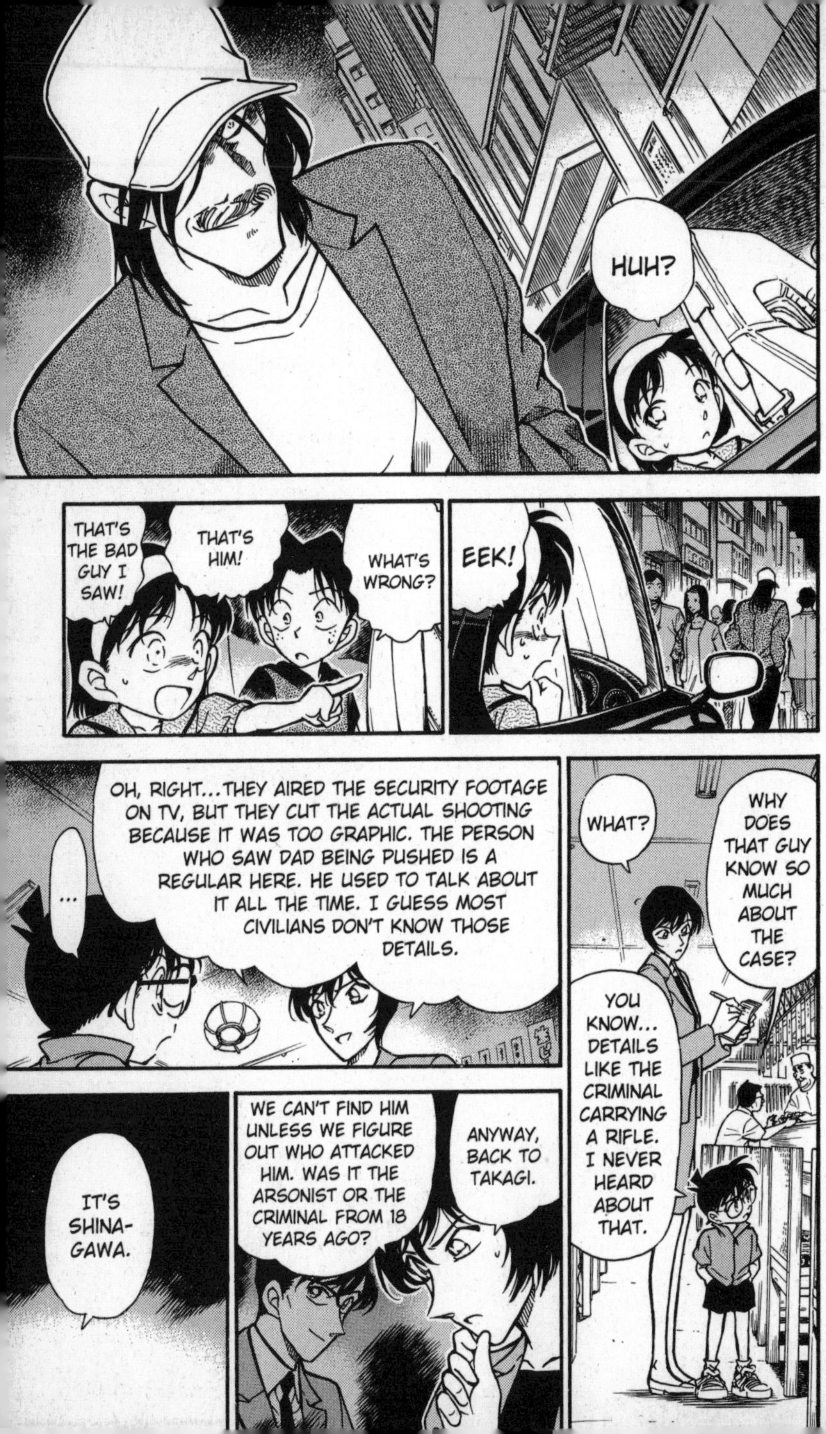
HUH?
EEK!
WHAT'S WRONG?
THAT'S HIM!
THAT'S THE BAD GUY I SAW!
WHY DOES THAT GUY KNOW SO MUCH ABOUT THE CASE?
WHAT?
YOU KNOW... DETAILS LIKE THE CRIMINAL CARRYING A RIFLE. I NEVER HEARD ABOUT THAT.
OH, RIGHT...THEY AIRED THE SECURITY FOOTAGE ON TV, BUT THEY CUT THE ACTUAL SHOOTING BECAUSE IT WAS TOO GRAPHIC. THE PERSON WHO SAW DAD BEING PUSHED IS A REGULAR HERE. HE USED TO TALK ABOUT IT ALL THE TIME. I GUESS MOST CIVILIANS DON'T KNOW THOSE DETAILS.
...
ANYWAY, BACK TO TAKAGI.
WE CAN'T FIND HIM UNLESS WE FIGURE OUT WHO ATTACKED HIM. WAS IT THE ARSONIST OR THE CRIMINAL FROM 18 YEARS AGO?
IT'S SHINA-GAWA.

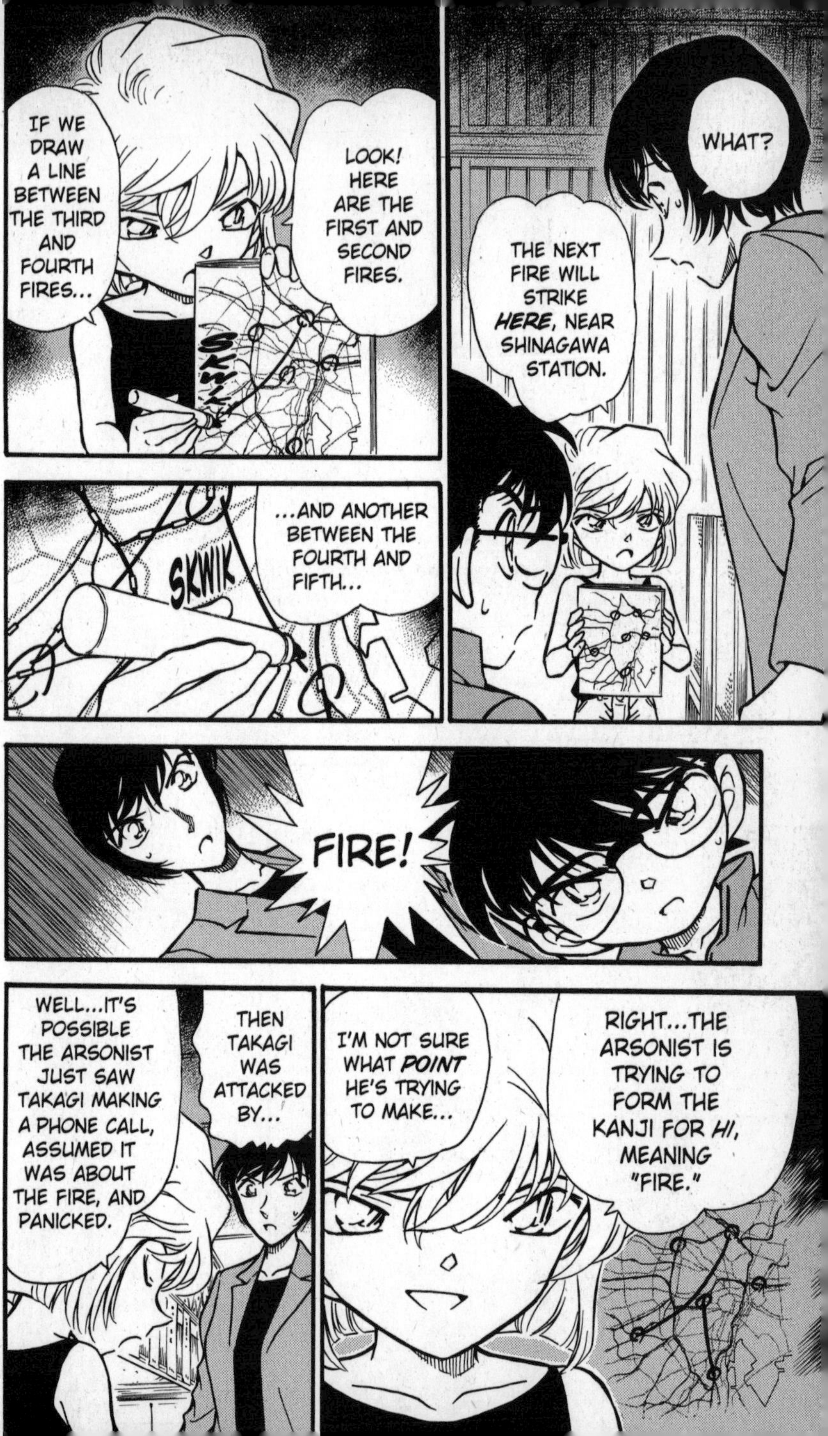
WHAT?
THE NEXT FIRE WILL STRIKE HERE, NEAR SHINAGAWA STATION.
LOOK! HERE ARE THE FIRST AND SECOND FIRES.
IF WE DRAW A LINE BETWEEN THE THIRD AND FOURTH FIRES...
SKWIK
...AND ANOTHER BETWEEN THE FOURTH AND FIFTH...
SKWIK
FIRE!
RIGHT...THE ARSONIST IS TRYING TO FORM THE KANJI FOR HI, MEANING "FIRE."
I'M NOT SURE WHAT POINT HE'S TRYING TO MAKE...
THEN TAKAGI WAS ATTACKED BY...
WELL...IT'S POSSIBLE THE ARSONIST JUST SAW TAKAGI MAKING A PHONE CALL, ASSUMED IT WAS ABOUT THE FIRE, AND PANICKED.

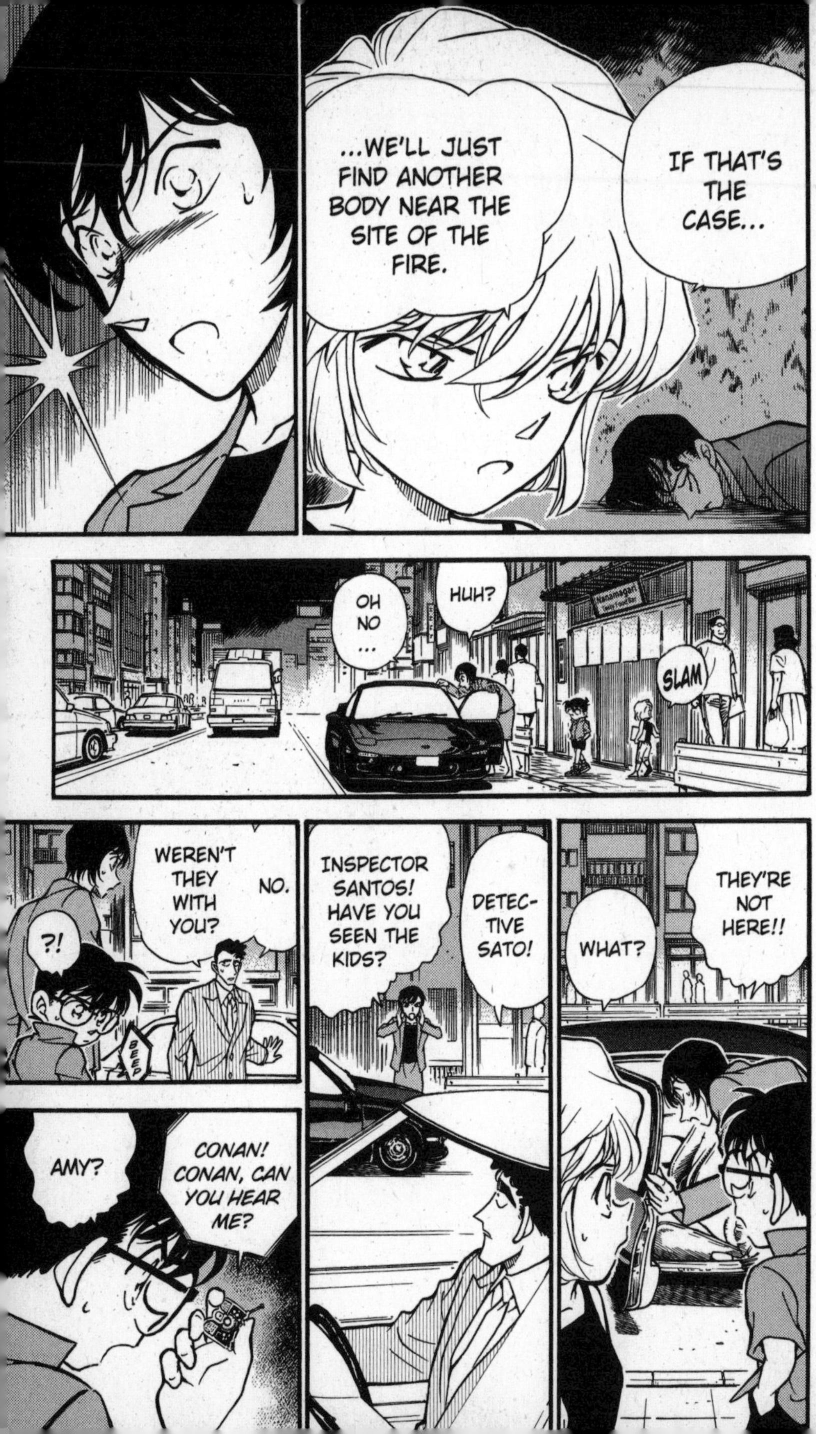
IF THAT'S THE CASE...
...WE'LL JUST FIND ANOTHER BODY NEAR THE SITE OF THE FIRE.
SLAM
HUH?
OH NO ...
THEY'RE NOT HERE!!
WHAT?
DETEC-TIVE SATO!
INSPECTOR SANTOS! HAVE YOU SEEN THE KIDS?
NO.
WEREN'T THEY WITH YOU?
?!
BEEP
CONAN! CONAN, CAN YOU HEAR ME?
AMY?

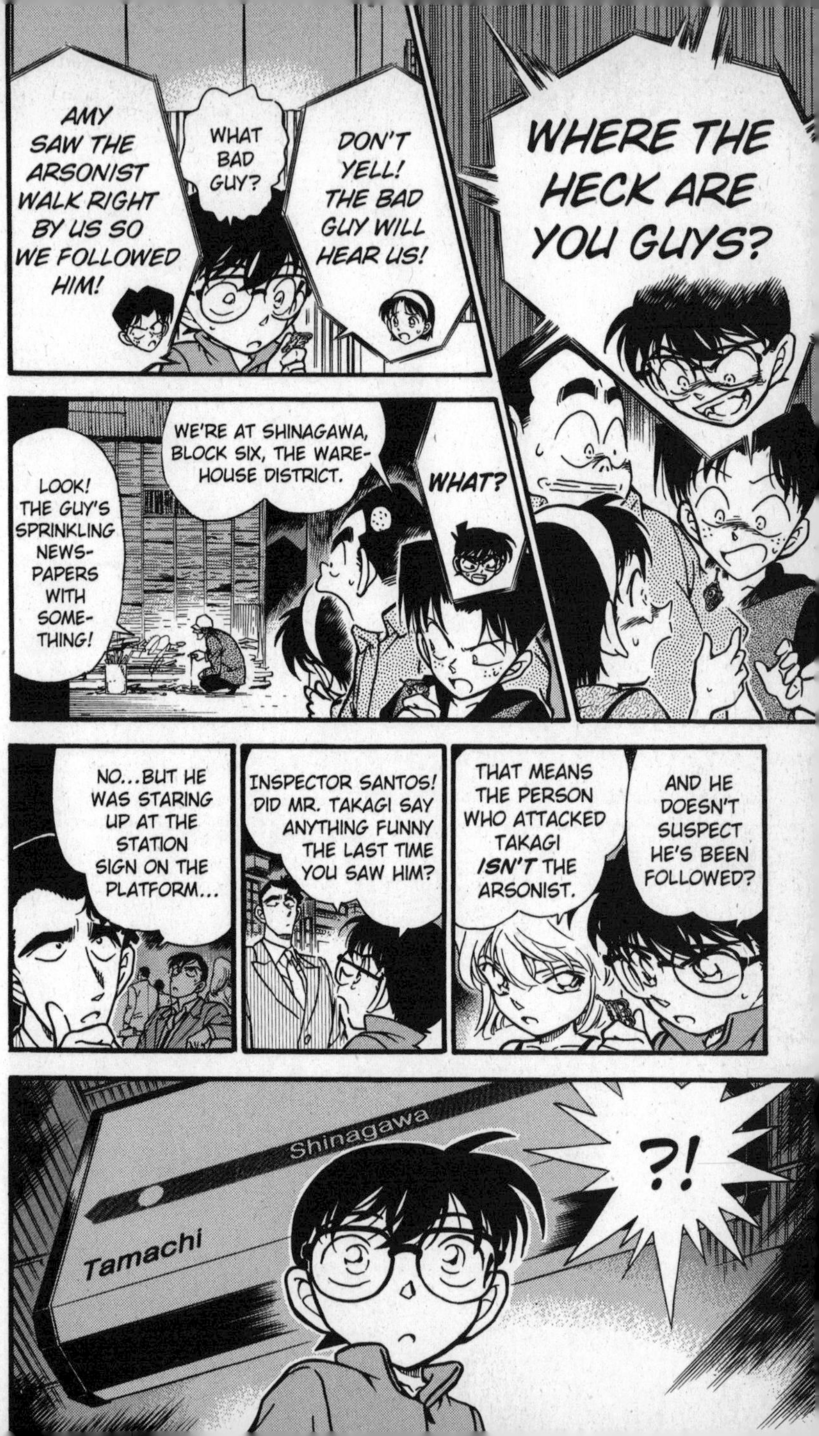
WHERE THE HECK ARE YOU GUYS?
DON'T YELL! THE BAD GUY WILL HEAR US!
WHAT BAD GUY?
AMY SAW THE ARSONIST WALK RIGHT BY US SO WE FOLLOWED HIM!
WHAT?
WE'RE AT SHINAGAWA, BLOCK SIX, THE WARE-HOUSE DISTRICT.
LOOK! THE GUY'S SPRINKLING NEWS-PAPERS WITH SOME-THING!
AND HE DOESN'T SUSPECT HE'S BEEN FOLLOWED?
THAT MEANS THE PERSON WHO ATTACKED TAKAGI *ISN'T* THE ARSONIST.
INSPECTOR SANTOS! DID MR. TAKAGI SAY ANYTHING FUNNY THE LAST TIME YOU SAW HIM?
NO...BUT HE WAS STARING UP AT THE STATION SIGN ON THE PLATFORM...
Shinagawa
Tamachi
?!

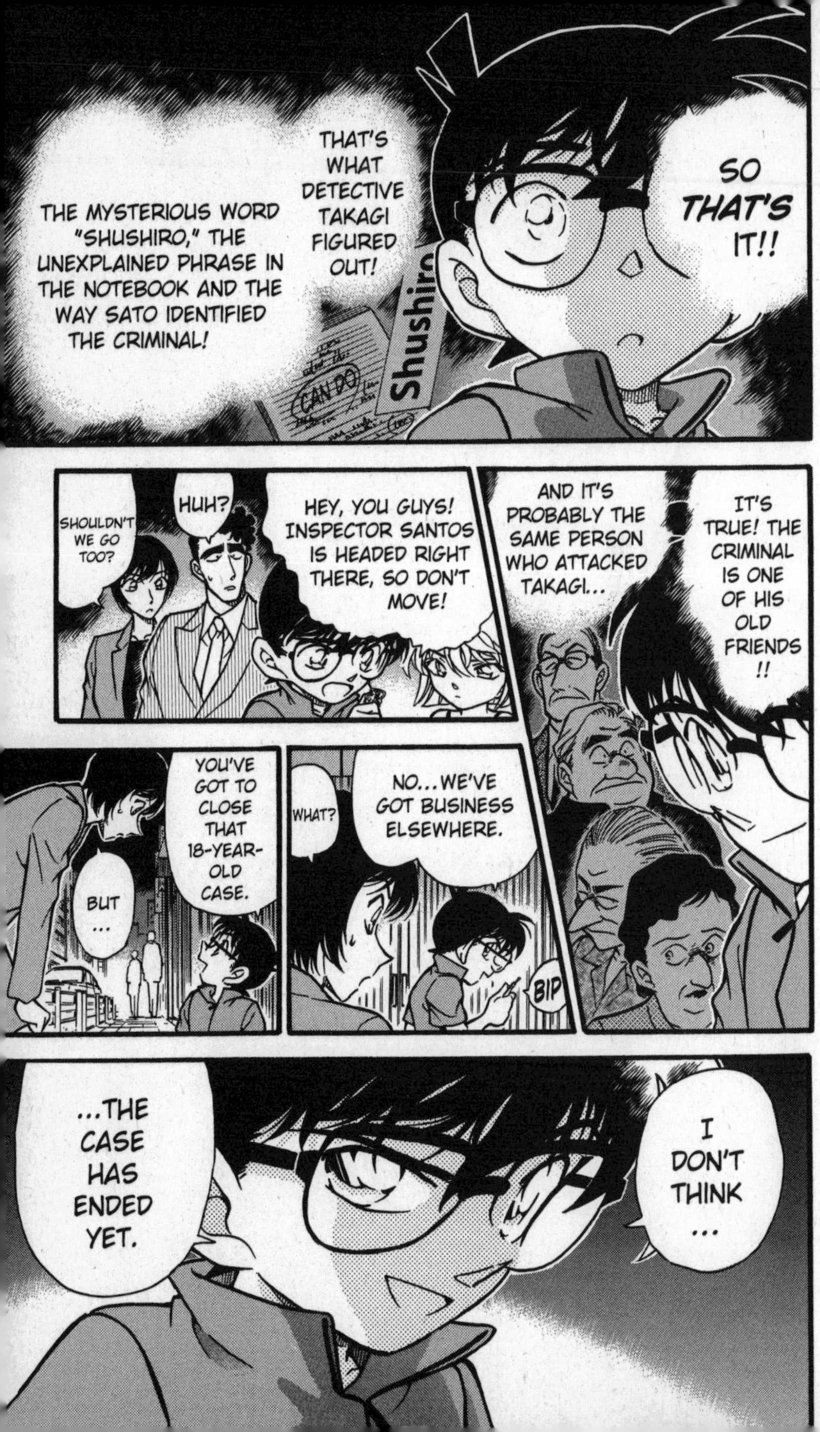

SO THAT'S IT!!
THAT'S WHAT DETECTIVE TAKAGI FIGURED OUT!
THE MYSTERIOUS WORD "SHUSHIRO," THE UNEXPLAINED PHRASE IN THE NOTEBOOK AND THE WAY SATO IDENTIFIED THE CRIMINAL!
Shushiro
CAN DO
IT'S TRUE! THE CRIMINAL IS ONE OF HIS OLD FRIENDS!!
AND IT'S PROBABLY THE SAME PERSON WHO ATTACKED TAKAGI...
HEY, YOU GUYS! INSPECTOR SANTOS IS HEADED RIGHT THERE, SO DON'T MOVE!
HUH?
SHOULDN'T WE GO TOO?
NO... WE'VE GOT BUSINESS ELSEWHERE.
WHAT?
BIP
YOU'VE GOT TO CLOSE THAT 18-YEAR-OLD CASE.
BUT...
I DON'T THINK...
...THE CASE HAS ENDED YET.

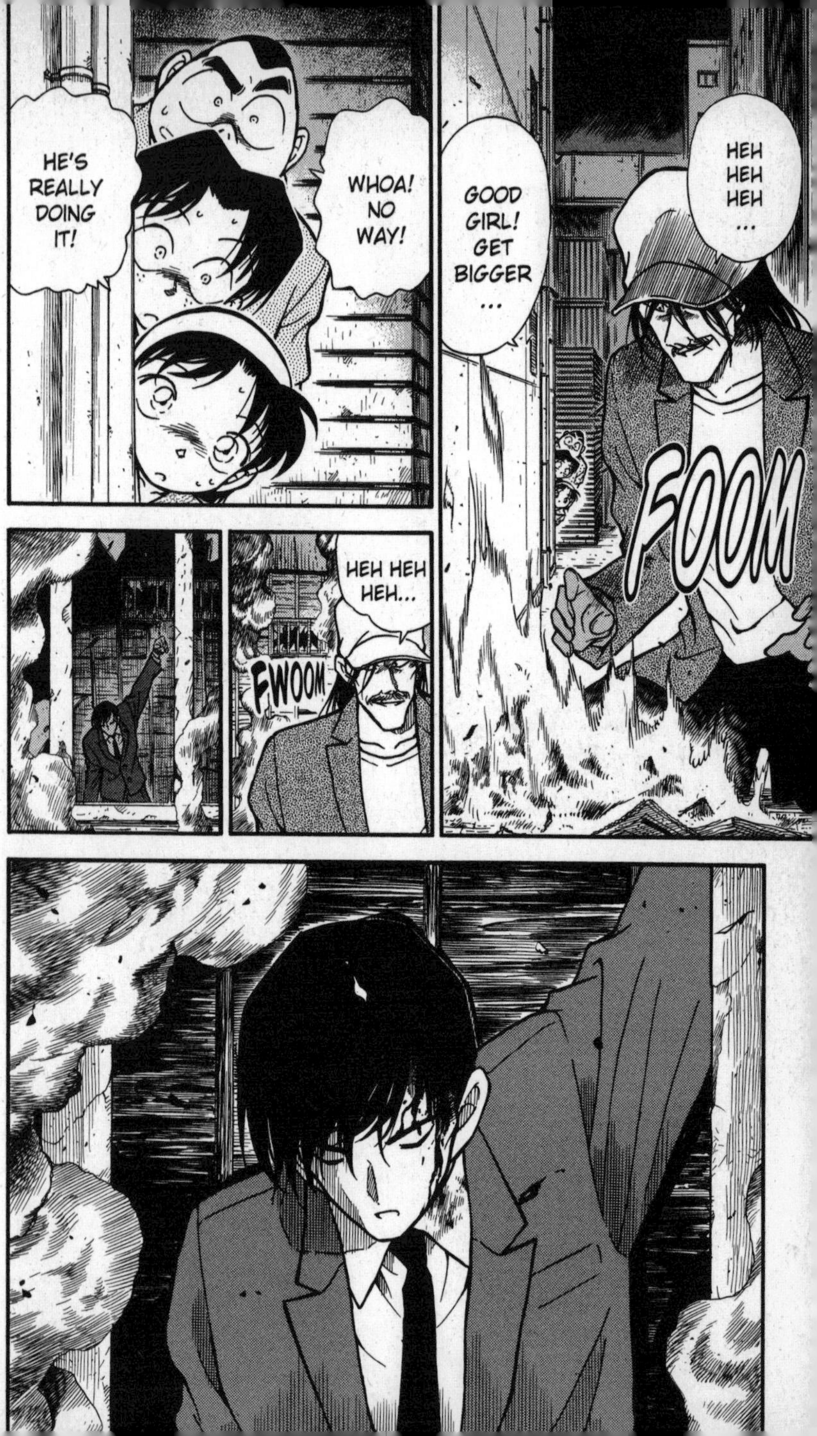
HEH HEH HEH ...
GOOD GIRL! GET BIGGER ...
FOOM
WHOA! NO WAY!
HE'S REALLY DOING IT!
HEH HEH HEH...
FWOOM

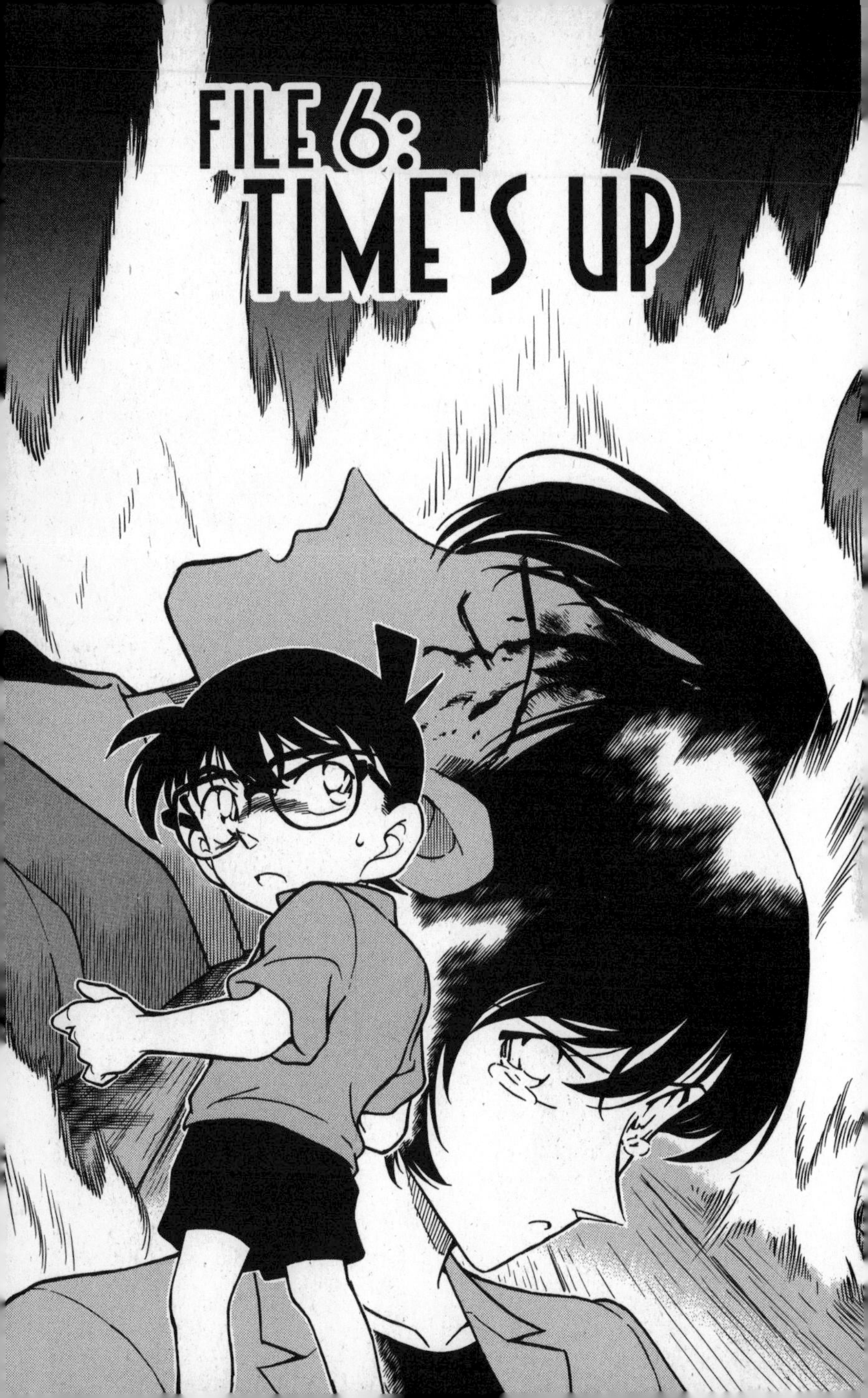
FILE 6:
TIME'S UP

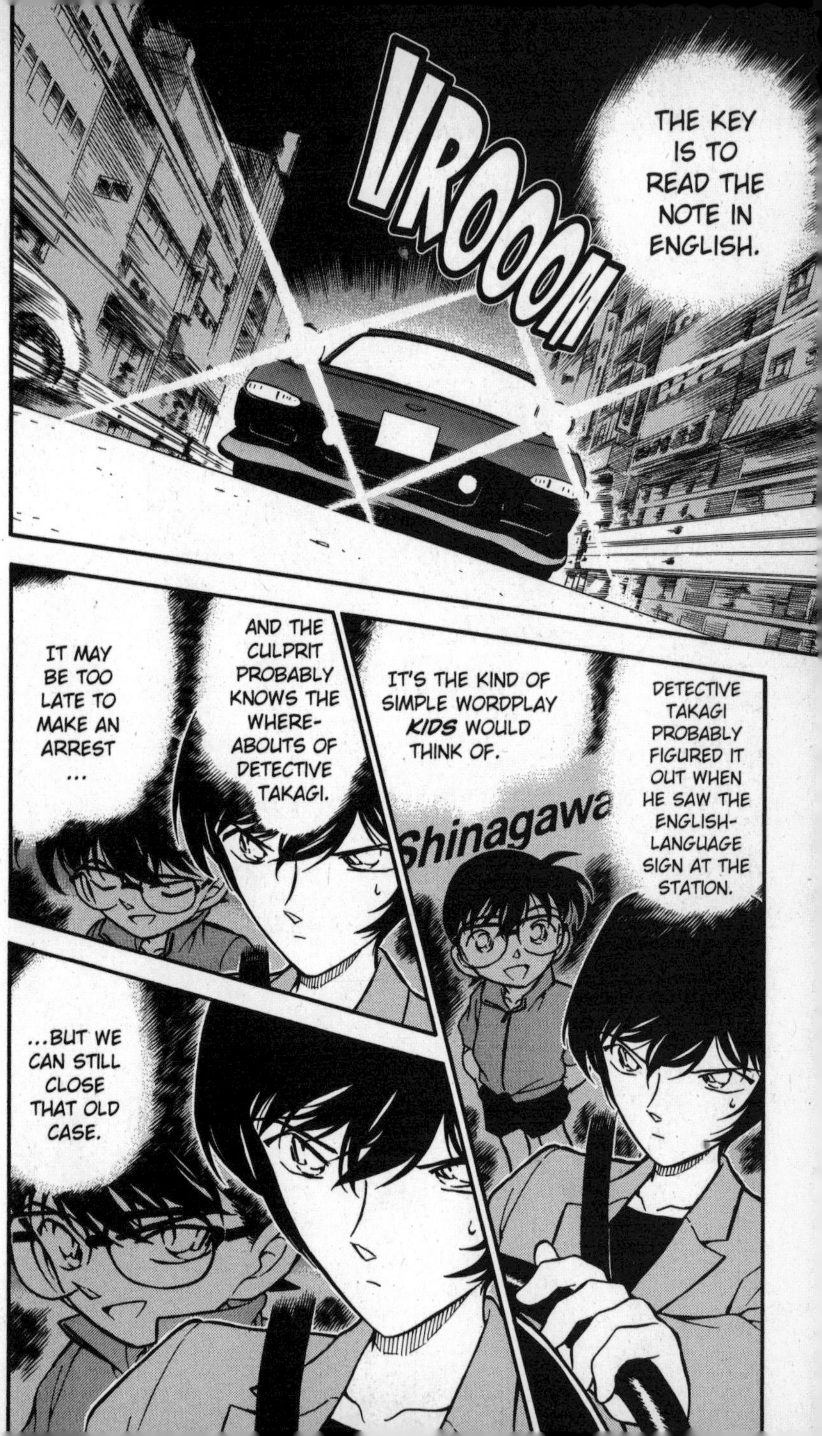
VROOOM
THE KEY IS TO READ THE NOTE IN ENGLISH.
DETECTIVE TAKAGI PROBABLY FIGURED IT OUT WHEN HE SAW THE ENGLISH-LANGUAGE SIGN AT THE STATION.
IT'S THE KIND OF SIMPLE WORDPLAY *KIDS* WOULD THINK OF.
Shinagawa
AND THE CULPRIT PROBABLY KNOWS THE WHERE-ABOUTS OF DETECTIVE TAKAGI.
IT MAY BE TOO LATE TO MAKE AN ARREST ...
...BUT WE CAN STILL CLOSE THAT OLD CASE.

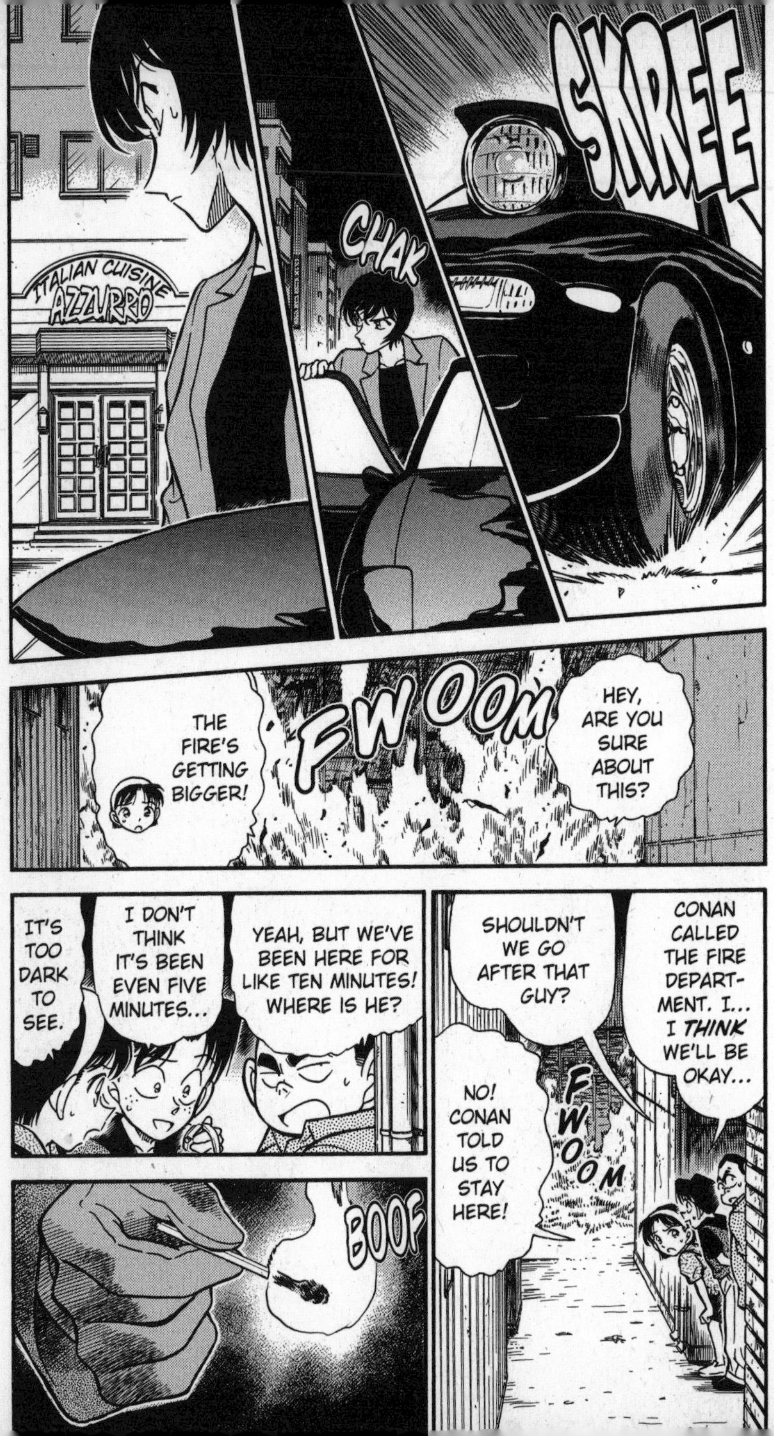
SKREE
CHAK
ITALIAN CUISINE
AZZURRO
HEY, ARE YOU SURE ABOUT THIS?
FWOOM
THE FIRE'S GETTING BIGGER!
CONAN CALLED THE FIRE DEPART-MENT. I... I *THINK* WE'LL BE OKAY...
SHOULDN'T WE GO AFTER THAT GUY?
FWOOM
NO! CONAN TOLD US TO STAY HERE!
YEAH, BUT WE'VE BEEN HERE FOR LIKE TEN MINUTES! WHERE IS HE?
I DON'T THINK IT'S BEEN EVEN FIVE MINUTES...
IT'S TOO DARK TO SEE.
BOOF

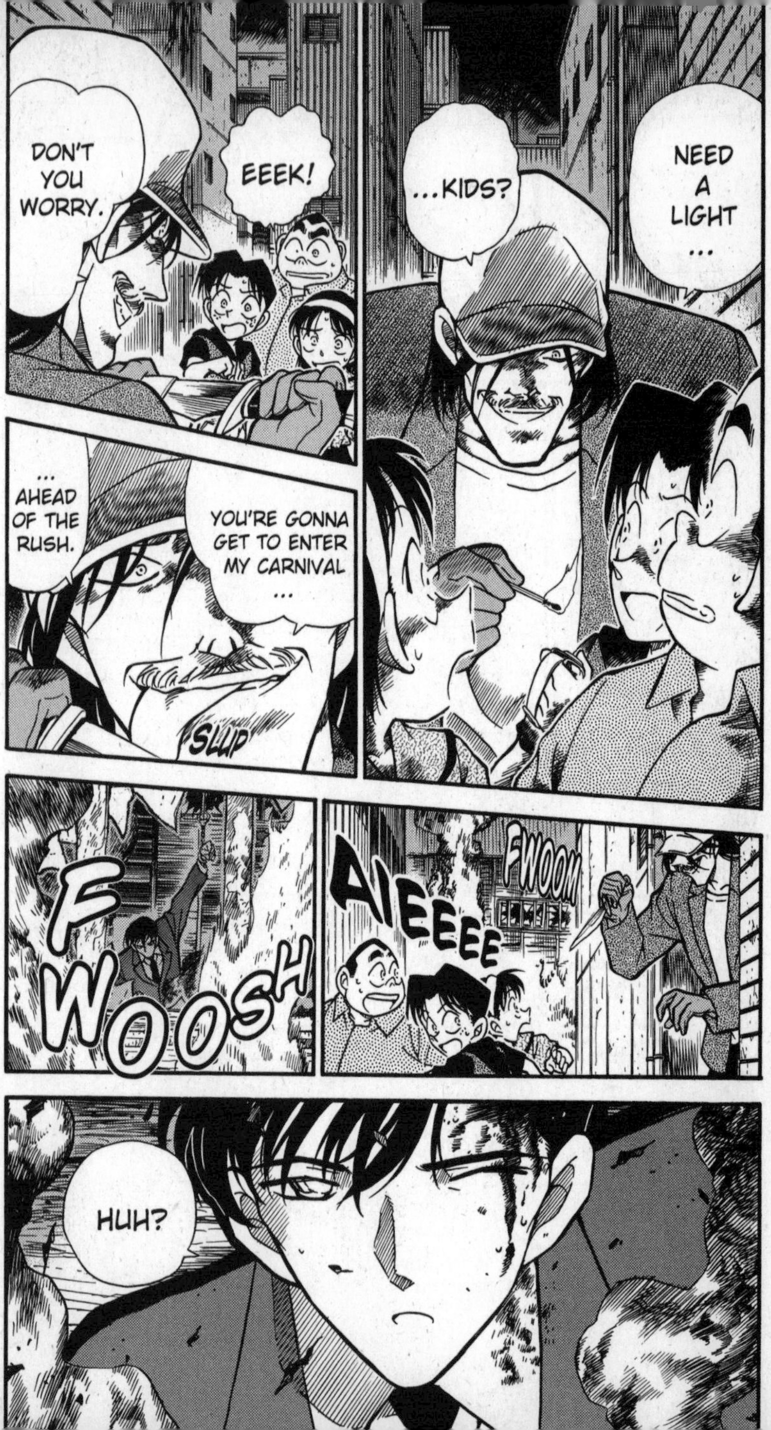
NEED A LIGHT...
...KIDS?
EEEK!
DON'T YOU WORRY.
YOU'RE GONNA GET TO ENTER MY CARNIVAL...
...AHEAD OF THE RUSH.
SLUP
FWOOM
AIEEEEE
FWOOSH
HUH?

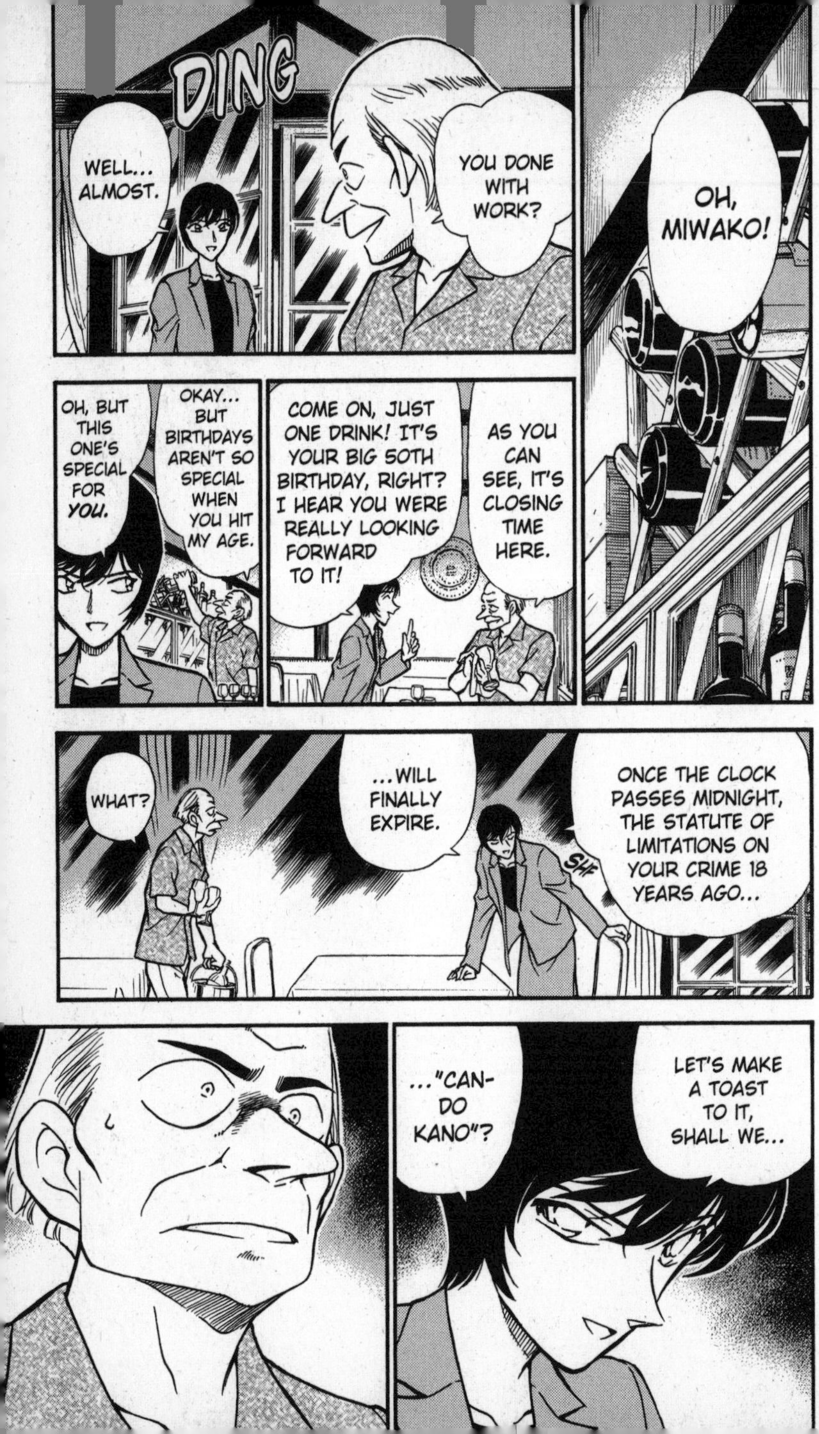
OH, MIWAKO!
DING
YOU DONE WITH WORK?
WELL... ALMOST.
AS YOU CAN SEE, IT'S CLOSING TIME HERE.
COME ON, JUST ONE DRINK! IT'S YOUR BIG 50TH BIRTHDAY, RIGHT? I HEAR YOU WERE REALLY LOOKING FORWARD TO IT!
OKAY... BUT BIRTHDAYS AREN'T SO SPECIAL WHEN YOU HIT MY AGE.
OH, BUT THIS ONE'S SPECIAL FOR *YOU*.
ONCE THE CLOCK PASSES MIDNIGHT, THE STATUTE OF LIMITATIONS ON YOUR CRIME 18 YEARS AGO...
SHF
...WILL FINALLY EXPIRE.
WHAT?
LET'S MAKE A TOAST TO IT, SHALL WE...
..."CAN-DO KANO"?

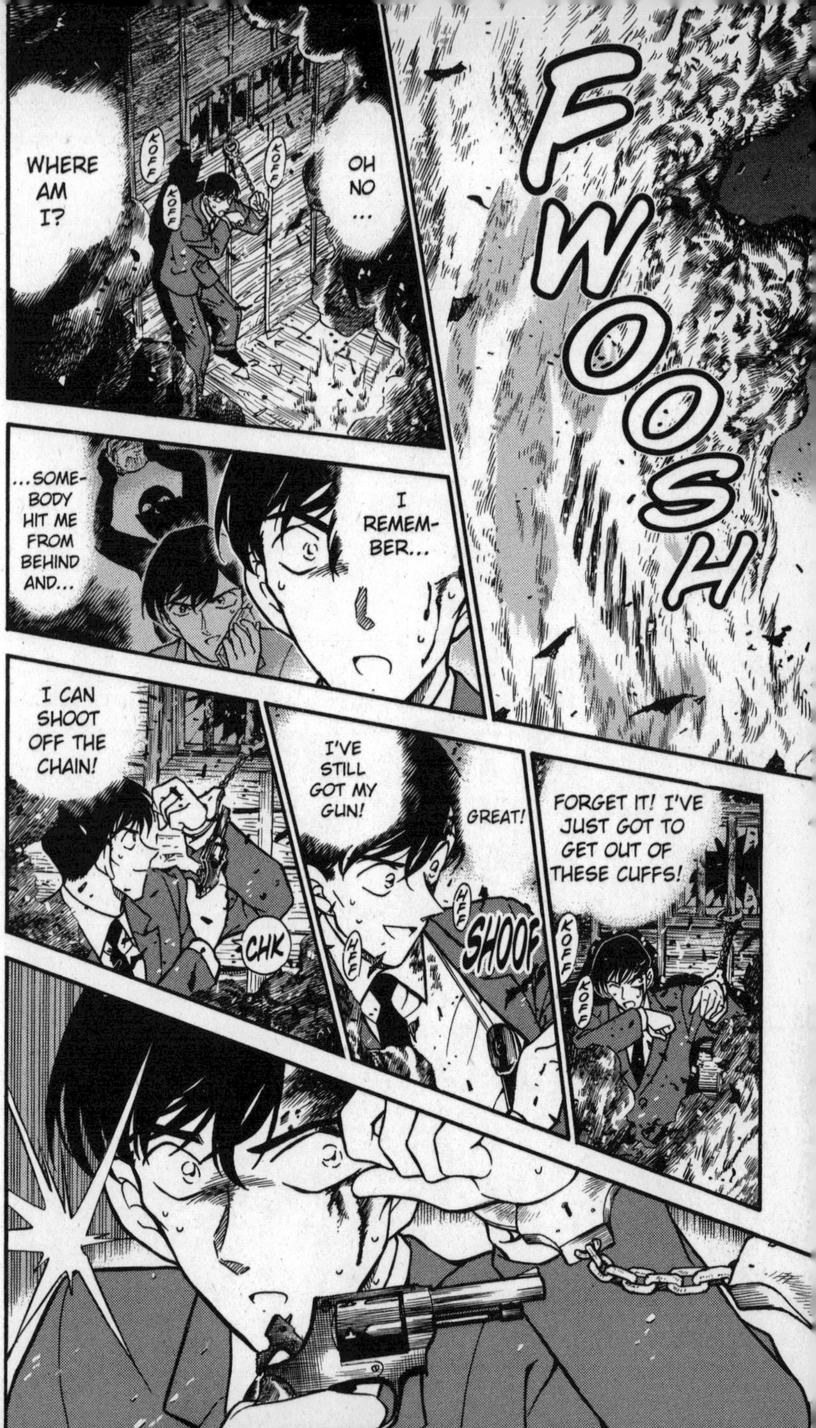
FWOOSH
OH NO ...
KOFF
KOFF
KOFF
WHERE AM I?
I REMEMBER...
...SOMEBODY HIT ME FROM BEHIND AND...
FORGET IT! I'VE JUST GOT TO GET OUT OF THESE CUFFS!
KOFF
KOFF
GREAT!
I'VE STILL GOT MY GUN!
HFF
SHOOF
HFF
I CAN SHOOT OFF THE CHAIN!
CHK

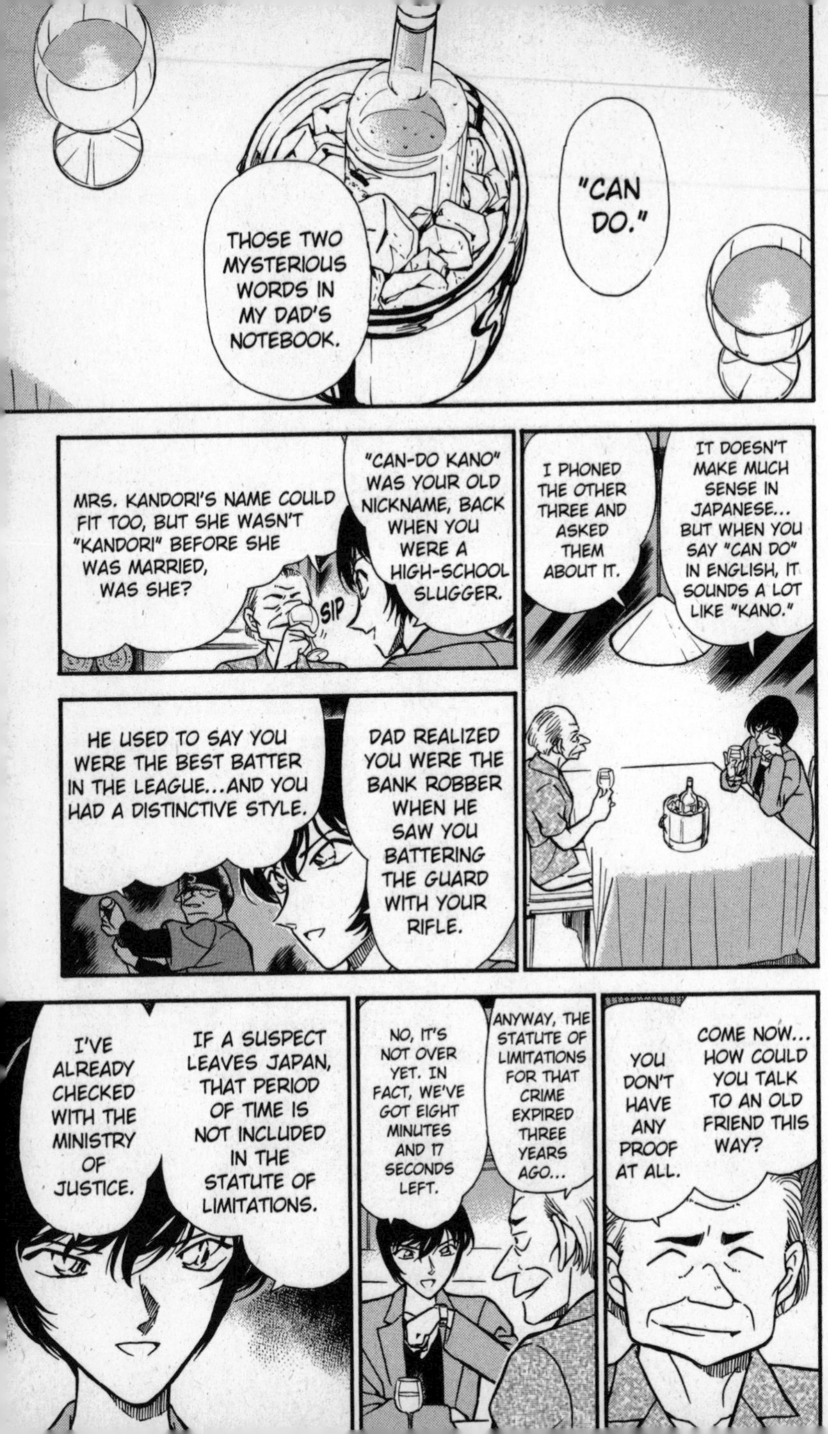
"CAN DO."
THOSE TWO MYSTERIOUS WORDS IN MY DAD'S NOTEBOOK.
IT DOESN'T MAKE MUCH SENSE IN JAPANESE... BUT WHEN YOU SAY "CAN DO" IN ENGLISH, IT SOUNDS A LOT LIKE "KANO."
I PHONED THE OTHER THREE AND ASKED THEM ABOUT IT.
"CAN-DO KANO" WAS YOUR OLD NICKNAME, BACK WHEN YOU WERE A HIGH-SCHOOL SLUGGER.
SIP
MRS. KANDORI'S NAME COULD FIT TOO, BUT SHE WASN'T "KANDORI" BEFORE SHE WAS MARRIED, WAS SHE?
DAD REALIZED YOU WERE THE BANK ROBBER WHEN HE SAW YOU BATTERING THE GUARD WITH YOUR RIFLE.
HE USED TO SAY YOU WERE THE BEST BATTER IN THE LEAGUE...AND YOU HAD A DISTINCTIVE STYLE.
COME NOW... HOW COULD YOU TALK TO AN OLD FRIEND THIS WAY?
YOU DON'T HAVE ANY PROOF AT ALL.
ANYWAY, THE STATUTE OF LIMITATIONS FOR THAT CRIME EXPIRED THREE YEARS AGO...
NO, IT'S NOT OVER YET. IN FACT, WE'VE GOT EIGHT MINUTES AND 17 SECONDS LEFT.
IF A SUSPECT LEAVES JAPAN, THAT PERIOD OF TIME IS NOT INCLUDED IN THE STATUTE OF LIMITATIONS.
I'VE ALREADY CHECKED WITH THE MINISTRY OF JUSTICE.

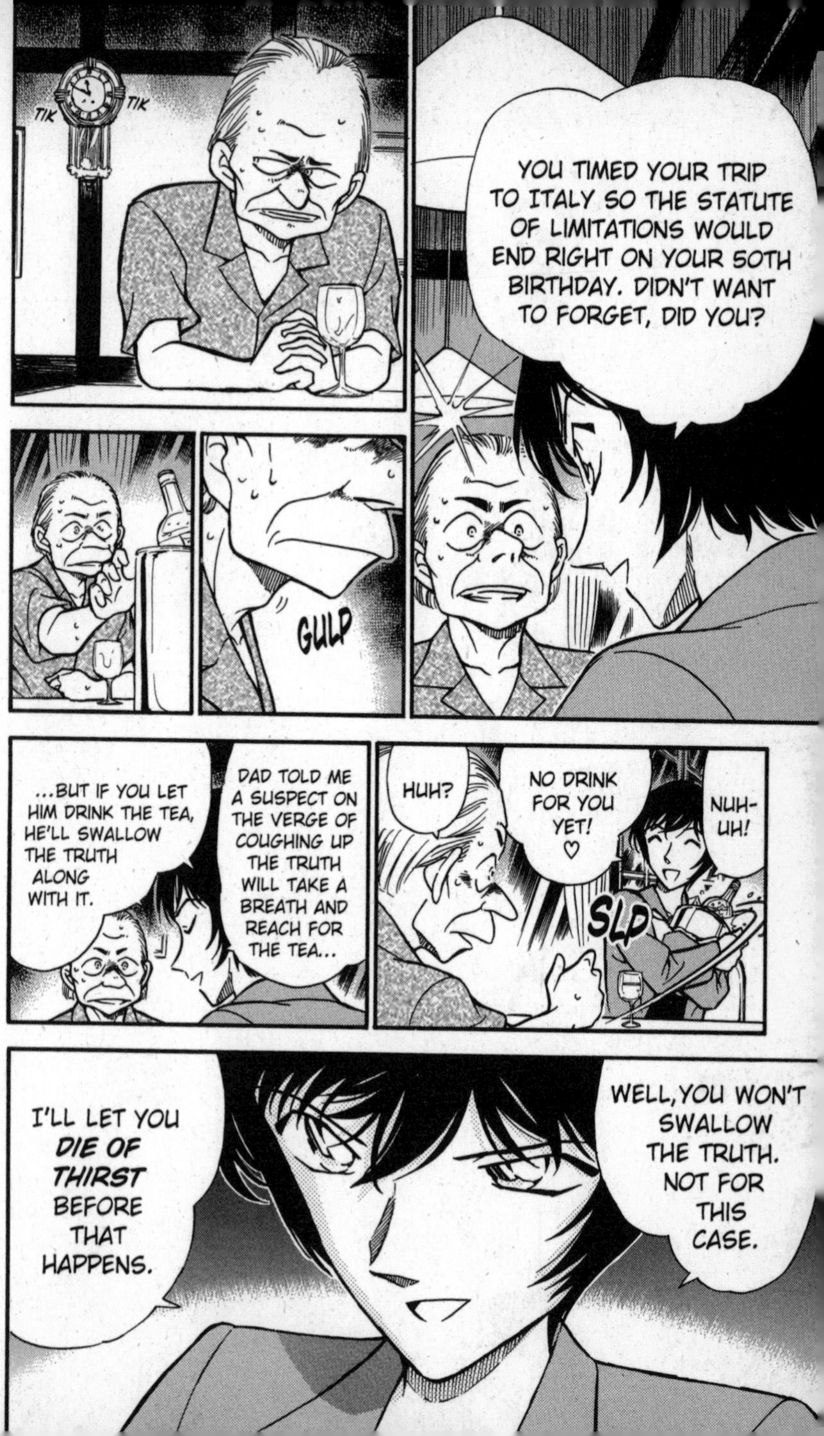
YOU TIMED YOUR TRIP TO ITALY SO THE STATUTE OF LIMITATIONS WOULD END RIGHT ON YOUR 50TH BIRTHDAY. DIDN'T WANT TO FORGET, DID YOU?
TIK
TIK
GULP
NUH-UH!
NO DRINK FOR YOU YET! ♡
HUH?
SLP
DAD TOLD ME A SUSPECT ON THE VERGE OF COUGHING UP THE TRUTH WILL TAKE A BREATH AND REACH FOR THE TEA...
...BUT IF YOU LET HIM DRINK THE TEA, HE'LL SWALLOW THE TRUTH ALONG WITH IT.
WELL, YOU WON'T SWALLOW THE TRUTH. NOT FOR THIS CASE.
I'LL LET YOU *DIE OF THIRST* BEFORE THAT HAPPENS.

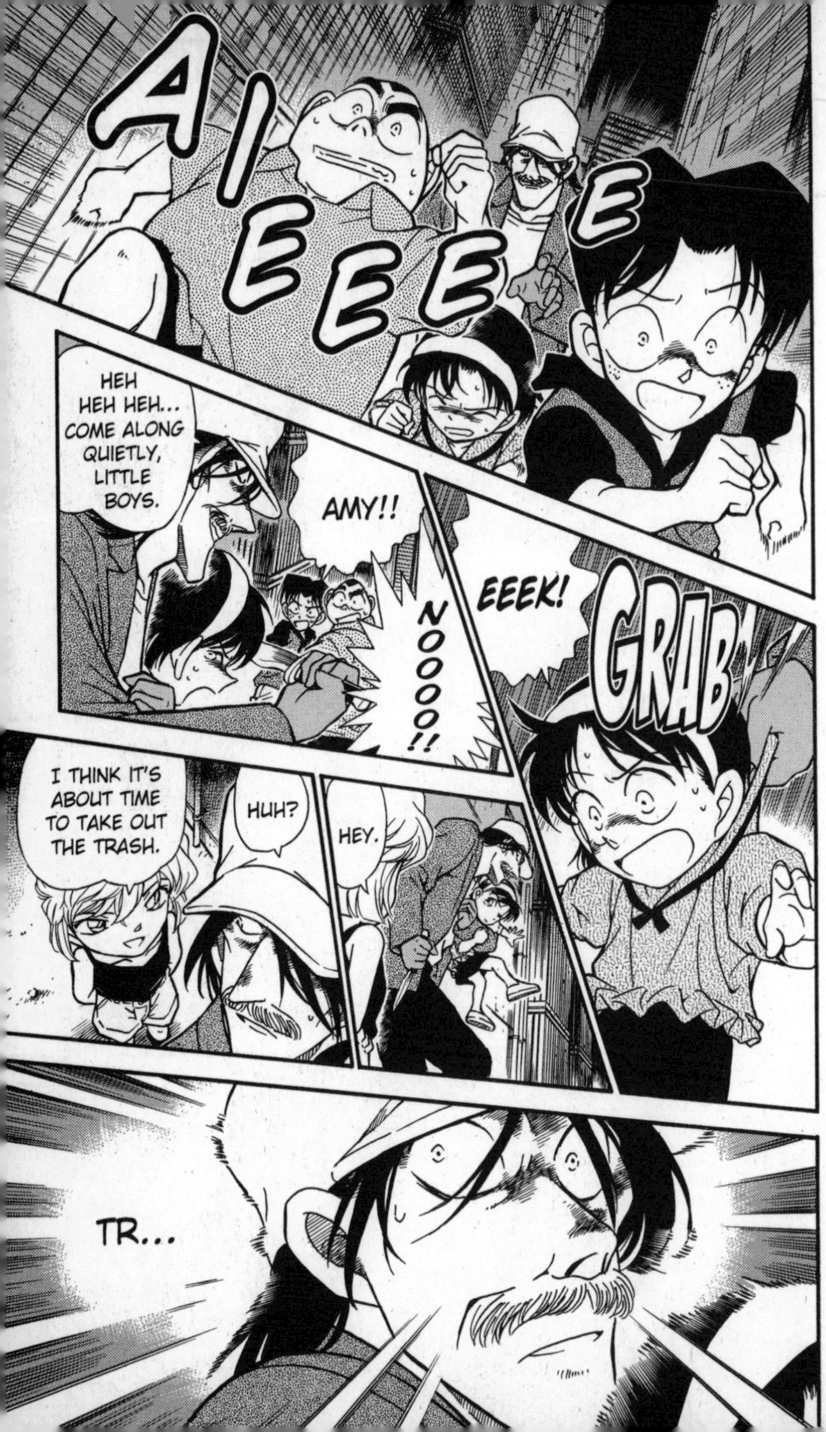
AIEEEEE
EEEK!
GRAB
HEH HEH HEH... COME ALONG QUIETLY, LITTLE BOYS.
AMY!!
NOOOOOO!!
HEY.
I THINK IT'S ABOUT TIME TO TAKE OUT THE TRASH.
HUH?
TR...

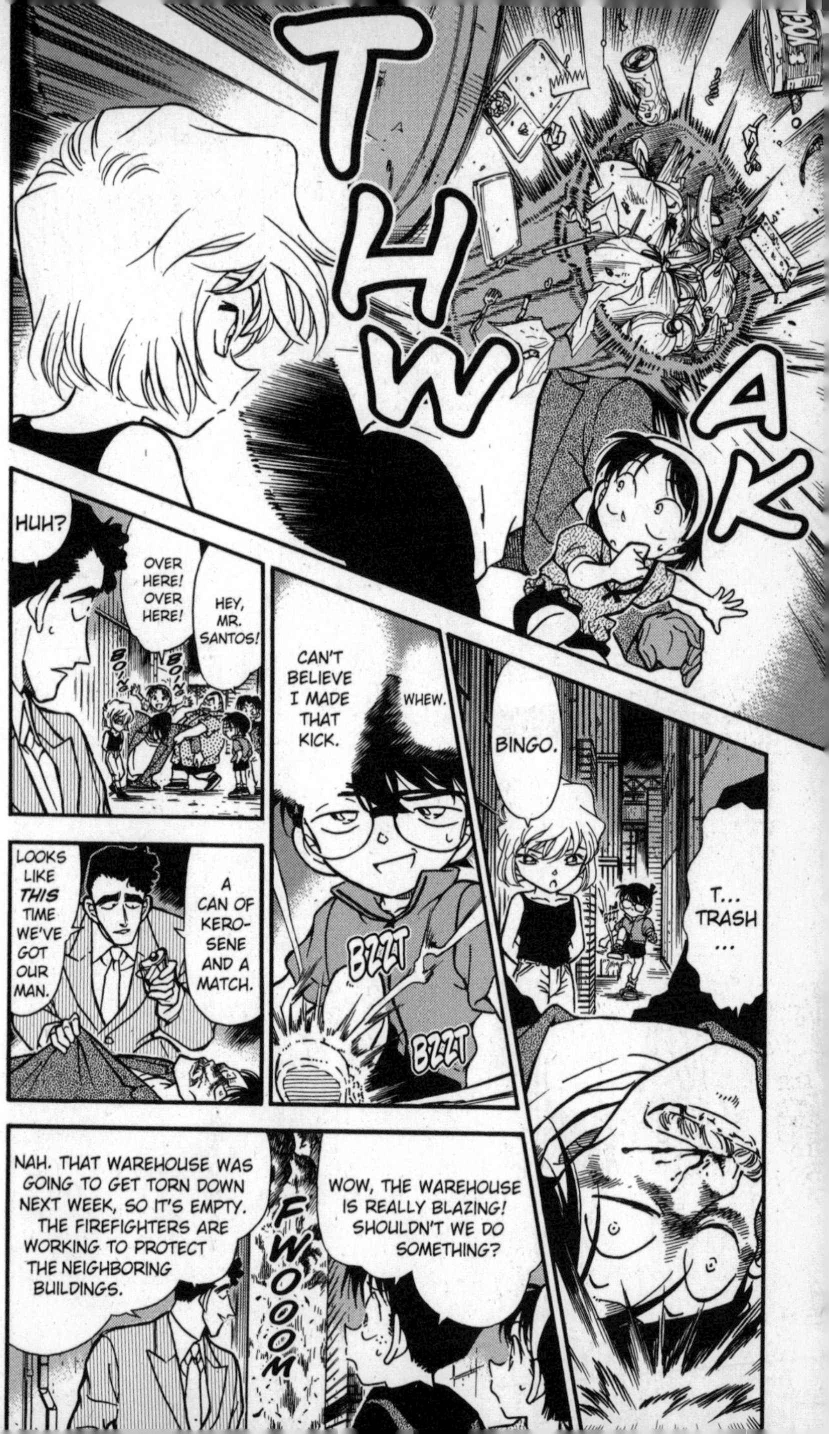
THWAK
BINGO.
T... TRASH...
WHEW.
CAN'T BELIEVE I MADE THAT KICK.
BZZT
BZZT
HEY, MR. SANTOS!
OVER HERE! OVER HERE!
BOING
BOING
HUH?
A CAN OF KEROSENE AND A MATCH.
LOOKS LIKE *THIS* TIME WE'VE GOT OUR MAN.
WOW, THE WAREHOUSE IS REALLY BLAZING! SHOULDN'T WE DO SOMETHING?
FWOOOOM
NAH. THAT WAREHOUSE WAS GOING TO GET TORN DOWN NEXT WEEK, SO IT'S EMPTY. THE FIREFIGHTERS ARE WORKING TO PROTECT THE NEIGHBORING BUILDINGS.

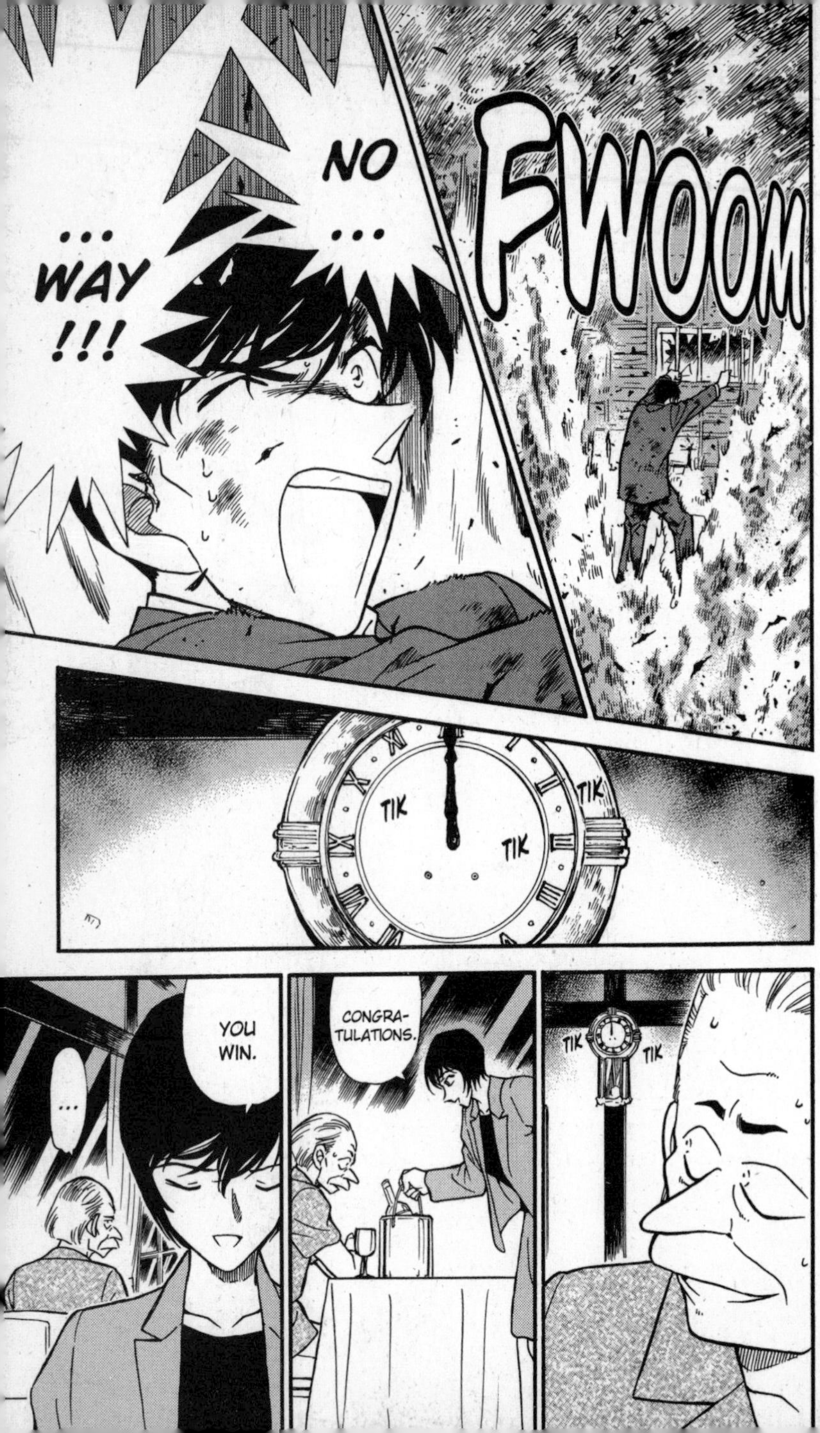
FWOOM
NO ...
... WAY !!!
TIK
TIK
TIK
TIK
TIK
CONGRA-TULATIONS.
YOU WIN.
...

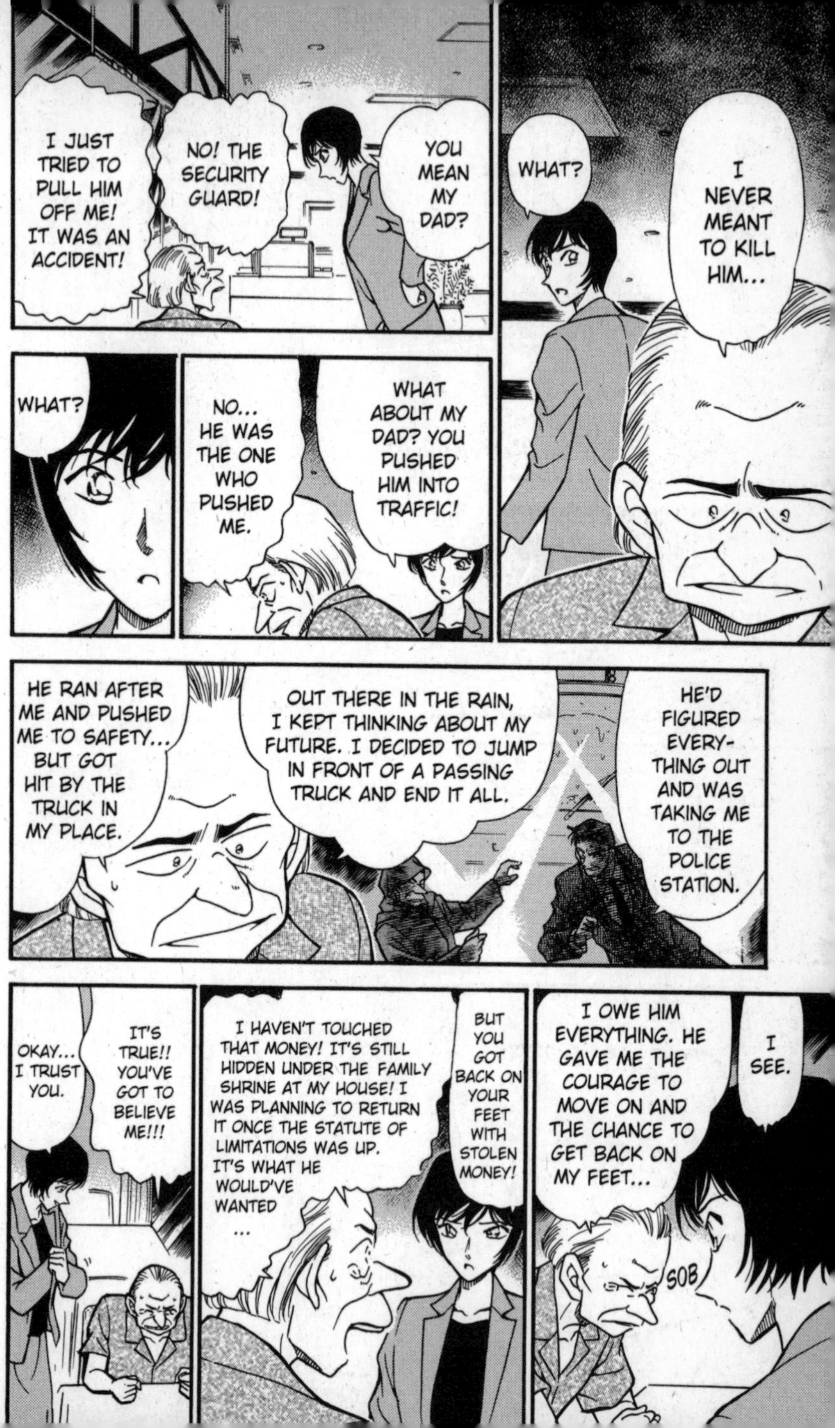
I NEVER MEANT TO KILL HIM...
WHAT?
YOU MEAN MY DAD?
NO! THE SECURITY GUARD!
I JUST TRIED TO PULL HIM OFF ME! IT WAS AN ACCIDENT!
WHAT ABOUT MY DAD? YOU PUSHED HIM INTO TRAFFIC!
NO... HE WAS THE ONE WHO PUSHED ME.
WHAT?
HE'D FIGURED EVERY-THING OUT AND WAS TAKING ME TO THE POLICE STATION.
OUT THERE IN THE RAIN, I KEPT THINKING ABOUT MY FUTURE. I DECIDED TO JUMP IN FRONT OF A PASSING TRUCK AND END IT ALL.
HE RAN AFTER ME AND PUSHED ME TO SAFETY... BUT GOT HIT BY THE TRUCK IN MY PLACE.
I SEE.
I OWE HIM EVERYTHING. HE GAVE ME THE COURAGE TO MOVE ON AND THE CHANCE TO GET BACK ON MY FEET...
SOB
BUT YOU GOT BACK ON YOUR FEET WITH STOLEN MONEY!
I HAVEN'T TOUCHED THAT MONEY! IT'S STILL HIDDEN UNDER THE FAMILY SHRINE AT MY HOUSE! I WAS PLANNING TO RETURN IT ONCE THE STATUTE OF LIMITATIONS WAS UP. IT'S WHAT HE WOULD'VE WANTED ...
IT'S TRUE!! YOU'VE GOT TO BELIEVE ME!!!
OKAY... I TRUST YOU.

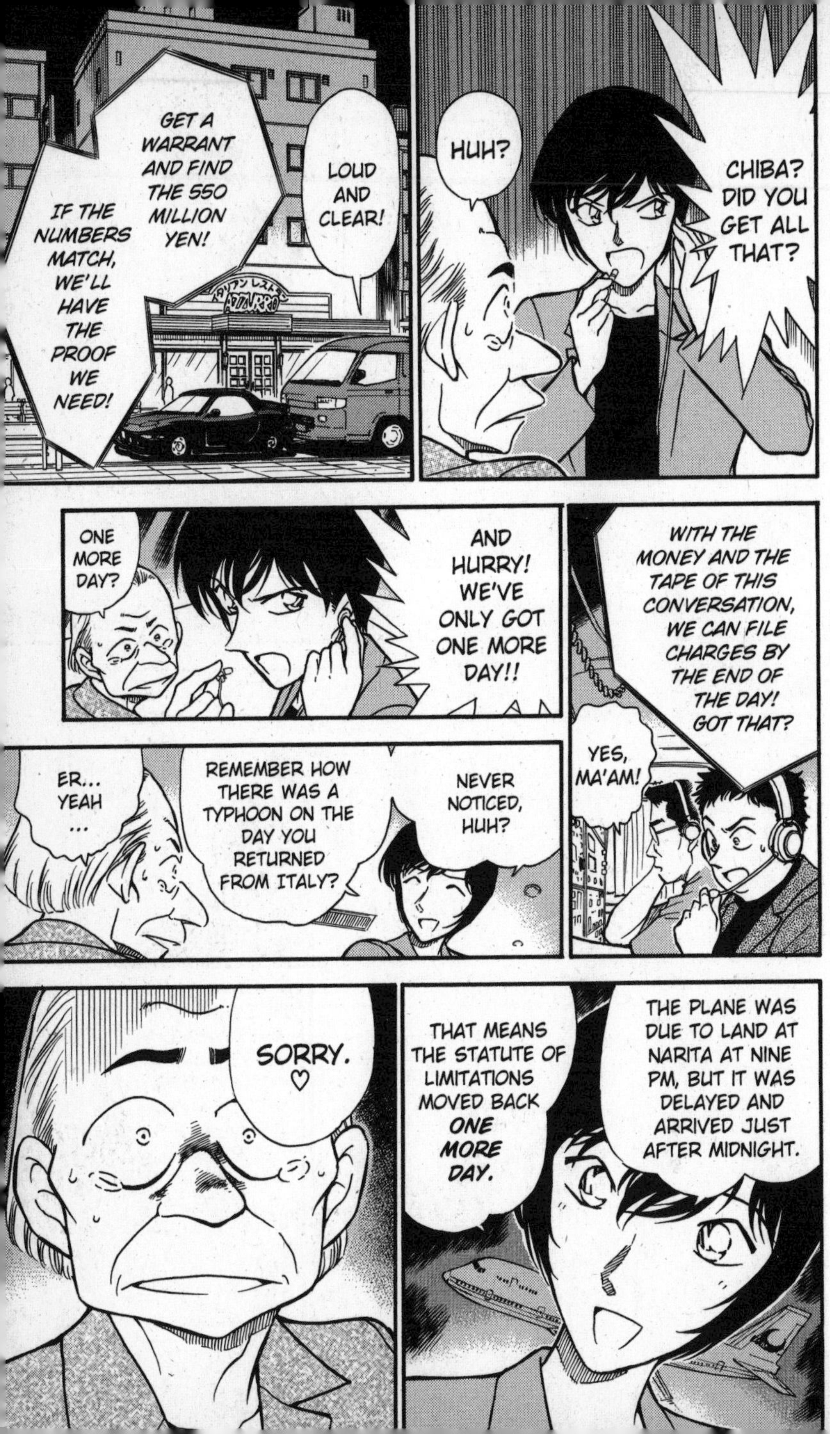
CHIBA? DID YOU GET ALL THAT?
HUH?
LOUD AND CLEAR!
GET A WARRANT AND FIND THE 550 MILLION YEN!
IF THE NUMBERS MATCH, WE'LL HAVE THE PROOF WE NEED!
WITH THE MONEY AND THE TAPE OF THIS CONVERSATION, WE CAN FILE CHARGES BY THE END OF THE DAY! GOT THAT?
YES, MA'AM!
AND HURRY! WE'VE ONLY GOT ONE MORE DAY!!
ONE MORE DAY?
NEVER NOTICED, HUH?
REMEMBER HOW THERE WAS A TYPHOON ON THE DAY YOU RETURNED FROM ITALY?
ER... YEAH ...
THE PLANE WAS DUE TO LAND AT NARITA AT NINE PM, BUT IT WAS DELAYED AND ARRIVED JUST AFTER MIDNIGHT.
THAT MEANS THE STATUTE OF LIMITATIONS MOVED BACK **ONE MORE DAY.**
SORRY. ♡

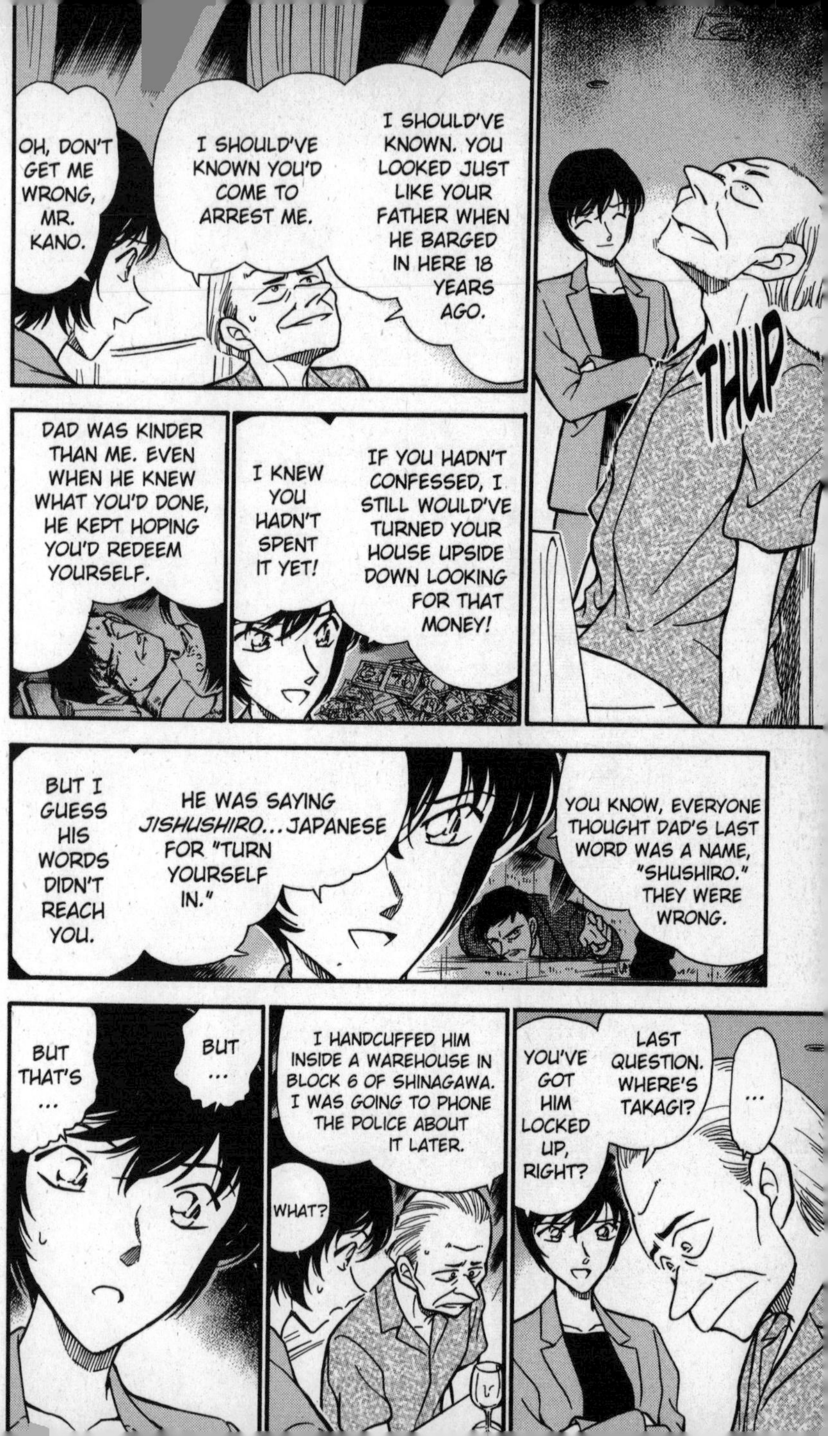
THUP
I SHOULD'VE KNOWN. YOU LOOKED JUST LIKE YOUR FATHER WHEN HE BARGED IN HERE 18 YEARS AGO.
I SHOULD'VE KNOWN YOU'D COME TO ARREST ME.
OH, DON'T GET ME WRONG, MR. KANO.
IF YOU HADN'T CONFESSED, I STILL WOULD'VE TURNED YOUR HOUSE UPSIDE DOWN LOOKING FOR THAT MONEY!
I KNEW YOU HADN'T SPENT IT YET!
DAD WAS KINDER THAN ME. EVEN WHEN HE KNEW WHAT YOU'D DONE, HE KEPT HOPING YOU'D REDEEM YOURSELF.
YOU KNOW, EVERYONE THOUGHT DAD'S LAST WORD WAS A NAME, "SHUSHIRO." THEY WERE WRONG.
HE WAS SAYING *JISHUSHIRO*... JAPANESE FOR "TURN YOURSELF IN."
BUT I GUESS HIS WORDS DIDN'T REACH YOU.
...
LAST QUESTION. WHERE'S TAKAGI?
YOU'VE GOT HIM LOCKED UP, RIGHT?
I HANDCUFFED HIM INSIDE A WAREHOUSE IN BLOCK 6 OF SHINAGAWA. I WAS GOING TO PHONE THE POLICE ABOUT IT LATER.
WHAT?
BUT ...
BUT THAT'S ...

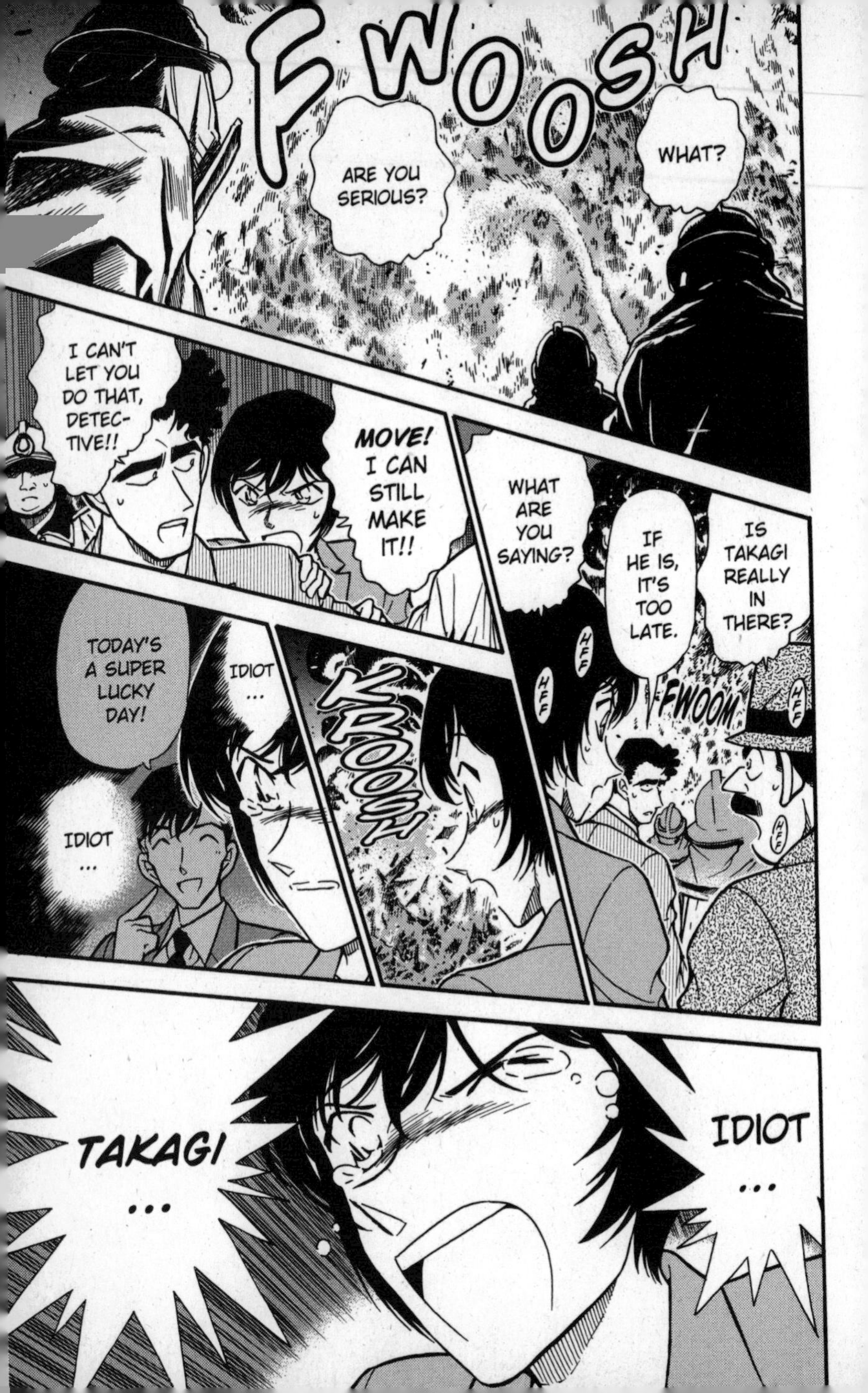
FWOOSH
WHAT?
ARE YOU SERIOUS?
IS TAKAGI REALLY IN THERE?
IF HE IS, IT'S TOO LATE.
WHAT ARE YOU SAYING?
HFF
HFF
FWOOM
HFF
HFF
MOVE! I CAN STILL MAKE IT!!
I CAN'T LET YOU DO THAT, DETECTIVE!!
KROOOOM
IDIOT …
TODAY'S A SUPER LUCKY DAY!
IDIOT …
IDIOT …
TAKAGI …

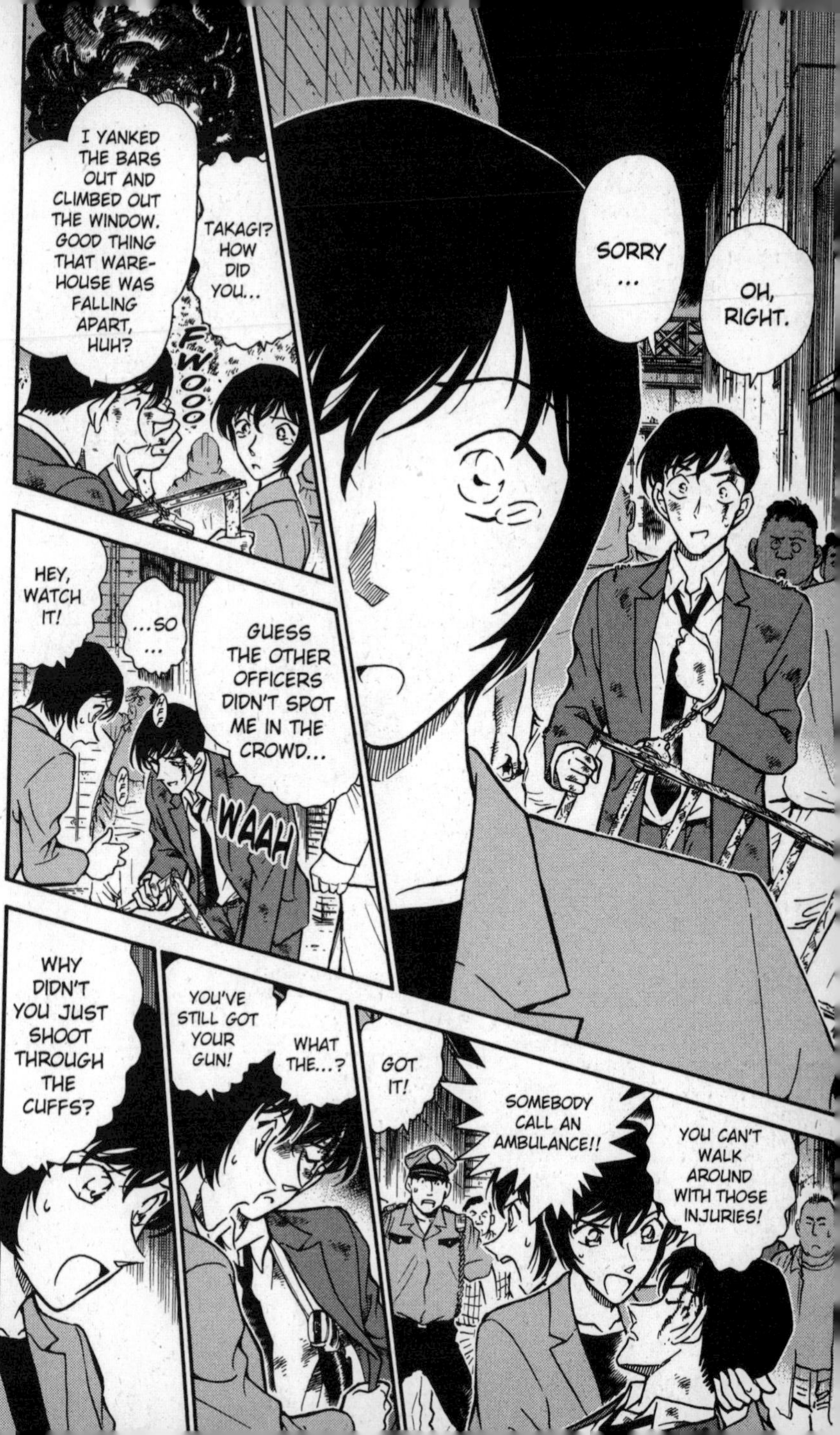
OH, RIGHT.
SORRY...
TAKAGI? HOW DID YOU...
I YANKED THE BARS OUT AND CLIMBED OUT THE WINDOW. GOOD THING THAT WARE-HOUSE WAS FALLING APART, HUH?
FWOOO
GUESS THE OTHER OFFICERS DIDN'T SPOT ME IN THE CROWD...
...SO...
HEY, WATCH IT!
WAAH
YOU CAN'T WALK AROUND WITH THOSE INJURIES!
SOMEBODY CALL AN AMBULANCE!!
GOT IT!
WHAT THE...?
YOU'VE STILL GOT YOUR GUN!
WHY DIDN'T YOU JUST SHOOT THROUGH THE CUFFS?

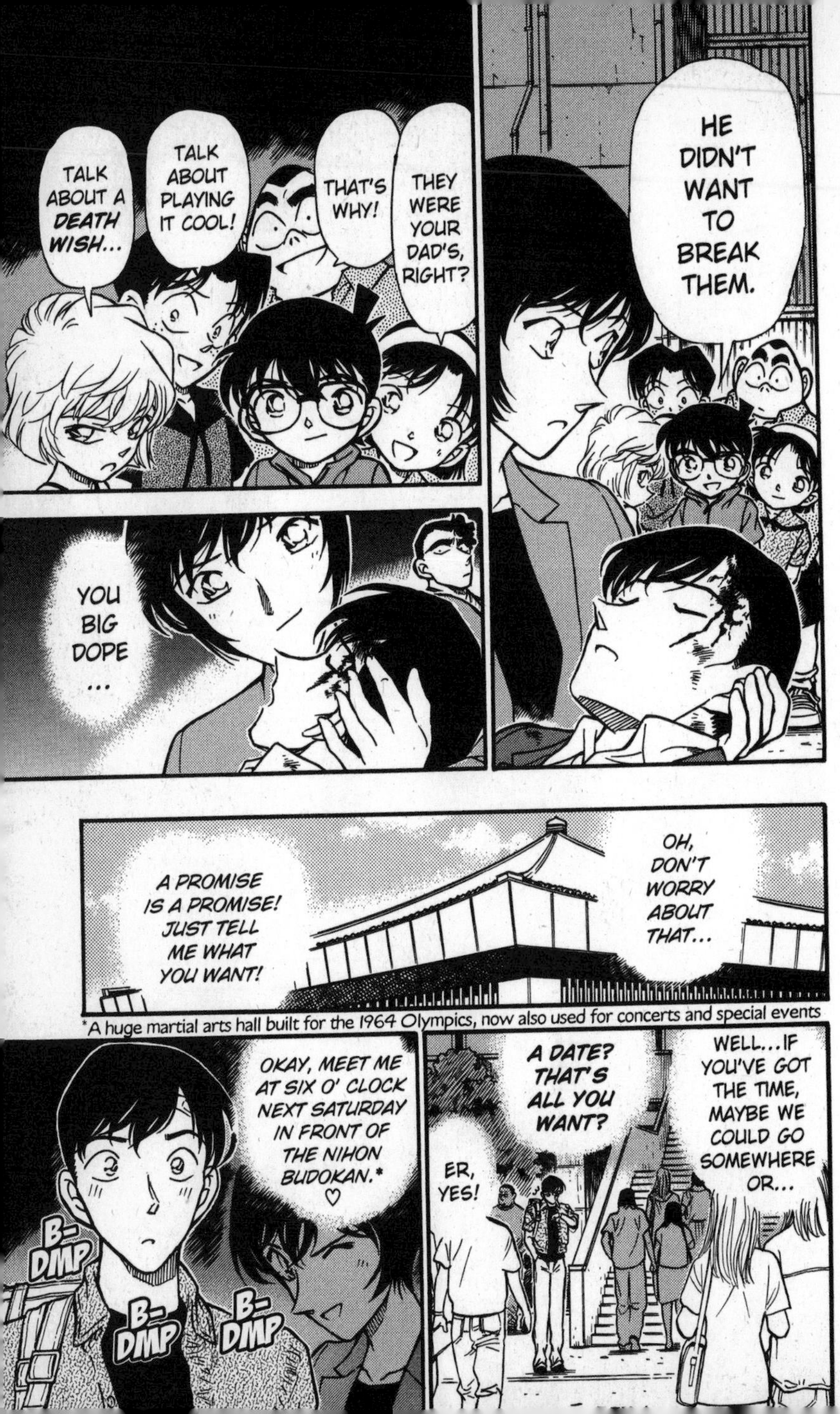
HE DIDN'T WANT TO BREAK THEM.
THEY WERE YOUR DAD'S, RIGHT?
THAT'S WHY!
TALK ABOUT PLAYING IT COOL!
TALK ABOUT A *DEATH WISH*...
YOU BIG DOPE ...
OH, DON'T WORRY ABOUT THAT...
A PROMISE IS A PROMISE! JUST TELL ME WHAT YOU WANT!
WELL...IF YOU'VE GOT THE TIME, MAYBE WE COULD GO SOMEWHERE OR...
A DATE? THAT'S ALL YOU WANT?
ER, YES!
OKAY, MEET ME AT SIX O' CLOCK NEXT SATURDAY IN FRONT OF THE NIHON BUDOKAN.* ♡
B-DMP
B-DMP
B-DMP
*A huge martial arts hall built for the 1964 Olympics, now also used for concerts and special events

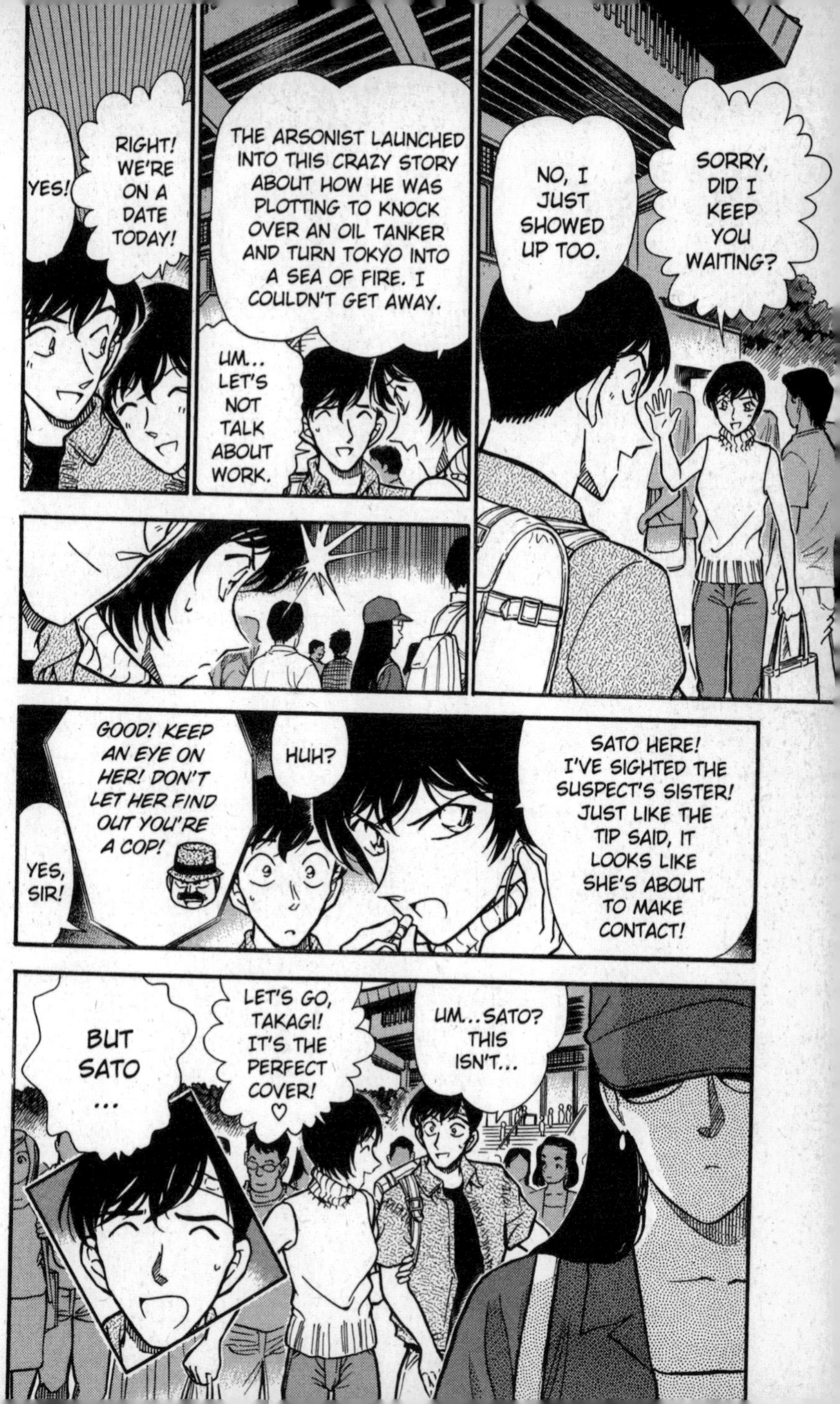
SORRY, DID I KEEP YOU WAITING?
NO, I JUST SHOWED UP TOO.
THE ARSONIST LAUNCHED INTO THIS CRAZY STORY ABOUT HOW HE WAS PLOTTING TO KNOCK OVER AN OIL TANKER AND TURN TOKYO INTO A SEA OF FIRE. I COULDN'T GET AWAY.
UM... LET'S NOT TALK ABOUT WORK.
RIGHT! WE'RE ON A DATE TODAY!
YES!
SATO HERE! I'VE SIGHTED THE SUSPECT'S SISTER! JUST LIKE THE TIP SAID, IT LOOKS LIKE SHE'S ABOUT TO MAKE CONTACT!
HUH?
GOOD! KEEP AN EYE ON HER! DON'T LET HER FIND OUT YOU'RE A COP!
YES, SIR!
UM...SATO? THIS ISN'T...
LET'S GO, TAKAGI! IT'S THE PERFECT COVER! ♡
BUT SATO ...

FILE 7: GAME ON

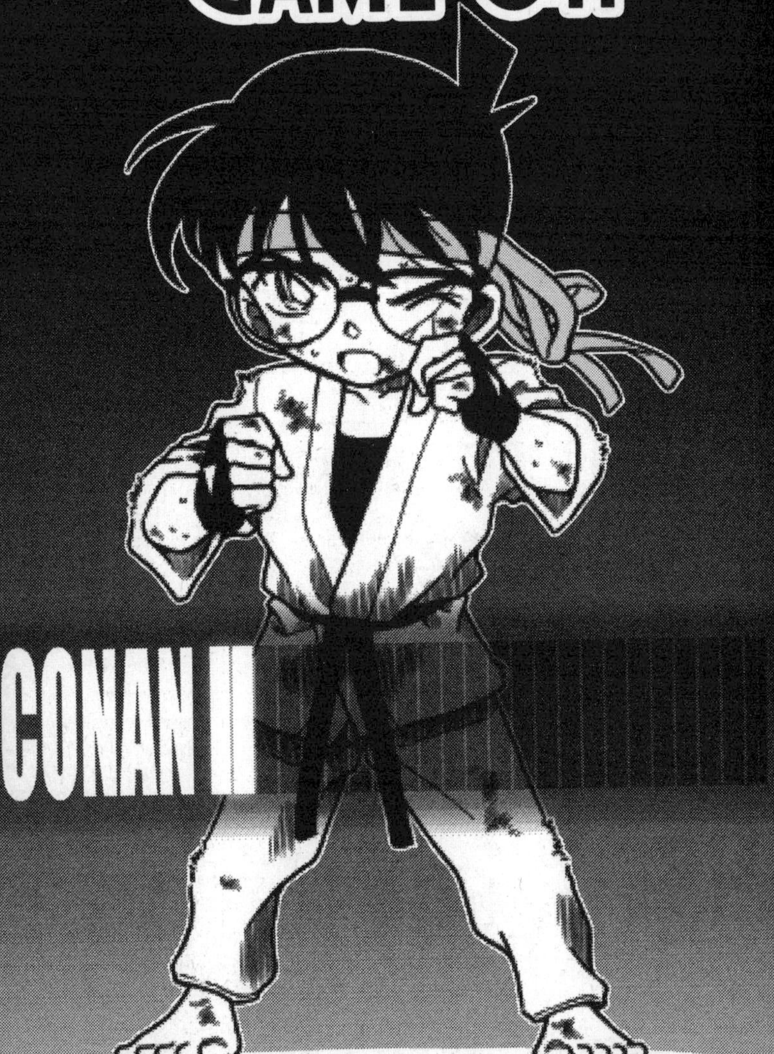
CONAN II

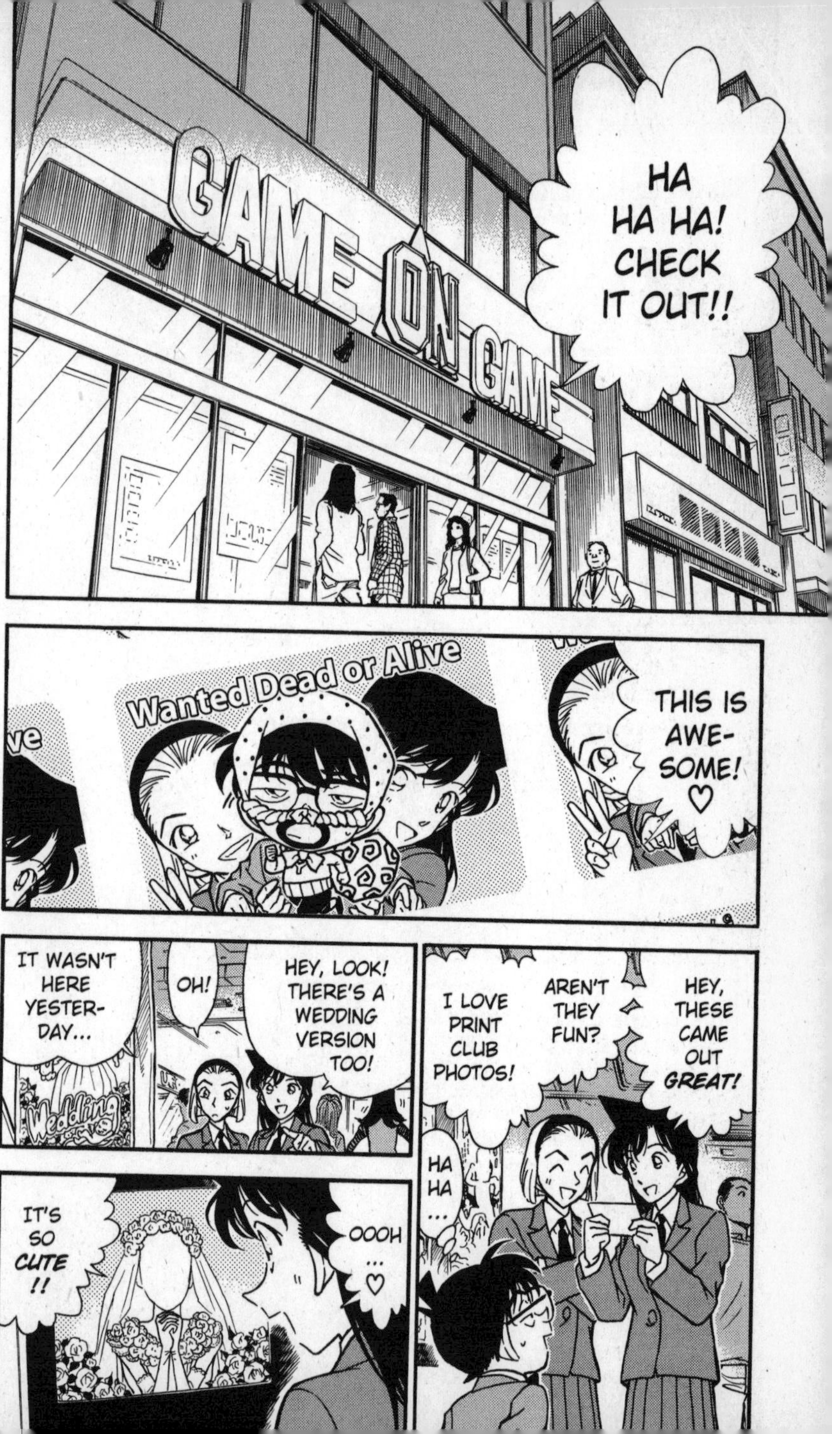
GAME ON GAME
HA HA HA! CHECK IT OUT!!
THIS IS AWE-SOME! ♡
Wanted Dead or Alive
HEY, THESE CAME OUT GREAT!
AREN'T THEY FUN?
I LOVE PRINT CLUB PHOTOS!
HA HA ...
HEY, LOOK! THERE'S A WEDDING VERSION TOO!
OH!
IT WASN'T HERE YESTER-DAY...
Wedding
OOOH ... ♡
IT'S SO CUTE !!

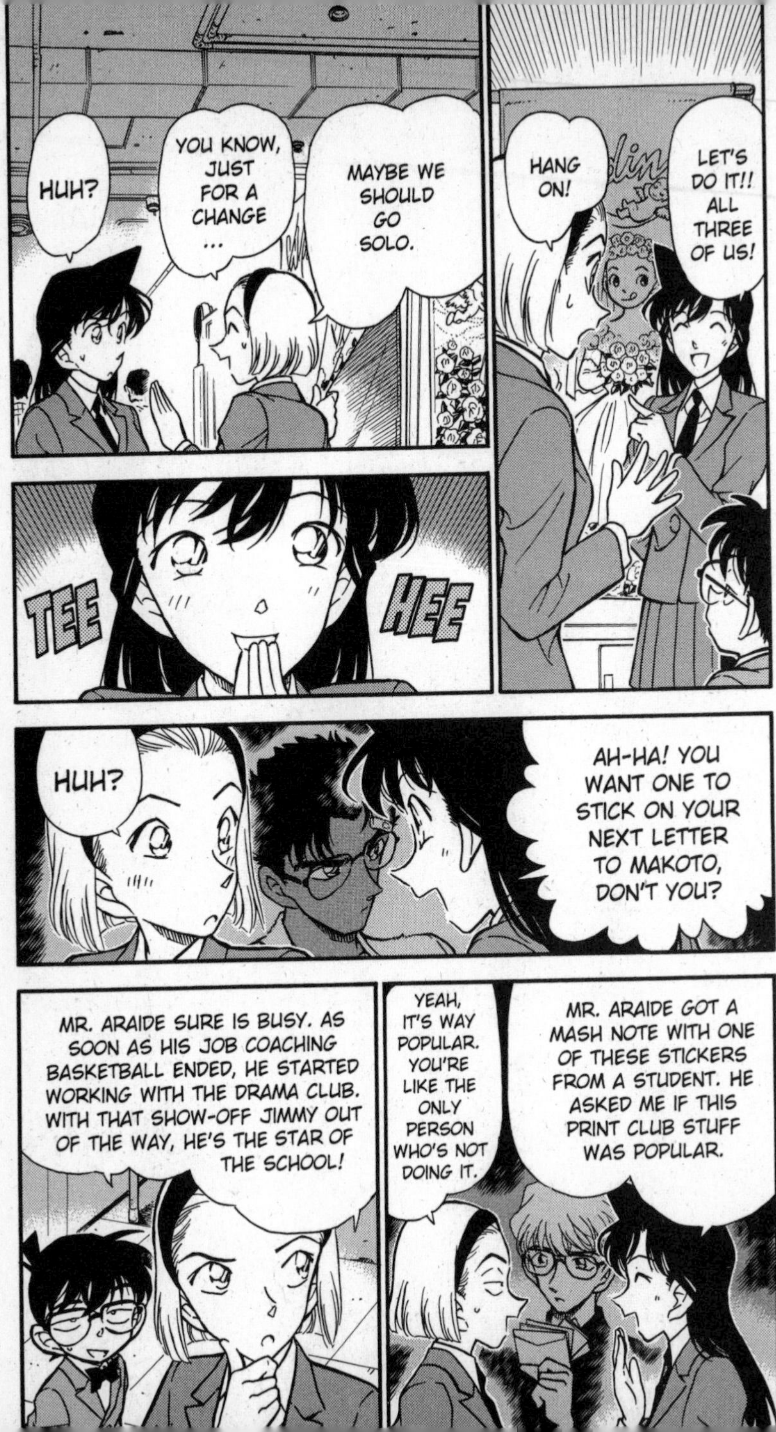
LET'S DO IT!! ALL THREE OF US!
HANG ON!
MAYBE WE SHOULD GO SOLO.
YOU KNOW, JUST FOR A CHANGE ...
HUH?
TEE
HEE
AH-HA! YOU WANT ONE TO STICK ON YOUR NEXT LETTER TO MAKOTO, DON'T YOU?
HUH?
MR. ARAIDE GOT A MASH NOTE WITH ONE OF THESE STICKERS FROM A STUDENT. HE ASKED ME IF THIS PRINT CLUB STUFF WAS POPULAR.
YEAH, IT'S WAY POPULAR. YOU'RE LIKE THE ONLY PERSON WHO'S NOT DOING IT.
MR. ARAIDE SURE IS BUSY. AS SOON AS HIS JOB COACHING BASKETBALL ENDED, HE STARTED WORKING WITH THE DRAMA CLUB. WITH THAT SHOW-OFF JIMMY OUT OF THE WAY, HE'S THE STAR OF THE SCHOOL!

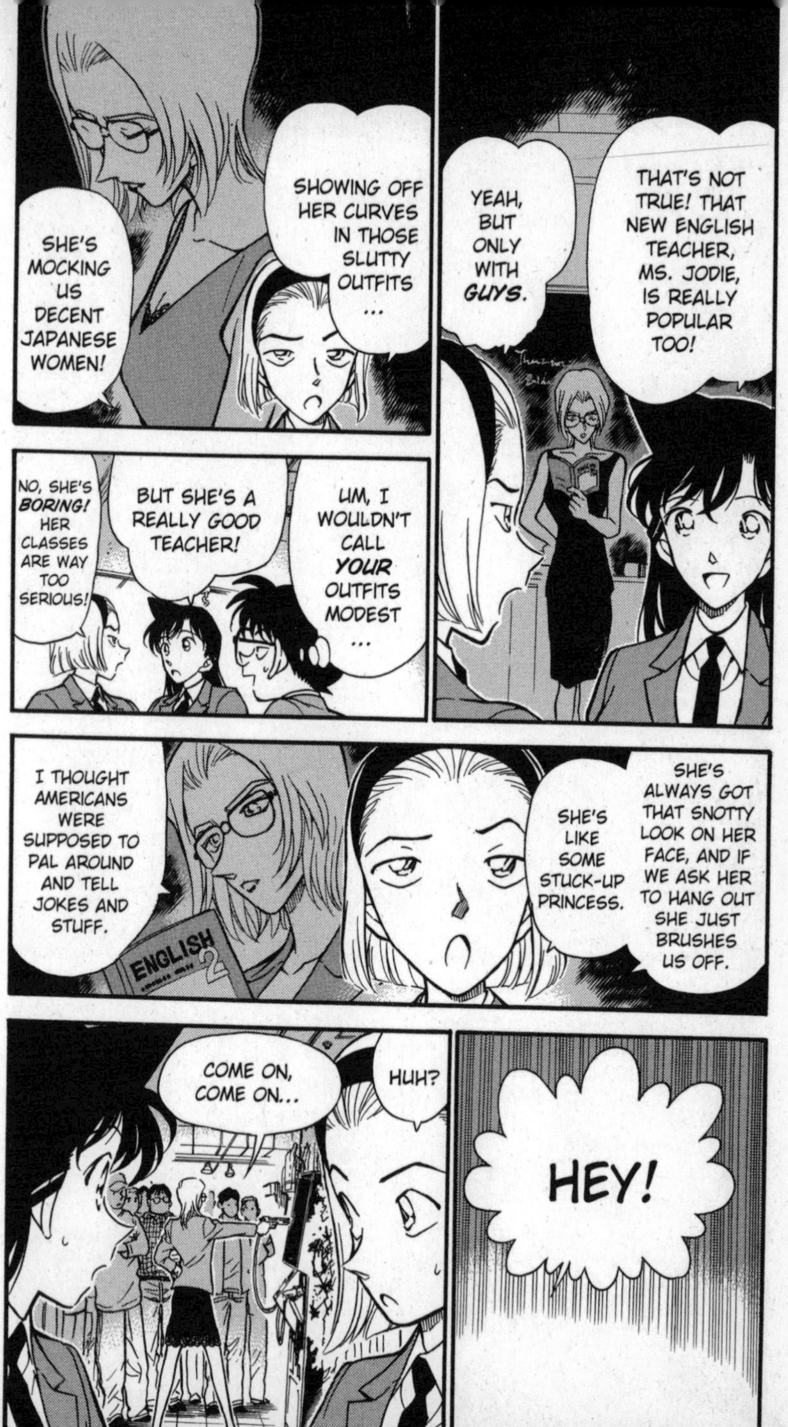
THAT'S NOT TRUE! THAT NEW ENGLISH TEACHER, MS. JODIE, IS REALLY POPULAR TOO!
YEAH, BUT ONLY WITH **GUYS**.
SHOWING OFF HER CURVES IN THOSE SLUTTY OUTFITS ...
SHE'S MOCKING US DECENT JAPANESE WOMEN!
UM, I WOULDN'T CALL **YOUR** OUTFITS MODEST ...
BUT SHE'S A REALLY GOOD TEACHER!
NO, SHE'S **BORING!** HER CLASSES ARE WAY TOO SERIOUS!
SHE'S ALWAYS GOT THAT SNOTTY LOOK ON HER FACE, AND IF WE ASK HER TO HANG OUT SHE JUST BRUSHES US OFF.
SHE'S LIKE SOME STUCK-UP PRINCESS.
I THOUGHT AMERICANS WERE SUPPOSED TO PAL AROUND AND TELL JOKES AND STUFF.
ENGLISH
HEY!
HUH?
COME ON, COME ON...

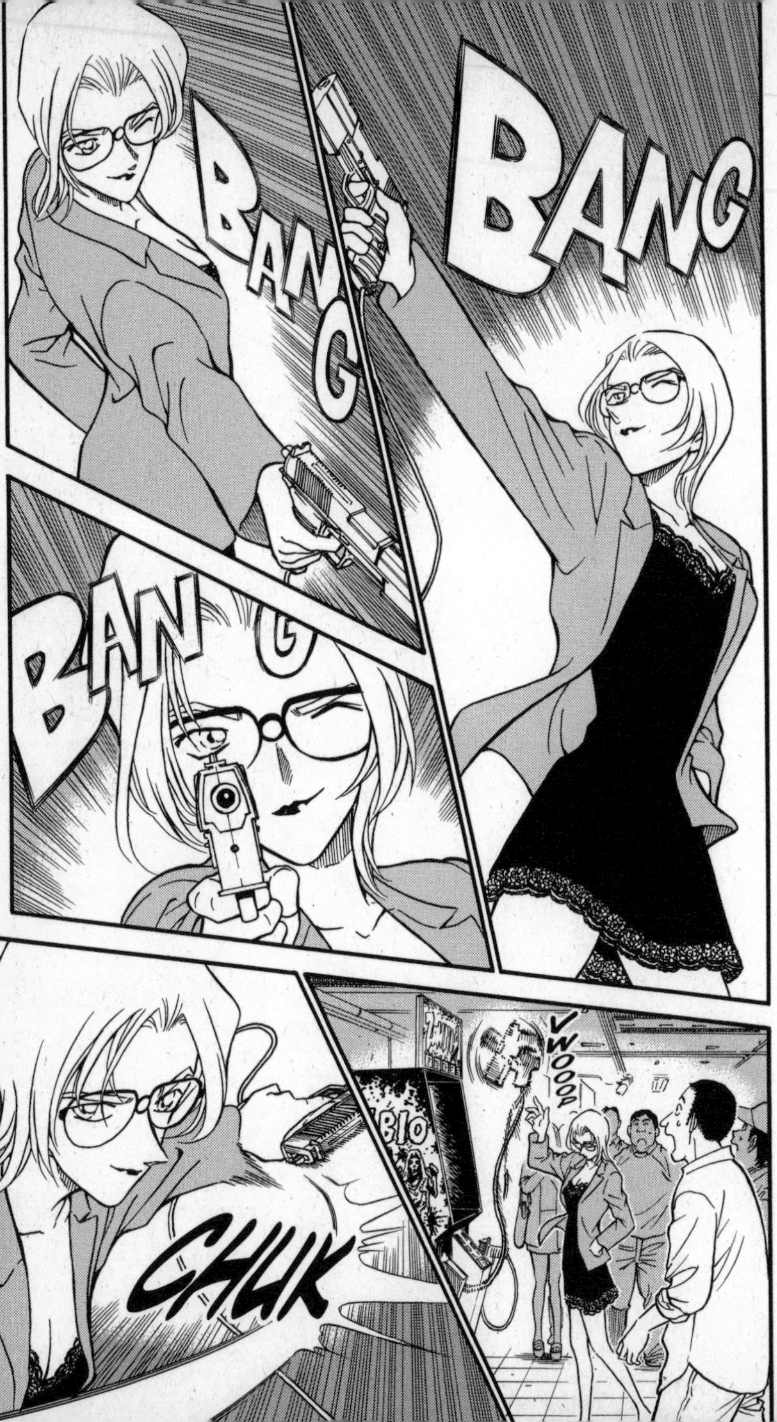
BANG
BANG
BANG
VWOOOP
CHUK

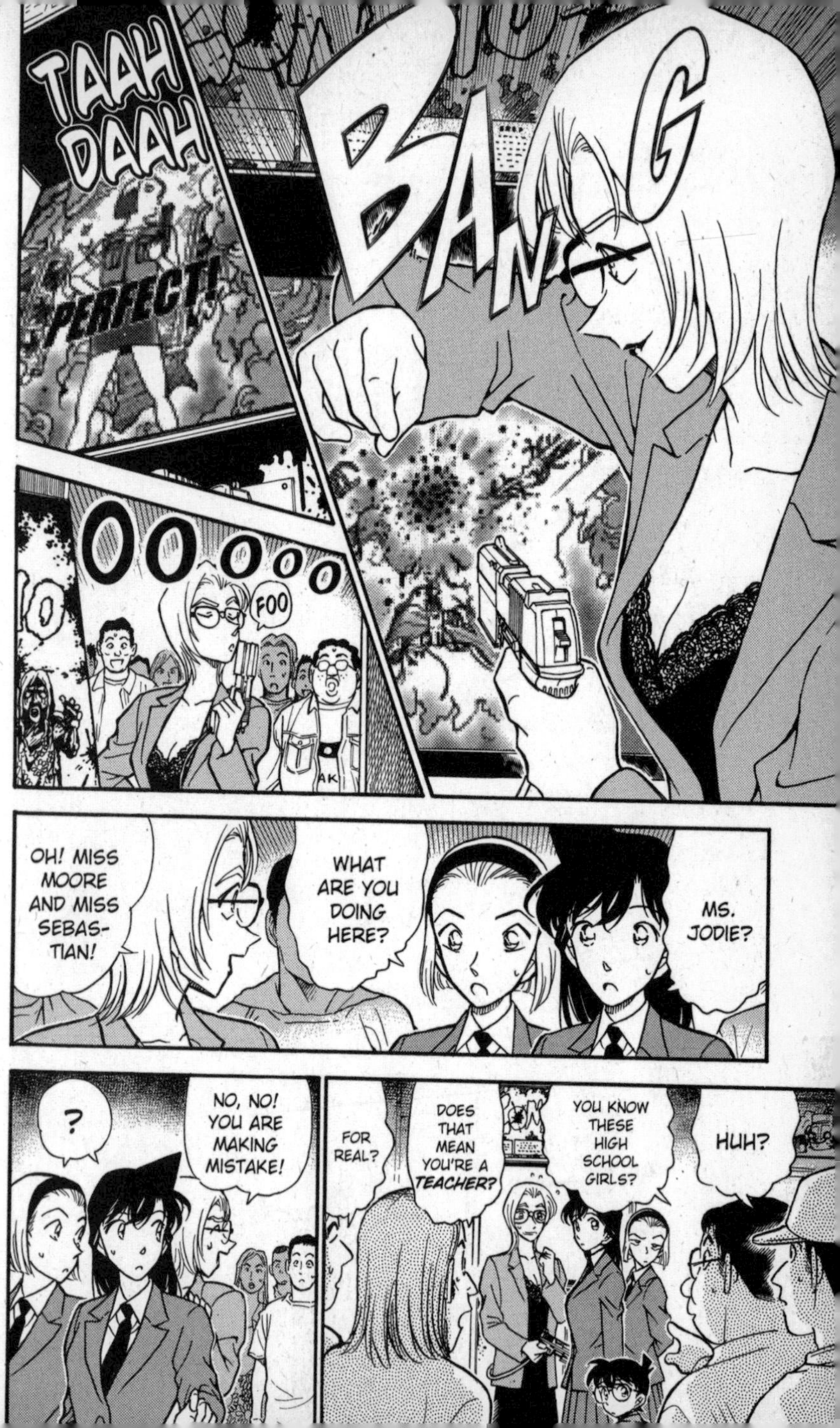
BANG
TAAH DAAH
PERFECT!
OOOOOO
FOO
MS. JODIE?
WHAT ARE YOU DOING HERE?
OH! MISS MOORE AND MISS SEBAS-TIAN!
HUH?
YOU KNOW THESE HIGH SCHOOL GIRLS?
DOES THAT MEAN YOU'RE A *TEACHER*?
FOR REAL?
NO, NO! YOU ARE MAKING MISTAKE!
?

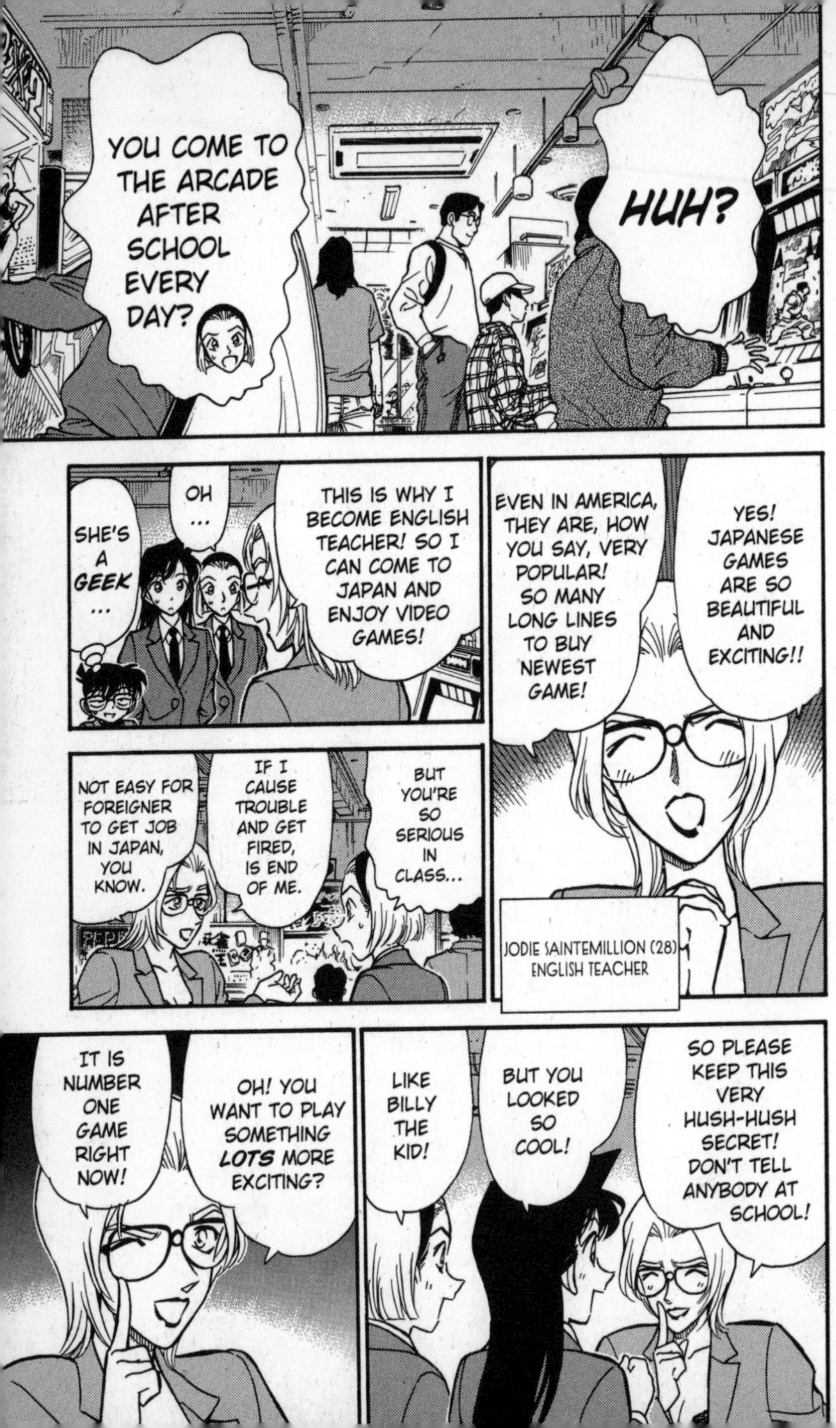

HUH?
YOU COME TO THE ARCADE AFTER SCHOOL EVERY DAY?
YES! JAPANESE GAMES ARE SO BEAUTIFUL AND EXCITING!!
EVEN IN AMERICA, THEY ARE, HOW YOU SAY, VERY POPULAR! SO MANY LONG LINES TO BUY NEWEST GAME!
JODIE SAINTEMILLION (28) ENGLISH TEACHER
THIS IS WHY I BECOME ENGLISH TEACHER! SO I CAN COME TO JAPAN AND ENJOY VIDEO GAMES!
OH ...
SHE'S A **GEEK** ...
BUT YOU'RE SO SERIOUS IN CLASS...
IF I CAUSE TROUBLE AND GET FIRED, IS END OF ME.
NOT EASY FOR FOREIGNER TO GET JOB IN JAPAN, YOU KNOW.
SO PLEASE KEEP THIS VERY HUSH-HUSH SECRET! DON'T TELL ANYBODY AT SCHOOL!
BUT YOU LOOKED SO COOL!
LIKE BILLY THE KID!
OH! YOU WANT TO PLAY SOMETHING **LOTS** MORE EXCITING?
IT IS NUMBER ONE GAME RIGHT NOW!

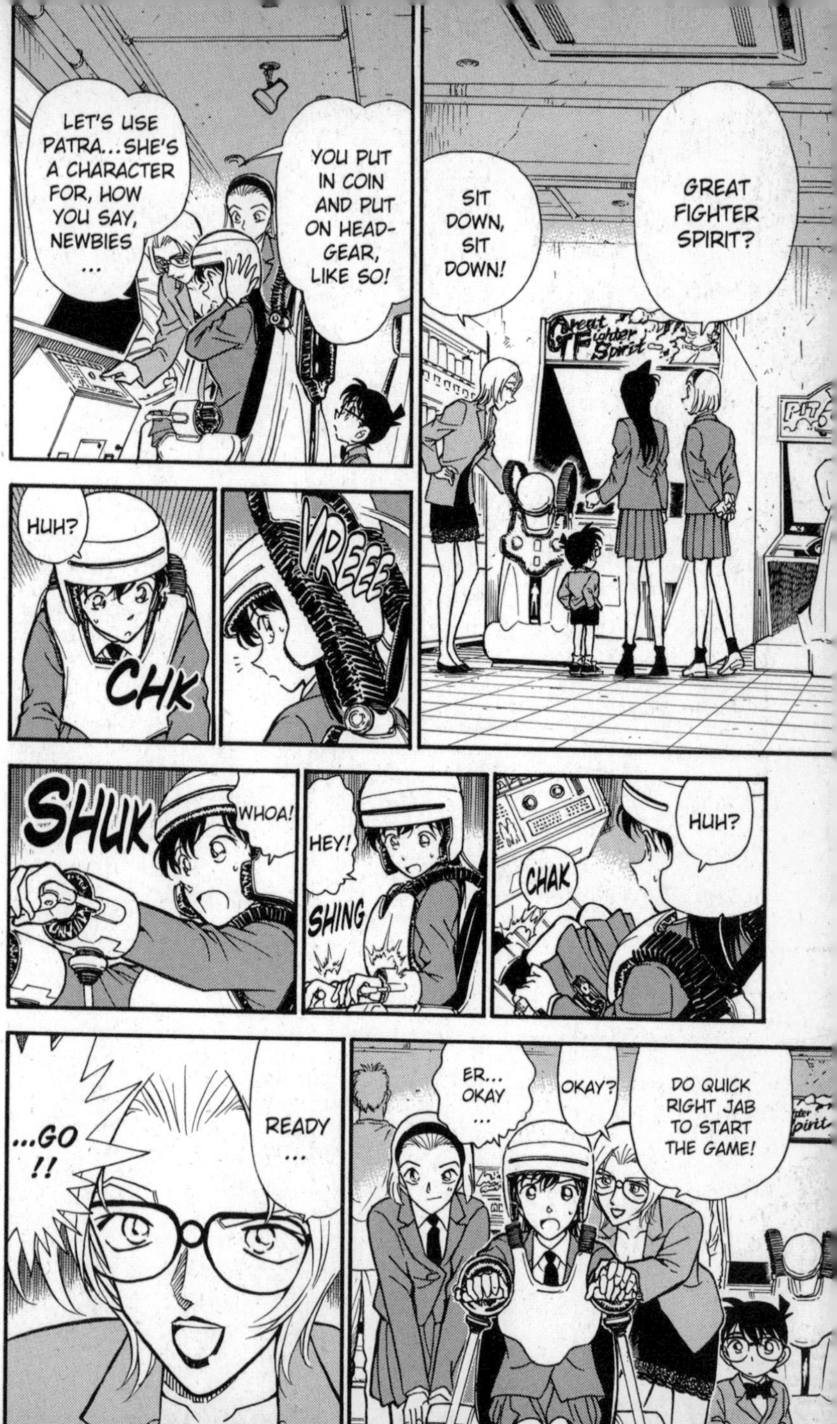
GREAT FIGHTER SPIRIT?
SIT DOWN, SIT DOWN!
Great Fighter Spirit
PIT
YOU PUT IN COIN AND PUT ON HEAD-GEAR, LIKE SO!
LET'S USE PATRA...SHE'S A CHARACTER FOR, HOW YOU SAY, NEWBIES ...
VREEEE
HUH?
CHK
HUH?
CHAK
HEY!
SHING
WHOA!
SHUK
DO QUICK RIGHT JAB TO START THE GAME!
OKAY?
ER... OKAY ...
READY ...
...GO !!

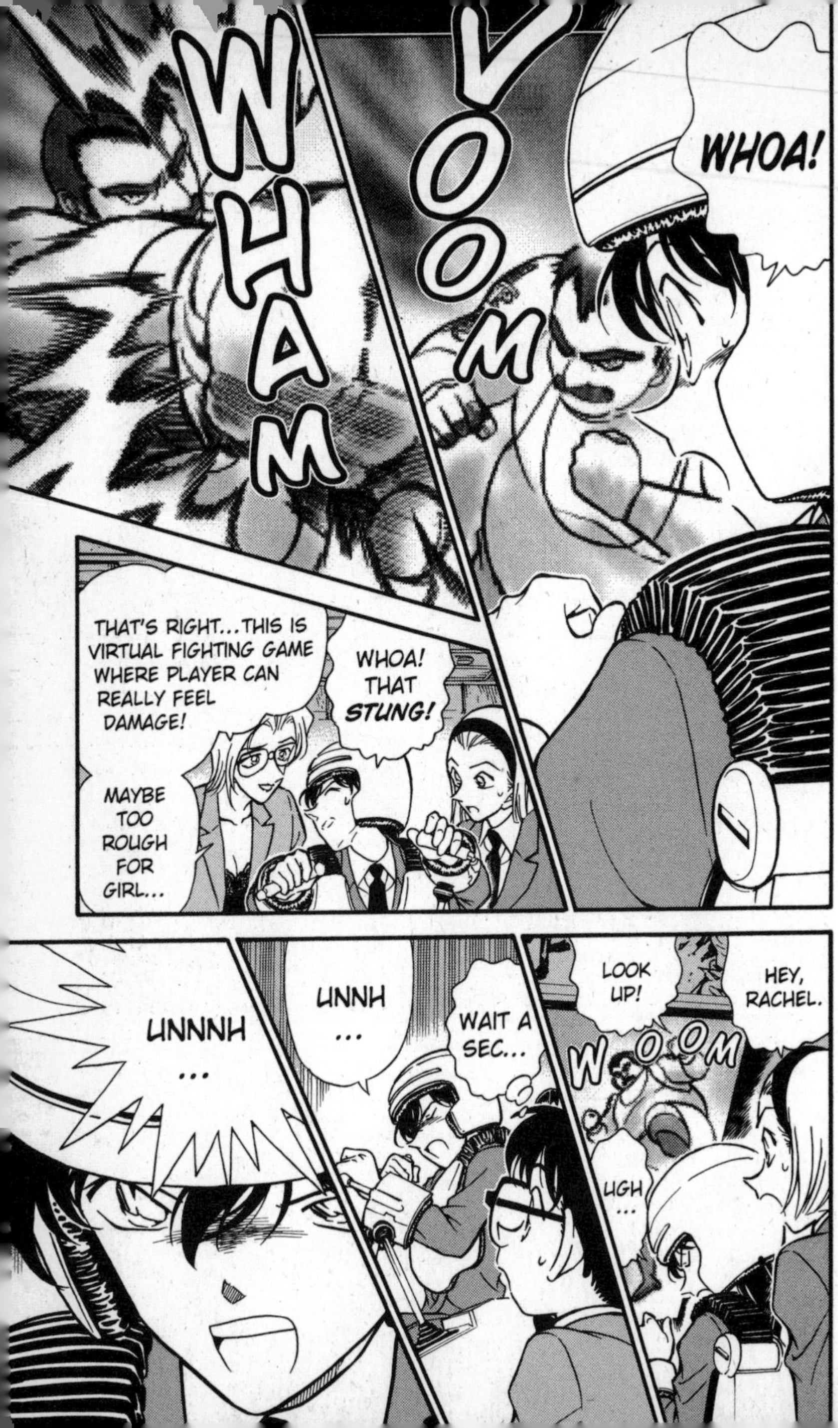
WHOA!
VOOM
WHAM
WHOA! THAT STUNG!
THAT'S RIGHT... THIS IS VIRTUAL FIGHTING GAME WHERE PLAYER CAN REALLY FEEL DAMAGE!
MAYBE TOO ROUGH FOR GIRL...
HEY, RACHEL.
LOOK UP!
WOOM
UGH...
WAIT A SEC...
UNNH...
UNNNH...

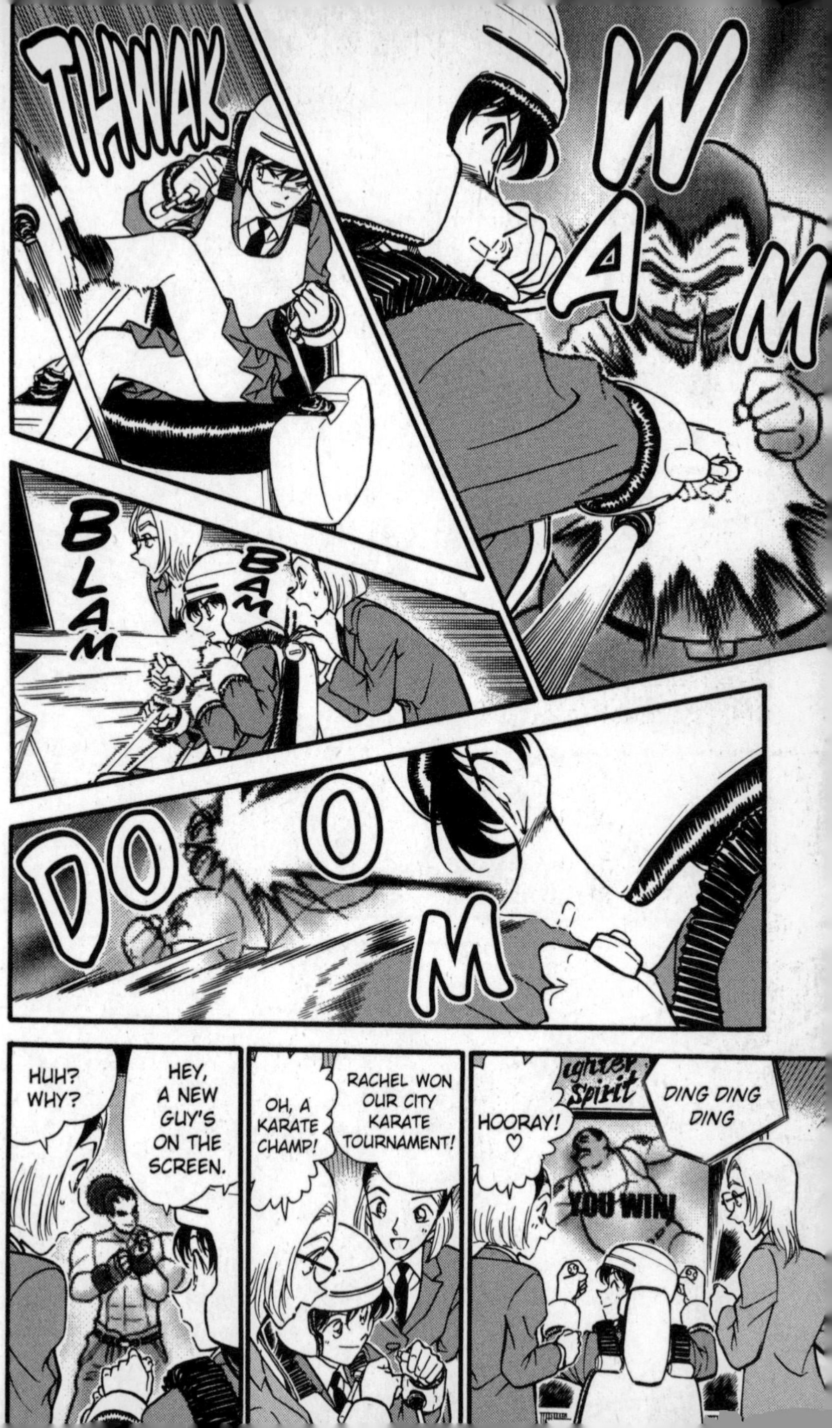
WAM
THWAK
BLAM
BAM
DOOM
DING DING DING
Spirit
HOORAY! ♡
YOU WIN!
RACHEL WON OUR CITY KARATE TOURNAMENT!
OH, A KARATE CHAMP!
HEY, A NEW GUY'S ON THE SCREEN.
HUH? WHY?

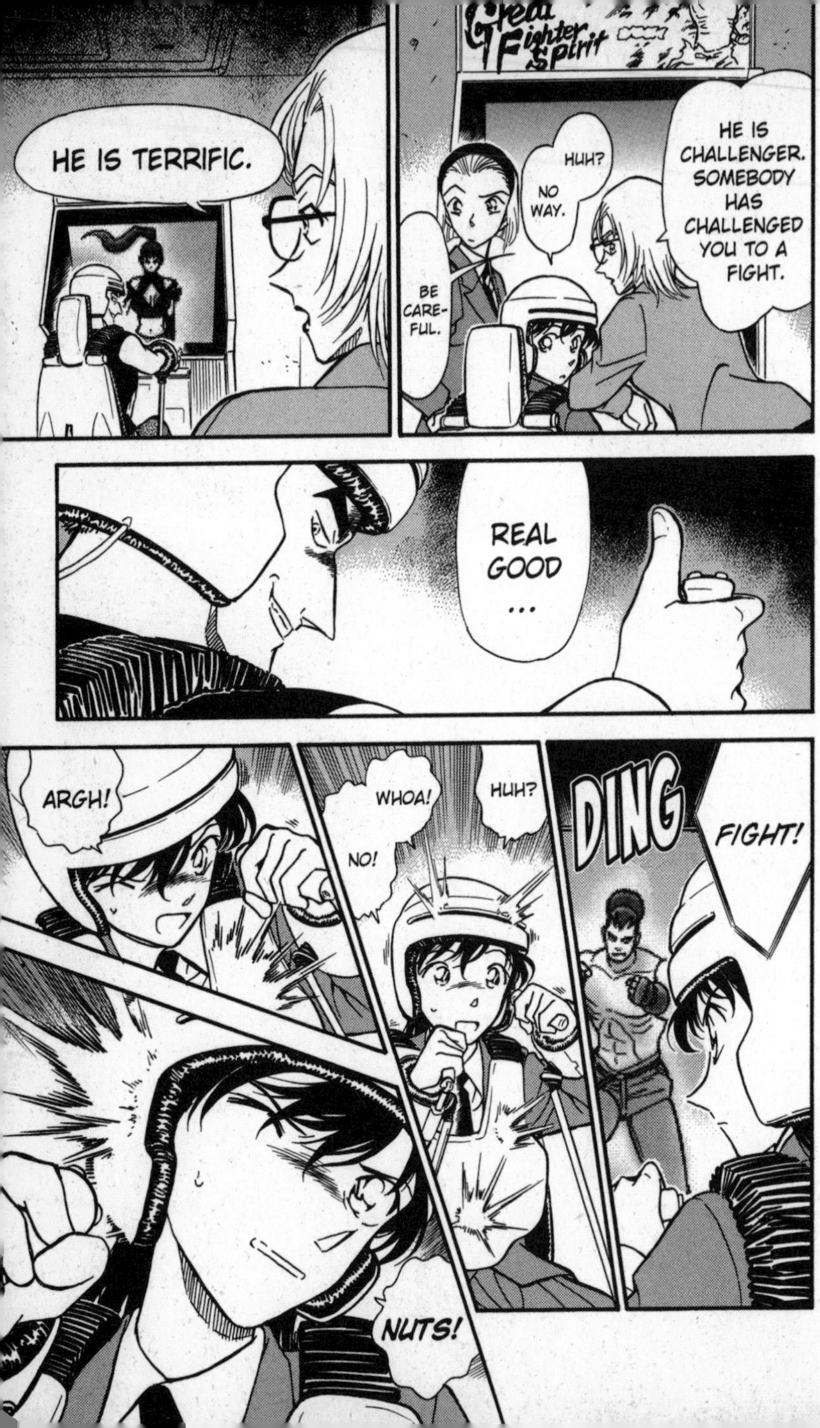
Great Fighter Spirit
HE IS CHALLENGER. SOMEBODY HAS CHALLENGED YOU TO A FIGHT.
HUH? NO WAY.
BE CARE-FUL.
HE IS TERRIFIC.
REAL GOOD ...
DING
FIGHT!
HUH?
WHOA!
NO!
ARGH!
NUTS!

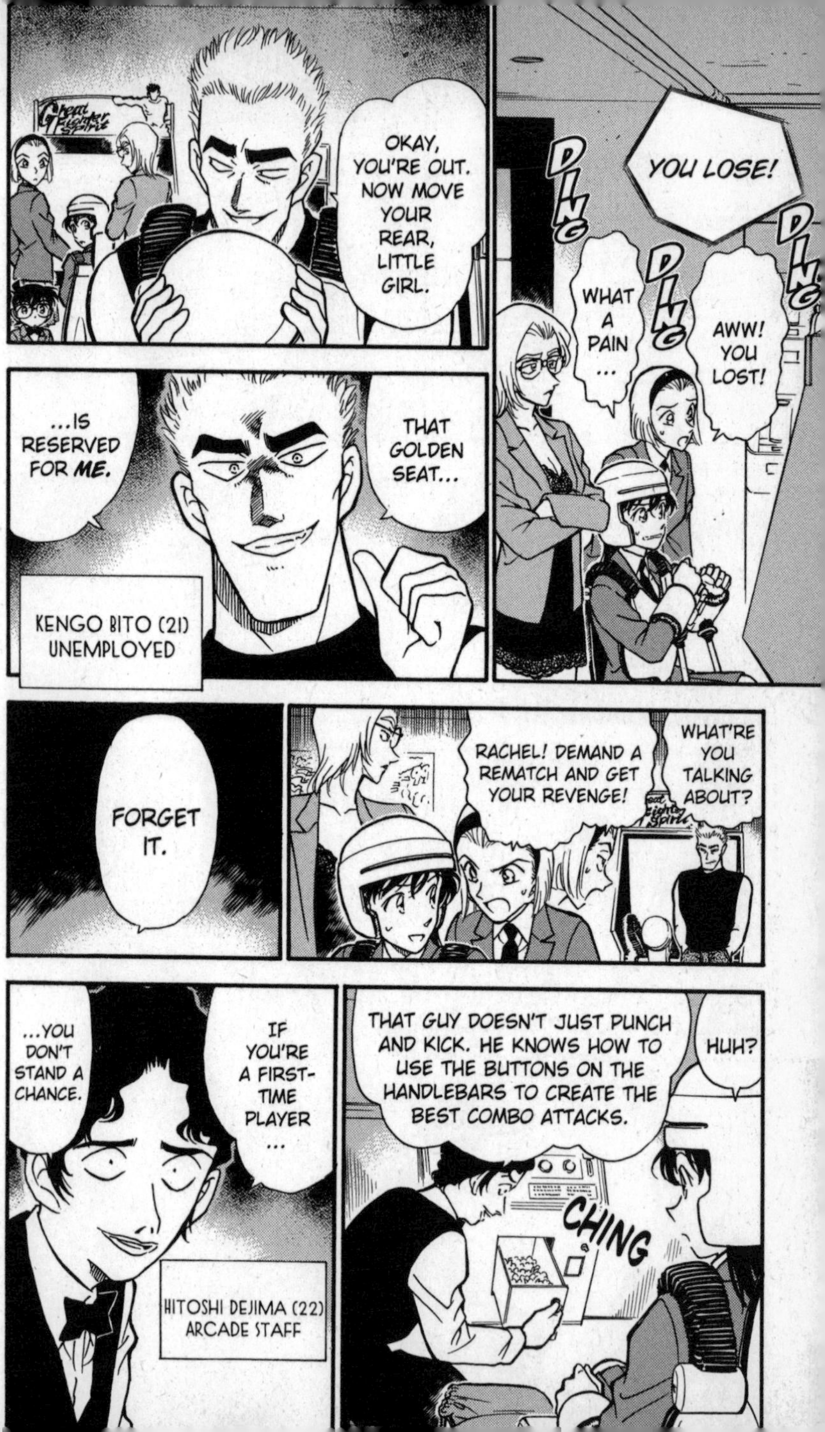
DING
YOU LOSE!
DING
AWW! YOU LOST!
DING
WHAT A PAIN ...
OKAY, YOU'RE OUT. NOW MOVE YOUR REAR, LITTLE GIRL.
THAT GOLDEN SEAT...
...IS RESERVED FOR ME.
KENGO BITO (21) UNEMPLOYED
WHAT'RE YOU TALKING ABOUT?
RACHEL! DEMAND A REMATCH AND GET YOUR REVENGE!
FORGET IT.
HUH?
THAT GUY DOESN'T JUST PUNCH AND KICK. HE KNOWS HOW TO USE THE BUTTONS ON THE HANDLEBARS TO CREATE THE BEST COMBO ATTACKS.
CHING
IF YOU'RE A FIRST-TIME PLAYER ...
...YOU DON'T STAND A CHANCE.
HITOSHI DEJIMA (22) ARCADE STAFF

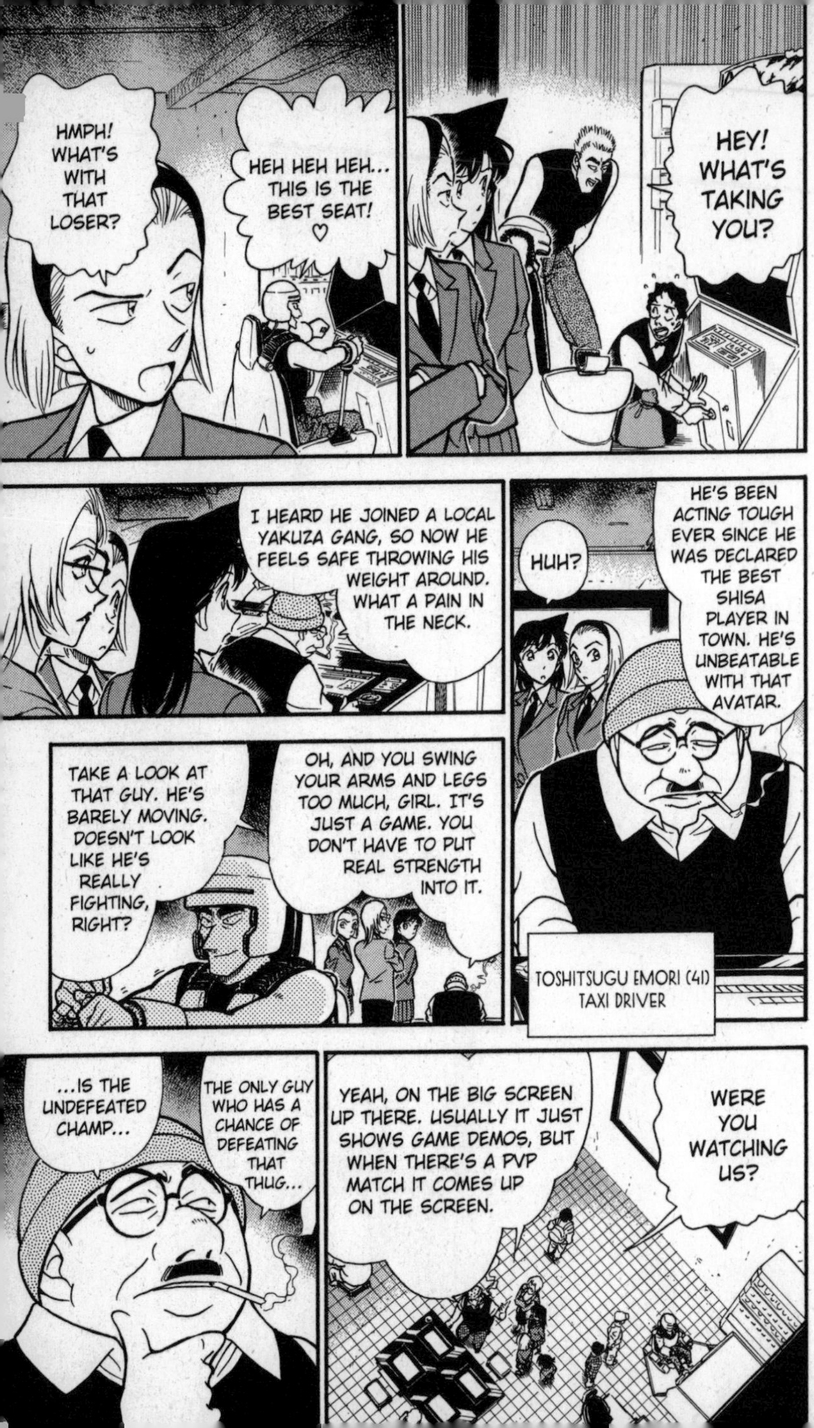
HEY! WHAT'S TAKING YOU?
HEH HEH HEH... THIS IS THE BEST SEAT! ♡
HMPH! WHAT'S WITH THAT LOSER?
HE'S BEEN ACTING TOUGH EVER SINCE HE WAS DECLARED THE BEST SHISA PLAYER IN TOWN. HE'S UNBEATABLE WITH THAT AVATAR.
HUH?
TOSHITSUGU EMORI (41) TAXI DRIVER
I HEARD HE JOINED A LOCAL YAKUZA GANG, SO NOW HE FEELS SAFE THROWING HIS WEIGHT AROUND. WHAT A PAIN IN THE NECK.
OH, AND YOU SWING YOUR ARMS AND LEGS TOO MUCH, GIRL. IT'S JUST A GAME. YOU DON'T HAVE TO PUT REAL STRENGTH INTO IT.
TAKE A LOOK AT THAT GUY. HE'S BARELY MOVING. DOESN'T LOOK LIKE HE'S REALLY FIGHTING, RIGHT?
WERE YOU WATCHING US?
YEAH, ON THE BIG SCREEN UP THERE. USUALLY IT JUST SHOWS GAME DEMOS, BUT WHEN THERE'S A PVP MATCH IT COMES UP ON THE SCREEN.
THE ONLY GUY WHO HAS A CHANCE OF DEFEATING THAT THUG...
...IS THE UNDEFEATED CHAMP...

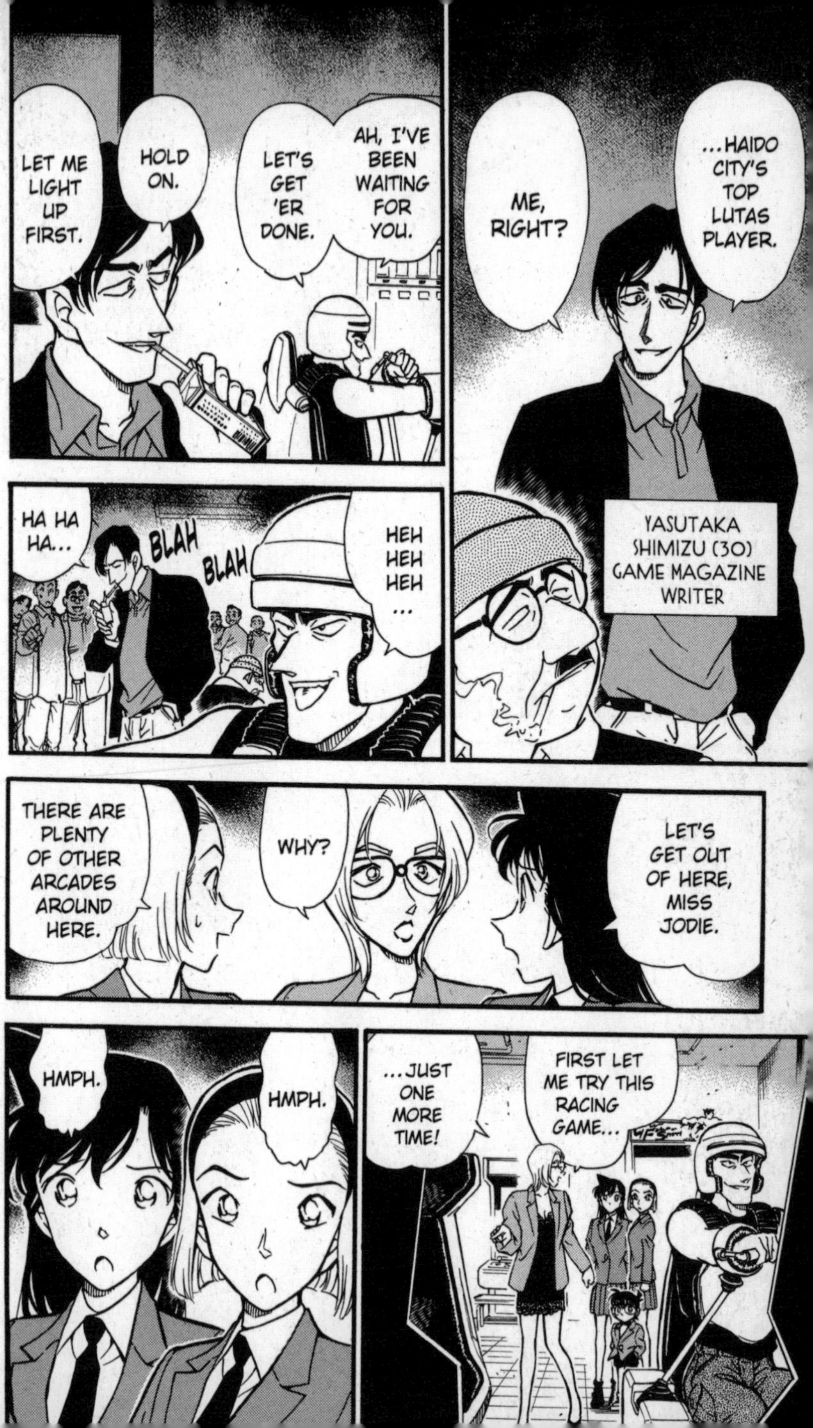
...HAIDO CITY'S TOP LUTAS PLAYER.
ME, RIGHT?
YASUTAKA SHIMIZU (30) GAME MAGAZINE WRITER
AH, I'VE BEEN WAITING FOR YOU.
LET'S GET 'ER DONE.
HOLD ON.
LET ME LIGHT UP FIRST.
HEH HEH HEH...
BLAH
BLAH
HA HA HA...
LET'S GET OUT OF HERE, MISS JODIE.
WHY?
THERE ARE PLENTY OF OTHER ARCADES AROUND HERE.
FIRST LET ME TRY THIS RACING GAME...
...JUST ONE MORE TIME!
HMPH.
HMPH.

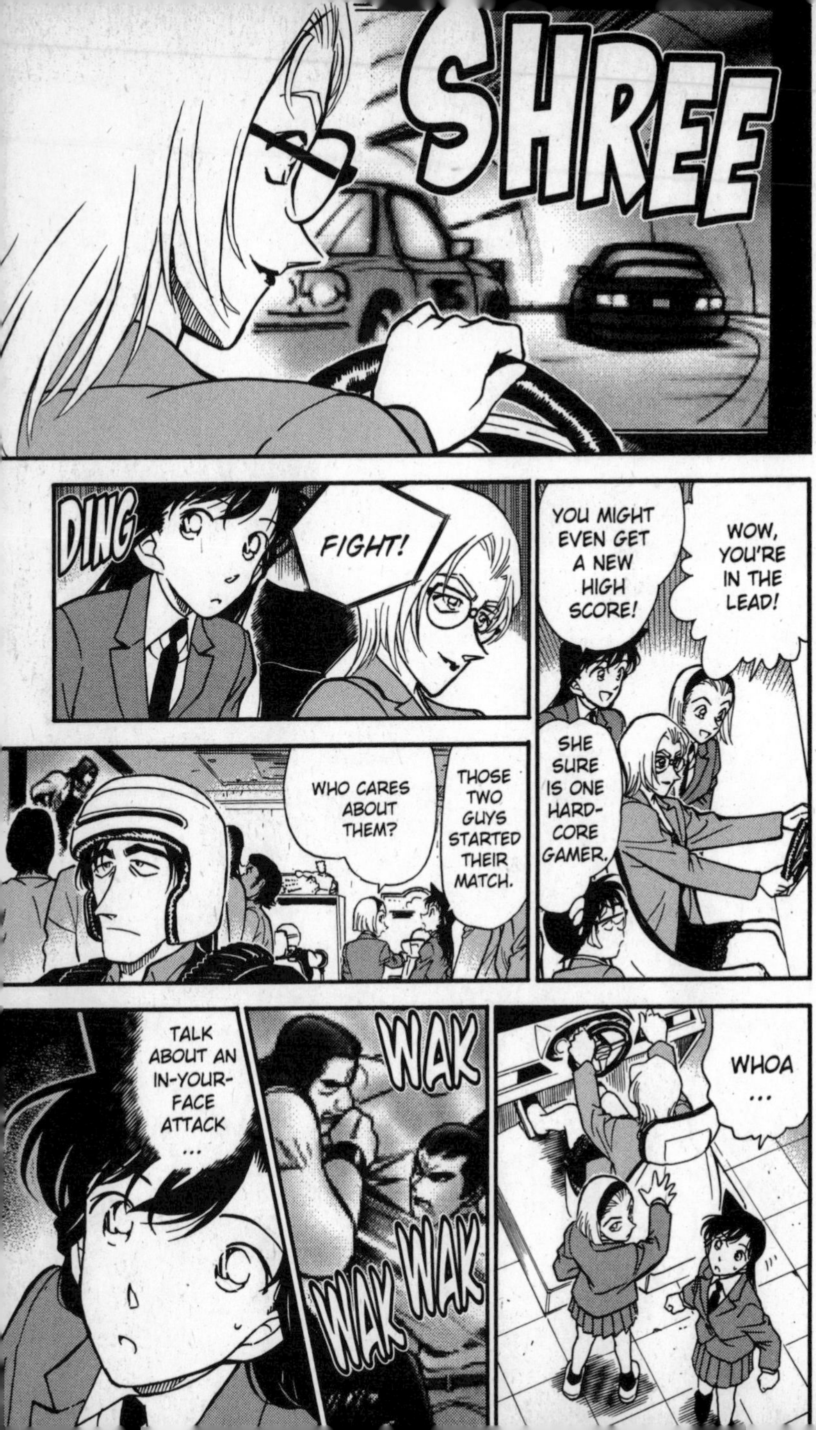
SHREE
WOW, YOU'RE IN THE LEAD!
YOU MIGHT EVEN GET A NEW HIGH SCORE!
SHE SURE IS ONE HARD-CORE GAMER.
DING
FIGHT!
THOSE TWO GUYS STARTED THEIR MATCH.
WHO CARES ABOUT THEM?
WHOA ...
WAK
WAK
WAK
TALK ABOUT AN IN-YOUR-FACE ATTACK ...

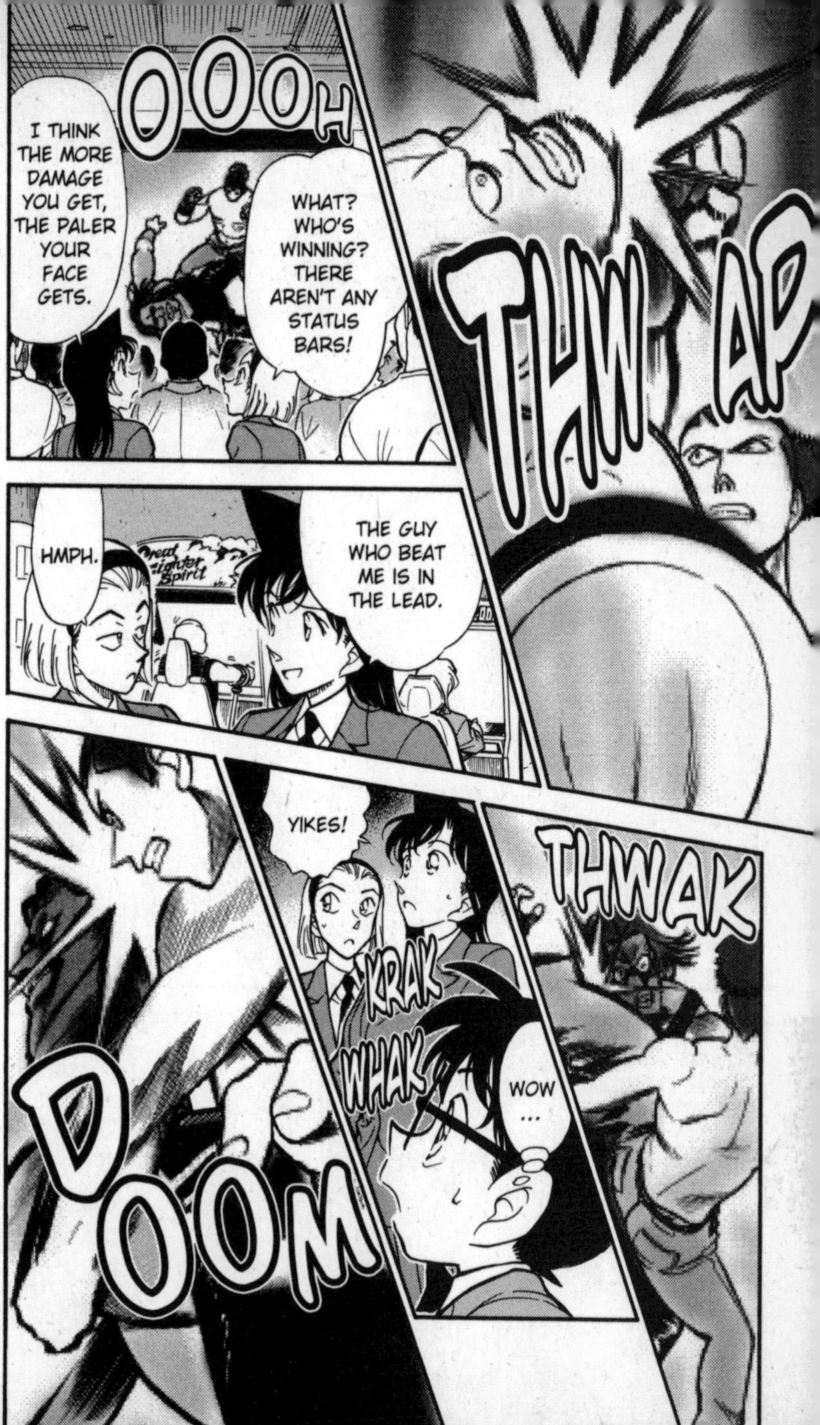
THWAP
OOOH
WHAT? WHO'S WINNING? THERE AREN'T ANY STATUS BARS!
I THINK THE MORE DAMAGE YOU GET, THE PALER YOUR FACE GETS.
THE GUY WHO BEAT ME IS IN THE LEAD.
HMPH.
Great Fighter Spirit
THWAK
YIKES!
KRAK
WHAK
WOW ...
DOOM

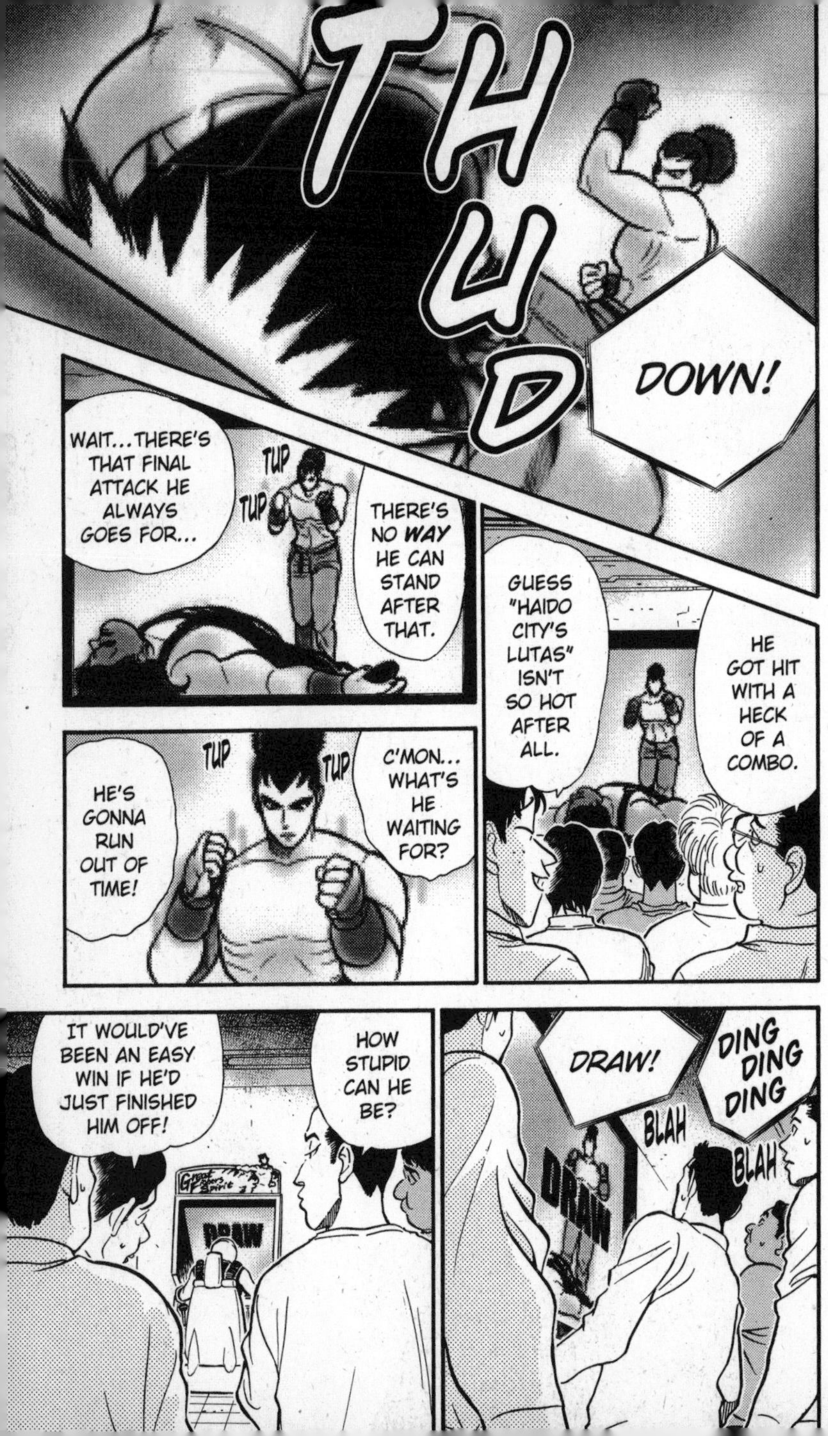
THUD
DOWN!
HE GOT HIT WITH A HECK OF A COMBO.
GUESS "HAIDO CITY'S LUTAS" ISN'T SO HOT AFTER ALL.
TUP
TUP
THERE'S NO ***WAY*** HE CAN STAND AFTER THAT.
WAIT...THERE'S THAT FINAL ATTACK HE ALWAYS GOES FOR...
C'MON... WHAT'S HE WAITING FOR?
TUP
TUP
HE'S GONNA RUN OUT OF TIME!
DING DING DING
DRAW!
BLAH
BLAH
HOW STUPID CAN HE BE?
IT WOULD'VE BEEN AN EASY WIN IF HE'D JUST FINISHED HIM OFF!

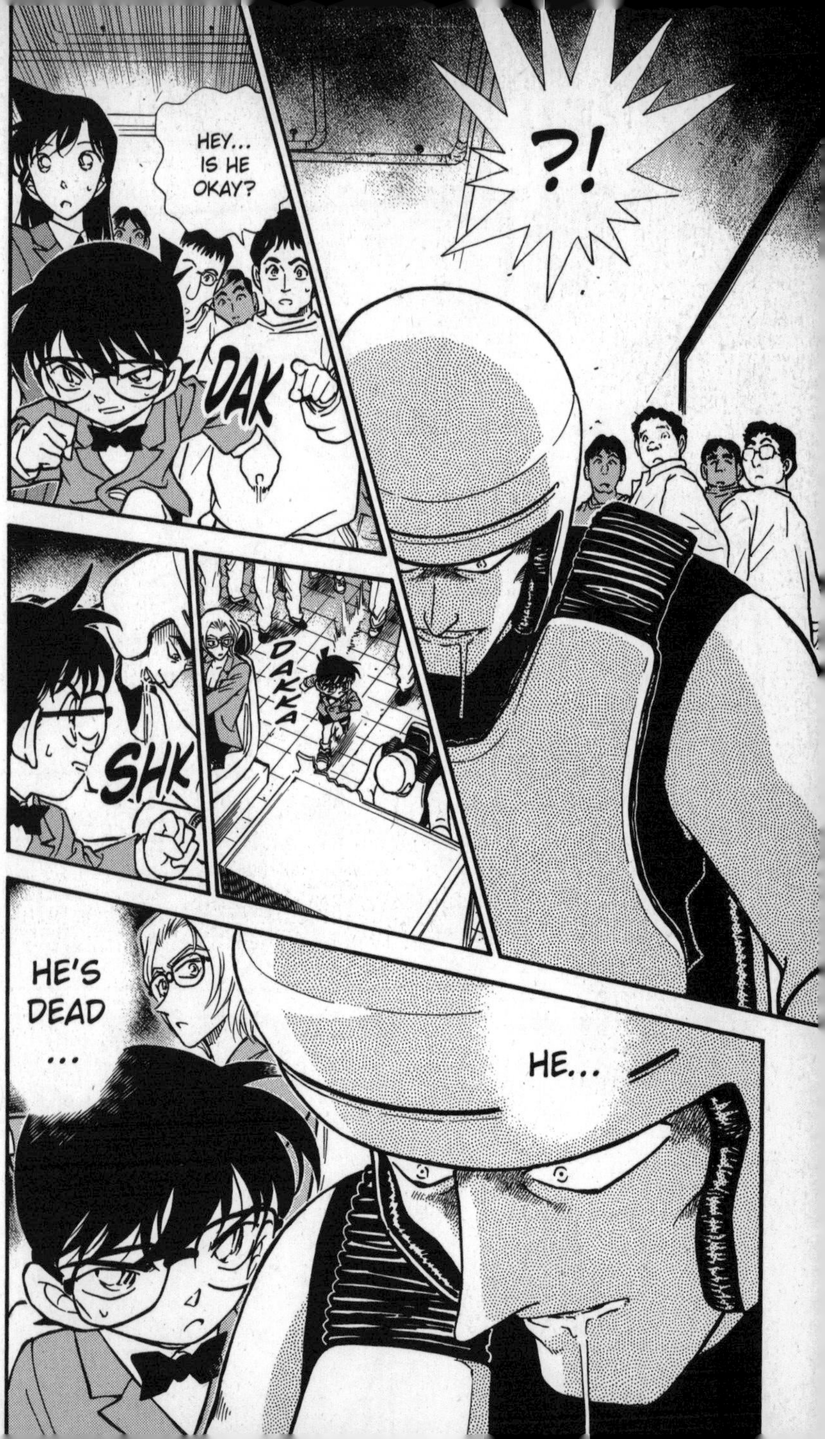
?!
HEY... IS HE OKAY?
DAK
DAKKA
SHK
HE...
HE'S DEAD ...

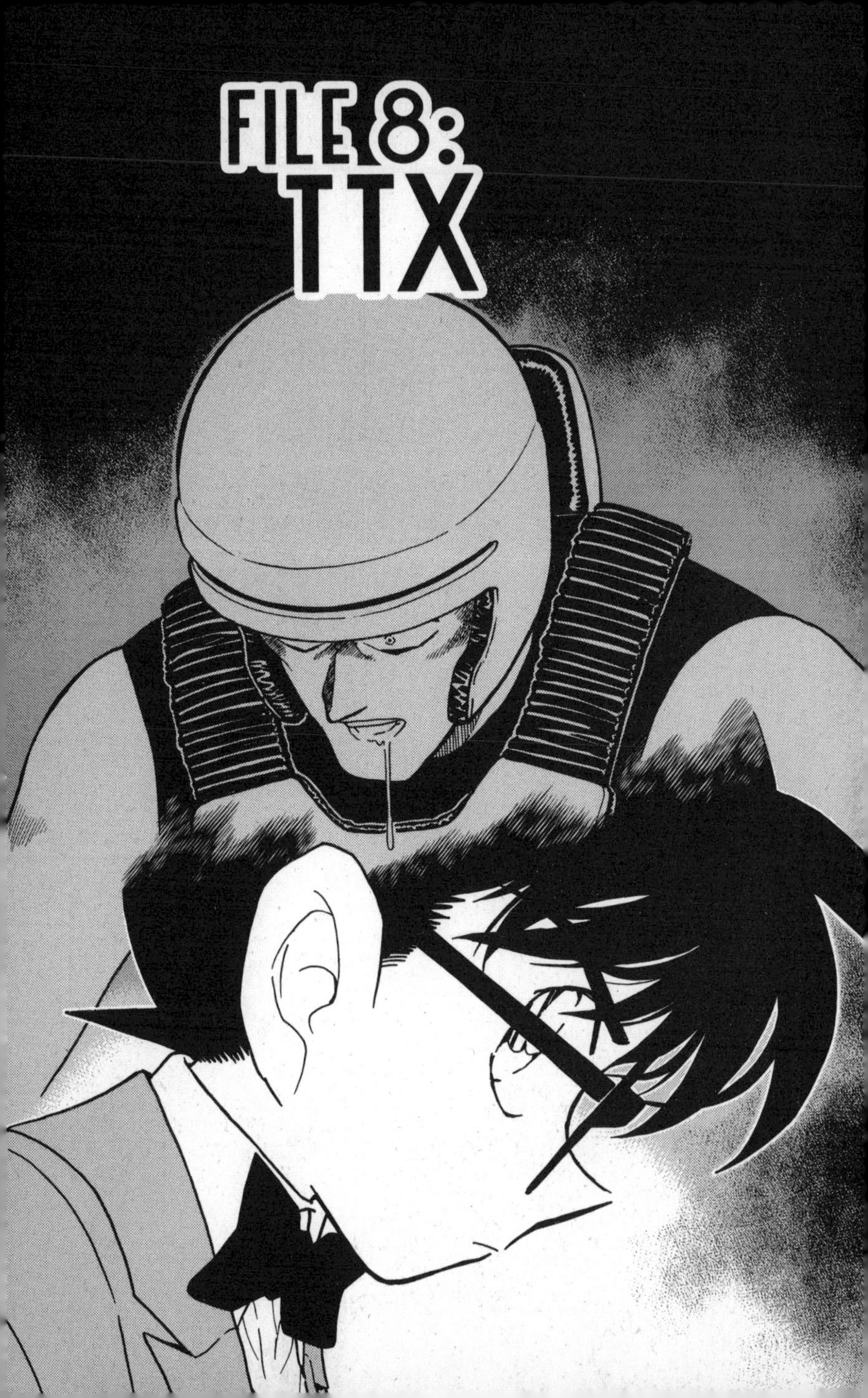
FILE 8:
TTX

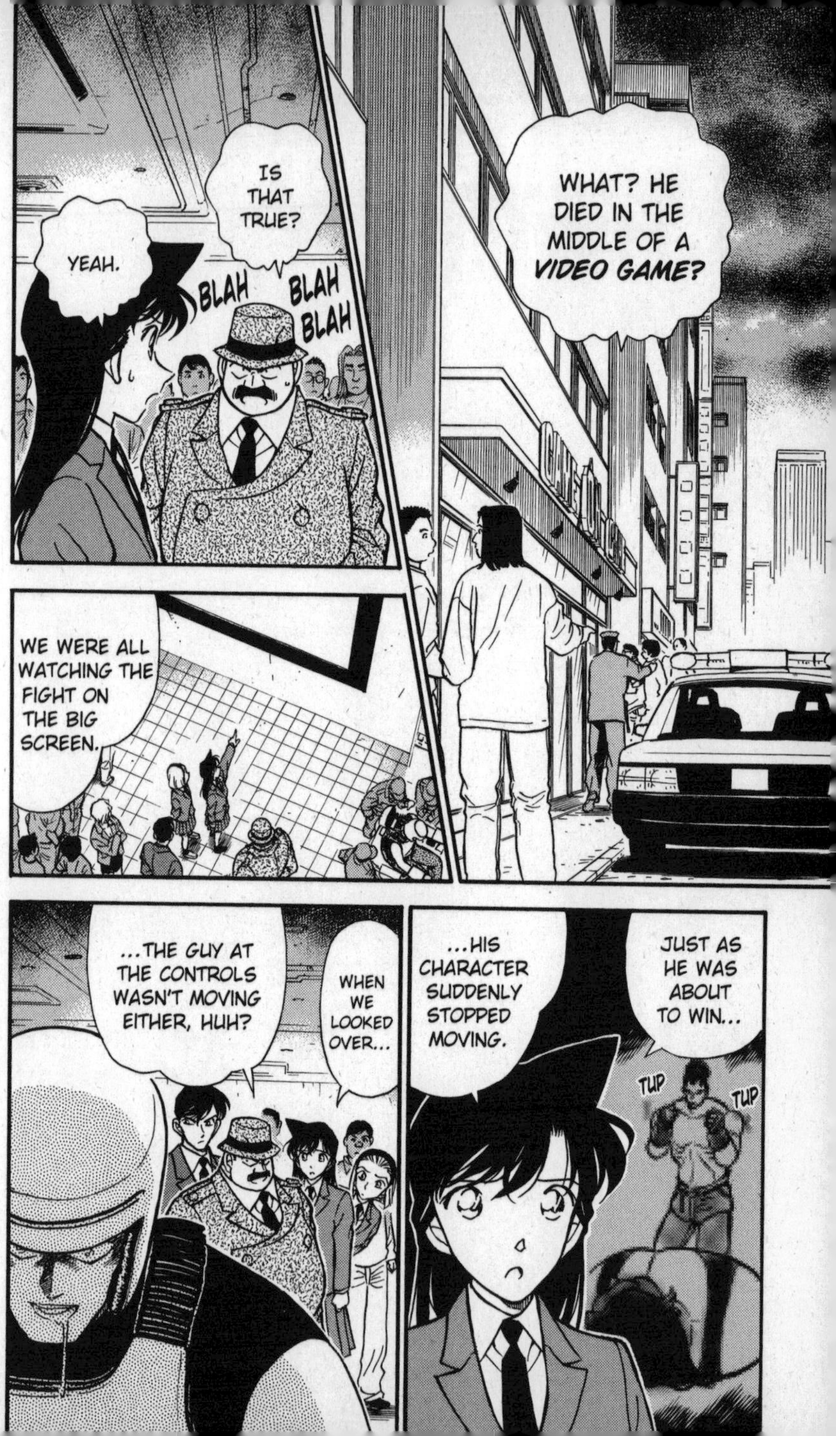
WHAT? HE DIED IN THE MIDDLE OF A *VIDEO GAME?*
IS THAT TRUE?
BLAH BLAH
BLAH
YEAH.
WE WERE ALL WATCHING THE FIGHT ON THE BIG SCREEN.
JUST AS HE WAS ABOUT TO WIN...
TUP
TUP
...HIS CHARACTER SUDDENLY STOPPED MOVING.
WHEN WE LOOKED OVER...
...THE GUY AT THE CONTROLS WASN'T MOVING EITHER, HUH?

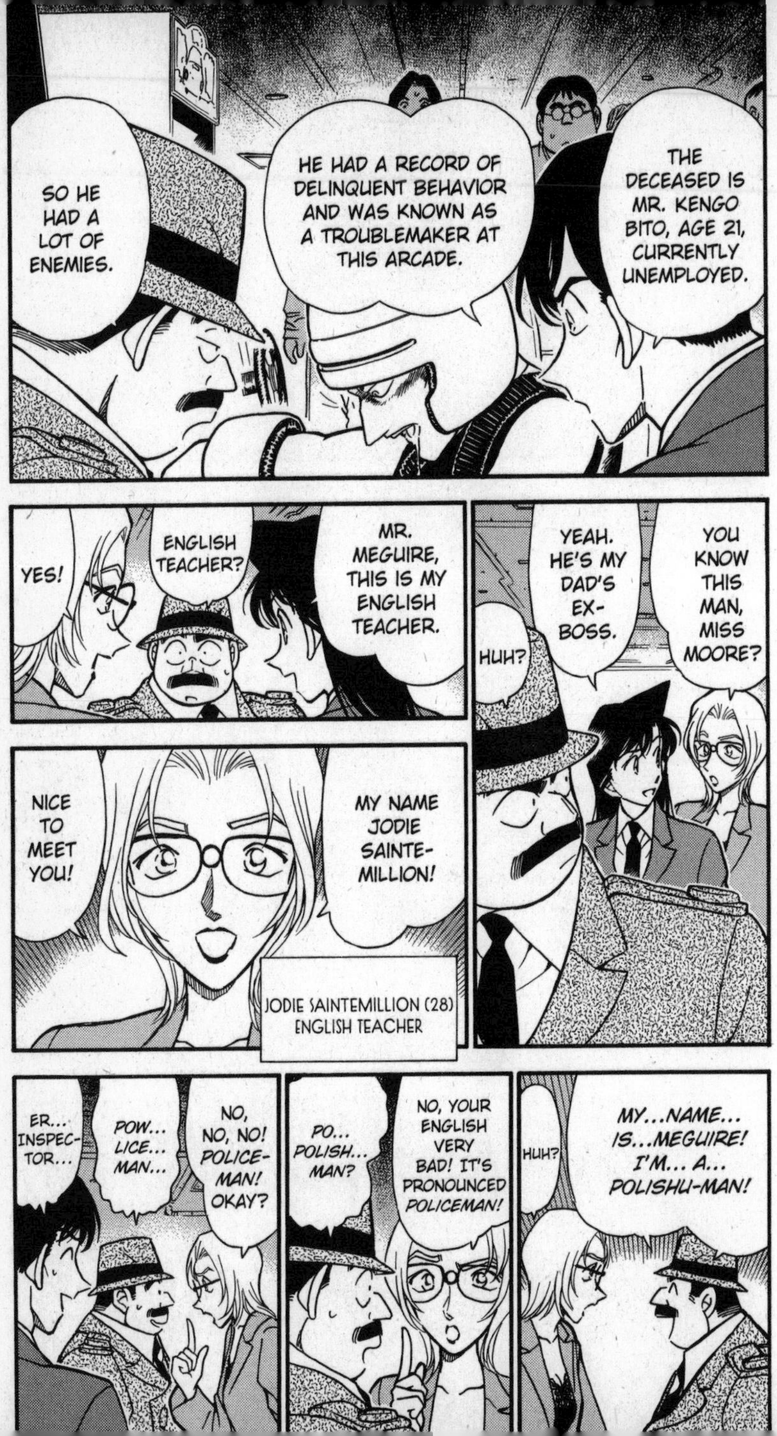
THE DECEASED IS MR. KENGO BITO, AGE 21, CURRENTLY UNEMPLOYED.
HE HAD A RECORD OF DELINQUENT BEHAVIOR AND WAS KNOWN AS A TROUBLEMAKER AT THIS ARCADE.
SO HE HAD A LOT OF ENEMIES.
YOU KNOW THIS MAN, MISS MOORE?
YEAH. HE'S MY DAD'S EX-BOSS.
HUH?
MR. MEGUIRE, THIS IS MY ENGLISH TEACHER.
ENGLISH TEACHER?
YES!
MY NAME JODIE SAINTE-MILLION!
NICE TO MEET YOU!
JODIE SAINTEMILLION (28) ENGLISH TEACHER
MY...NAME... IS...MEGUIRE! I'M... A... POLISHU-MAN!
HUH?
NO, YOUR ENGLISH VERY BAD! IT'S PRONOUNCED *POLICEMAN!*
PO... POLISH... MAN?
NO, NO, NO! *POLICE-MAN!* OKAY?
POW... LICE... MAN...
ER... INSPECTOR...

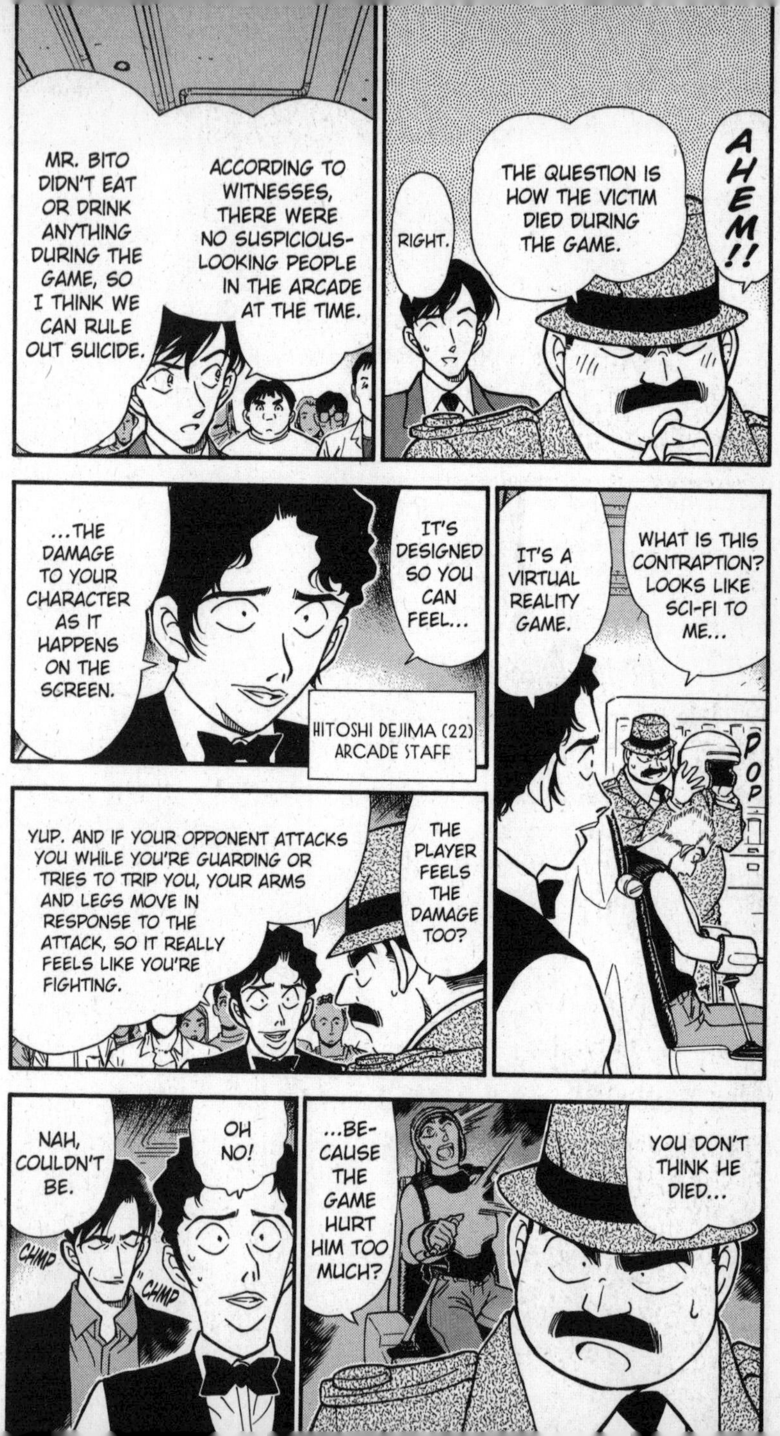
AHEM!!
THE QUESTION IS HOW THE VICTIM DIED DURING THE GAME.
RIGHT.
ACCORDING TO WITNESSES, THERE WERE NO SUSPICIOUS-LOOKING PEOPLE IN THE ARCADE AT THE TIME.
MR. BITO DIDN'T EAT OR DRINK ANYTHING DURING THE GAME, SO I THINK WE CAN RULE OUT SUICIDE.
WHAT IS THIS CONTRAPTION? LOOKS LIKE SCI-FI TO ME...
IT'S A VIRTUAL REALITY GAME.
POP
IT'S DESIGNED SO YOU CAN FEEL...
...THE DAMAGE TO YOUR CHARACTER AS IT HAPPENS ON THE SCREEN.
HITOSHI DEJIMA (22) ARCADE STAFF
THE PLAYER FEELS THE DAMAGE TOO?
YUP. AND IF YOUR OPPONENT ATTACKS YOU WHILE YOU'RE GUARDING OR TRIES TO TRIP YOU, YOUR ARMS AND LEGS MOVE IN RESPONSE TO THE ATTACK, SO IT REALLY FEELS LIKE YOU'RE FIGHTING.
YOU DON'T THINK HE DIED...
...BE-CAUSE THE GAME HURT HIM TOO MUCH?
OH NO!
NAH, COULDN'T BE.
CHMP
CHMP

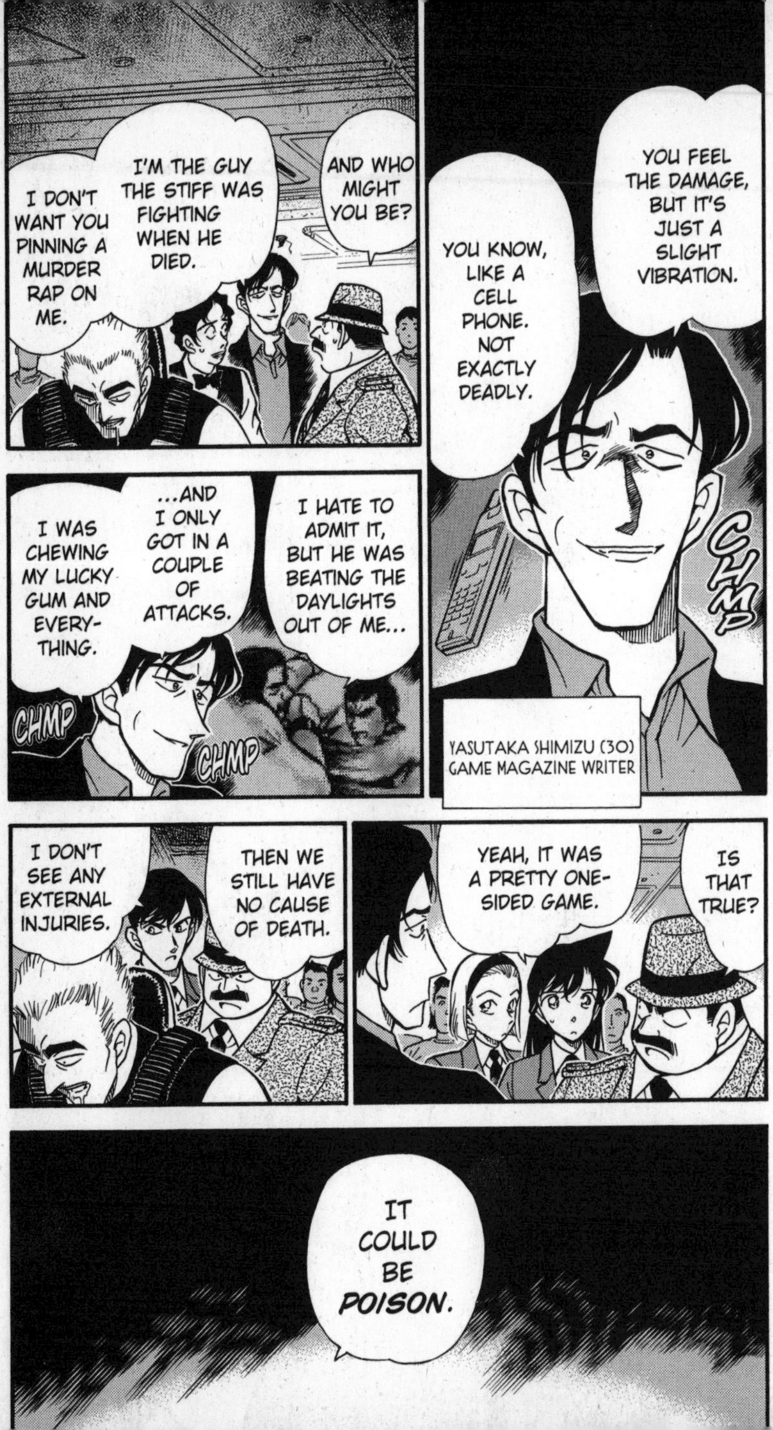
YOU FEEL THE DAMAGE, BUT IT'S JUST A SLIGHT VIBRATION.
YOU KNOW, LIKE A CELL PHONE. NOT EXACTLY DEADLY.
CHMP
YASUTAKA SHIMIZU (30) GAME MAGAZINE WRITER
AND WHO MIGHT YOU BE?
I'M THE GUY THE STIFF WAS FIGHTING WHEN HE DIED.
I DON'T WANT YOU PINNING A MURDER RAP ON ME.
I HATE TO ADMIT IT, BUT HE WAS BEATING THE DAYLIGHTS OUT OF ME...
...AND I ONLY GOT IN A COUPLE OF ATTACKS.
I WAS CHEWING MY LUCKY GUM AND EVERY-THING.
CHMP
CHMP
IS THAT TRUE?
YEAH, IT WAS A PRETTY ONE-SIDED GAME.
THEN WE STILL HAVE NO CAUSE OF DEATH.
I DON'T SEE ANY EXTERNAL INJURIES.
IT COULD BE POISON.

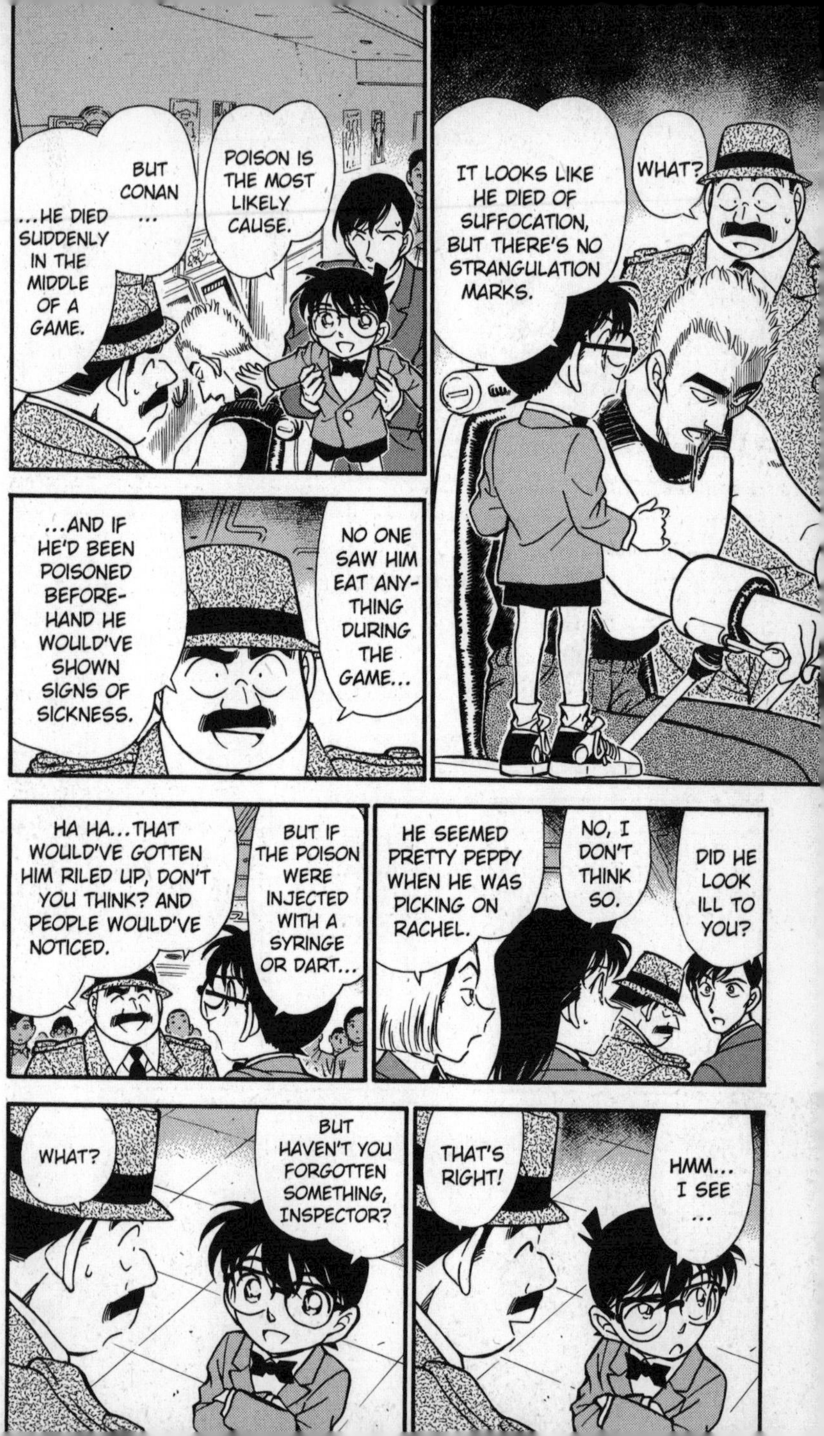
WHAT?
IT LOOKS LIKE HE DIED OF SUFFOCATION, BUT THERE'S NO STRANGULATION MARKS.
POISON IS THE MOST LIKELY CAUSE.
BUT CONAN...
...HE DIED SUDDENLY IN THE MIDDLE OF A GAME.
NO ONE SAW HIM EAT ANY-THING DURING THE GAME...
...AND IF HE'D BEEN POISONED BEFORE-HAND HE WOULD'VE SHOWN SIGNS OF SICKNESS.
DID HE LOOK ILL TO YOU?
NO, I DON'T THINK SO.
HE SEEMED PRETTY PEPPY WHEN HE WAS PICKING ON RACHEL.
BUT IF THE POISON WERE INJECTED WITH A SYRINGE OR DART...
HA HA...THAT WOULD'VE GOTTEN HIM RILED UP, DON'T YOU THINK? AND PEOPLE WOULD'VE NOTICED.
HMM... I SEE...
THAT'S RIGHT!
BUT HAVEN'T YOU FORGOTTEN SOMETHING, INSPECTOR?
WHAT?

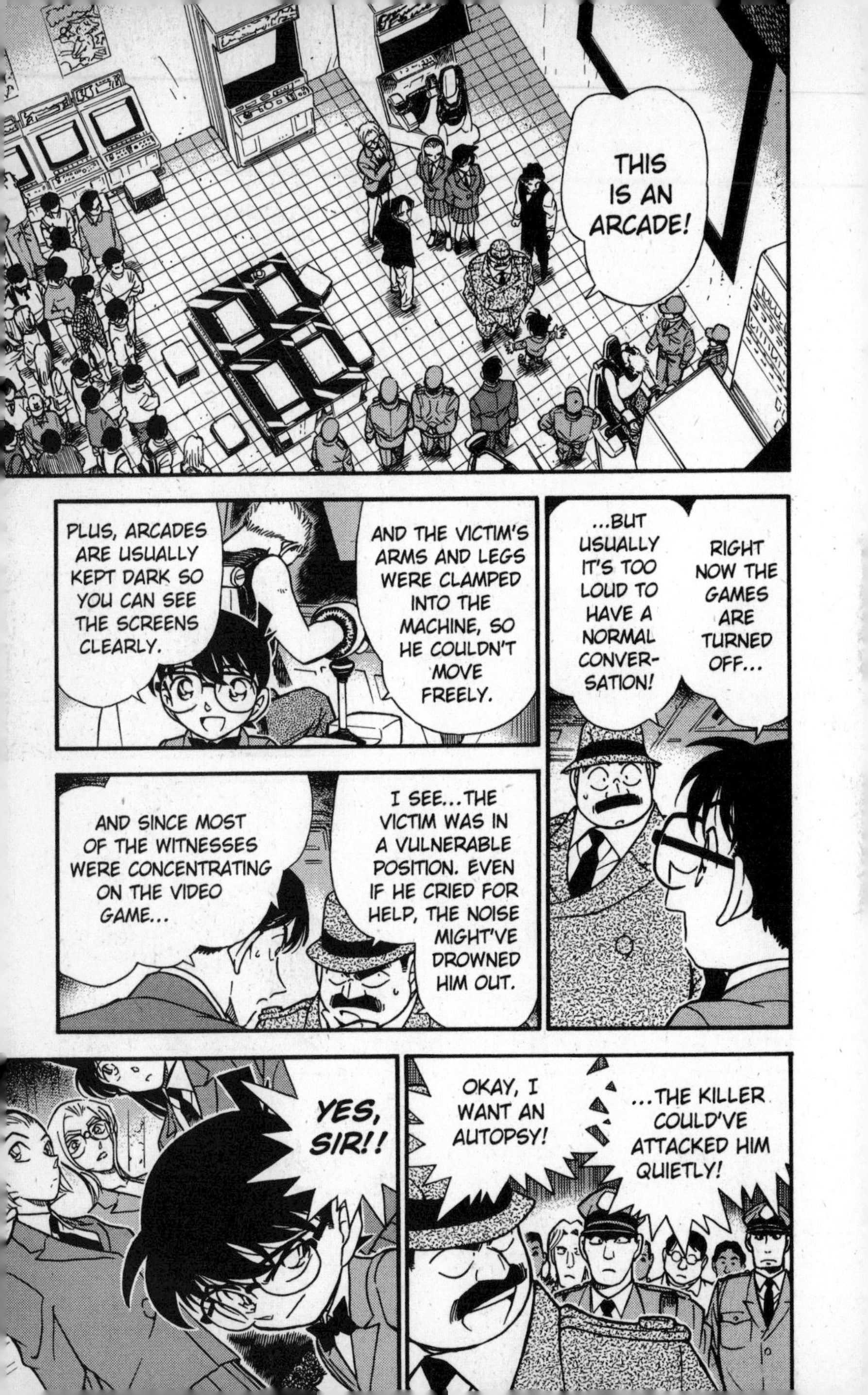
THIS IS AN ARCADE!
RIGHT NOW THE GAMES ARE TURNED OFF...
...BUT USUALLY IT'S TOO LOUD TO HAVE A NORMAL CONVERSATION!
AND THE VICTIM'S ARMS AND LEGS WERE CLAMPED INTO THE MACHINE, SO HE COULDN'T MOVE FREELY.
PLUS, ARCADES ARE USUALLY KEPT DARK SO YOU CAN SEE THE SCREENS CLEARLY.
I SEE...THE VICTIM WAS IN A VULNERABLE POSITION. EVEN IF HE CRIED FOR HELP, THE NOISE MIGHT'VE DROWNED HIM OUT.
AND SINCE MOST OF THE WITNESSES WERE CONCENTRATING ON THE VIDEO GAME...
...THE KILLER COULD'VE ATTACKED HIM QUIETLY!
OKAY, I WANT AN AUTOPSY!
YES, SIR!!

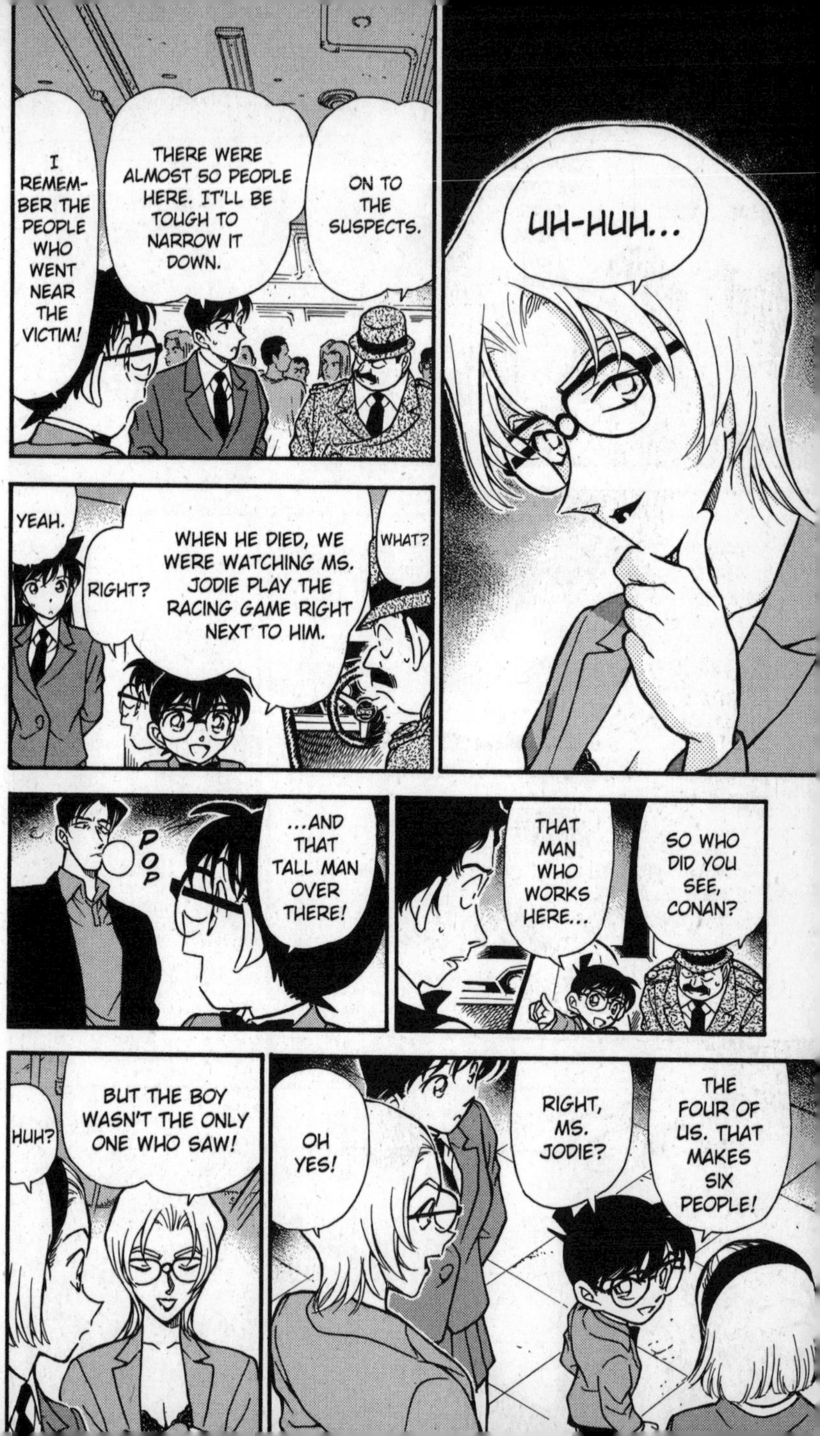
UH-HUH...
ON TO THE SUSPECTS.
THERE WERE ALMOST 50 PEOPLE HERE. IT'LL BE TOUGH TO NARROW IT DOWN.
I REMEMBER THE PEOPLE WHO WENT NEAR THE VICTIM!
WHAT?
WHEN HE DIED, WE WERE WATCHING MS. JODIE PLAY THE RACING GAME RIGHT NEXT TO HIM.
RIGHT?
YEAH.
SO WHO DID YOU SEE, CONAN?
THAT MAN WHO WORKS HERE...
...AND THAT TALL MAN OVER THERE!
POP
THE FOUR OF US. THAT MAKES SIX PEOPLE!
RIGHT, MS. JODIE?
OH YES!
BUT THE BOY WASN'T THE ONLY ONE WHO SAW!
HUH?

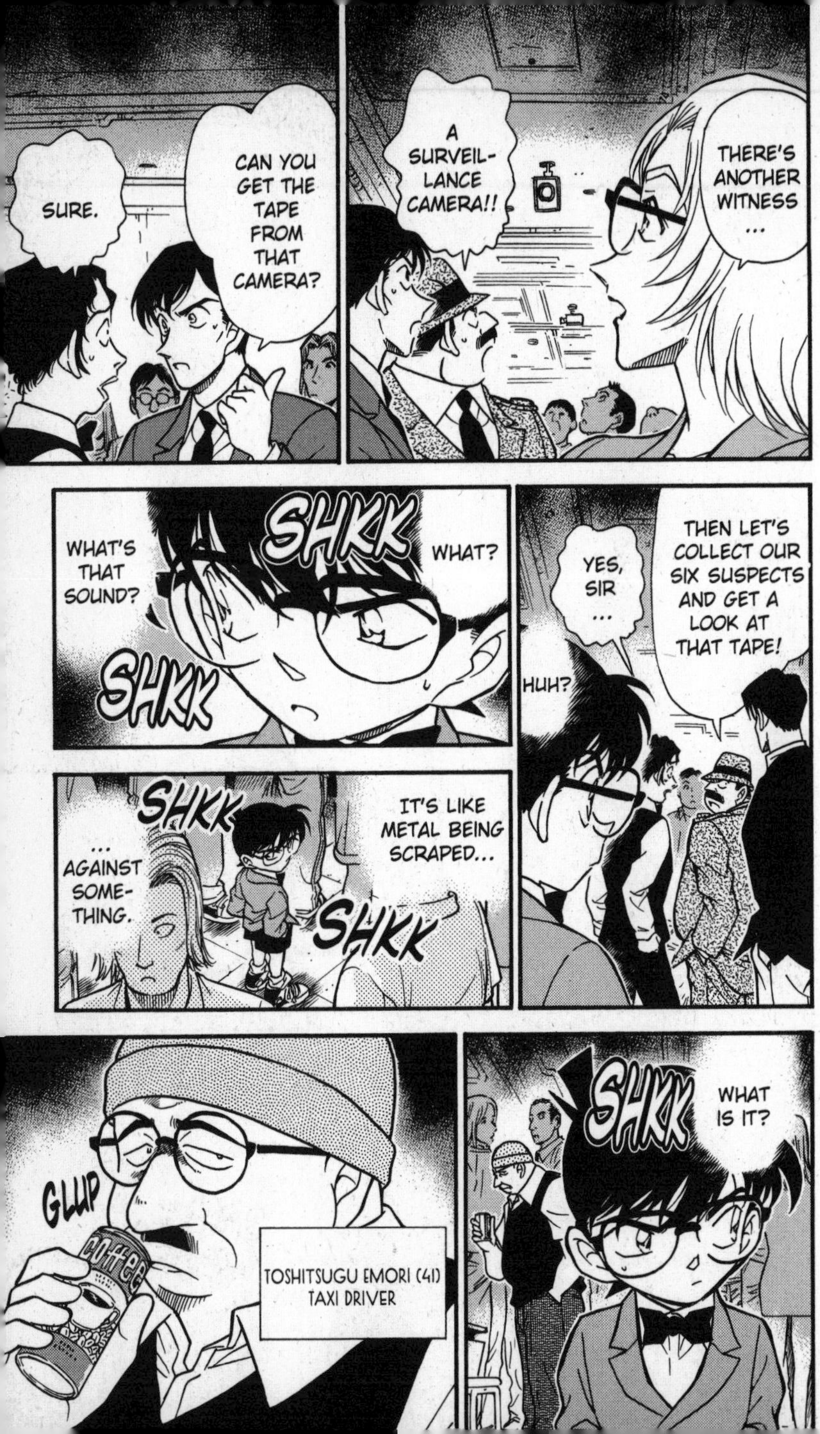
THERE'S ANOTHER WITNESS ...
A SURVEIL-LANCE CAMERA!!
CAN YOU GET THE TAPE FROM THAT CAMERA?
SURE.
THEN LET'S COLLECT OUR SIX SUSPECTS AND GET A LOOK AT THAT TAPE!
YES, SIR ...
HUH?
SHKK
WHAT?
WHAT'S THAT SOUND?
SHKK
IT'S LIKE METAL BEING SCRAPED...
SHKK
... AGAINST SOME-THING.
SHKK
SHKK
WHAT IS IT?
GLUP
TOSHITSUGU EMORI (41)
TAXI DRIVER
Coffee

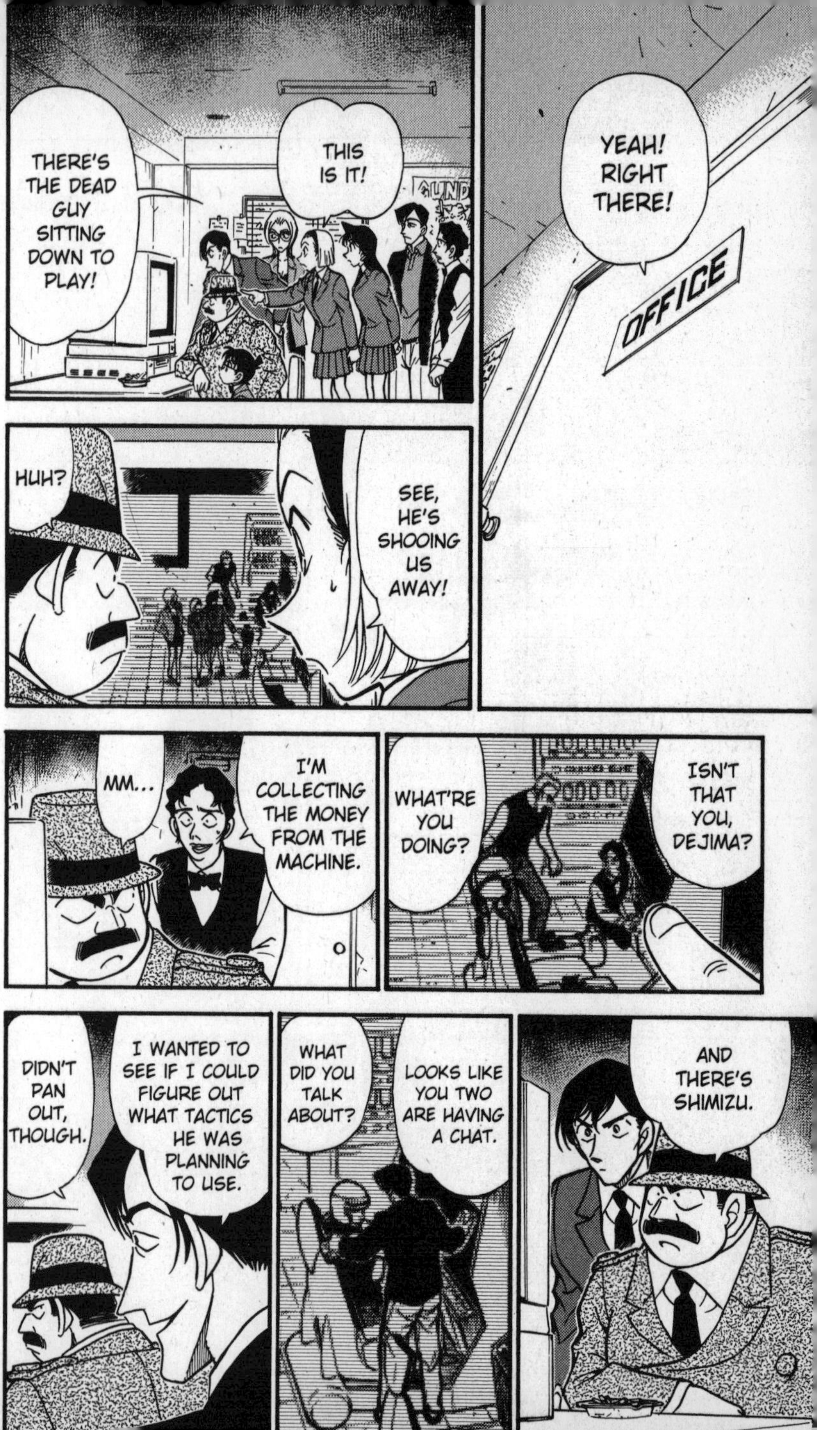
YEAH! RIGHT THERE!
OFFICE
THIS IS IT!
THERE'S THE DEAD GUY SITTING DOWN TO PLAY!
SEE, HE'S SHOOING US AWAY!
HUH?
ISN'T THAT YOU, DEJIMA?
WHAT'RE YOU DOING?
I'M COLLECTING THE MONEY FROM THE MACHINE.
MM...
AND THERE'S SHIMIZU.
LOOKS LIKE YOU TWO ARE HAVING A CHAT.
WHAT DID YOU TALK ABOUT?
I WANTED TO SEE IF I COULD FIGURE OUT WHAT TACTICS HE WAS PLANNING TO USE.
DIDN'T PAN OUT, THOUGH.

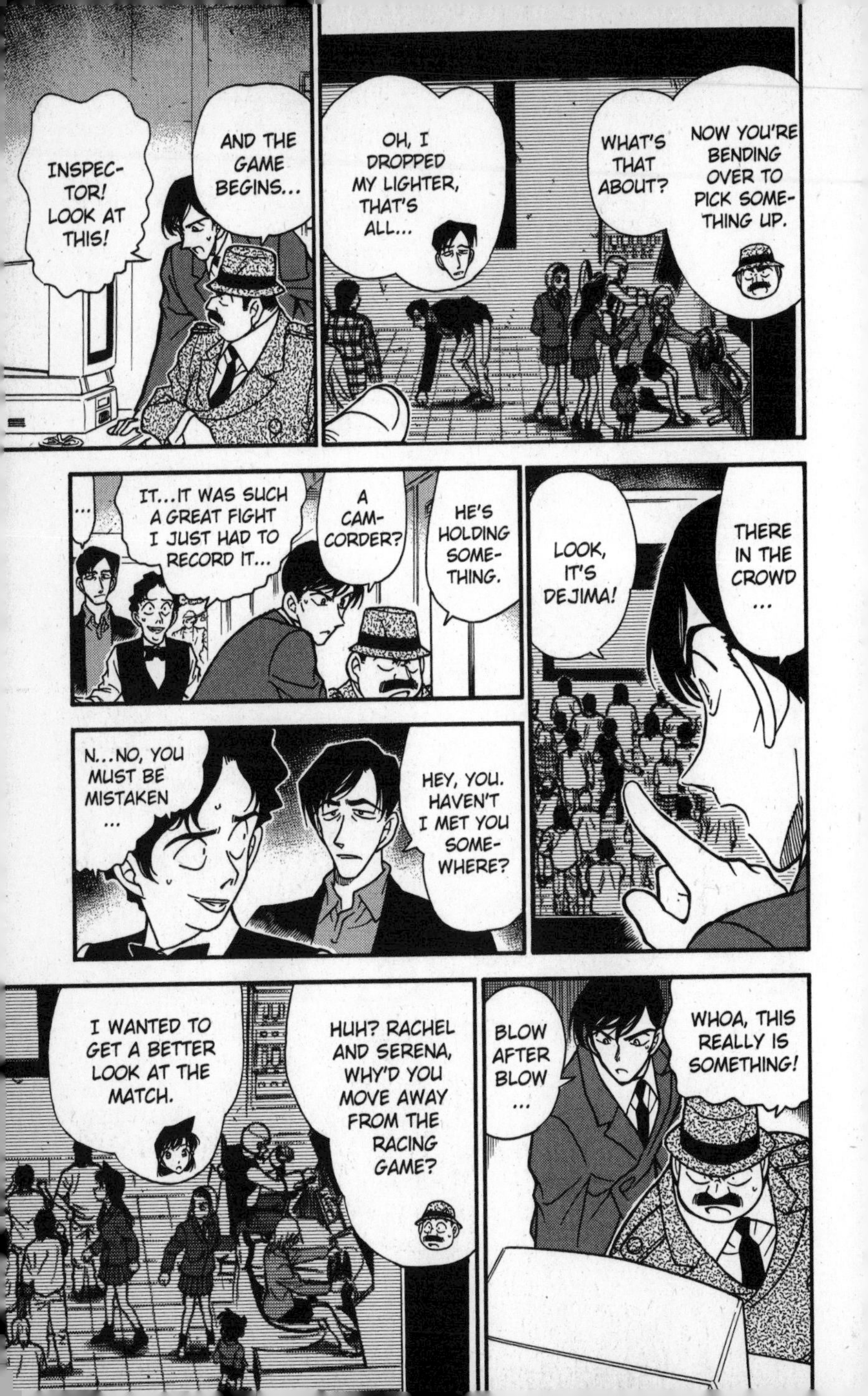
NOW YOU'RE BENDING OVER TO PICK SOME-THING UP.
WHAT'S THAT ABOUT?
OH, I DROPPED MY LIGHTER, THAT'S ALL...
AND THE GAME BEGINS...
INSPEC-TOR! LOOK AT THIS!
THERE IN THE CROWD...
LOOK, IT'S DEJIMA!
HE'S HOLDING SOME-THING.
A CAM-CORDER?
IT...IT WAS SUCH A GREAT FIGHT I JUST HAD TO RECORD IT...
...
HEY, YOU. HAVEN'T I MET YOU SOME-WHERE?
N...NO, YOU MUST BE MISTAKEN...
WHOA, THIS REALLY IS SOMETHING!
BLOW AFTER BLOW...
HUH? RACHEL AND SERENA, WHY'D YOU MOVE AWAY FROM THE RACING GAME?
I WANTED TO GET A BETTER LOOK AT THE MATCH.

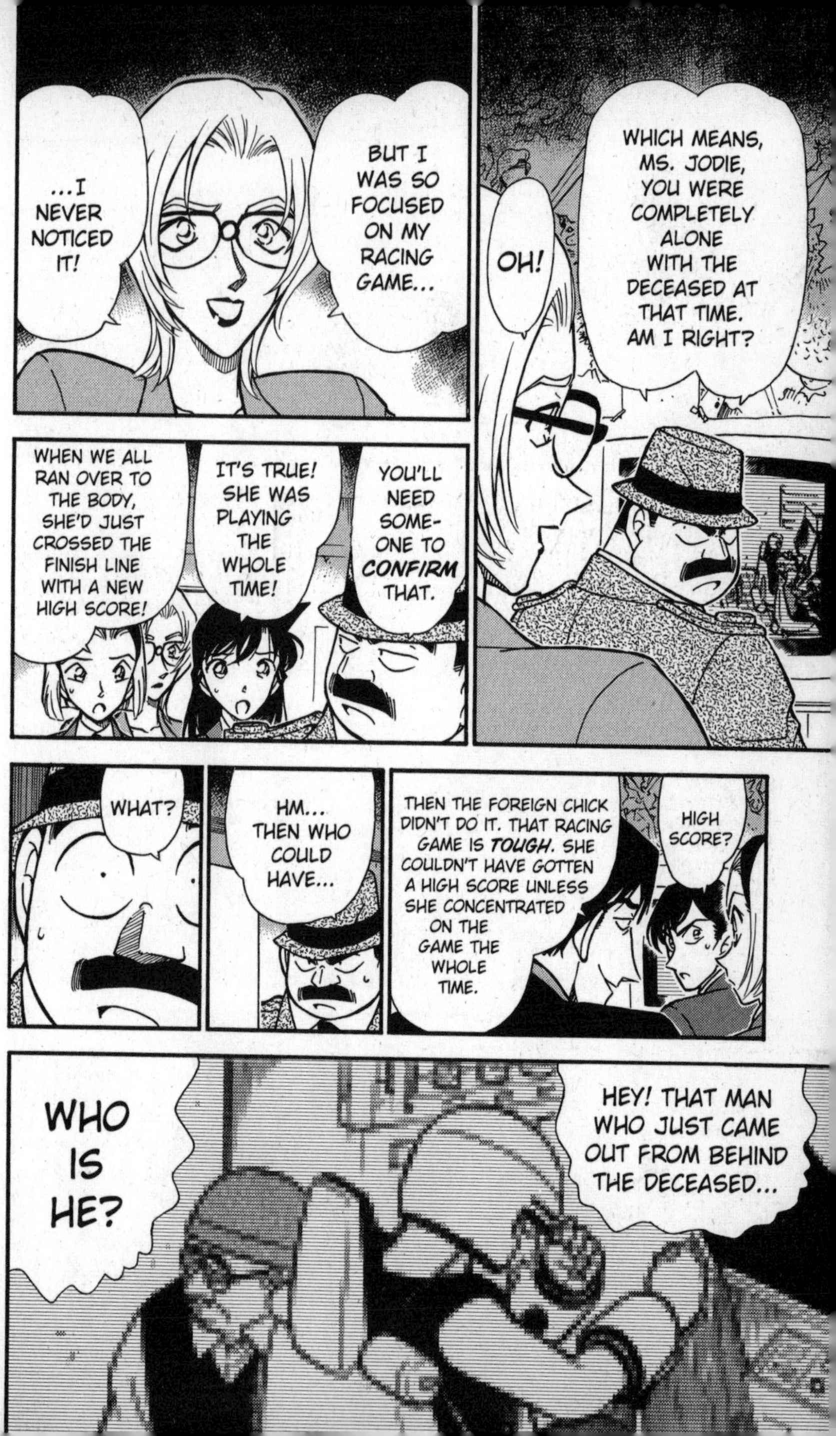
WHICH MEANS, MS. JODIE, YOU WERE COMPLETELY ALONE WITH THE DECEASED AT THAT TIME. AM I RIGHT?
OH!
BUT I WAS SO FOCUSED ON MY RACING GAME...
...I NEVER NOTICED IT!
YOU'LL NEED SOME-ONE TO **CONFIRM** THAT.
IT'S TRUE! SHE WAS PLAYING THE WHOLE TIME!
WHEN WE ALL RAN OVER TO THE BODY, SHE'D JUST CROSSED THE FINISH LINE WITH A NEW HIGH SCORE!
HIGH SCORE?
THEN THE FOREIGN CHICK DIDN'T DO IT. THAT RACING GAME IS **TOUGH**. SHE COULDN'T HAVE GOTTEN A HIGH SCORE UNLESS SHE CONCENTRATED ON THE GAME THE WHOLE TIME.
HM... THEN WHO COULD HAVE...
WHAT?
HEY! THAT MAN WHO JUST CAME OUT FROM BEHIND THE DECEASED...
WHO IS HE?

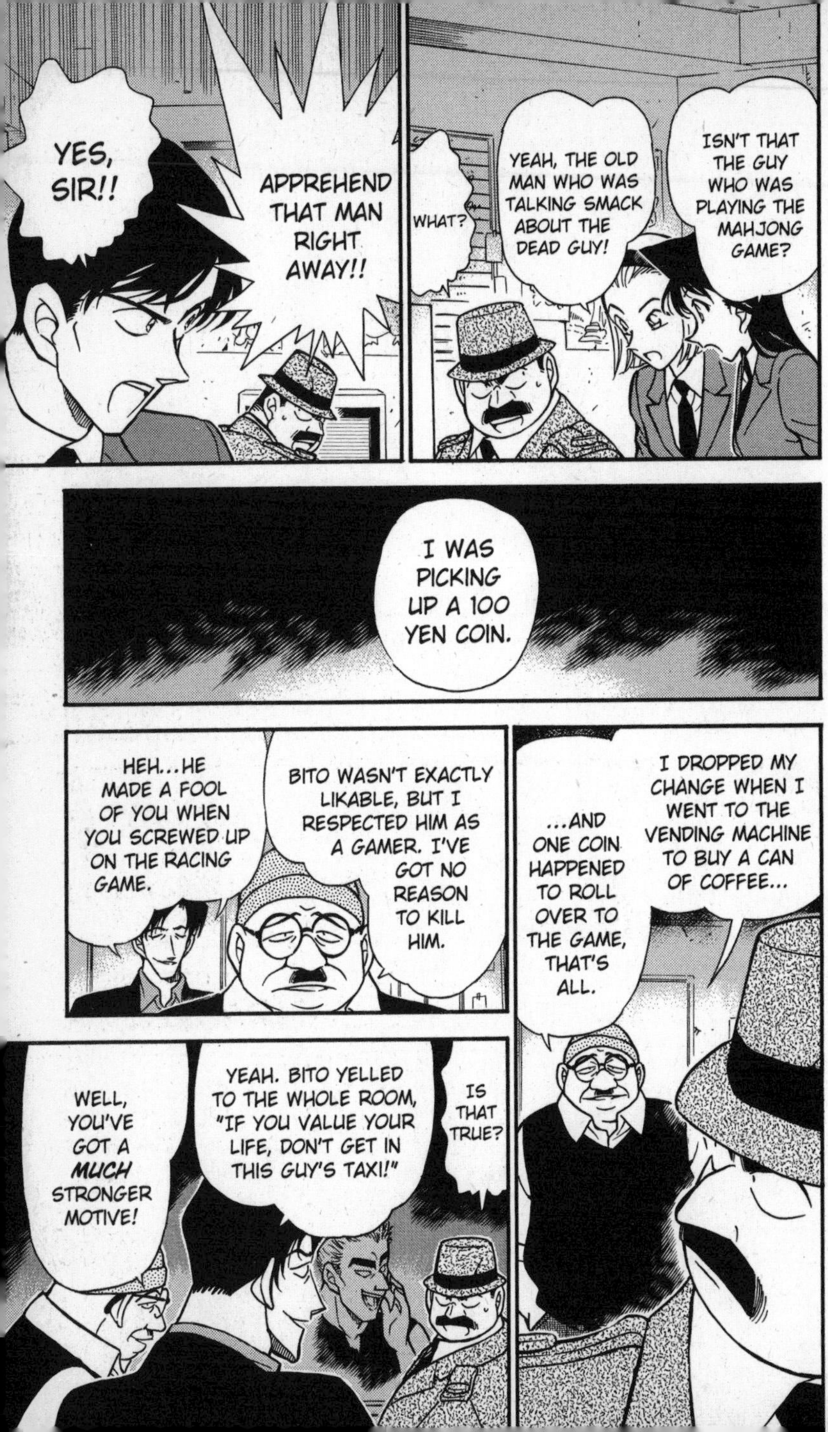
ISN'T THAT THE GUY WHO WAS PLAYING THE MAHJONG GAME?
YEAH, THE OLD MAN WHO WAS TALKING SMACK ABOUT THE DEAD GUY!
WHAT?
APPREHEND THAT MAN RIGHT AWAY!!
YES, SIR!!
I WAS PICKING UP A 100 YEN COIN.
I DROPPED MY CHANGE WHEN I WENT TO THE VENDING MACHINE TO BUY A CAN OF COFFEE...
...AND ONE COIN HAPPENED TO ROLL OVER TO THE GAME, THAT'S ALL.
BITO WASN'T EXACTLY LIKABLE, BUT I RESPECTED HIM AS A GAMER. I'VE GOT NO REASON TO KILL HIM.
HEH...HE MADE A FOOL OF YOU WHEN YOU SCREWED UP ON THE RACING GAME.
IS THAT TRUE?
YEAH. BITO YELLED TO THE WHOLE ROOM, "IF YOU VALUE YOUR LIFE, DON'T GET IN THIS GUY'S TAXI!"
WELL, YOU'VE GOT A *MUCH* STRONGER MOTIVE!

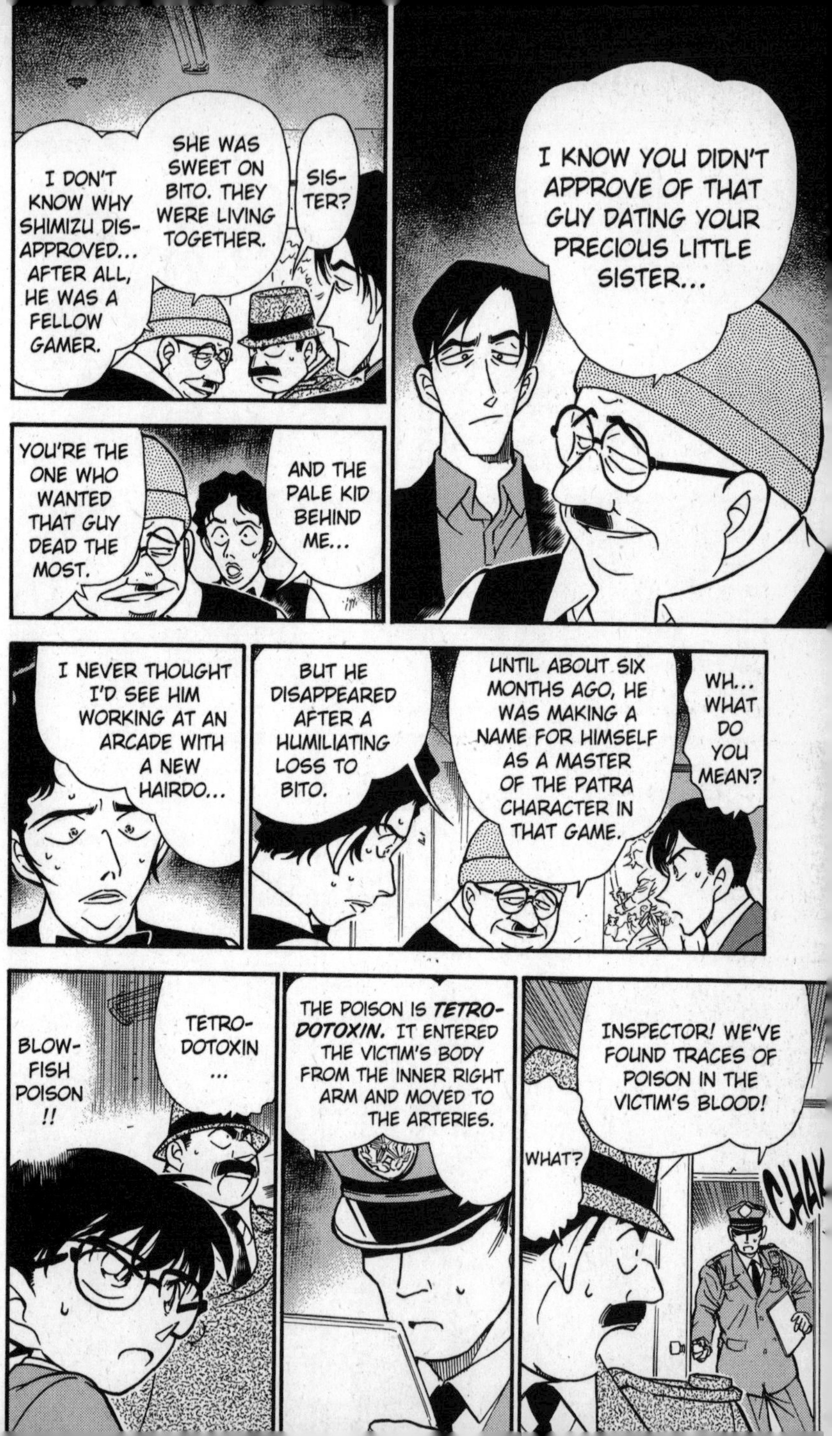

I KNOW YOU DIDN'T APPROVE OF THAT GUY DATING YOUR PRECIOUS LITTLE SISTER...
SISTER?
SHE WAS SWEET ON BITO. THEY WERE LIVING TOGETHER.
I DON'T KNOW WHY SHIMIZU DISAPPROVED... AFTER ALL, HE WAS A FELLOW GAMER.
AND THE PALE KID BEHIND ME...
YOU'RE THE ONE WHO WANTED THAT GUY DEAD THE MOST.
WH... WHAT DO YOU MEAN?
UNTIL ABOUT SIX MONTHS AGO, HE WAS MAKING A NAME FOR HIMSELF AS A MASTER OF THE PATRA CHARACTER IN THAT GAME.
BUT HE DISAPPEARED AFTER A HUMILIATING LOSS TO BITO.
I NEVER THOUGHT I'D SEE HIM WORKING AT AN ARCADE WITH A NEW HAIRDO...
INSPECTOR! WE'VE FOUND TRACES OF POISON IN THE VICTIM'S BLOOD!
CHAK
WHAT?
THE POISON IS *TETRODOTOXIN.* IT ENTERED THE VICTIM'S BODY FROM THE INNER RIGHT ARM AND MOVED TO THE ARTERIES.
TETRODOTOXIN ...
BLOWFISH POISON !!

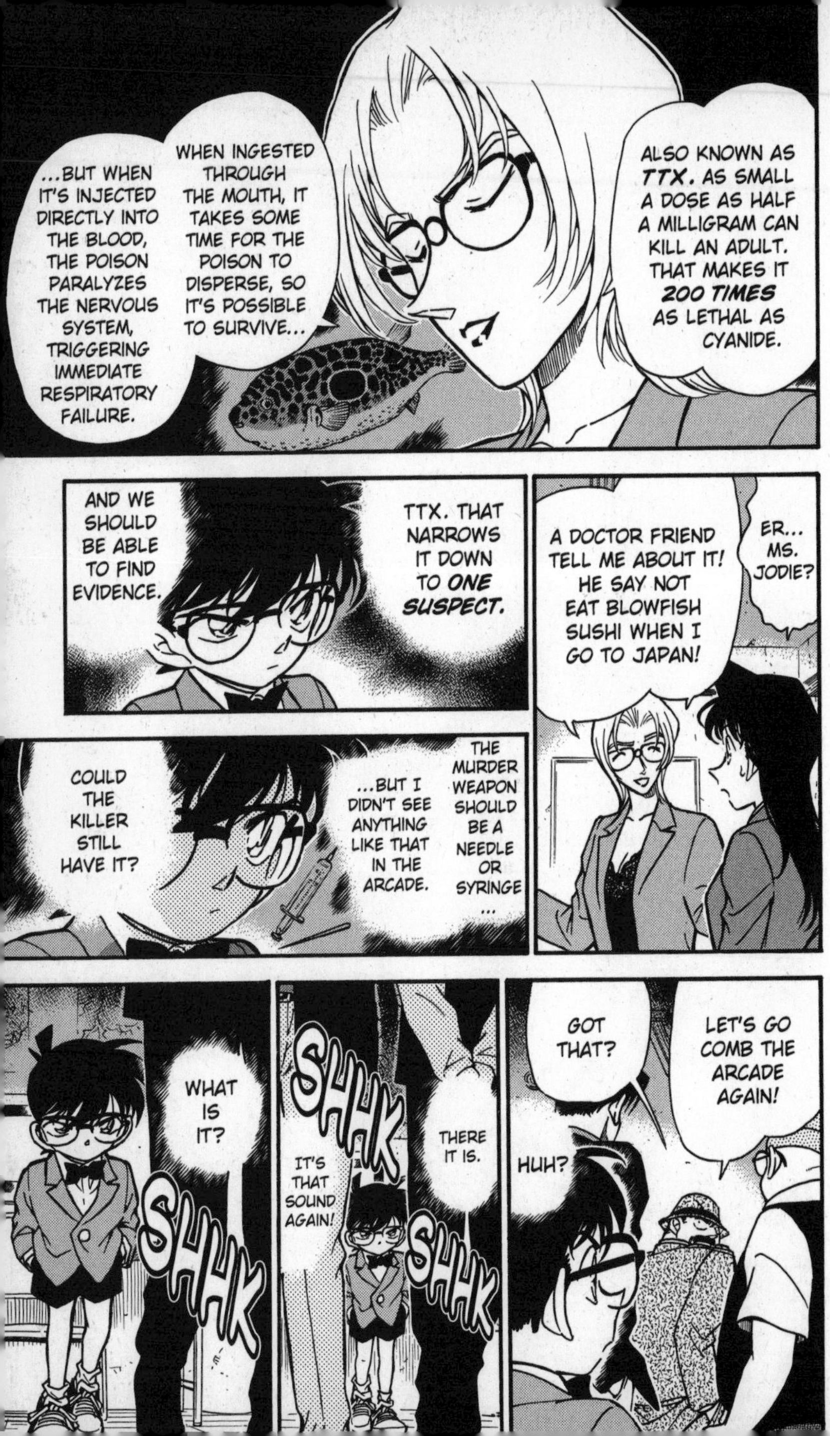
ALSO KNOWN AS TTX. AS SMALL A DOSE AS HALF A MILLIGRAM CAN KILL AN ADULT. THAT MAKES IT 200 TIMES AS LETHAL AS CYANIDE.
WHEN INGESTED THROUGH THE MOUTH, IT TAKES SOME TIME FOR THE POISON TO DISPERSE, SO IT'S POSSIBLE TO SURVIVE...
...BUT WHEN IT'S INJECTED DIRECTLY INTO THE BLOOD, THE POISON PARALYZES THE NERVOUS SYSTEM, TRIGGERING IMMEDIATE RESPIRATORY FAILURE.
ER... MS. JODIE?
A DOCTOR FRIEND TELL ME ABOUT IT! HE SAY NOT EAT BLOWFISH SUSHI WHEN I GO TO JAPAN!
TTX. THAT NARROWS IT DOWN TO ONE SUSPECT.
AND WE SHOULD BE ABLE TO FIND EVIDENCE.
THE MURDER WEAPON SHOULD BE A NEEDLE OR SYRINGE ...
...BUT I DIDN'T SEE ANYTHING LIKE THAT IN THE ARCADE.
COULD THE KILLER STILL HAVE IT?
LET'S GO COMB THE ARCADE AGAIN!
GOT THAT?
HUH?
THERE IT IS.
SHHK
IT'S THAT SOUND AGAIN!
SHHK
WHAT IS IT?
SHHK

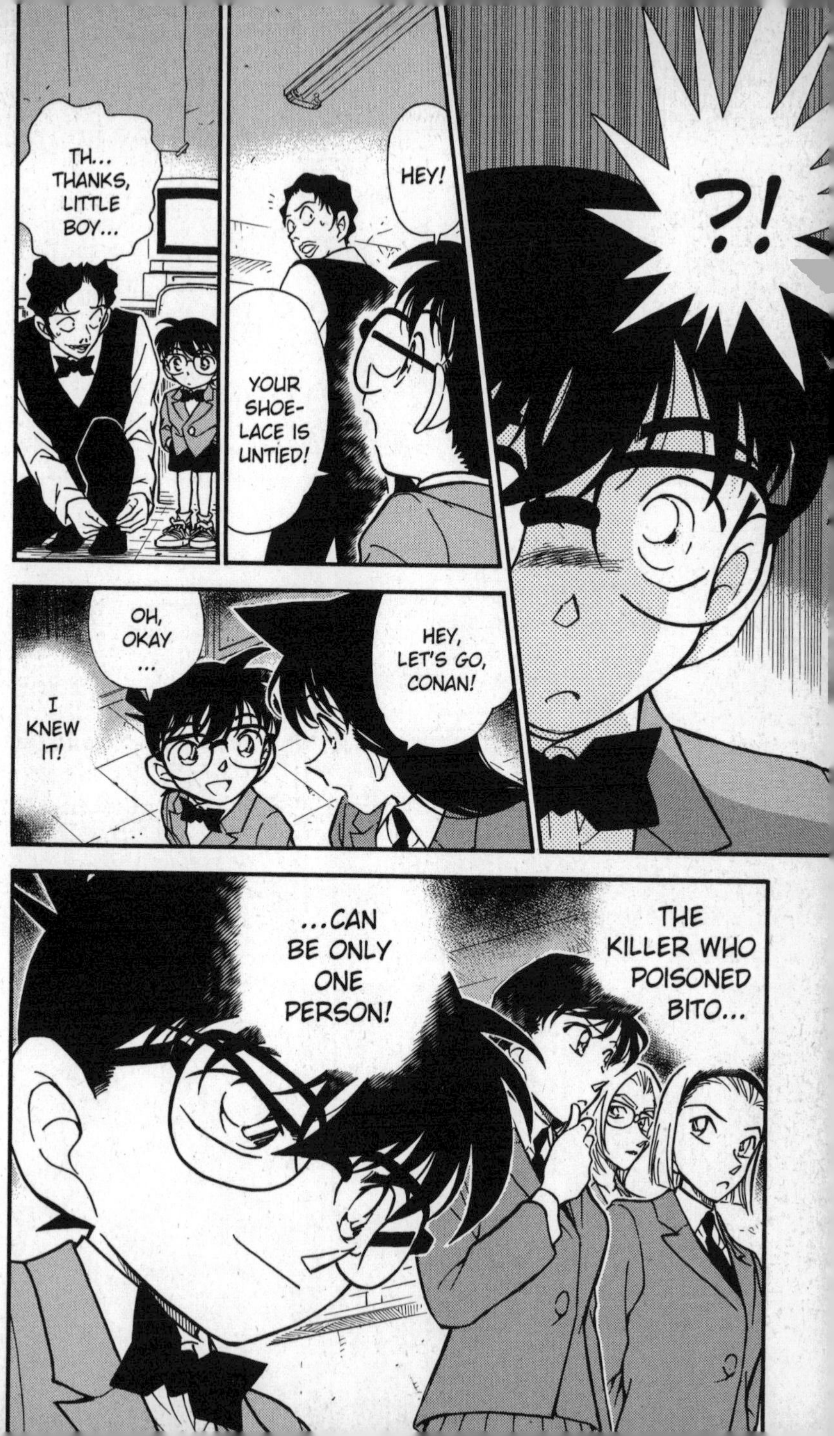
?!
HEY!
YOUR SHOE-LACE IS UNTIED!
TH... THANKS, LITTLE BOY...
HEY, LET'S GO, CONAN!
OH, OKAY ...
I KNEW IT!
THE KILLER WHO POISONED BITO...
...CAN BE ONLY ONE PERSON!

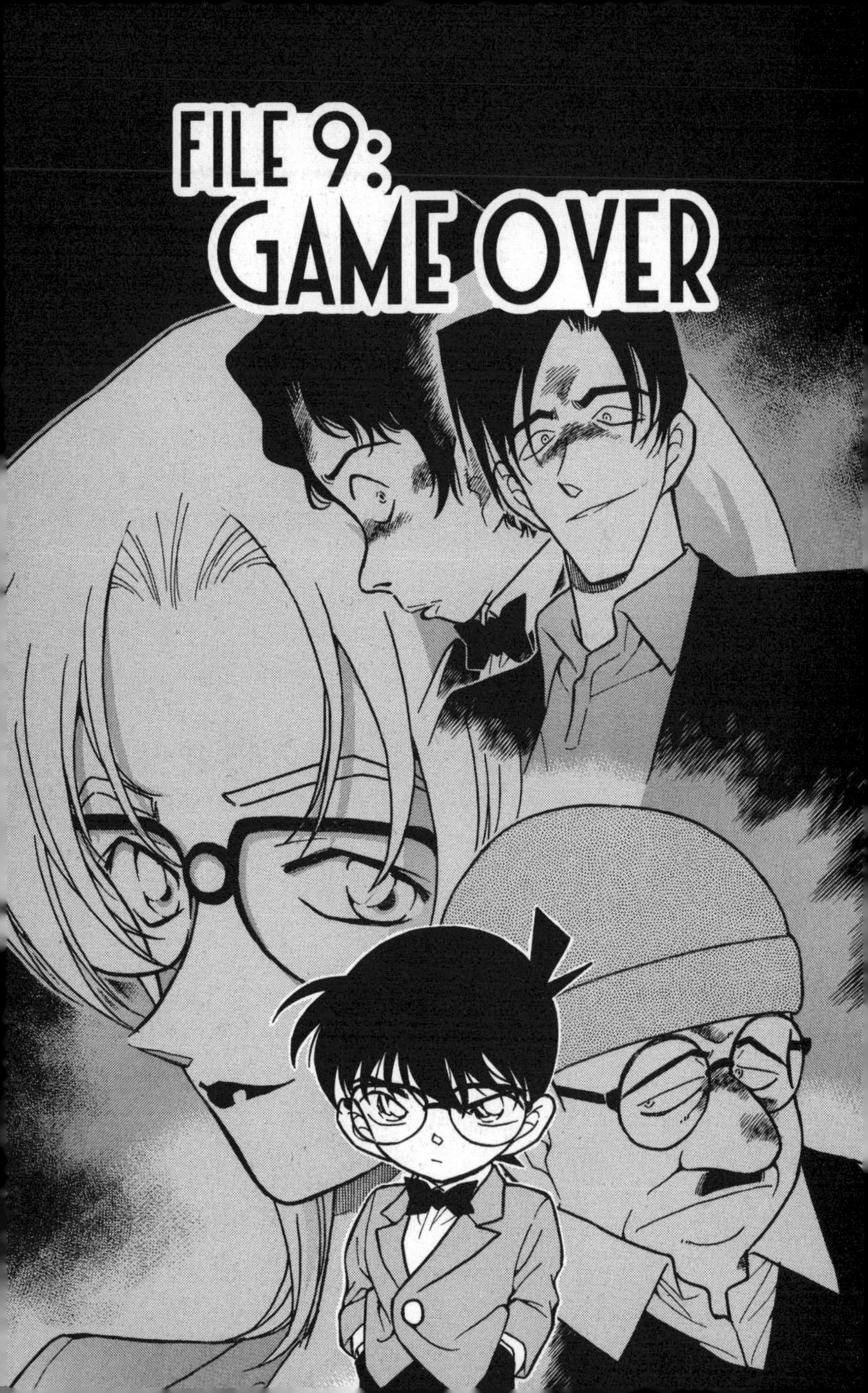
FILE 9:
GAME OVER

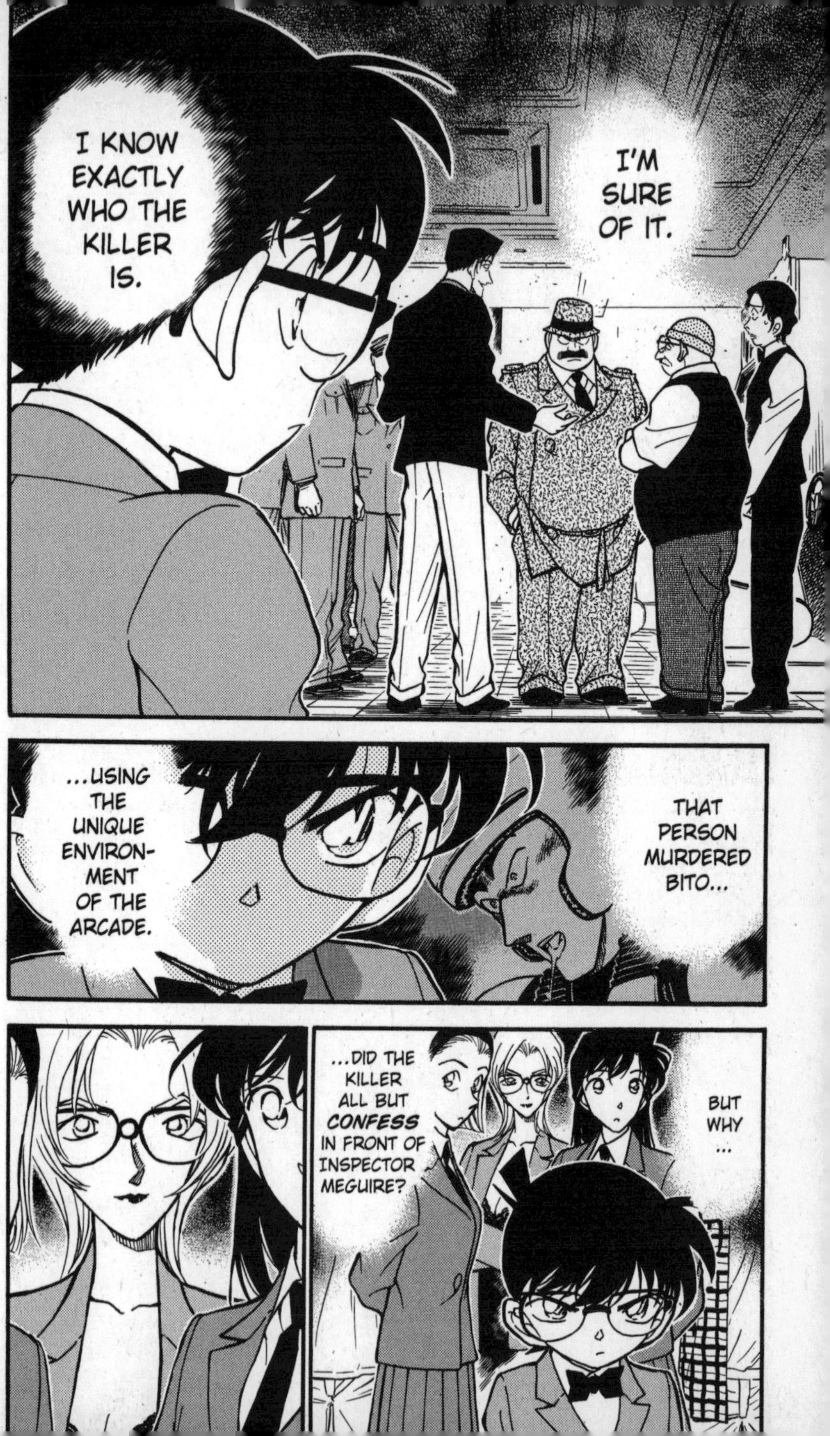
I'M SURE OF IT.
I KNOW EXACTLY WHO THE KILLER IS.
THAT PERSON MURDERED BITO...
...USING THE UNIQUE ENVIRONMENT OF THE ARCADE.
BUT WHY...
...DID THE KILLER ALL BUT **CONFESS** IN FRONT OF INSPECTOR MEGUIRE?

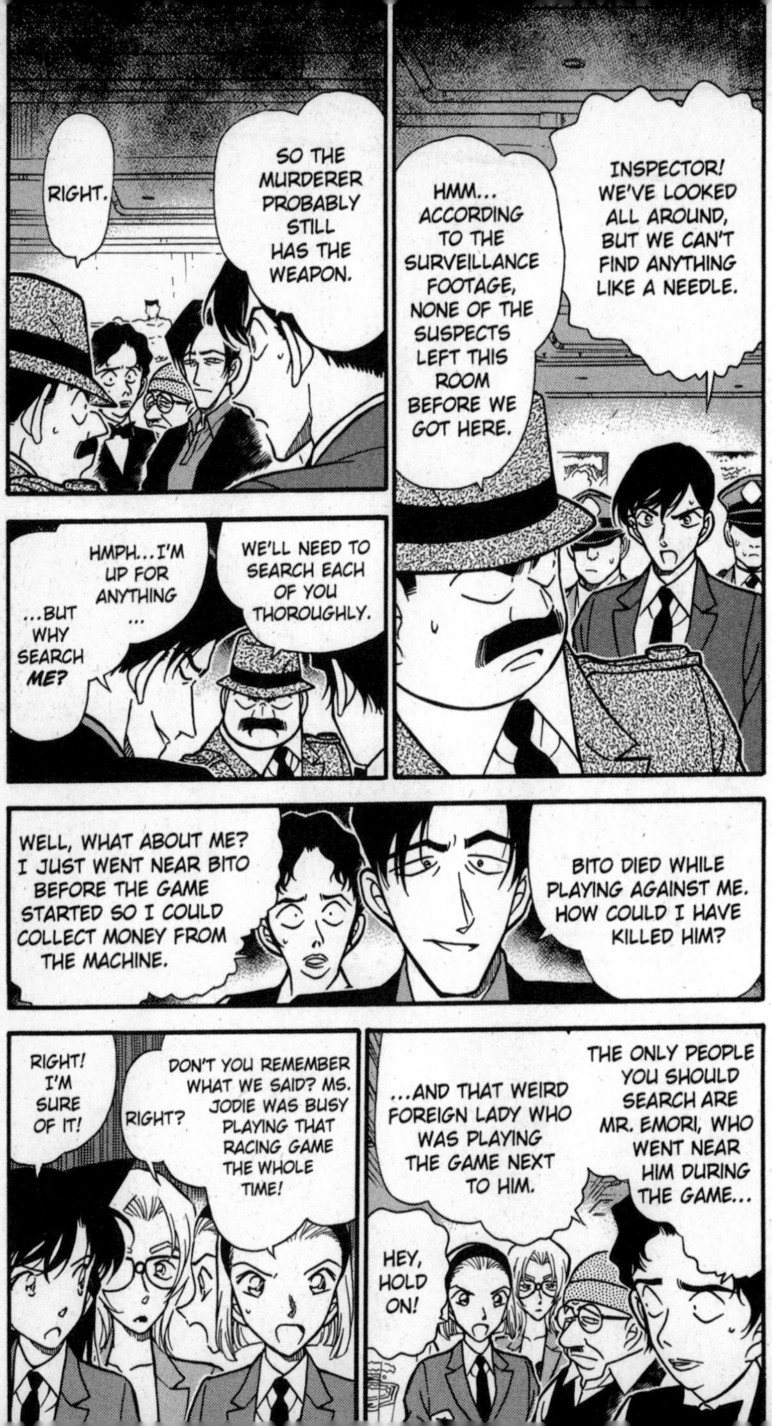
INSPECTOR! WE'VE LOOKED ALL AROUND, BUT WE CAN'T FIND ANYTHING LIKE A NEEDLE.
HMM... ACCORDING TO THE SURVEILLANCE FOOTAGE, NONE OF THE SUSPECTS LEFT THIS ROOM BEFORE WE GOT HERE.
SO THE MURDERER PROBABLY STILL HAS THE WEAPON.
RIGHT.
WE'LL NEED TO SEARCH EACH OF YOU THOROUGHLY.
HMPH...I'M UP FOR ANYTHING ...
...BUT WHY SEARCH *ME?*
BITO DIED WHILE PLAYING AGAINST ME. HOW COULD I HAVE KILLED HIM?
WELL, WHAT ABOUT ME? I JUST WENT NEAR BITO BEFORE THE GAME STARTED SO I COULD COLLECT MONEY FROM THE MACHINE.
THE ONLY PEOPLE YOU SHOULD SEARCH ARE MR. EMORI, WHO WENT NEAR HIM DURING THE GAME...
...AND THAT WEIRD FOREIGN LADY WHO WAS PLAYING THE GAME NEXT TO HIM.
HEY, HOLD ON!
DON'T YOU REMEMBER WHAT WE SAID? MS. JODIE WAS BUSY PLAYING THAT RACING GAME THE WHOLE TIME!
RIGHT?
RIGHT! I'M SURE OF IT!

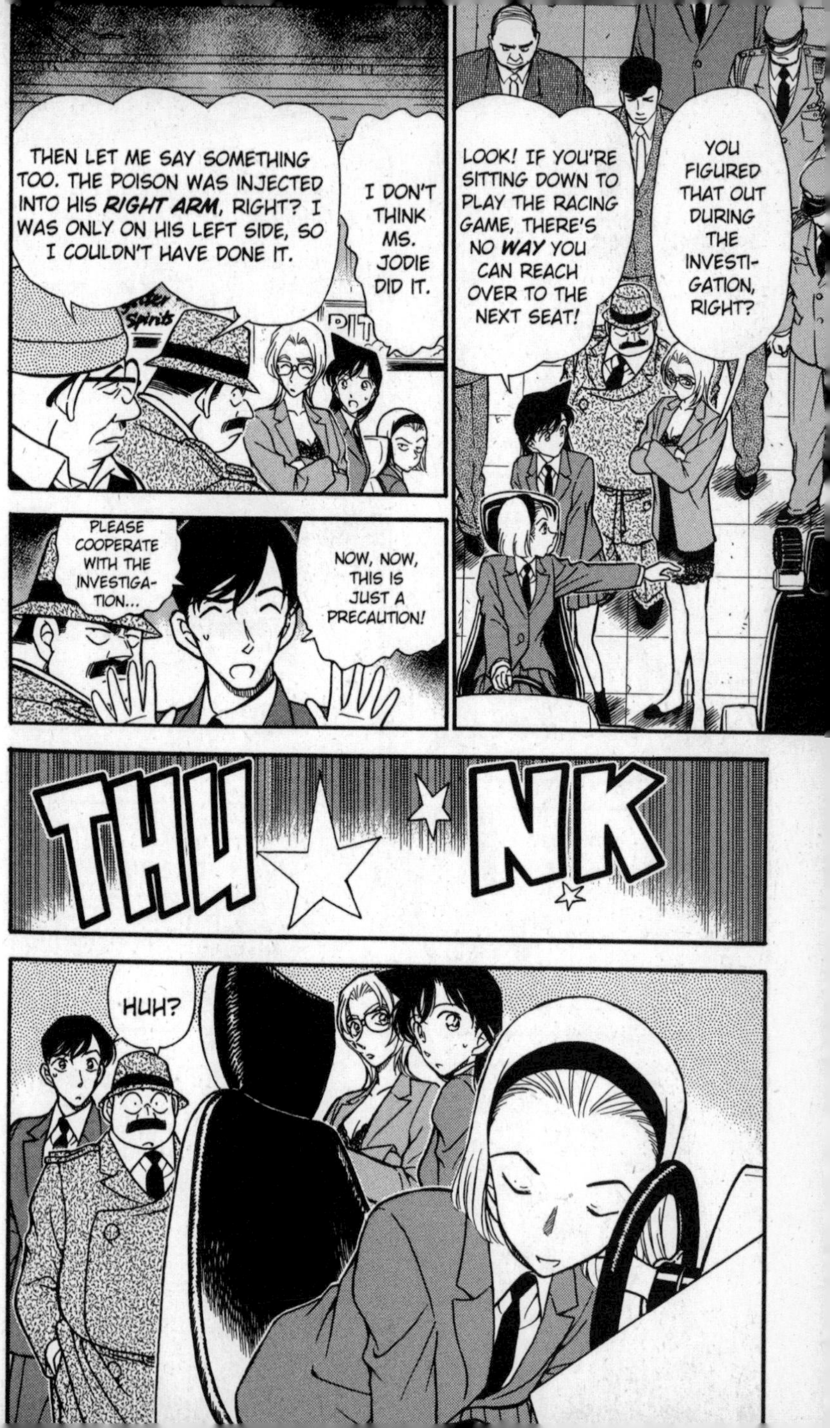
YOU FIGURED THAT OUT DURING THE INVESTIGATION, RIGHT?
LOOK! IF YOU'RE SITTING DOWN TO PLAY THE RACING GAME, THERE'S NO WAY YOU CAN REACH OVER TO THE NEXT SEAT!
I DON'T THINK MS. JODIE DID IT.
THEN LET ME SAY SOMETHING TOO. THE POISON WAS INJECTED INTO HIS RIGHT ARM, RIGHT? I WAS ONLY ON HIS LEFT SIDE, SO I COULDN'T HAVE DONE IT.
NOW, NOW, THIS IS JUST A PRECAUTION!
PLEASE COOPERATE WITH THE INVESTIGATION...
THU★NK
HUH?

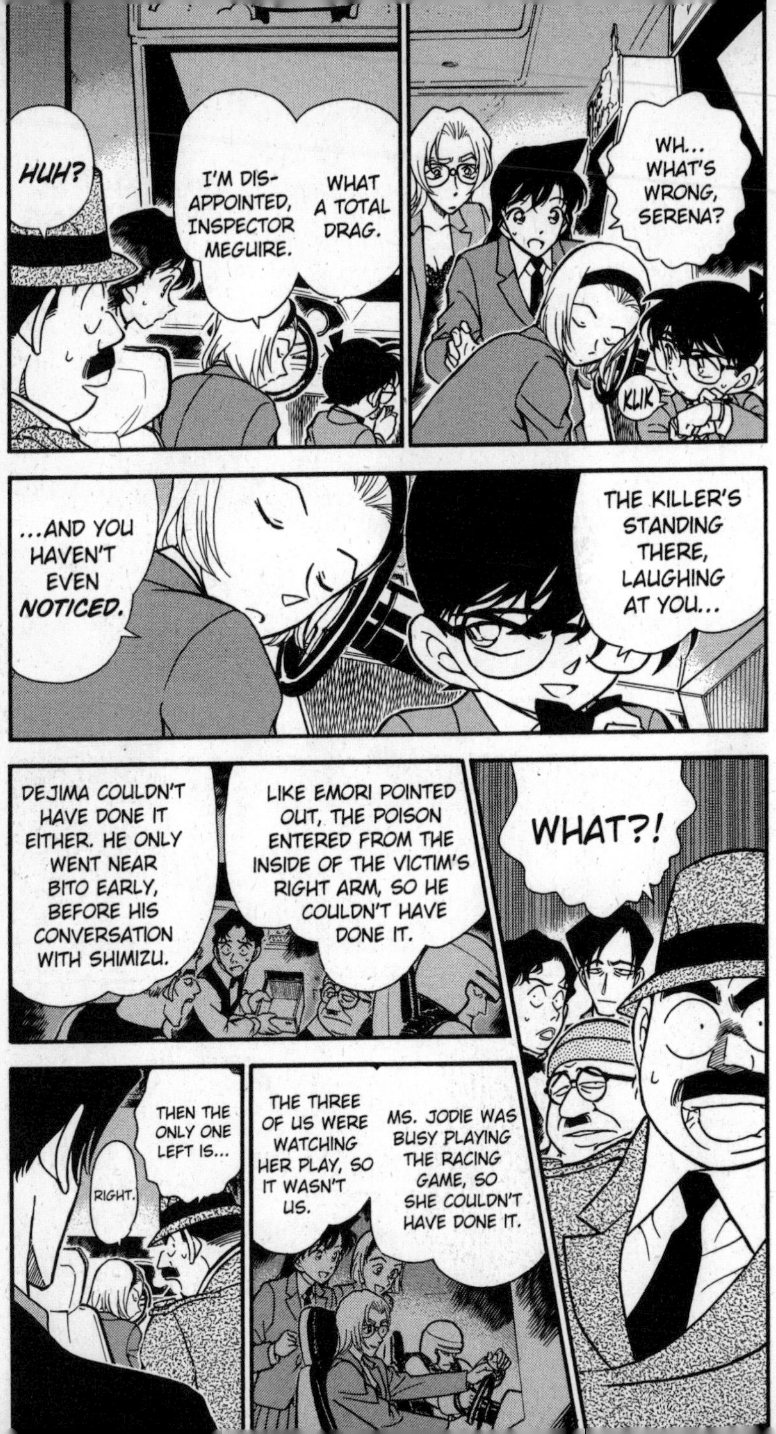
WH... WHAT'S WRONG, SERENA?
KLIK
WHAT A TOTAL DRAG.
I'M DIS-APPOINTED, INSPECTOR MEGUIRE.
HUH?
THE KILLER'S STANDING THERE, LAUGHING AT YOU...
...AND YOU HAVEN'T EVEN NOTICED.
WHAT?!
LIKE EMORI POINTED OUT, THE POISON ENTERED FROM THE INSIDE OF THE VICTIM'S RIGHT ARM, SO HE COULDN'T HAVE DONE IT.
DEJIMA COULDN'T HAVE DONE IT EITHER. HE ONLY WENT NEAR BITO EARLY, BEFORE HIS CONVERSATION WITH SHIMIZU.
MS. JODIE WAS BUSY PLAYING THE RACING GAME, SO SHE COULDN'T HAVE DONE IT.
THE THREE OF US WERE WATCHING HER PLAY, SO IT WASN'T US.
THEN THE ONLY ONE LEFT IS...
RIGHT.

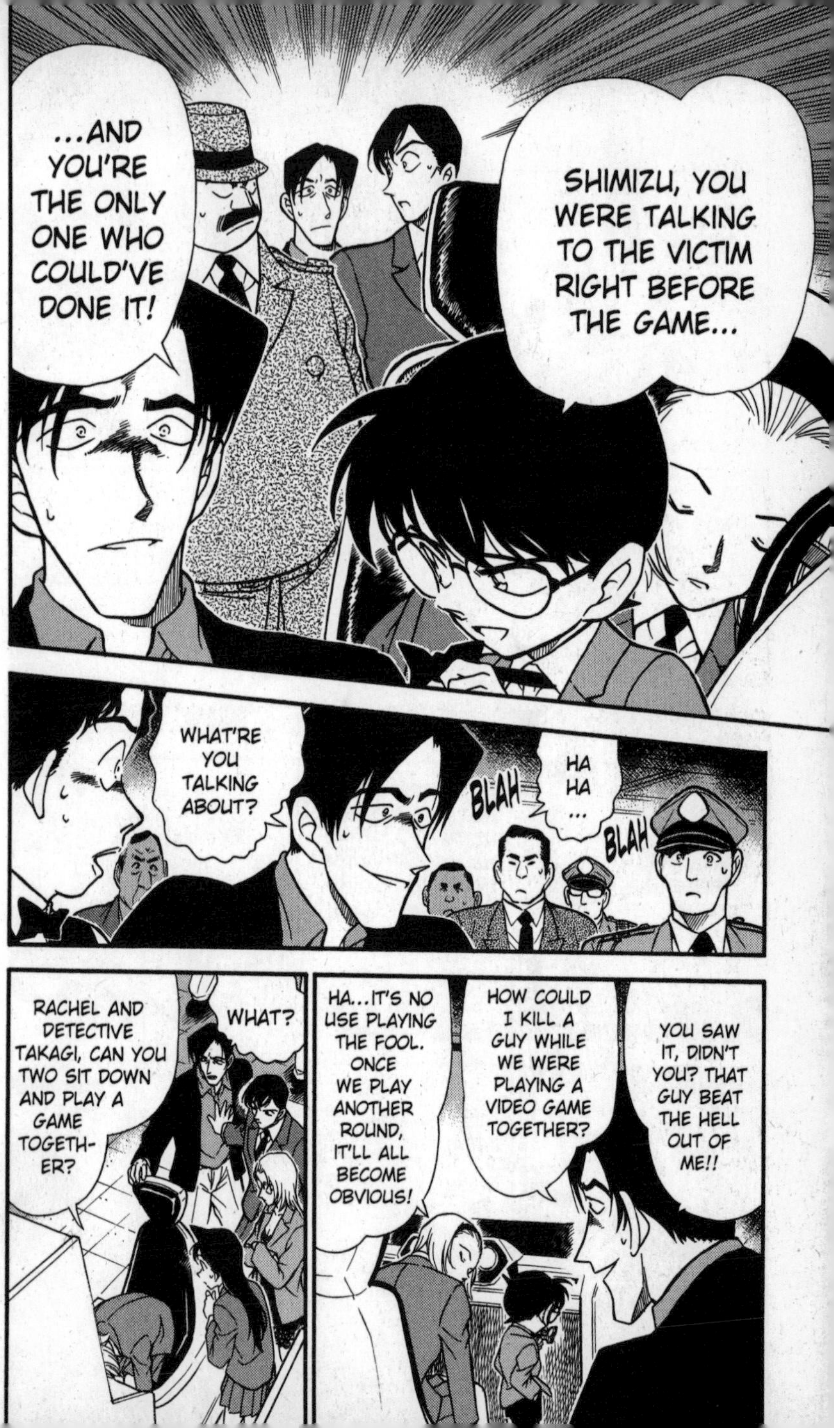
SHIMIZU, YOU WERE TALKING TO THE VICTIM RIGHT BEFORE THE GAME...
...AND YOU'RE THE ONLY ONE WHO COULD'VE DONE IT!
HA HA ...
BLAH
BLAH
WHAT'RE YOU TALKING ABOUT?
YOU SAW IT, DIDN'T YOU? THAT GUY BEAT THE HELL OUT OF ME!!
HOW COULD I KILL A GUY WHILE WE WERE PLAYING A VIDEO GAME TOGETHER?
HA...IT'S NO USE PLAYING THE FOOL. ONCE WE PLAY ANOTHER ROUND, IT'LL ALL BECOME OBVIOUS!
WHAT?
RACHEL AND DETECTIVE TAKAGI, CAN YOU TWO SIT DOWN AND PLAY A GAME TOGETH-ER?

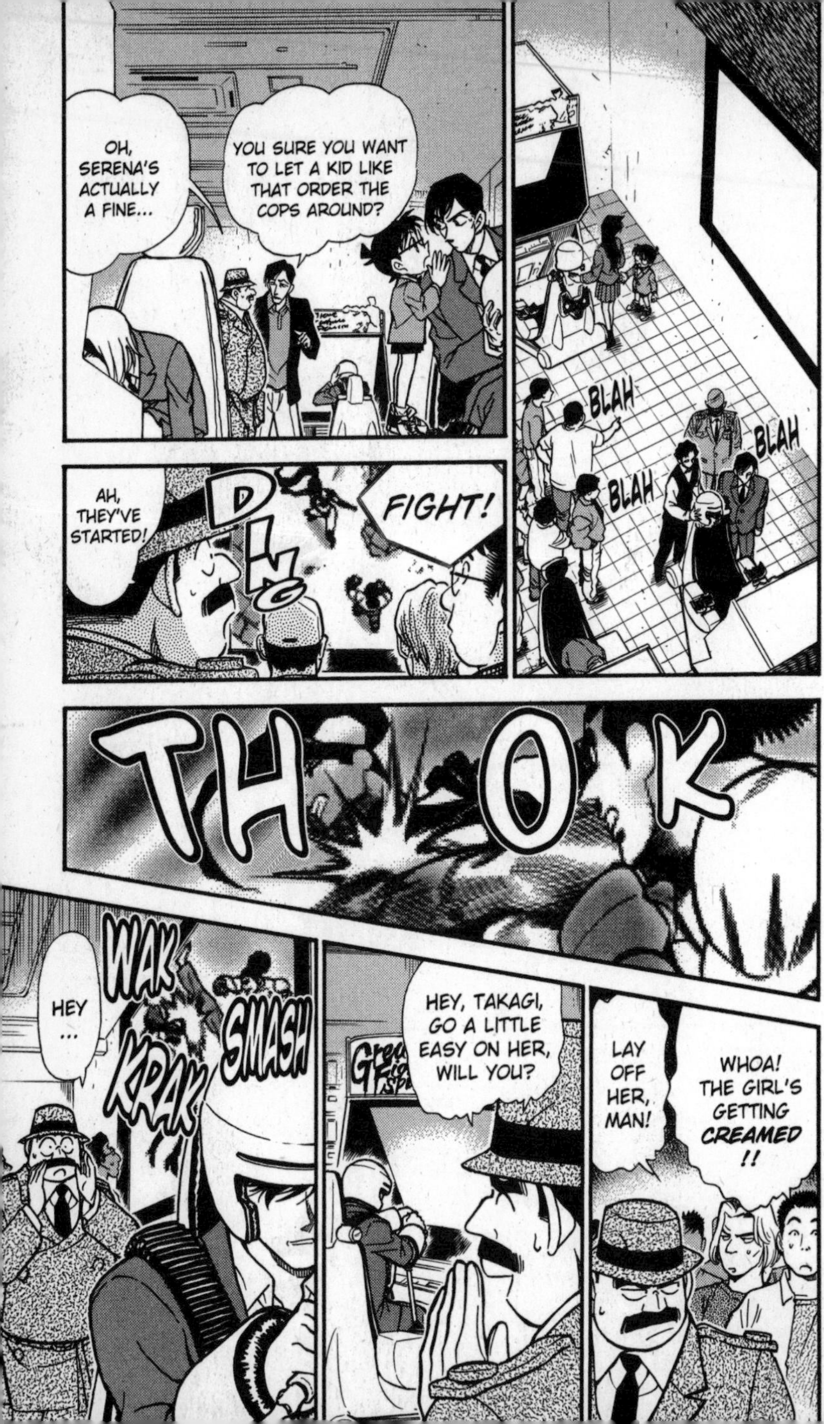
BLAH
BLAH
BLAH
YOU SURE YOU WANT TO LET A KID LIKE THAT ORDER THE COPS AROUND?
OH, SERENA'S ACTUALLY A FINE...
FIGHT!
DING
AH, THEY'VE STARTED!
THOK
WHOA! THE GIRL'S GETTING **CREAMED** !!
LAY OFF HER, MAN!
HEY, TAKAGI, GO A LITTLE EASY ON HER, WILL YOU?
SMASH
KRAK
WAK
HEY ...

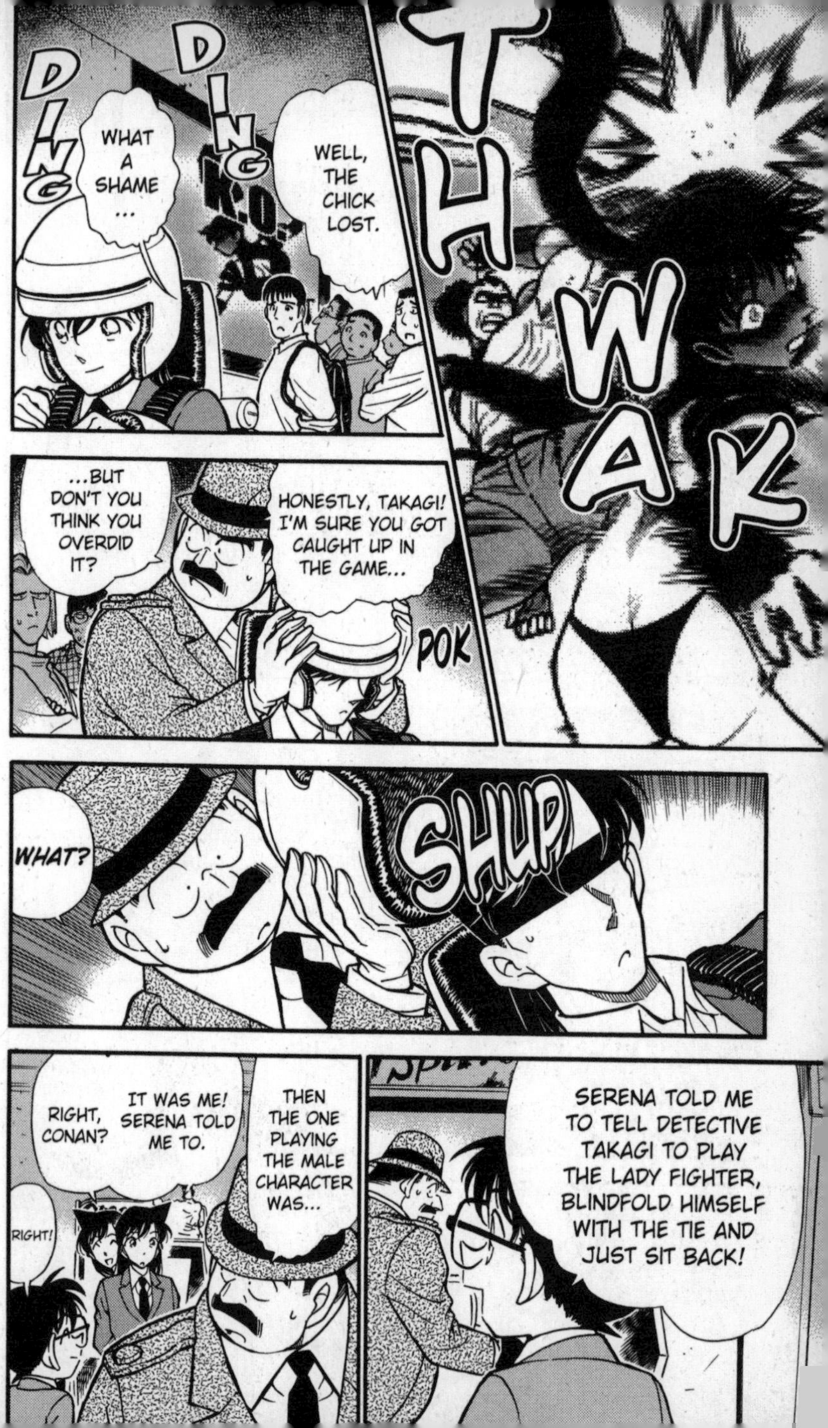
THWAK
DING
DING
WELL, THE CHICK LOST.
WHAT A SHAME ...
HONESTLY, TAKAGI! I'M SURE YOU GOT CAUGHT UP IN THE GAME...
...BUT DON'T YOU THINK YOU OVERDID IT?
POK
SHUP
WHAT?
SERENA TOLD ME TO TELL DETECTIVE TAKAGI TO PLAY THE LADY FIGHTER, BLINDFOLD HIMSELF WITH THE TIE AND JUST SIT BACK!
THEN THE ONE PLAYING THE MALE CHARACTER WAS...
IT WAS ME! SERENA TOLD ME TO.
RIGHT, CONAN?
RIGHT!

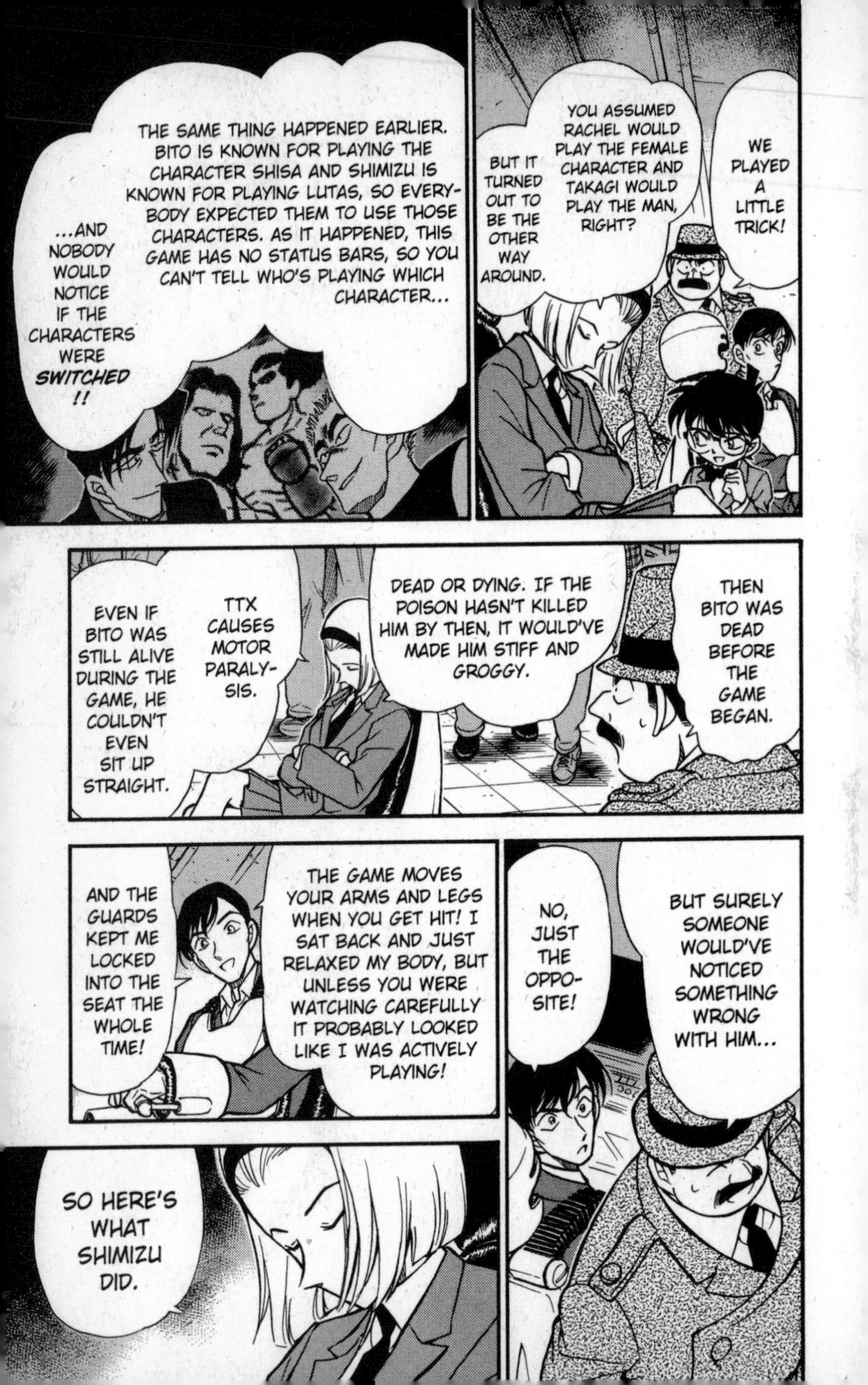
WE PLAYED A LITTLE TRICK!
YOU ASSUMED RACHEL WOULD PLAY THE FEMALE CHARACTER AND TAKAGI WOULD PLAY THE MAN, RIGHT?
BUT IT TURNED OUT TO BE THE OTHER WAY AROUND.
THE SAME THING HAPPENED EARLIER. BITO IS KNOWN FOR PLAYING THE CHARACTER SHISA AND SHIMIZU IS KNOWN FOR PLAYING LUTAS, SO EVERYBODY EXPECTED THEM TO USE THOSE CHARACTERS. AS IT HAPPENED, THIS GAME HAS NO STATUS BARS, SO YOU CAN'T TELL WHO'S PLAYING WHICH CHARACTER...
...AND NOBODY WOULD NOTICE IF THE CHARACTERS WERE ***SWITCHED*** !!
THEN BITO WAS DEAD BEFORE THE GAME BEGAN.
DEAD OR DYING. IF THE POISON HASN'T KILLED HIM BY THEN, IT WOULD'VE MADE HIM STIFF AND GROGGY.
TTX CAUSES MOTOR PARALYSIS.
EVEN IF BITO WAS STILL ALIVE DURING THE GAME, HE COULDN'T EVEN SIT UP STRAIGHT.
BUT SURELY SOMEONE WOULD'VE NOTICED SOMETHING WRONG WITH HIM...
NO, JUST THE OPPOSITE!
THE GAME MOVES YOUR ARMS AND LEGS WHEN YOU GET HIT! I SAT BACK AND JUST RELAXED MY BODY, BUT UNLESS YOU WERE WATCHING CAREFULLY IT PROBABLY LOOKED LIKE I WAS ACTIVELY PLAYING!
AND THE GUARDS KEPT ME LOCKED INTO THE SEAT THE WHOLE TIME!
SO HERE'S WHAT SHIMIZU DID.

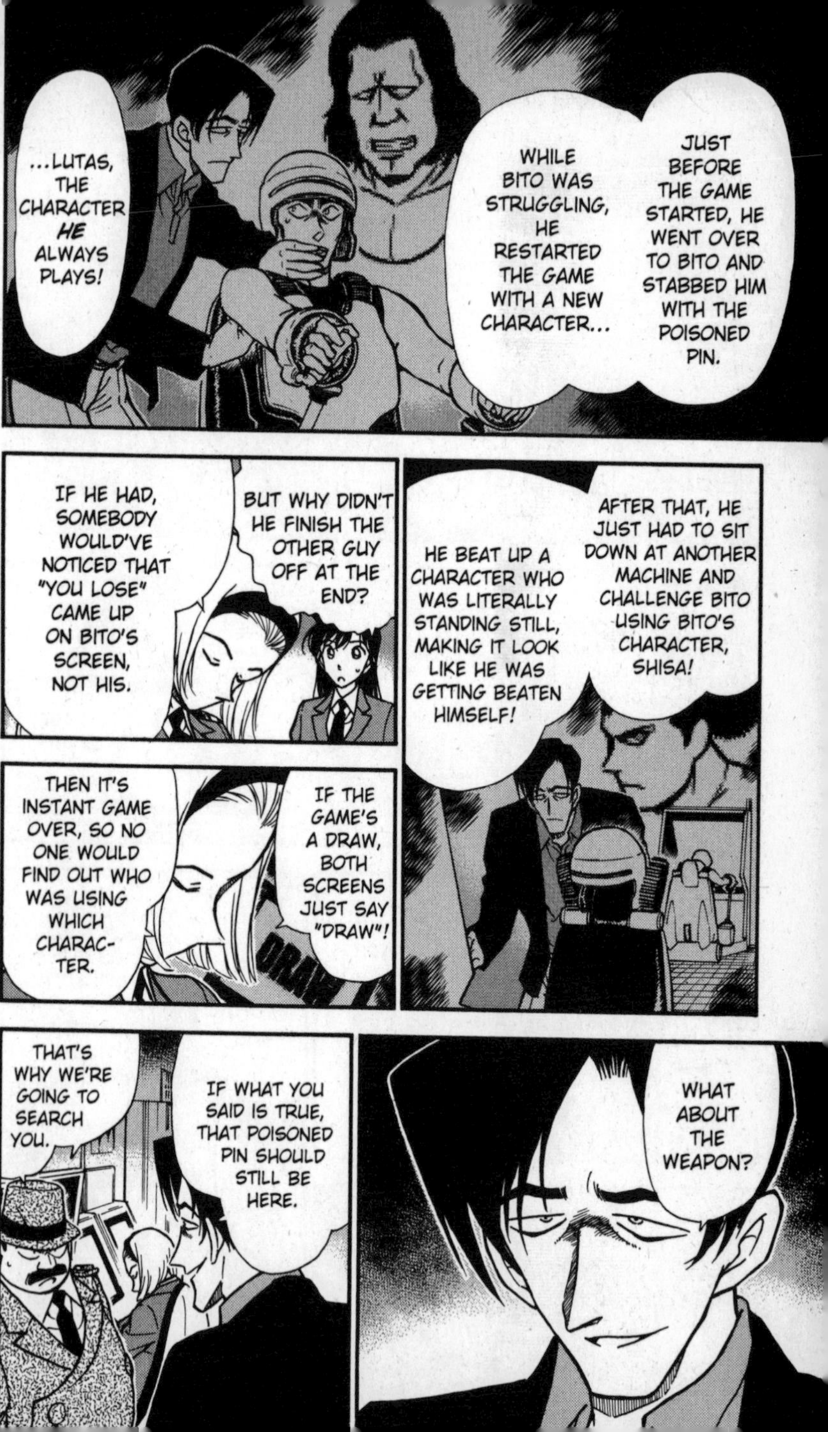
JUST BEFORE THE GAME STARTED, HE WENT OVER TO BITO AND STABBED HIM WITH THE POISONED PIN.
WHILE BITO WAS STRUGGLING, HE RESTARTED THE GAME WITH A NEW CHARACTER...
...LUTAS, THE CHARACTER *HE* ALWAYS PLAYS!
AFTER THAT, HE JUST HAD TO SIT DOWN AT ANOTHER MACHINE AND CHALLENGE BITO USING BITO'S CHARACTER, SHISA!
HE BEAT UP A CHARACTER WHO WAS LITERALLY STANDING STILL, MAKING IT LOOK LIKE HE WAS GETTING BEATEN HIMSELF!
BUT WHY DIDN'T HE FINISH THE OTHER GUY OFF AT THE END?
IF HE HAD, SOMEBODY WOULD'VE NOTICED THAT "YOU LOSE" CAME UP ON BITO'S SCREEN, NOT HIS.
IF THE GAME'S A DRAW, BOTH SCREENS JUST SAY "DRAW"!
THEN IT'S INSTANT GAME OVER, SO NO ONE WOULD FIND OUT WHO WAS USING WHICH CHARAC-TER.
WHAT ABOUT THE WEAPON?
IF WHAT YOU SAID IS TRUE, THAT POISONED PIN SHOULD STILL BE HERE.
THAT'S WHY WE'RE GOING TO SEARCH YOU.

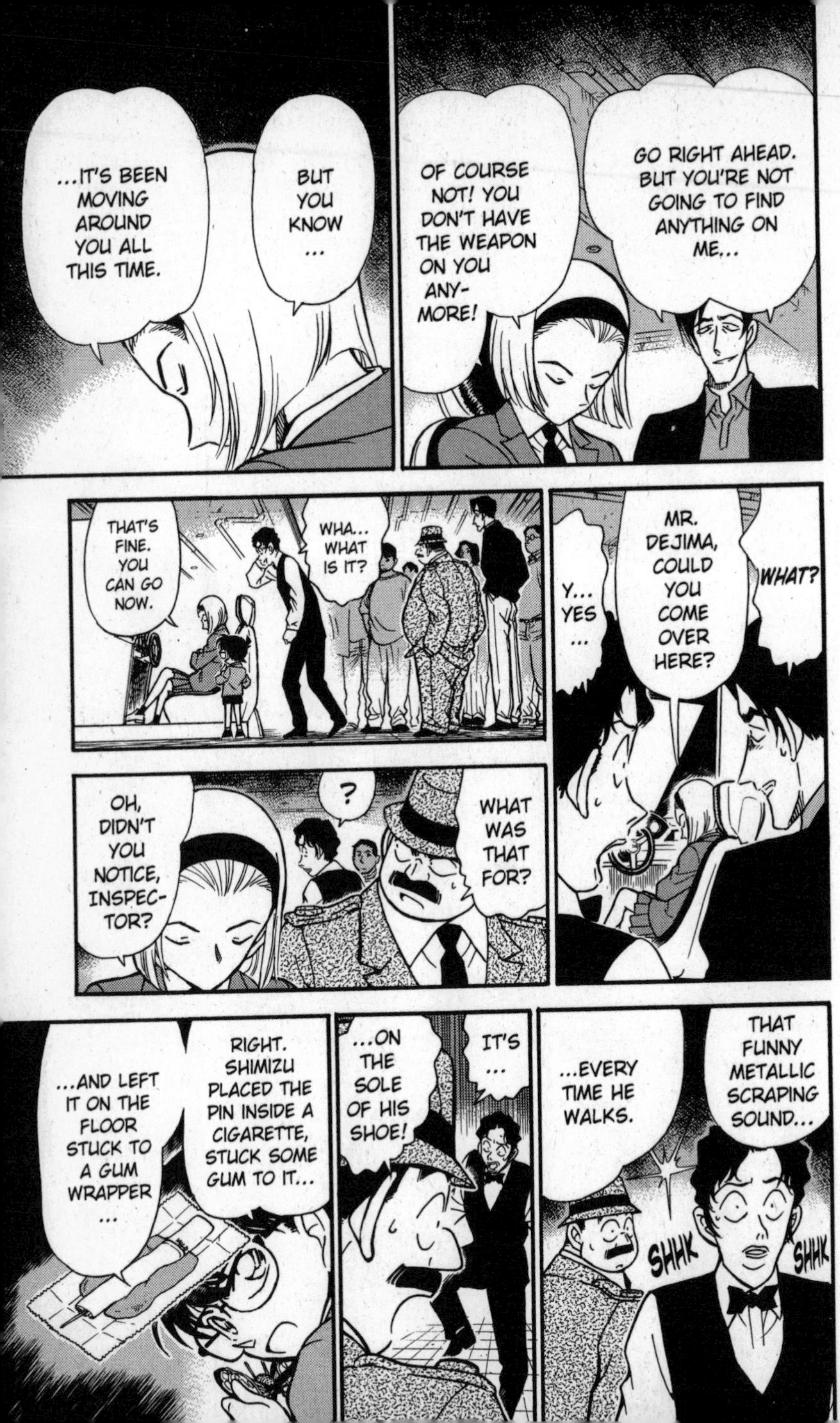
GO RIGHT AHEAD. BUT YOU'RE NOT GOING TO FIND ANYTHING ON ME...
OF COURSE NOT! YOU DON'T HAVE THE WEAPON ON YOU ANYMORE!
BUT YOU KNOW ...
...IT'S BEEN MOVING AROUND YOU ALL THIS TIME.
WHAT?
MR. DEJIMA, COULD YOU COME OVER HERE?
Y... YES ...
WHA... WHAT IS IT?
THAT'S FINE. YOU CAN GO NOW.
WHAT WAS THAT FOR?
?
OH, DIDN'T YOU NOTICE, INSPECTOR?
THAT FUNNY METALLIC SCRAPING SOUND...
...EVERY TIME HE WALKS.
SHHK
SHHK
IT'S ...
...ON THE SOLE OF HIS SHOE!
RIGHT. SHIMIZU PLACED THE PIN INSIDE A CIGARETTE, STUCK SOME GUM TO IT...
...AND LEFT IT ON THE FLOOR STUCK TO A GUM WRAPPER ...

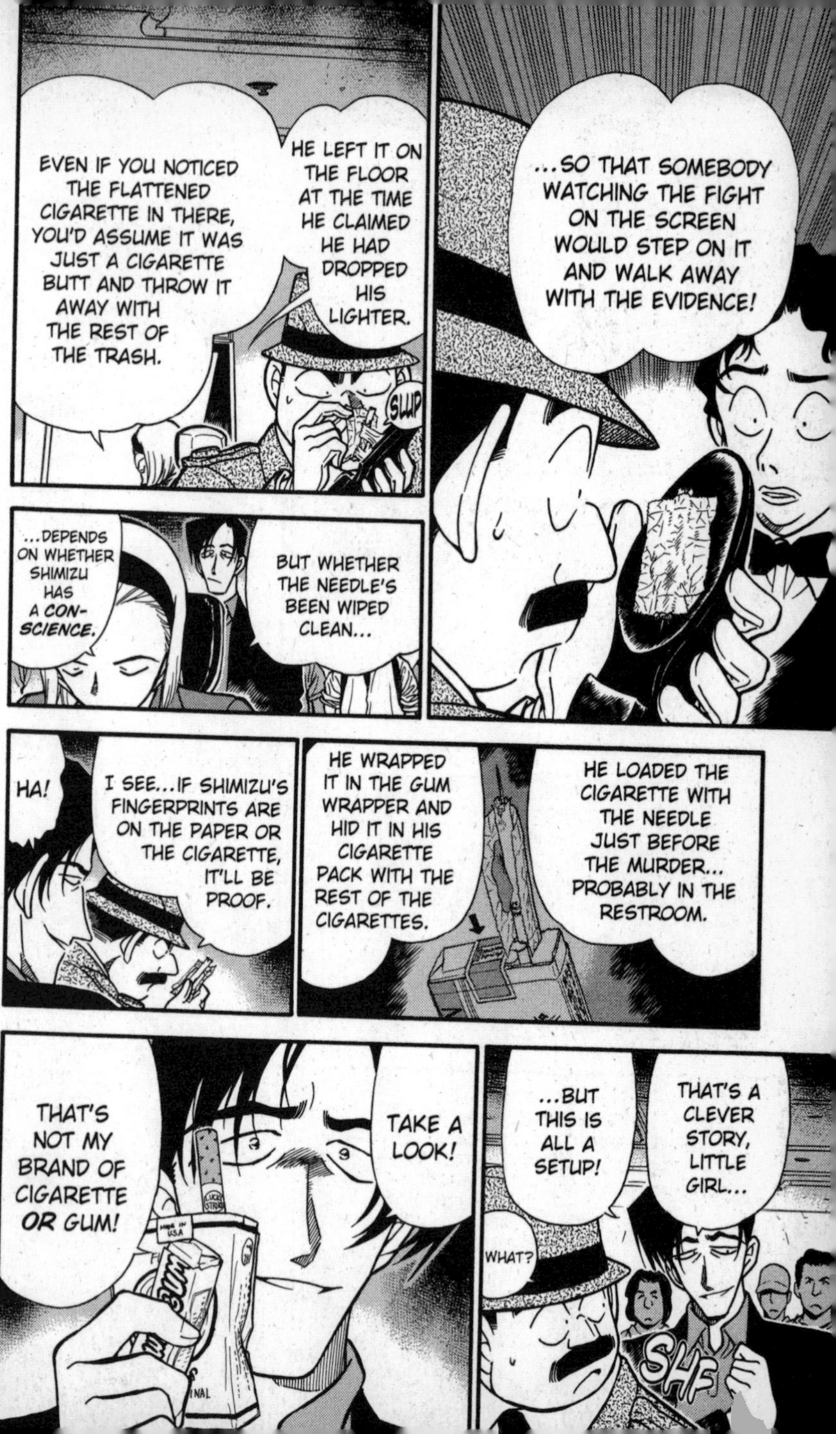
...SO THAT SOMEBODY WATCHING THE FIGHT ON THE SCREEN WOULD STEP ON IT AND WALK AWAY WITH THE EVIDENCE!
HE LEFT IT ON THE FLOOR AT THE TIME HE CLAIMED HE HAD DROPPED HIS LIGHTER.
EVEN IF YOU NOTICED THE FLATTENED CIGARETTE IN THERE, YOU'D ASSUME IT WAS JUST A CIGARETTE BUTT AND THROW IT AWAY WITH THE REST OF THE TRASH.
SLIP
BUT WHETHER THE NEEDLE'S BEEN WIPED CLEAN...
...DEPENDS ON WHETHER SHIMIZU HAS A **CON-SCIENCE.**
HE LOADED THE CIGARETTE WITH THE NEEDLE JUST BEFORE THE MURDER... PROBABLY IN THE RESTROOM.
HE WRAPPED IT IN THE GUM WRAPPER AND HID IT IN HIS CIGARETTE PACK WITH THE REST OF THE CIGARETTES.
I SEE...IF SHIMIZU'S FINGERPRINTS ARE ON THE PAPER OR THE CIGARETTE, IT'LL BE PROOF.
HA!
THAT'S A CLEVER STORY, LITTLE GIRL...
...BUT THIS IS ALL A SETUP!
WHAT?
SHF
TAKE A LOOK!
THAT'S NOT MY BRAND OF CIGARETTE **OR** GUM!

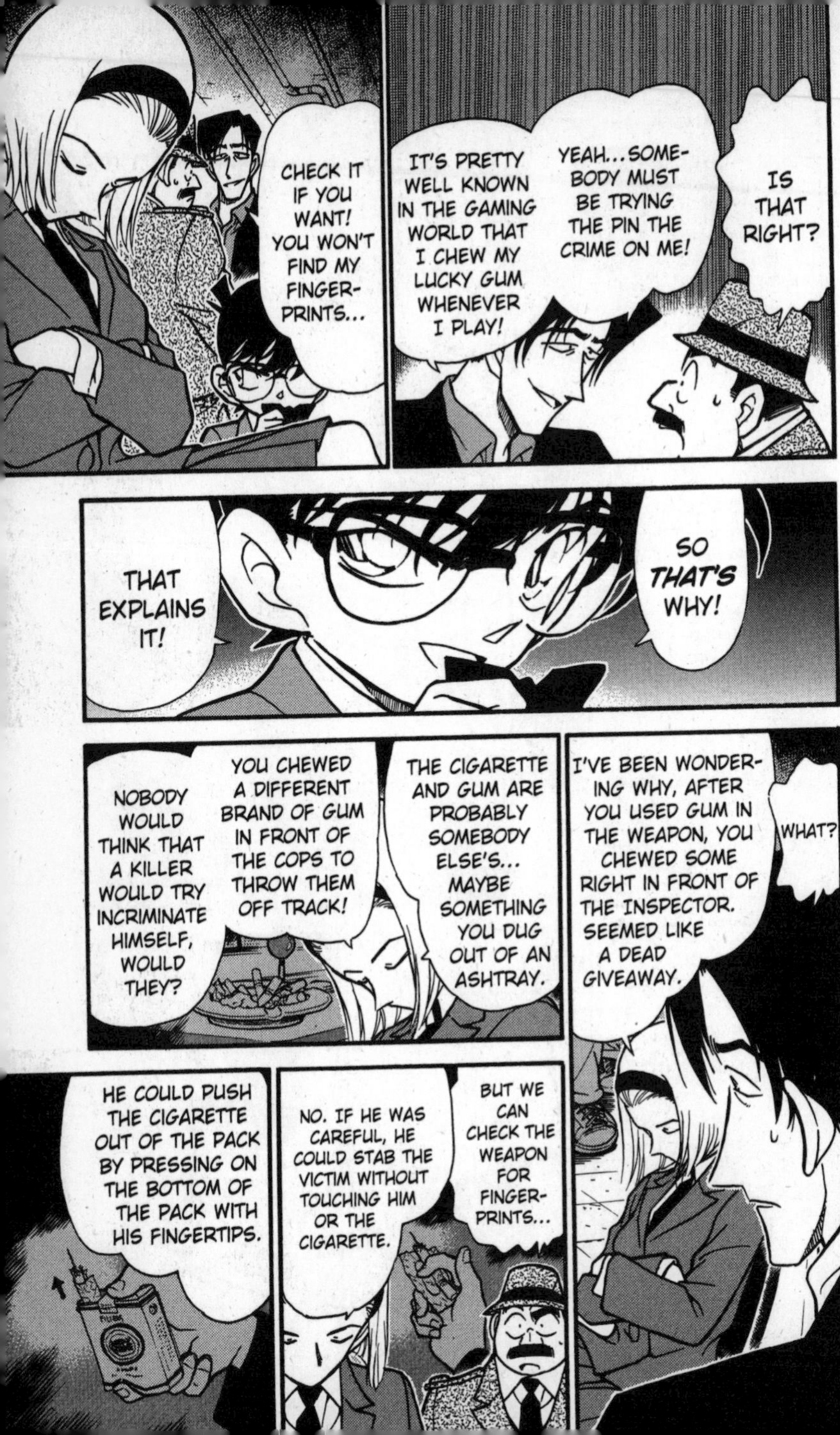
IS THAT RIGHT?
YEAH...SOMEBODY MUST BE TRYING THE PIN THE CRIME ON ME!
IT'S PRETTY WELL KNOWN IN THE GAMING WORLD THAT I CHEW MY LUCKY GUM WHENEVER I PLAY!
CHECK IT IF YOU WANT! YOU WON'T FIND MY FINGERPRINTS...
SO *THAT'S* WHY!
THAT EXPLAINS IT!
WHAT?
I'VE BEEN WONDERING WHY, AFTER YOU USED GUM IN THE WEAPON, YOU CHEWED SOME RIGHT IN FRONT OF THE INSPECTOR. SEEMED LIKE A DEAD GIVEAWAY.
THE CIGARETTE AND GUM ARE PROBABLY SOMEBODY ELSE'S... MAYBE SOMETHING YOU DUG OUT OF AN ASHTRAY.
YOU CHEWED A DIFFERENT BRAND OF GUM IN FRONT OF THE COPS TO THROW THEM OFF TRACK!
NOBODY WOULD THINK THAT A KILLER WOULD TRY INCRIMINATE HIMSELF, WOULD THEY?
BUT WE CAN CHECK THE WEAPON FOR FINGERPRINTS...
NO. IF HE WAS CAREFUL, HE COULD STAB THE VICTIM WITHOUT TOUCHING HIM OR THE CIGARETTE.
HE COULD PUSH THE CIGARETTE OUT OF THE PACK BY PRESSING ON THE BOTTOM OF THE PACK WITH HIS FINGERTIPS.

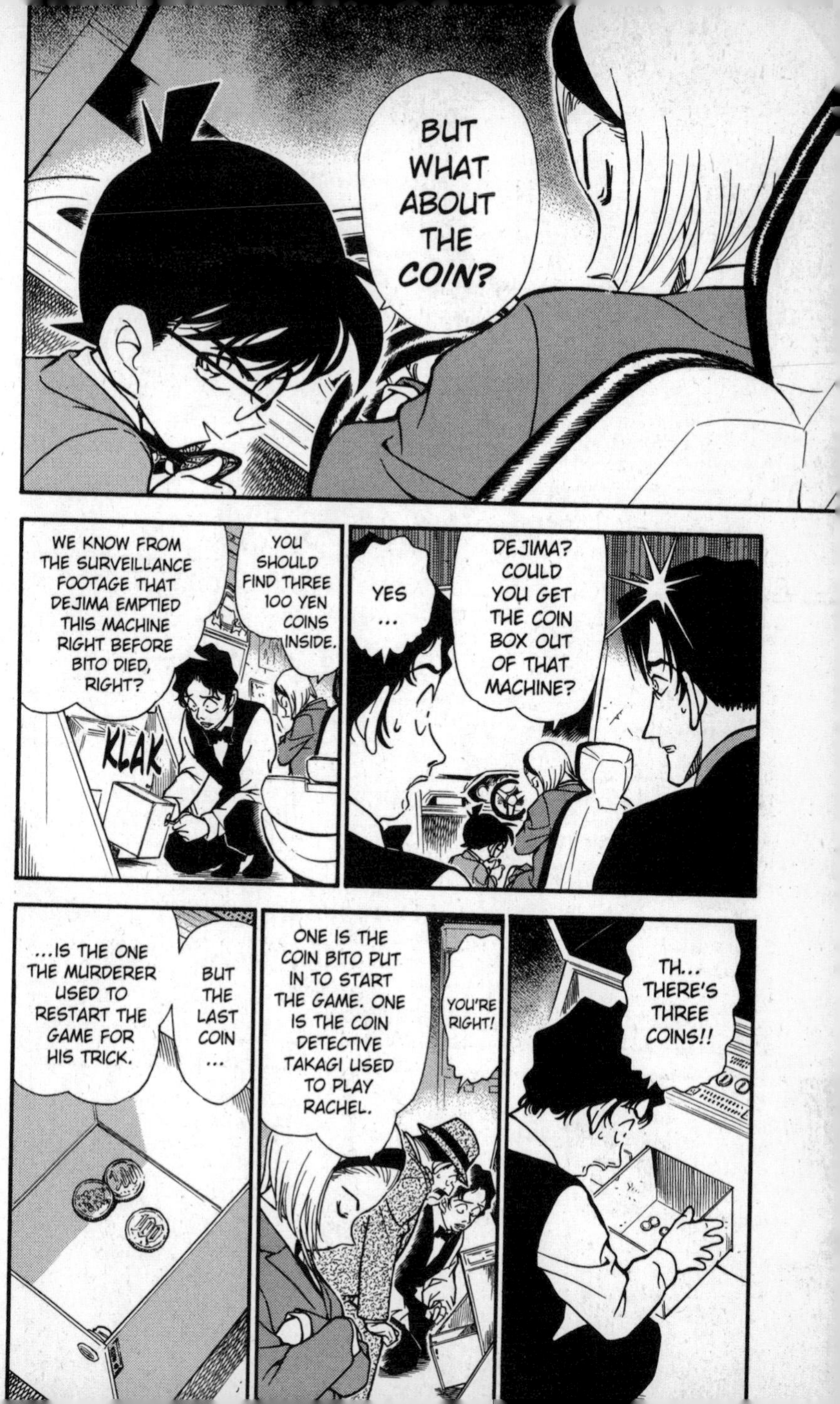
BUT WHAT ABOUT THE COIN?
DEJIMA? COULD YOU GET THE COIN BOX OUT OF THAT MACHINE?
YES ...
YOU SHOULD FIND THREE 100 YEN COINS INSIDE.
WE KNOW FROM THE SURVEILLANCE FOOTAGE THAT DEJIMA EMPTIED THIS MACHINE RIGHT BEFORE BITO DIED, RIGHT?
KLAK
TH... THERE'S THREE COINS!!
YOU'RE RIGHT!
ONE IS THE COIN BITO PUT IN TO START THE GAME. ONE IS THE COIN DETECTIVE TAKAGI USED TO PLAY RACHEL.
BUT THE LAST COIN ...
...IS THE ONE THE MURDERER USED TO RESTART THE GAME FOR HIS TRICK.

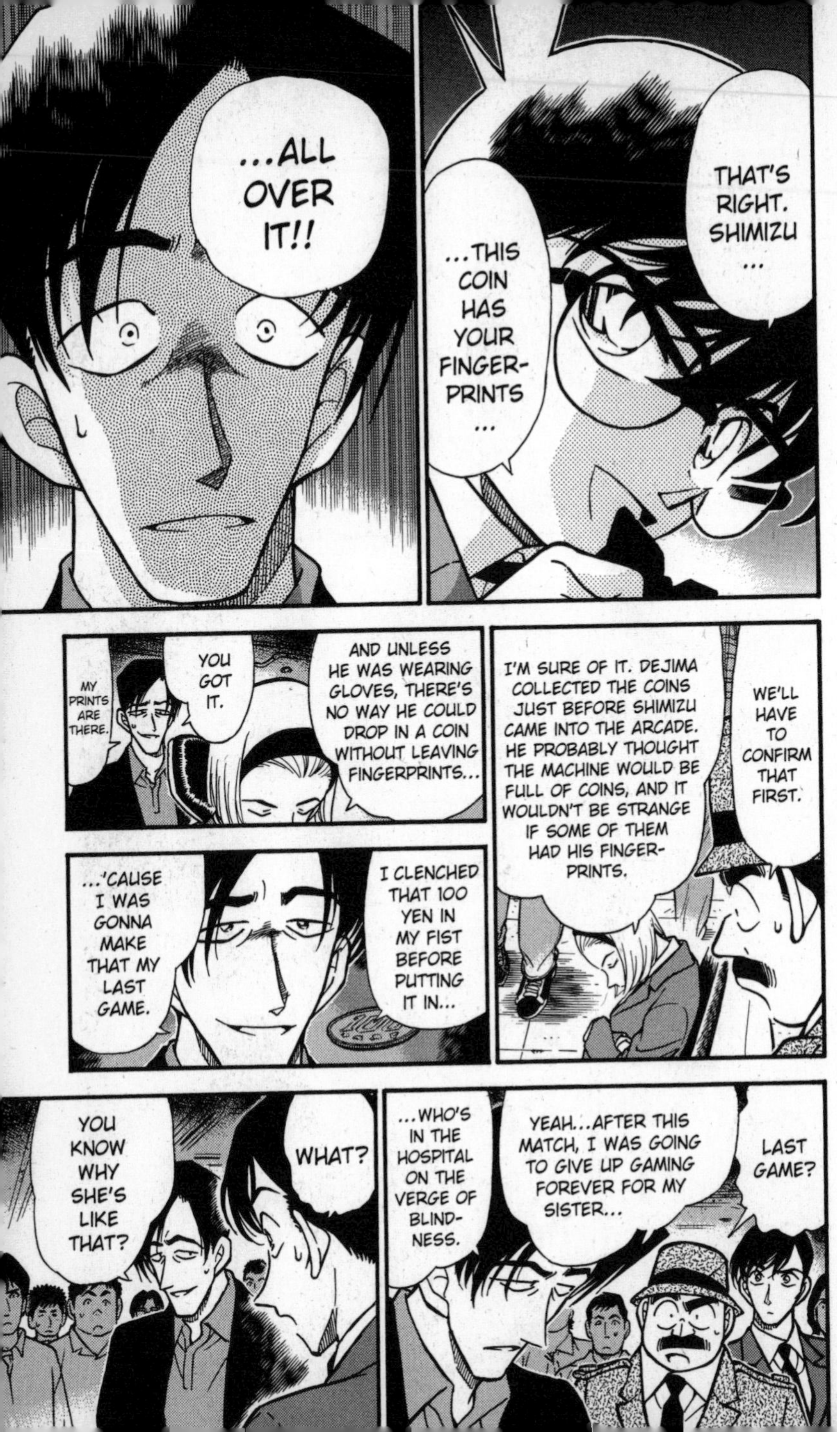
THAT'S RIGHT. SHIMIZU ...
...THIS COIN HAS YOUR FINGER-PRINTS ...
...ALL OVER IT!!
WE'LL HAVE TO CONFIRM THAT FIRST.
I'M SURE OF IT. DEJIMA COLLECTED THE COINS JUST BEFORE SHIMIZU CAME INTO THE ARCADE. HE PROBABLY THOUGHT THE MACHINE WOULD BE FULL OF COINS, AND IT WOULDN'T BE STRANGE IF SOME OF THEM HAD HIS FINGER-PRINTS.
AND UNLESS HE WAS WEARING GLOVES, THERE'S NO WAY HE COULD DROP IN A COIN WITHOUT LEAVING FINGERPRINTS...
YOU GOT IT.
MY PRINTS ARE THERE.
I CLENCHED THAT 100 YEN IN MY FIST BEFORE PUTTING IT IN...
...'CAUSE I WAS GONNA MAKE THAT MY LAST GAME.
LAST GAME?
YEAH...AFTER THIS MATCH, I WAS GOING TO GIVE UP GAMING FOREVER FOR MY SISTER...
...WHO'S IN THE HOSPITAL ON THE VERGE OF BLIND-NESS.
WHAT?
YOU KNOW WHY SHE'S LIKE THAT?

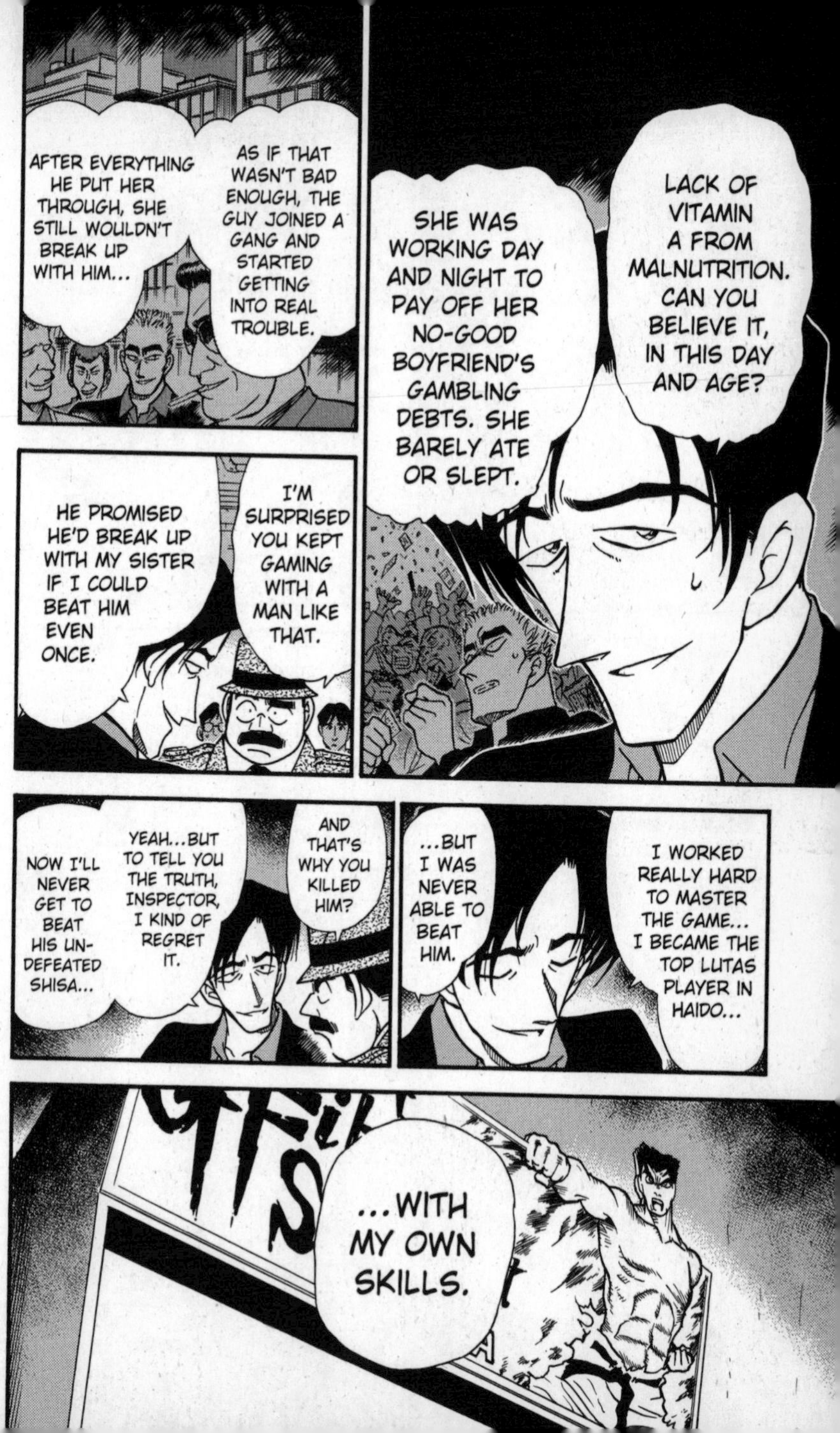
LACK OF VITAMIN A FROM MALNUTRITION. CAN YOU BELIEVE IT, IN THIS DAY AND AGE?
SHE WAS WORKING DAY AND NIGHT TO PAY OFF HER NO-GOOD BOYFRIEND'S GAMBLING DEBTS. SHE BARELY ATE OR SLEPT.
AS IF THAT WASN'T BAD ENOUGH, THE GUY JOINED A GANG AND STARTED GETTING INTO REAL TROUBLE.
AFTER EVERYTHING HE PUT HER THROUGH, SHE STILL WOULDN'T BREAK UP WITH HIM...
I'M SURPRISED YOU KEPT GAMING WITH A MAN LIKE THAT.
HE PROMISED HE'D BREAK UP WITH MY SISTER IF I COULD BEAT HIM EVEN ONCE.
I WORKED REALLY HARD TO MASTER THE GAME... I BECAME THE TOP LUTAS PLAYER IN HAIDO...
...BUT I WAS NEVER ABLE TO BEAT HIM.
AND THAT'S WHY YOU KILLED HIM?
YEAH...BUT TO TELL YOU THE TRUTH, INSPECTOR, I KIND OF REGRET IT.
NOW I'LL NEVER GET TO BEAT HIS UN-DEFEATED SHISA...
...WITH MY OWN SKILLS.

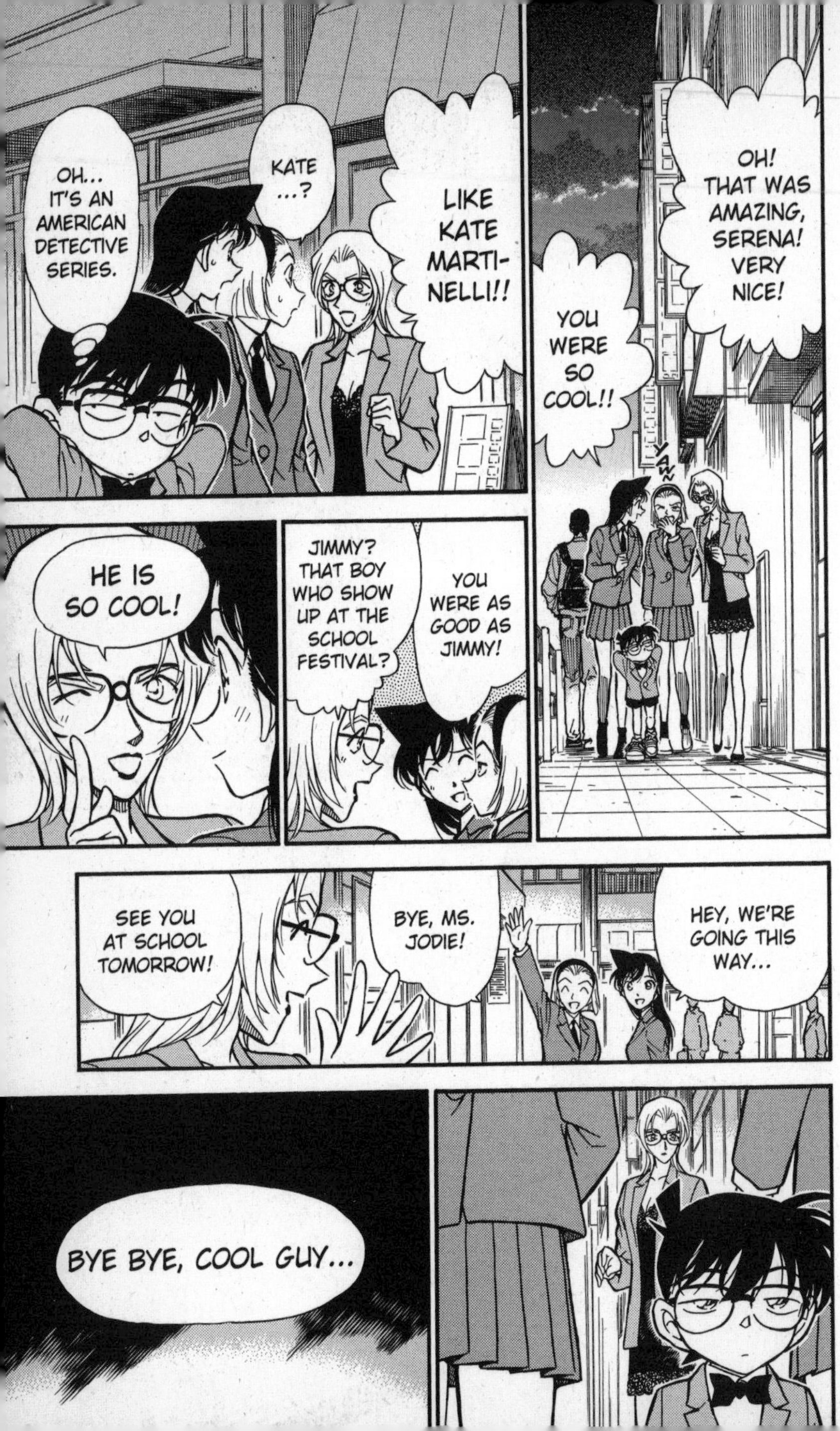
OH! THAT WAS AMAZING, SERENA! VERY NICE!
YOU WERE SO COOL!!
YAWN
LIKE KATE MARTI-NELLI!!
KATE ...?
OH... IT'S AN AMERICAN DETECTIVE SERIES.
YOU WERE AS GOOD AS JIMMY!
JIMMY? THAT BOY WHO SHOW UP AT THE SCHOOL FESTIVAL?
HE IS SO COOL!
HEY, WE'RE GOING THIS WAY...
BYE, MS. JODIE!
SEE YOU AT SCHOOL TOMORROW!
BYE BYE, COOL GUY...

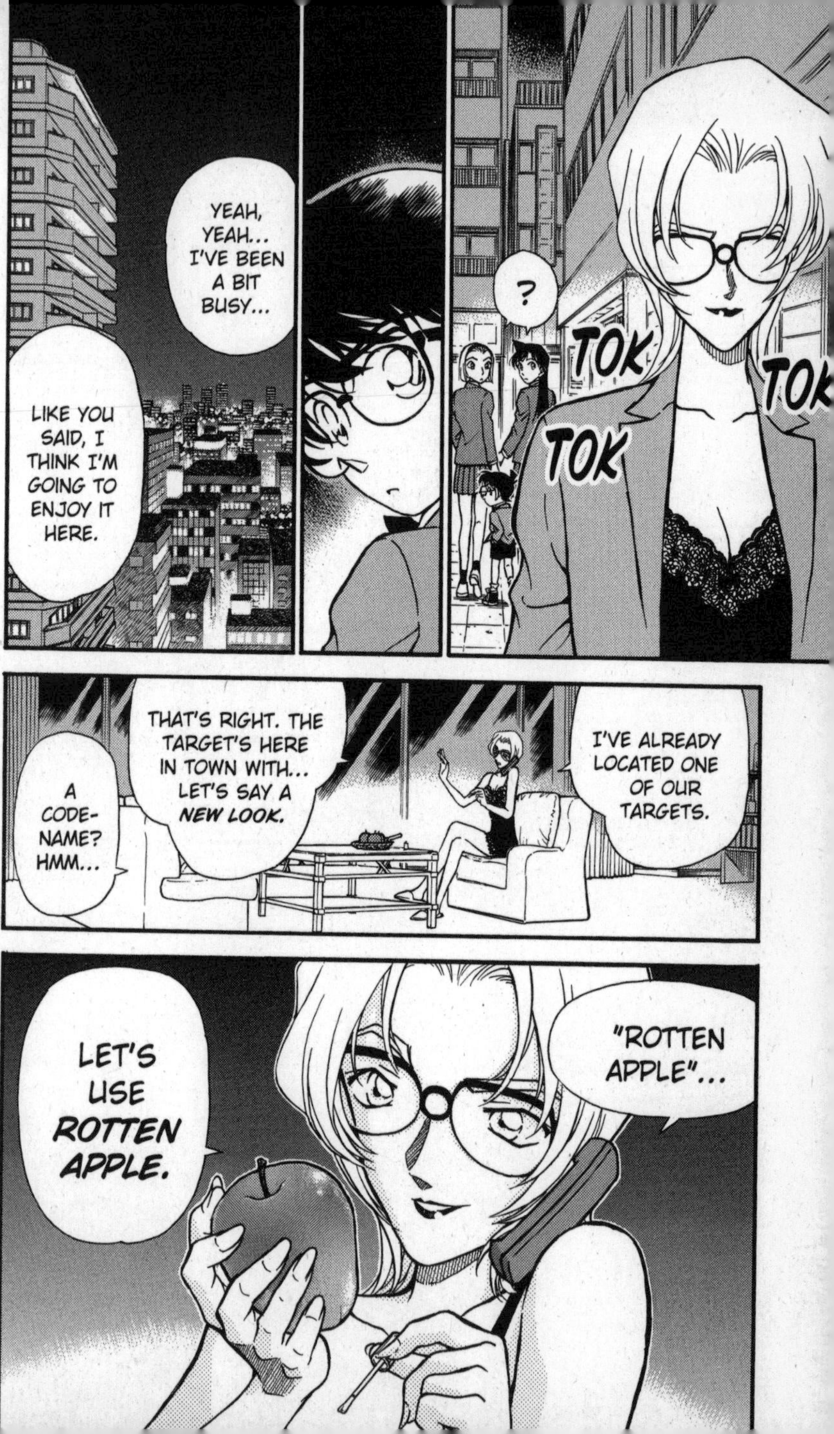
TOK
TOK
?
TOK
YEAH, YEAH... I'VE BEEN A BIT BUSY...
LIKE YOU SAID, I THINK I'M GOING TO ENJOY IT HERE.
I'VE ALREADY LOCATED ONE OF OUR TARGETS.
THAT'S RIGHT. THE TARGET'S HERE IN TOWN WITH... LET'S SAY A *NEW LOOK.*
A CODE-NAME? HMM...
"ROTTEN APPLE"...
LET'S USE ***ROTTEN APPLE.***

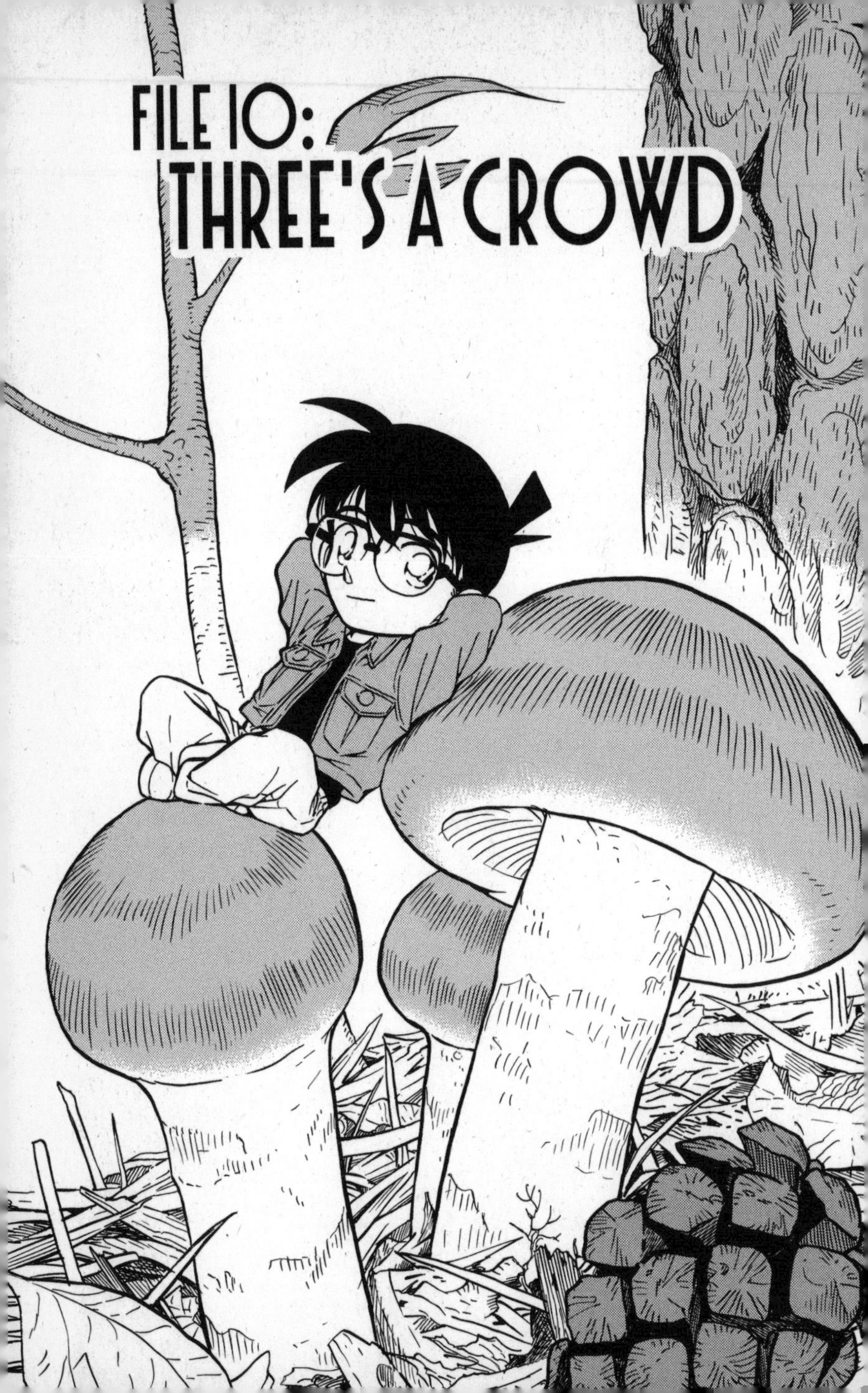
FILE 10:
THREE'S A CROWD

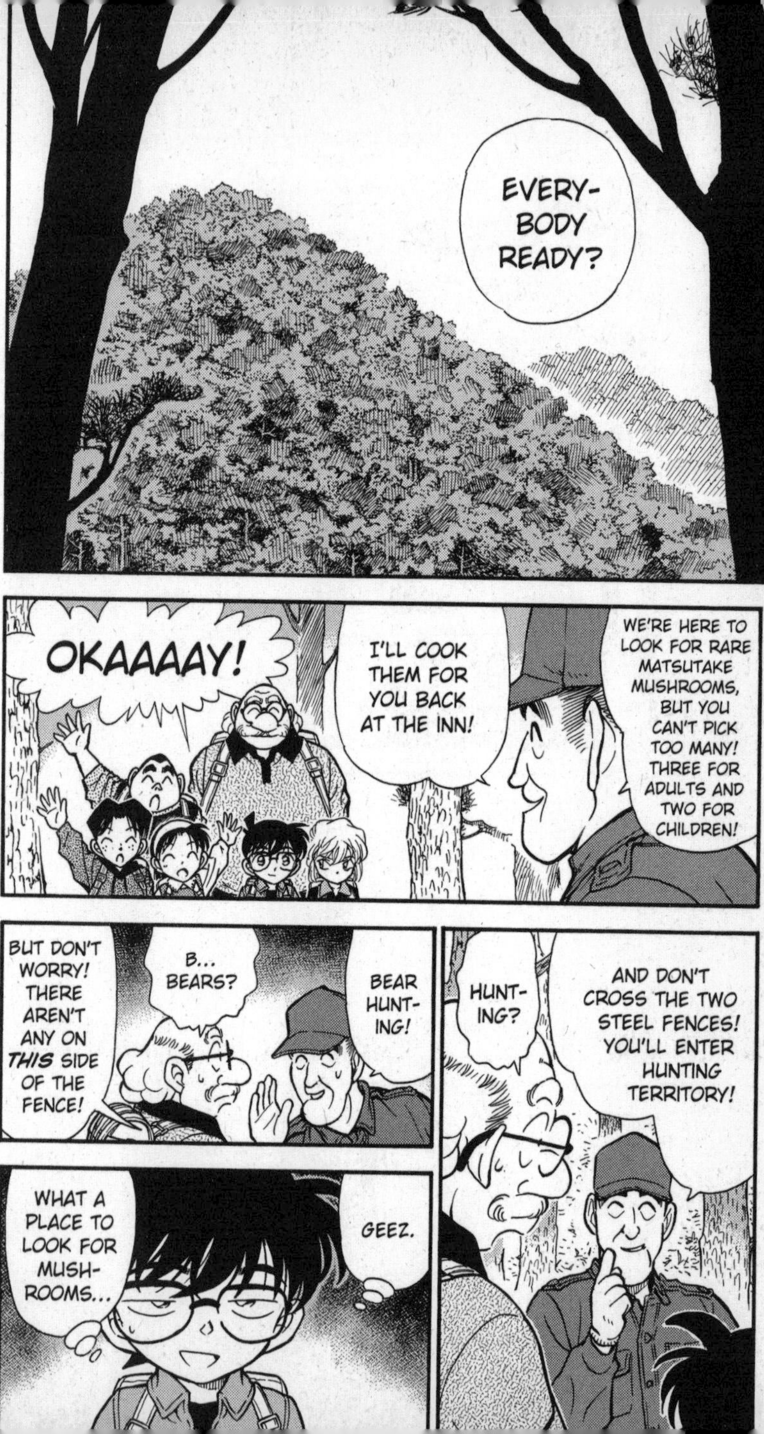
EVERY-BODY READY?
WE'RE HERE TO LOOK FOR RARE MATSUTAKE MUSHROOMS, BUT YOU CAN'T PICK TOO MANY! THREE FOR ADULTS AND TWO FOR CHILDREN!
I'LL COOK THEM FOR YOU BACK AT THE INN!
OKAAAAY!
AND DON'T CROSS THE TWO STEEL FENCES! YOU'LL ENTER HUNTING TERRITORY!
HUNT-ING?
BEAR HUNT-ING!
B... BEARS?
BUT DON'T WORRY! THERE AREN'T ANY ON *THIS* SIDE OF THE FENCE!
GEEZ.
WHAT A PLACE TO LOOK FOR MUSH-ROOMS...

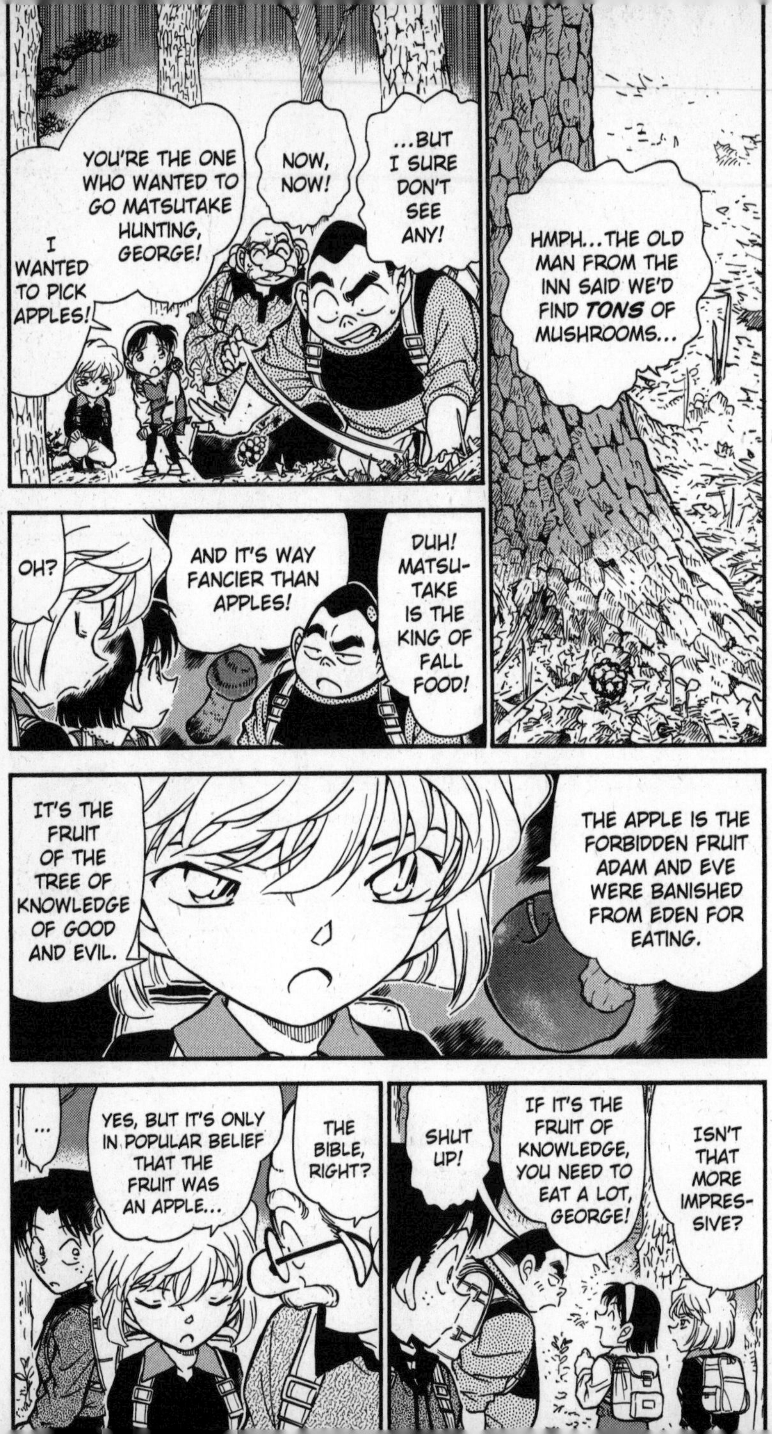
HMPH...THE OLD MAN FROM THE INN SAID WE'D FIND ***TONS*** OF MUSHROOMS...
...BUT I SURE DON'T SEE ANY!
NOW, NOW!
YOU'RE THE ONE WHO WANTED TO GO MATSUTAKE HUNTING, GEORGE!
I WANTED TO PICK APPLES!
DUH! MATSU-TAKE IS THE KING OF FALL FOOD!
AND IT'S WAY FANCIER THAN APPLES!
OH?
THE APPLE IS THE FORBIDDEN FRUIT ADAM AND EVE WERE BANISHED FROM EDEN FOR EATING.
IT'S THE FRUIT OF THE TREE OF KNOWLEDGE OF GOOD AND EVIL.
ISN'T THAT MORE IMPRES-SIVE?
IF IT'S THE FRUIT OF KNOWLEDGE, YOU NEED TO EAT A LOT, GEORGE!
SHUT UP!
THE BIBLE, RIGHT?
YES, BUT IT'S ONLY IN POPULAR BELIEF THAT THE FRUIT WAS AN APPLE...
...

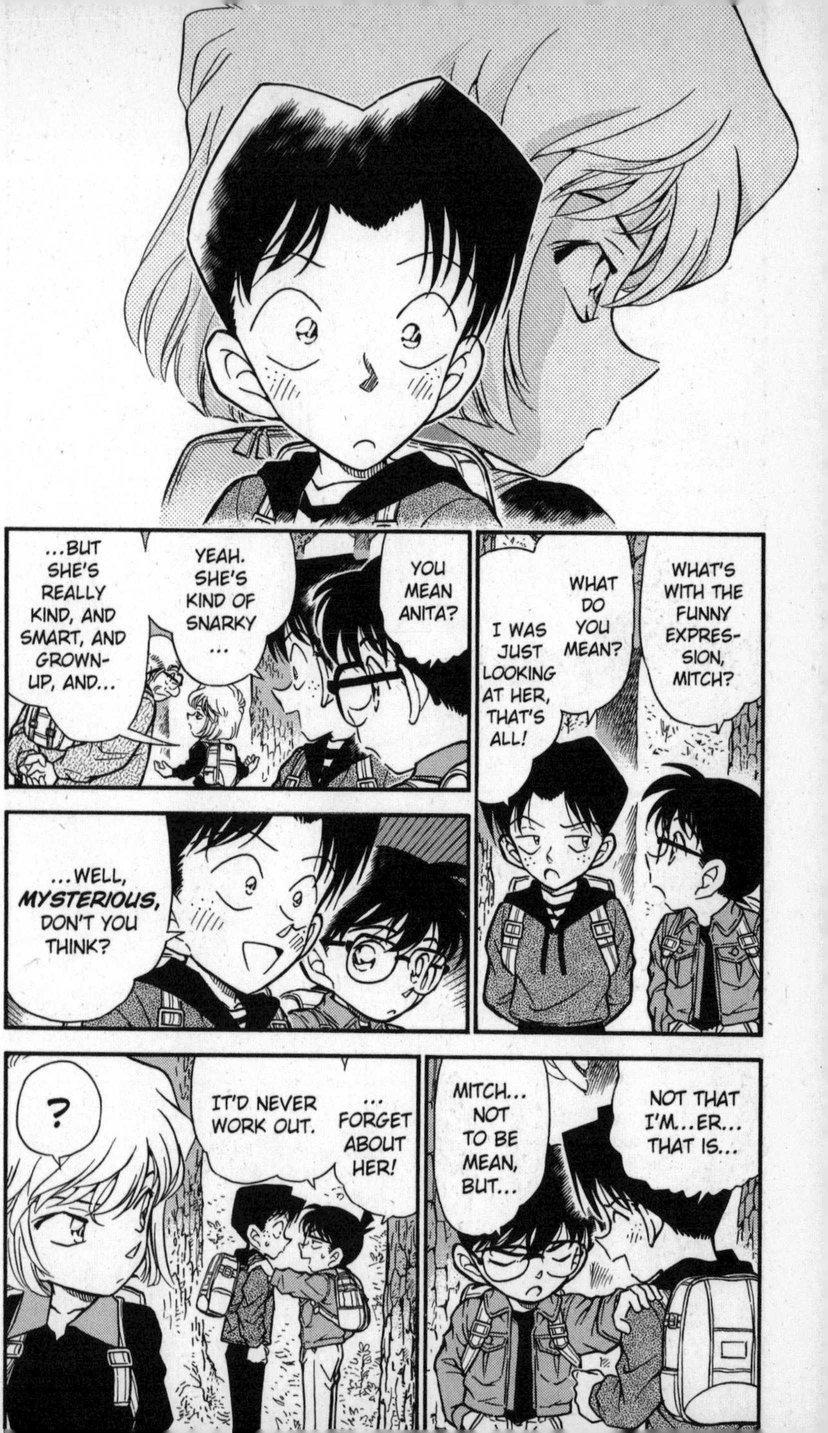
WHAT'S WITH THE FUNNY EXPRESSION, MITCH?
WHAT DO YOU MEAN?
I WAS JUST LOOKING AT HER, THAT'S ALL!
YOU MEAN ANITA?
YEAH. SHE'S KIND OF SNARKY...
...BUT SHE'S REALLY KIND, AND SMART, AND GROWN-UP, AND...
...WELL, *MYSTERIOUS,* DON'T YOU THINK?
NOT THAT I'M...ER... THAT IS...
MITCH... NOT TO BE MEAN, BUT...
...FORGET ABOUT HER!
IT'D NEVER WORK OUT.
?

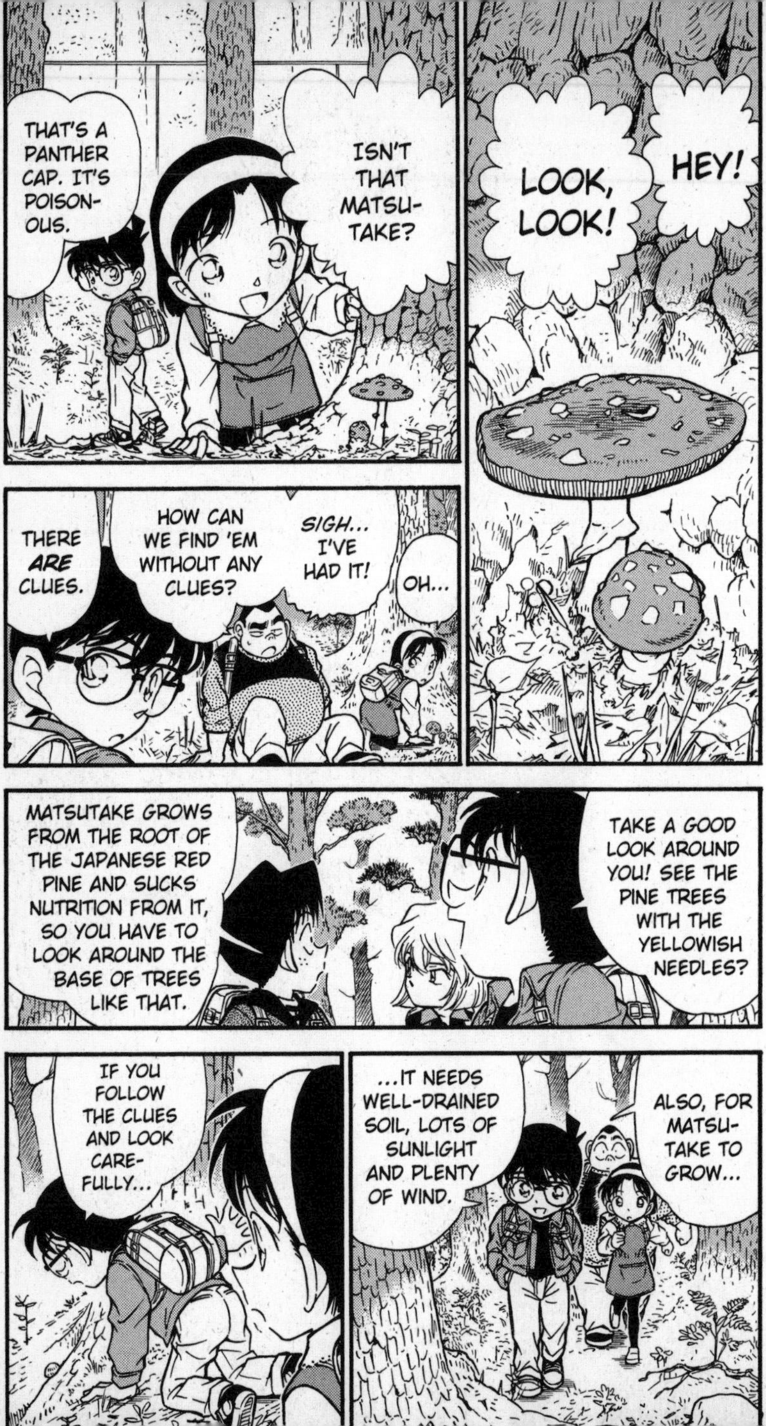
HEY!
LOOK, LOOK!
ISN'T THAT MATSU-TAKE?
THAT'S A PANTHER CAP. IT'S POISON-OUS.
OH...
SIGH... I'VE HAD IT!
HOW CAN WE FIND 'EM WITHOUT ANY CLUES?
THERE ***ARE*** CLUES.
TAKE A GOOD LOOK AROUND YOU! SEE THE PINE TREES WITH THE YELLOWISH NEEDLES?
MATSUTAKE GROWS FROM THE ROOT OF THE JAPANESE RED PINE AND SUCKS NUTRITION FROM IT, SO YOU HAVE TO LOOK AROUND THE BASE OF TREES LIKE THAT.
ALSO, FOR MATSU-TAKE TO GROW...
...IT NEEDS WELL-DRAINED SOIL, LOTS OF SUNLIGHT AND PLENTY OF WIND.
IF YOU FOLLOW THE CLUES AND LOOK CARE-FULLY...

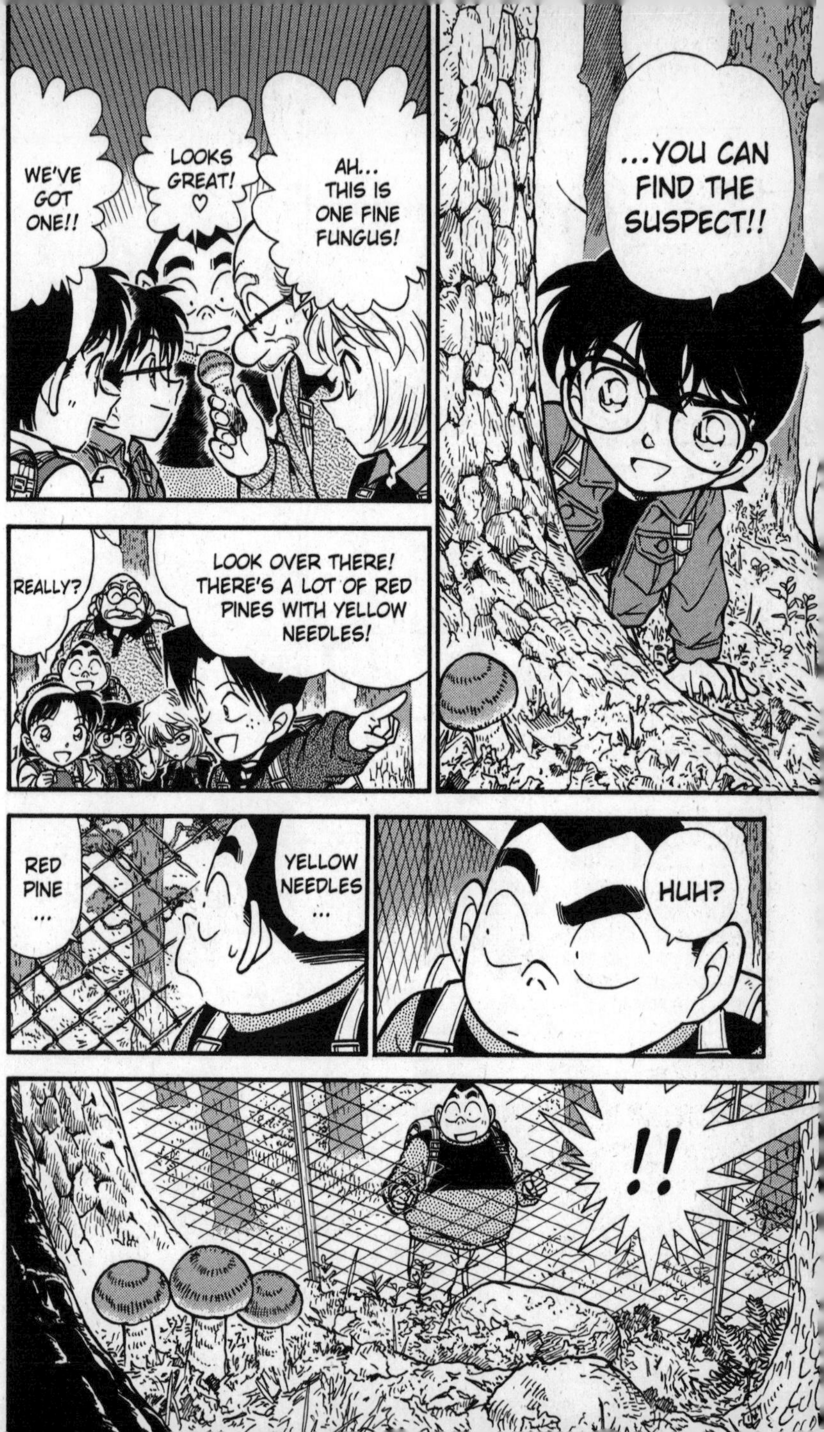
...YOU CAN FIND THE SUSPECT!!
AH... THIS IS ONE FINE FUNGUS!
LOOKS GREAT! ♡
WE'VE GOT ONE!!
LOOK OVER THERE! THERE'S A LOT OF RED PINES WITH YELLOW NEEDLES!
REALLY?
HUH?
YELLOW NEEDLES ...
RED PINE ...
!!

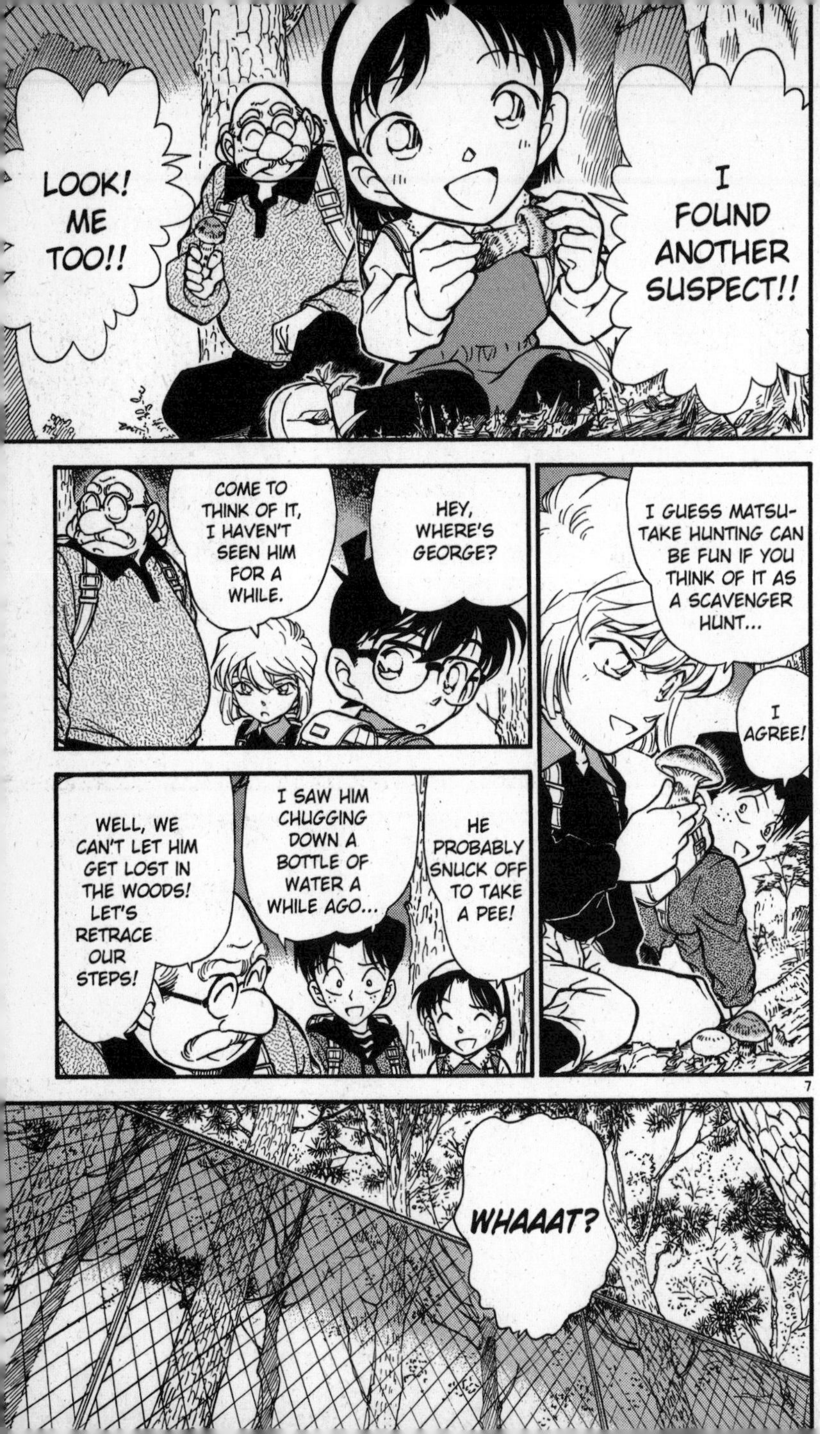
I FOUND ANOTHER SUSPECT!!
LOOK! ME TOO!!
I GUESS MATSU-TAKE HUNTING CAN BE FUN IF YOU THINK OF IT AS A SCAVENGER HUNT...
I AGREE!
HEY, WHERE'S GEORGE?
COME TO THINK OF IT, I HAVEN'T SEEN HIM FOR A WHILE.
HE PROBABLY SNUCK OFF TO TAKE A PEE!
I SAW HIM CHUGGING DOWN A BOTTLE OF WATER A WHILE AGO...
WELL, WE CAN'T LET HIM GET LOST IN THE WOODS! LET'S RETRACE OUR STEPS!
WHAAAT?

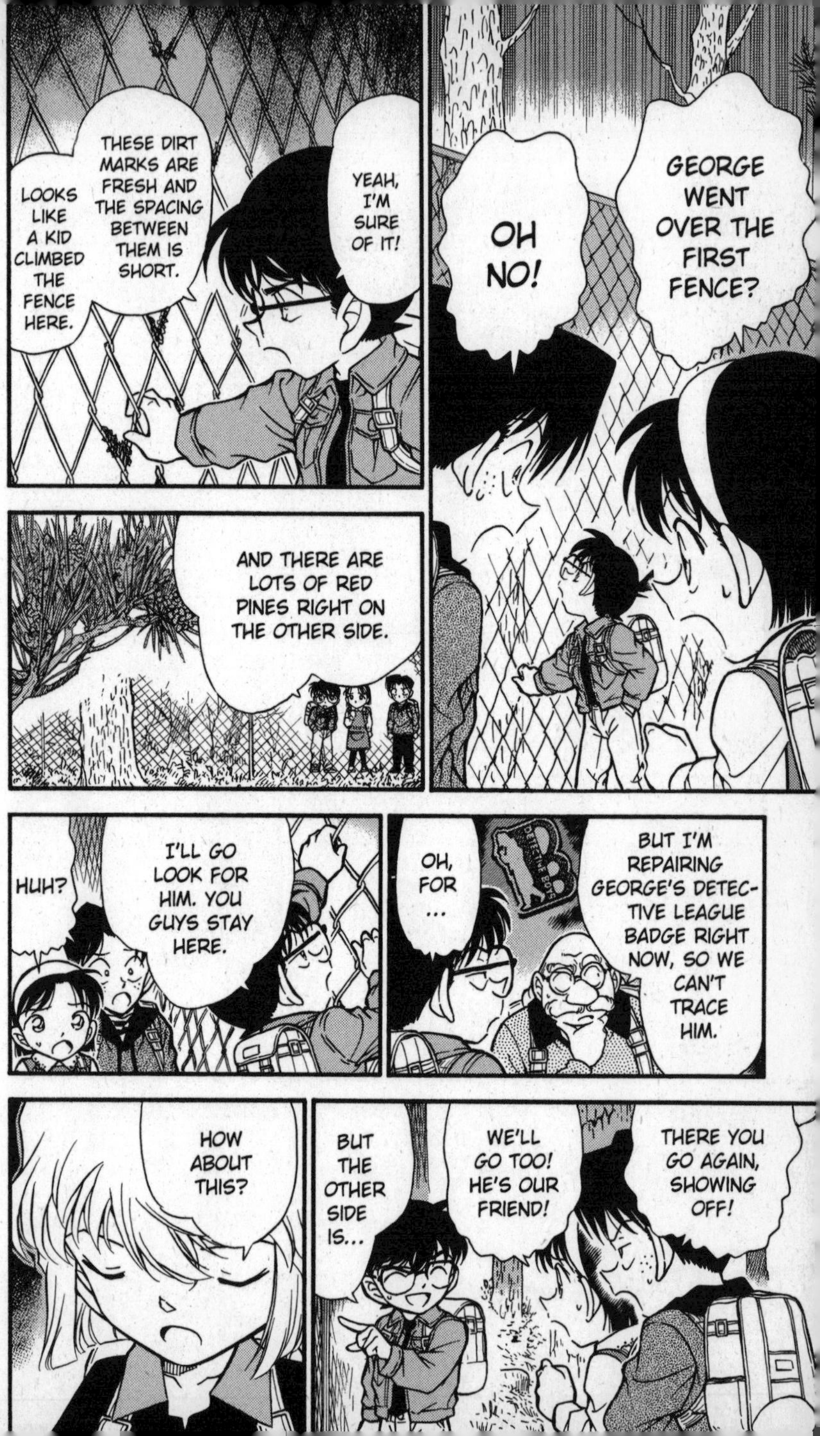
GEORGE WENT OVER THE FIRST FENCE?
OH NO!
YEAH, I'M SURE OF IT!
THESE DIRT MARKS ARE FRESH AND THE SPACING BETWEEN THEM IS SHORT.
LOOKS LIKE A KID CLIMBED THE FENCE HERE.
AND THERE ARE LOTS OF RED PINES RIGHT ON THE OTHER SIDE.
BUT I'M REPAIRING GEORGE'S DETECTIVE LEAGUE BADGE RIGHT NOW, SO WE CAN'T TRACE HIM.
OH, FOR ...
I'LL GO LOOK FOR HIM. YOU GUYS STAY HERE.
HUH?
THERE YOU GO AGAIN, SHOWING OFF!
WE'LL GO TOO! HE'S OUR FRIEND!
BUT THE OTHER SIDE IS...
HOW ABOUT THIS?

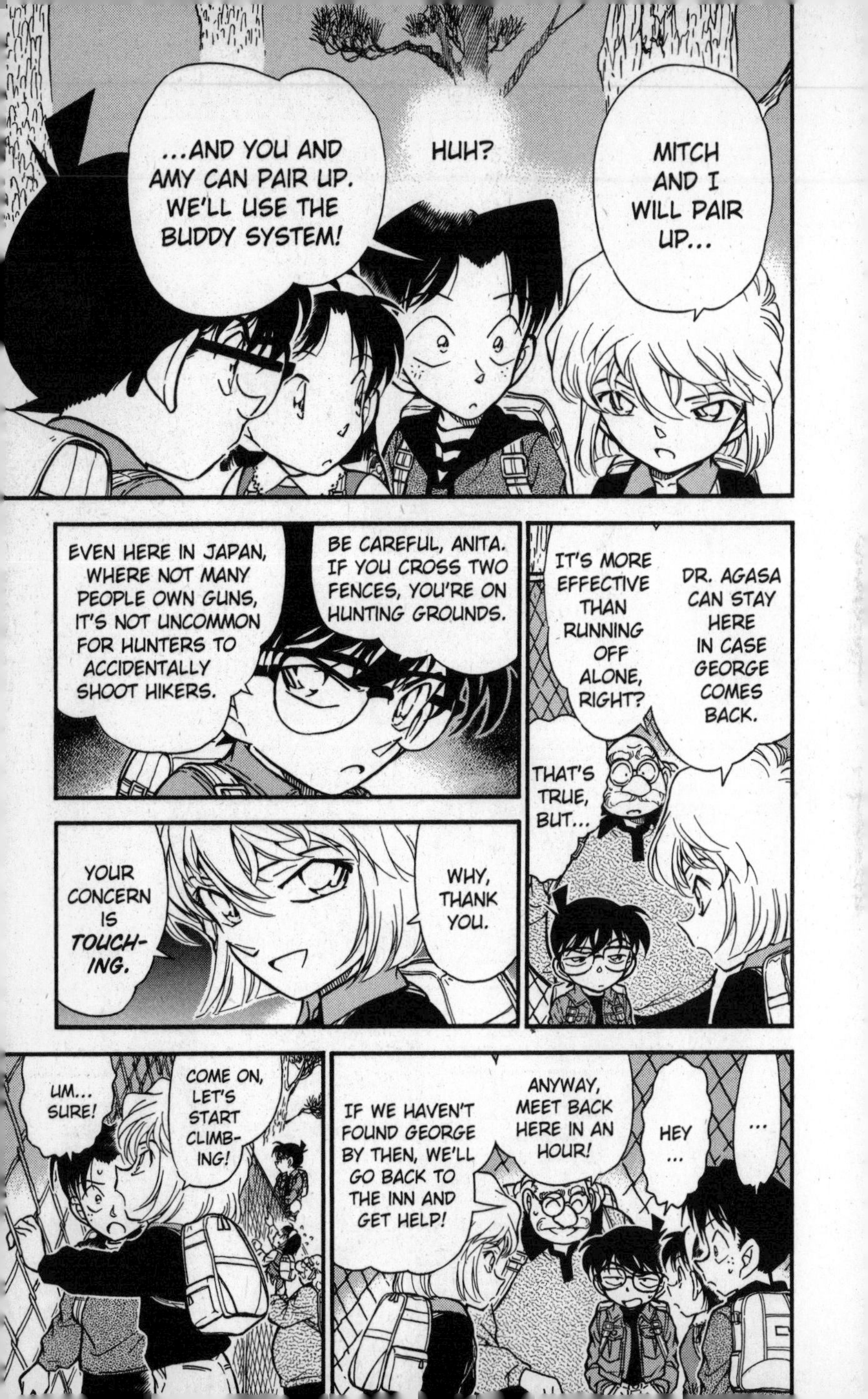
MITCH AND I WILL PAIR UP...
HUH?
...AND YOU AND AMY CAN PAIR UP. WE'LL USE THE BUDDY SYSTEM!
DR. AGASA CAN STAY HERE IN CASE GEORGE COMES BACK.
IT'S MORE EFFECTIVE THAN RUNNING OFF ALONE, RIGHT?
THAT'S TRUE, BUT...
BE CAREFUL, ANITA. IF YOU CROSS TWO FENCES, YOU'RE ON HUNTING GROUNDS.
EVEN HERE IN JAPAN, WHERE NOT MANY PEOPLE OWN GUNS, IT'S NOT UNCOMMON FOR HUNTERS TO ACCIDENTALLY SHOOT HIKERS.
WHY, THANK YOU.
YOUR CONCERN IS *TOUCHING*.
...
HEY ...
ANYWAY, MEET BACK HERE IN AN HOUR!
IF WE HAVEN'T FOUND GEORGE BY THEN, WE'LL GO BACK TO THE INN AND GET HELP!
COME ON, LET'S START CLIMBING!
UM... SURE!

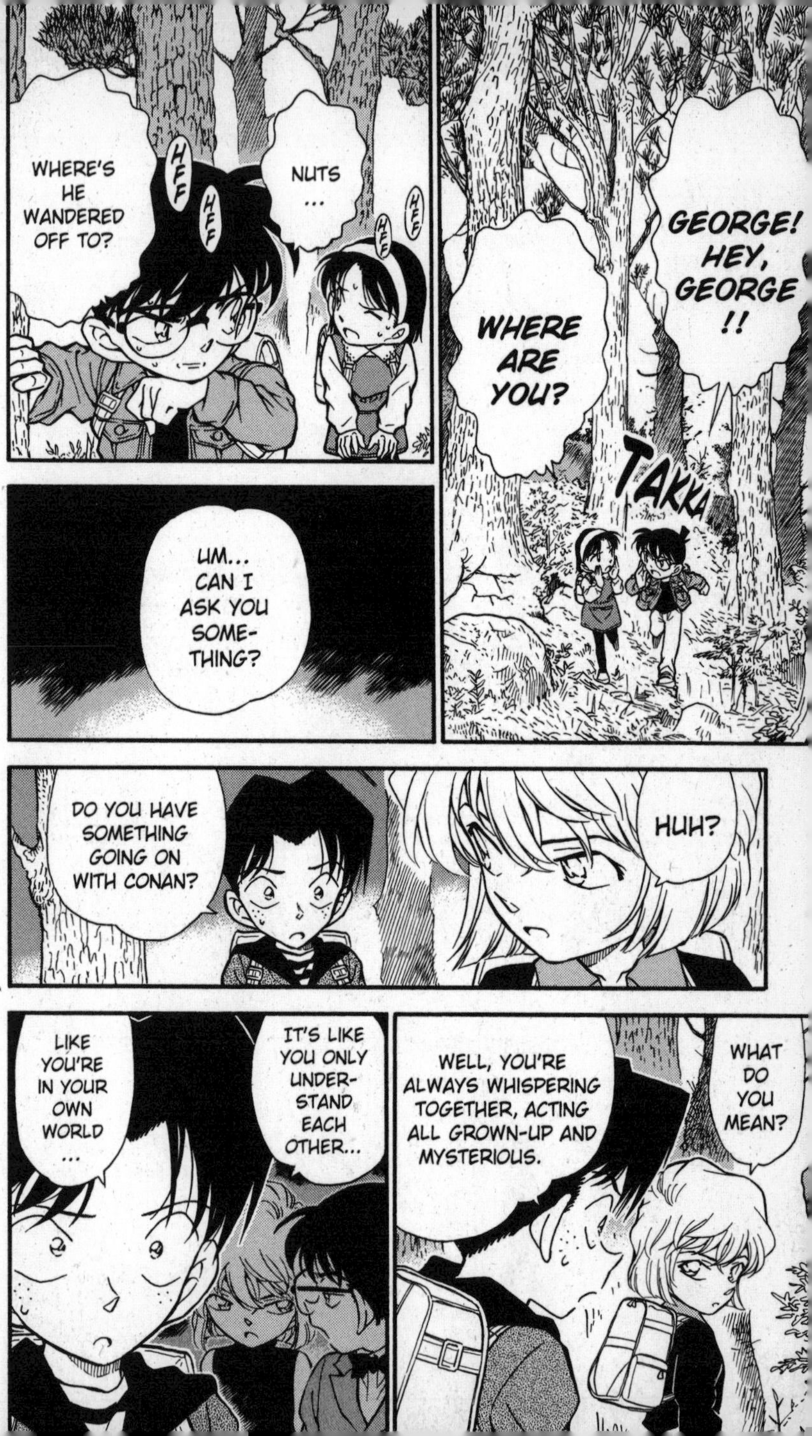
GEORGE! HEY, GEORGE!!
WHERE ARE YOU?
TAKKA
HEFF
NUTS...
HEFF
HEFF
HEFF
WHERE'S HE WANDERED OFF TO?
UM... CAN I ASK YOU SOME-THING?
HUH?
DO YOU HAVE SOMETHING GOING ON WITH CONAN?
WHAT DO YOU MEAN?
WELL, YOU'RE ALWAYS WHISPERING TOGETHER, ACTING ALL GROWN-UP AND MYSTERIOUS.
IT'S LIKE YOU ONLY UNDER-STAND EACH OTHER...
LIKE YOU'RE IN YOUR OWN WORLD...

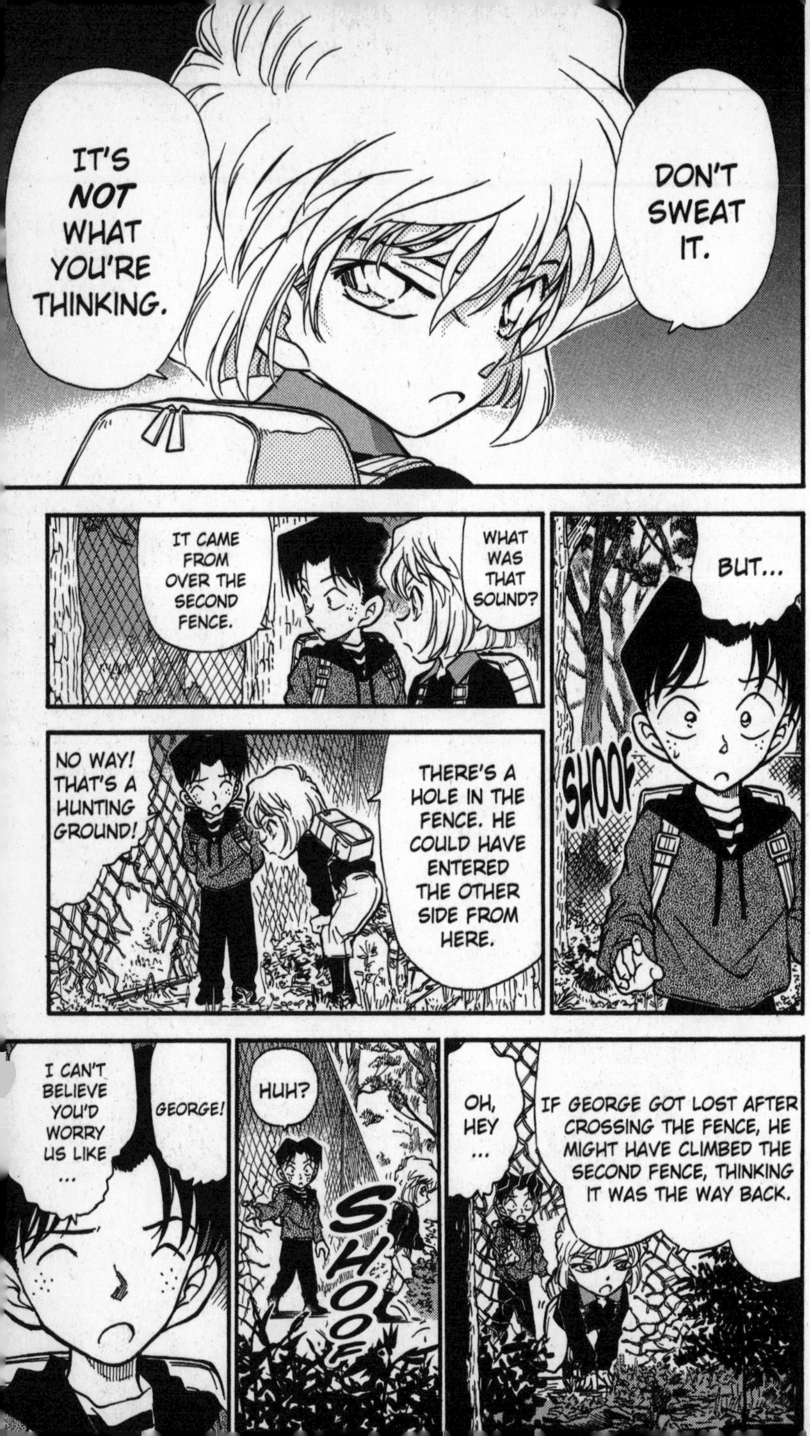
DON'T SWEAT IT.
IT'S NOT WHAT YOU'RE THINKING.
BUT...
SHOOF
WHAT WAS THAT SOUND?
IT CAME FROM OVER THE SECOND FENCE.
THERE'S A HOLE IN THE FENCE. HE COULD HAVE ENTERED THE OTHER SIDE FROM HERE.
NO WAY! THAT'S A HUNTING GROUND!
IF GEORGE GOT LOST AFTER CROSSING THE FENCE, HE MIGHT HAVE CLIMBED THE SECOND FENCE, THINKING IT WAS THE WAY BACK.
OH, HEY ...
HUH?
SHOOOOF
GEORGE!
I CAN'T BELIEVE YOU'D WORRY US LIKE ...

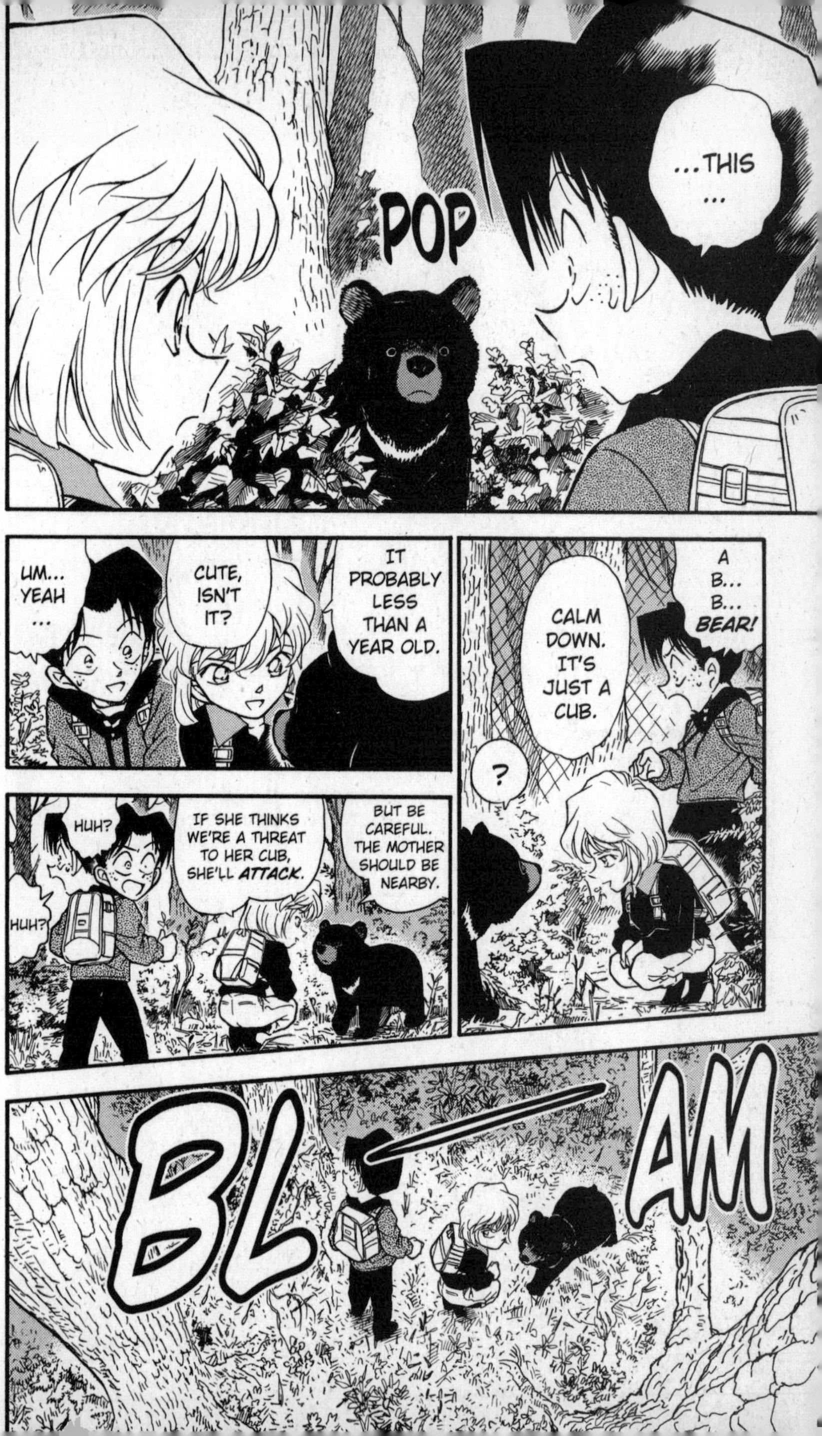
...THIS ...
POP
A B... B... BEAR!
CALM DOWN. IT'S JUST A CUB.
?
IT PROBABLY LESS THAN A YEAR OLD.
CUTE, ISN'T IT?
UM... YEAH ...
BUT BE CAREFUL. THE MOTHER SHOULD BE NEARBY.
IF SHE THINKS WE'RE A THREAT TO HER CUB, SHE'LL ATTACK.
HUH?
HUH?
BL—AM

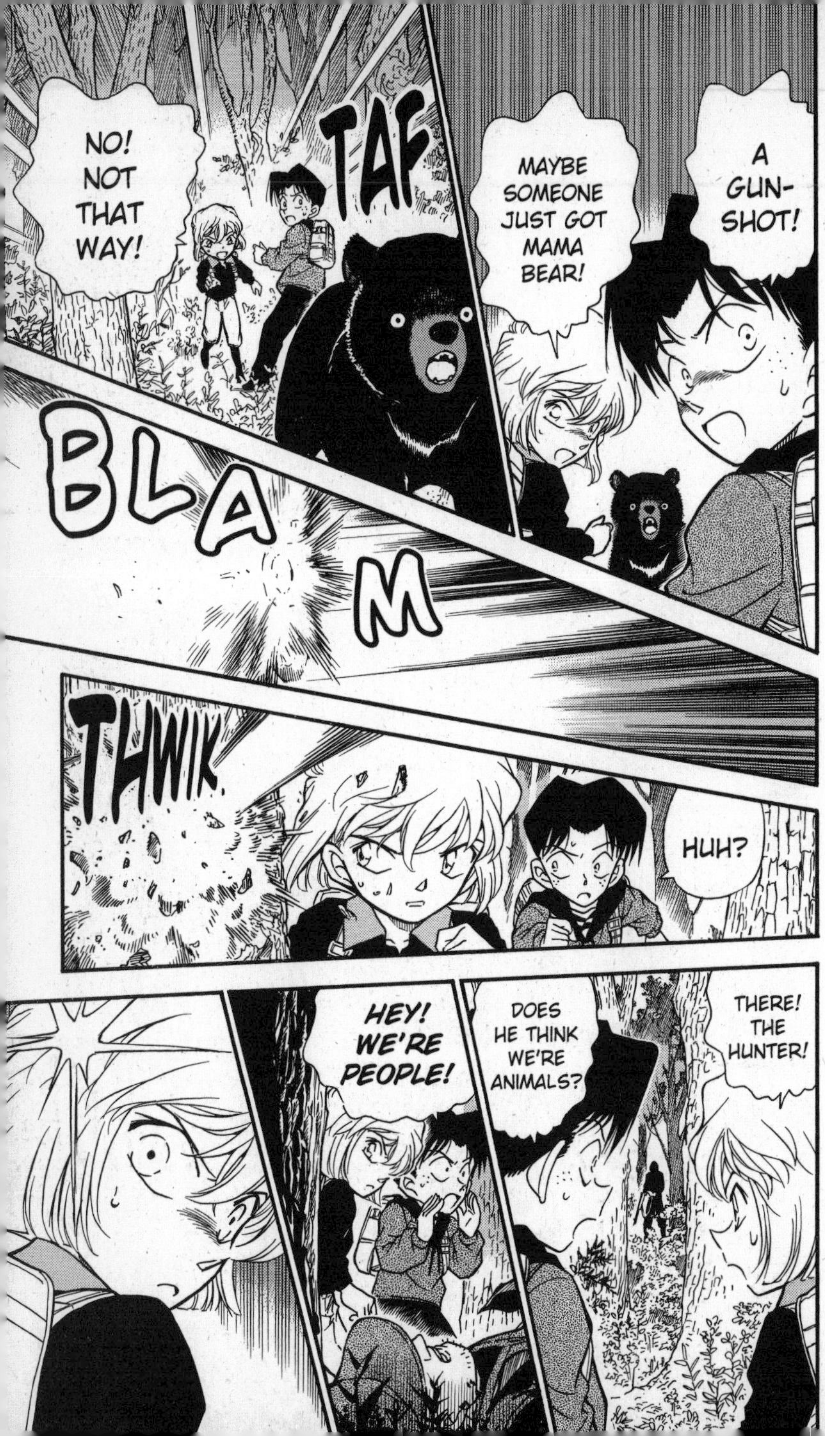
A GUN-SHOT!
MAYBE SOMEONE JUST GOT MAMA BEAR!
TAF
NO! NOT THAT WAY!
BLAM
HUH?
THWIK
THERE! THE HUNTER!
DOES HE THINK WE'RE ANIMALS?
HEY! WE'RE PEOPLE!

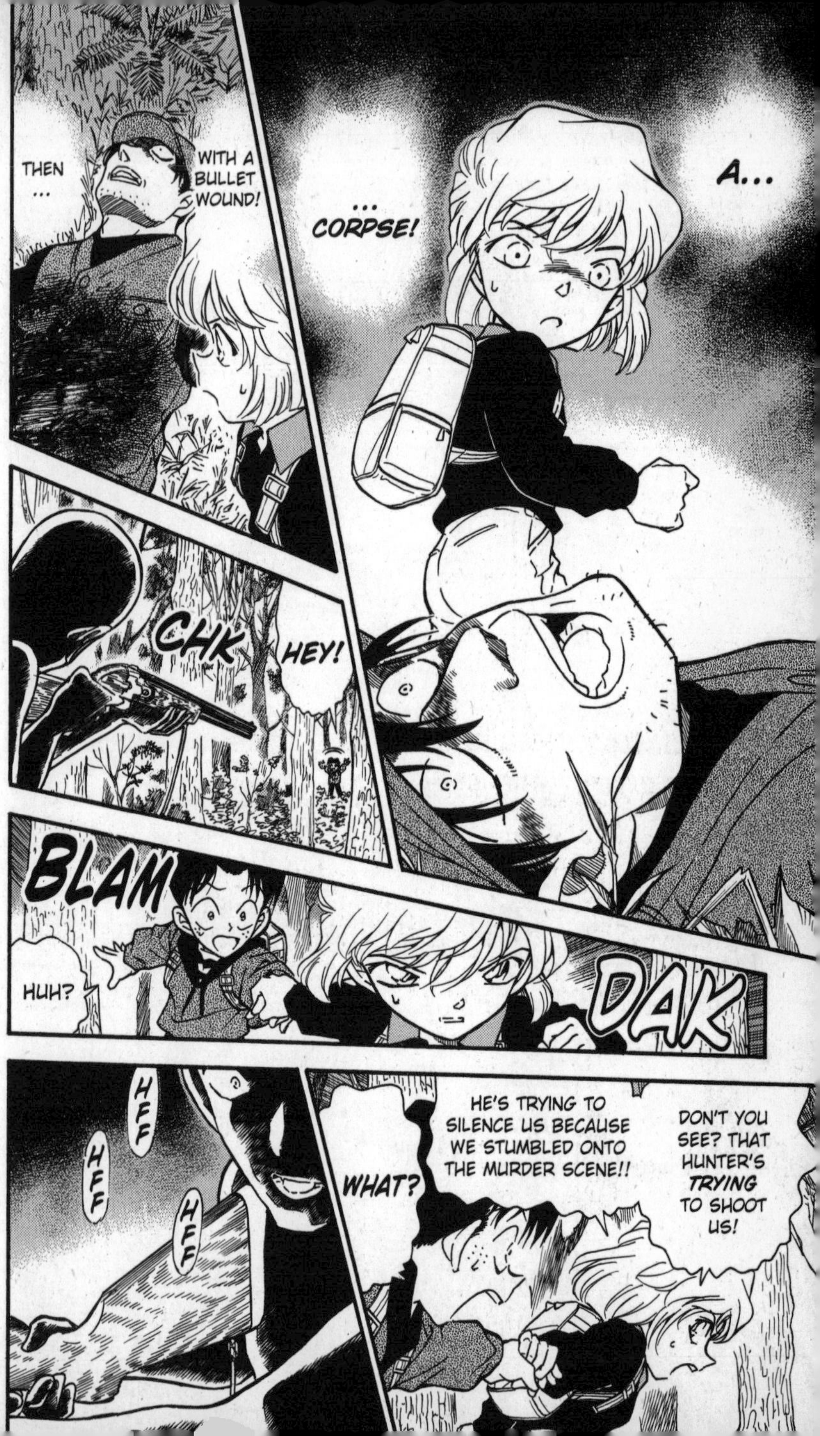
A...
... CORPSE!
THEN ...
WITH A BULLET WOUND!
HEY!
CHK
DAK
BLAM
HUH?
DON'T YOU SEE? THAT HUNTER'S *TRYING* TO SHOOT US!
HE'S TRYING TO SILENCE US BECAUSE WE STUMBLED ONTO THE MURDER SCENE!!
WHAT?
HFF
HFF
HFF

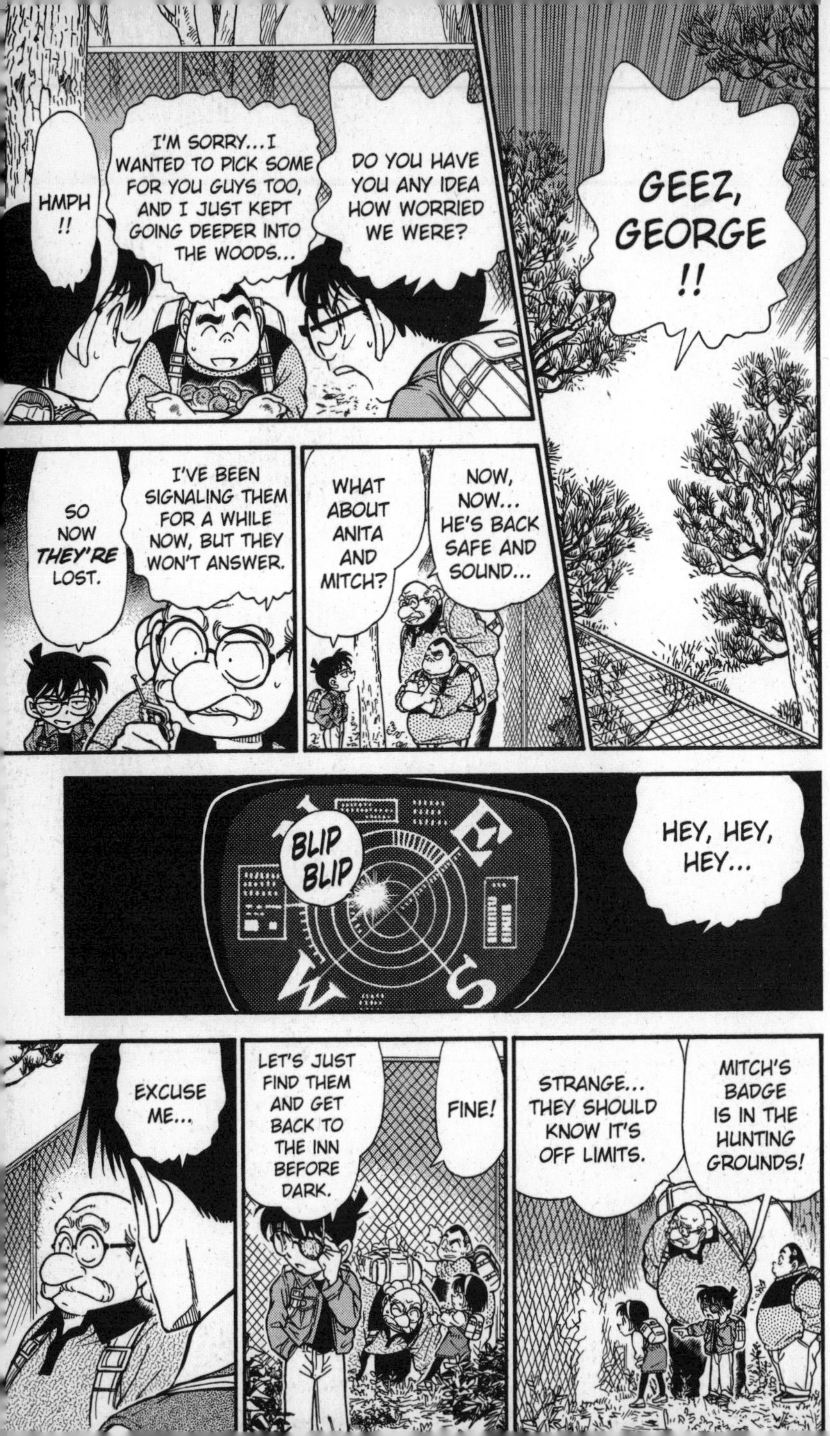
GEEZ, GEORGE !!
DO YOU HAVE YOU ANY IDEA HOW WORRIED WE WERE?
I'M SORRY... I WANTED TO PICK SOME FOR YOU GUYS TOO, AND I JUST KEPT GOING DEEPER INTO THE WOODS...
HMPH !!
NOW, NOW... HE'S BACK SAFE AND SOUND...
WHAT ABOUT ANITA AND MITCH?
I'VE BEEN SIGNALING THEM FOR A WHILE NOW, BUT THEY WON'T ANSWER.
SO NOW *THEY'RE* LOST.
HEY, HEY, HEY...
BLIP BLIP
MITCH'S BADGE IS IN THE HUNTING GROUNDS!
STRANGE... THEY SHOULD KNOW IT'S OFF LIMITS.
FINE!
LET'S JUST FIND THEM AND GET BACK TO THE INN BEFORE DARK.
EXCUSE ME...

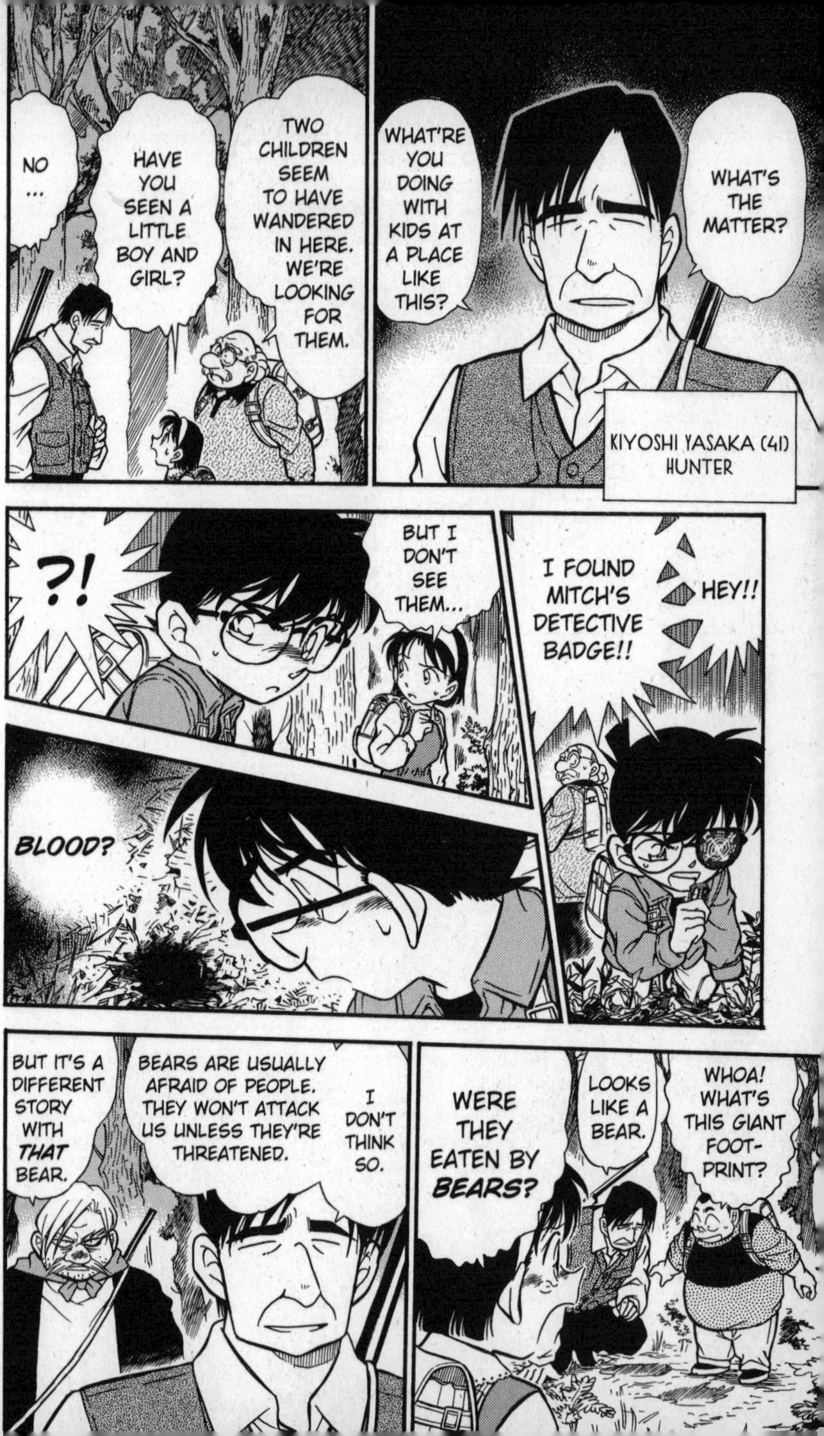
WHAT'S THE MATTER?
KIYOSHI YASAKA (41) HUNTER
WHAT'RE YOU DOING WITH KIDS AT A PLACE LIKE THIS?
TWO CHILDREN SEEM TO HAVE WANDERED IN HERE. WE'RE LOOKING FOR THEM.
HAVE YOU SEEN A LITTLE BOY AND GIRL?
NO ...
HEY!!
I FOUND MITCH'S DETECTIVE BADGE!!
BUT I DON'T SEE THEM...
?!
BLOOD?
WHOA! WHAT'S THIS GIANT FOOT-PRINT?
LOOKS LIKE A BEAR.
WERE THEY EATEN BY BEARS?
I DON'T THINK SO.
BEARS ARE USUALLY AFRAID OF PEOPLE. THEY WON'T ATTACK US UNLESS THEY'RE THREATENED.
BUT IT'S A DIFFERENT STORY WITH THAT BEAR.

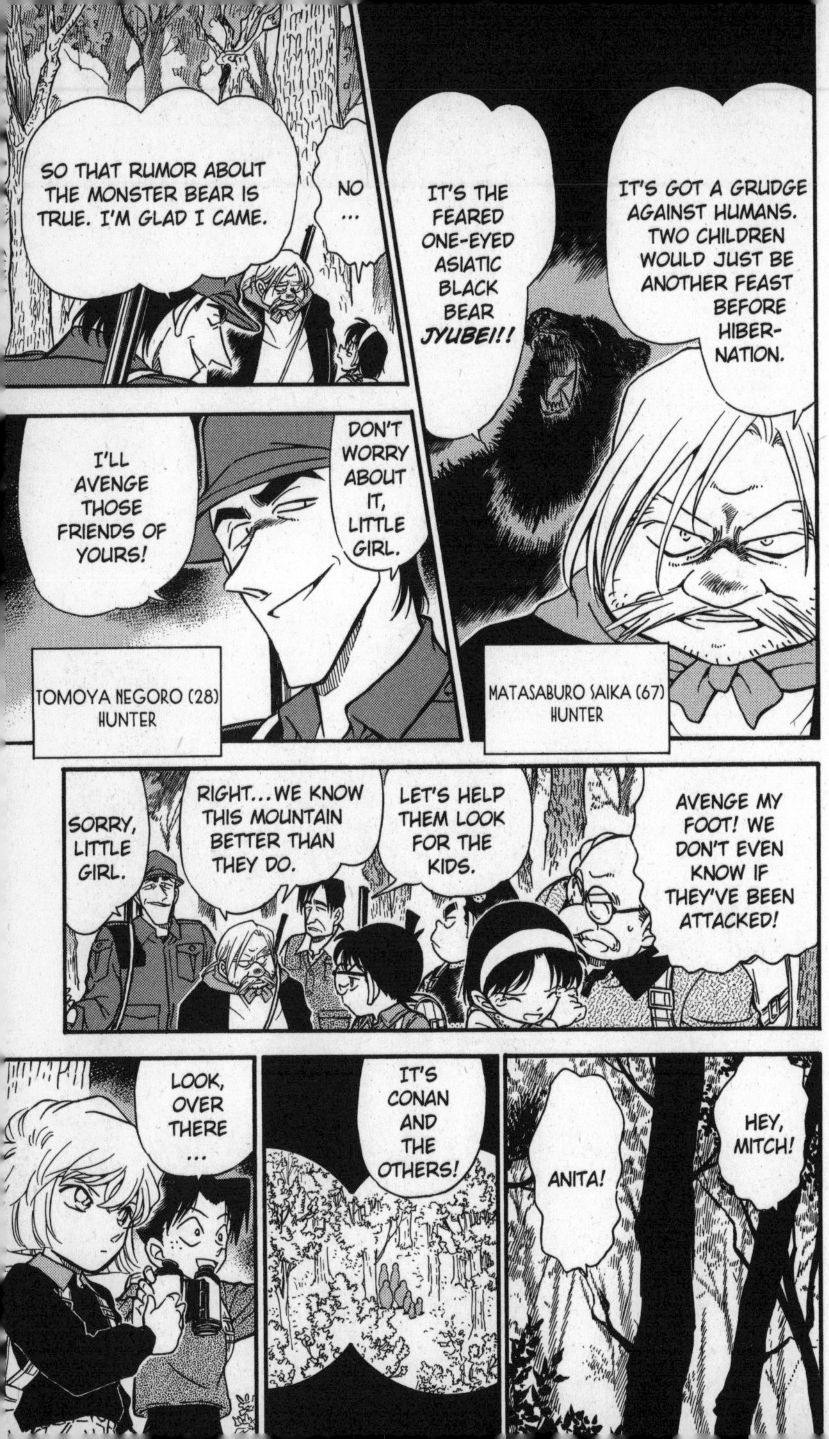
IT'S GOT A GRUDGE AGAINST HUMANS. TWO CHILDREN WOULD JUST BE ANOTHER FEAST BEFORE HIBER-NATION.
IT'S THE FEARED ONE-EYED ASIATIC BLACK BEAR JYUBEI!!
MATASABURO SAIKA (67) HUNTER
NO ...
SO THAT RUMOR ABOUT THE MONSTER BEAR IS TRUE. I'M GLAD I CAME.
DON'T WORRY ABOUT IT, LITTLE GIRL.
I'LL AVENGE THOSE FRIENDS OF YOURS!
TOMOYA NEGORO (28) HUNTER
AVENGE MY FOOT! WE DON'T EVEN KNOW IF THEY'VE BEEN ATTACKED!
LET'S HELP THEM LOOK FOR THE KIDS.
RIGHT... WE KNOW THIS MOUNTAIN BETTER THAN THEY DO.
SORRY, LITTLE GIRL.
HEY, MITCH!
ANITA!
IT'S CONAN AND THE OTHERS!
LOOK, OVER THERE ...

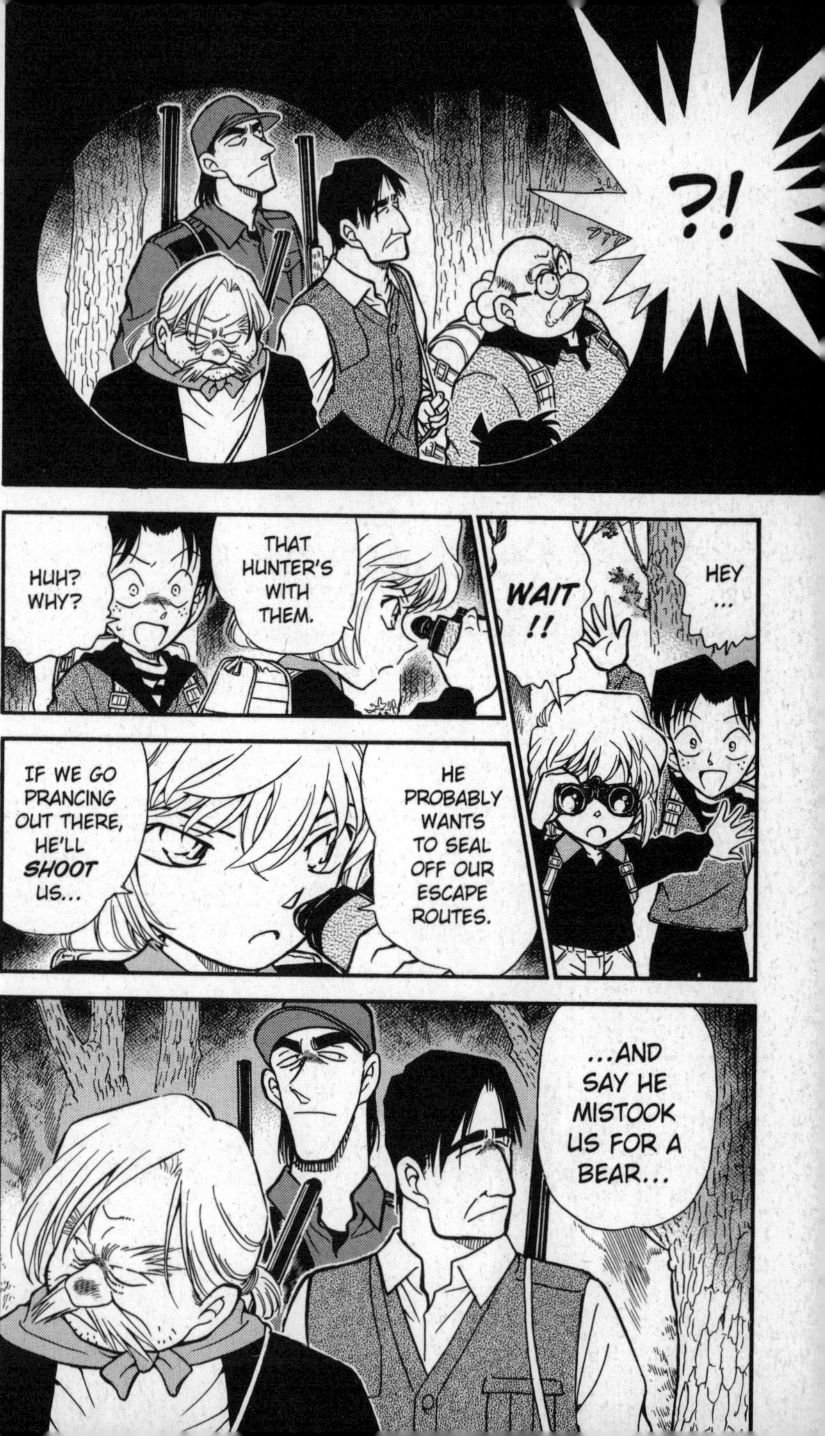
?!
HEY ...
WAIT !!
THAT HUNTER'S WITH THEM.
HUH? WHY?
HE PROBABLY WANTS TO SEAL OFF OUR ESCAPE ROUTES.
IF WE GO PRANCING OUT THERE, HE'LL SHOOT US...
...AND SAY HE MISTOOK US FOR A BEAR...

Hello, Aoyama here.

My hometown, Daieicho, now has a Conan Bridge! Whoa...
this is embarrassing!

But it's a relaxing town with plenty of fresh air. You there!
Stressed out from reading too many murder stories?
Why not drop by and take a look?

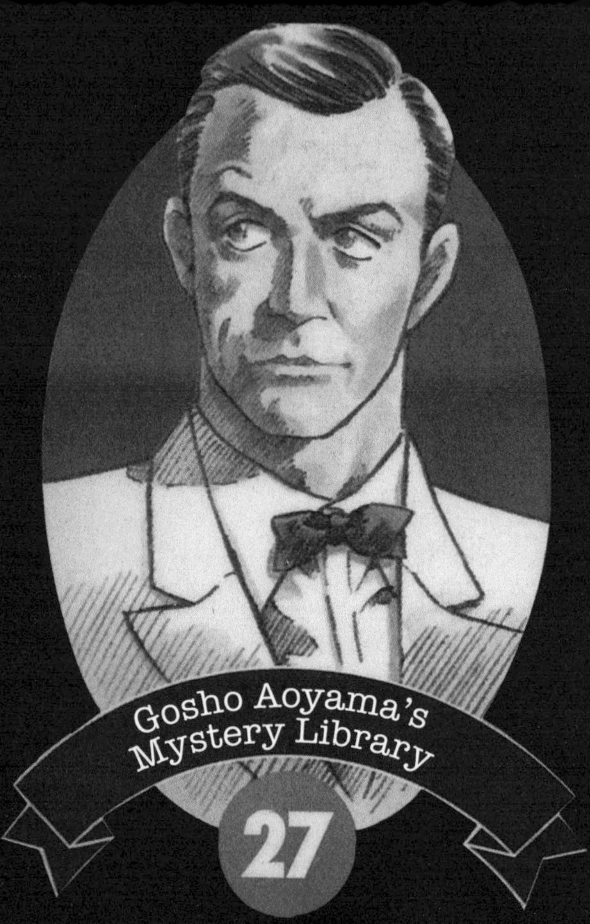
Gosho Aoyama's
Mystery Library
27

JAMES BOND

It's not just cops and detectives who fight criminals. There's also a certain employee of MI-6, the British secret service, who's been given a license to kill in his fight against terrorists and criminal organizations. It's James Bond, code number 007! Bond prefers the best of everything, from his clothes and shoes to his cigarettes and martinis—shaken, not stirred. He's a connoisseur of fine food and drink. He's also a master of foreign languages, excels in all sports, has extensive technological expertise and is extremely popular with the world's most beautiful women. He's a spy who seems to have everything heaven could bestow upon him. ❤ His trusty friend "Q," the head of MI-6's research and development team, produces unique gadgets that save Bond from many tight spots.

Bond's creator, Ian Fleming, was a former intelligence officer for the Royal Navy. It's said that the code name he used back then was "James Bond"...

I recommend *Goldfinger*.

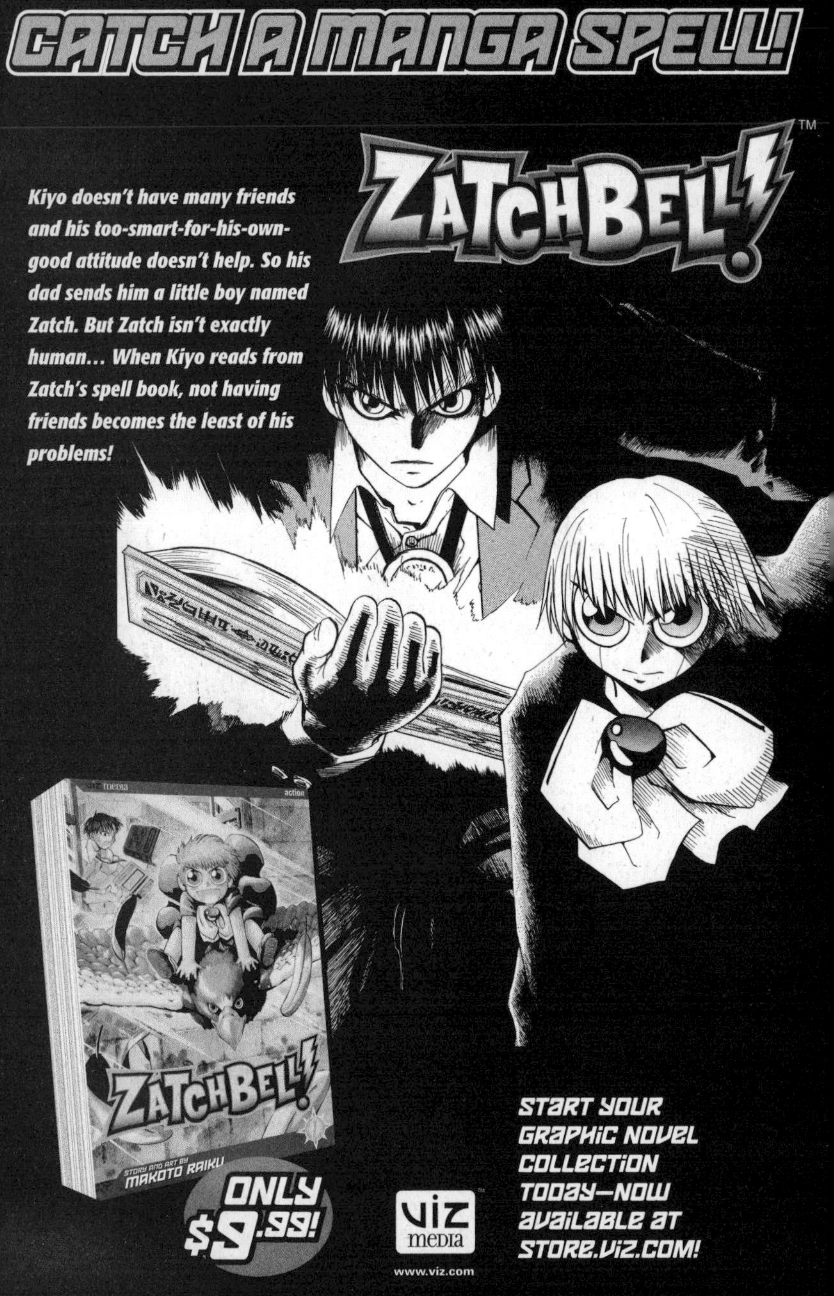
CATCH A MANGA SPELL!
ZATCH BELL!™
Kiyo doesn't have many friends and his too-smart-for-his-own-good attitude doesn't help. So his dad sends him a little boy named Zatch. But Zatch isn't exactly human… When Kiyo reads from Zatch's spell book, not having friends becomes the least of his problems!
viz media
action
ZATCH BELL!
STORY AND ART BY
MAKOTO RAIKU
ONLY $9.99!
viz media
www.viz.com
START YOUR GRAPHIC NOVEL COLLECTION TODAY—NOW AVAILABLE AT STORE.VIZ.COM!

A Comedy that Redefines a

Due to an unfortunate accident, when martial artist Ranma gets splashed with cold water, he becomes a buxom young girl! Hot water reverses the effect, but when blamed for offenses both real and imagined, and pursued by lovesick suitors of both genders, what's a half-boy, half-girl to do?

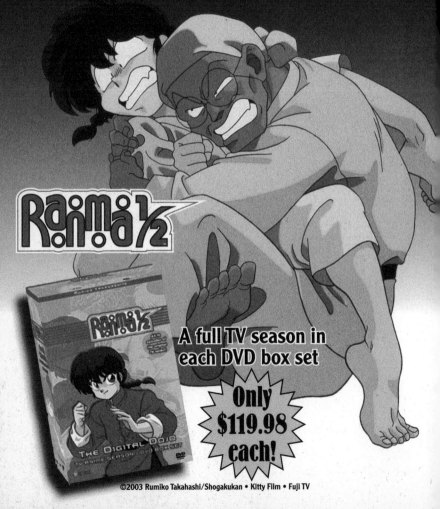

A full TV season in each DVD box set

Only $119.98 each!